INSIGHT GUIDES MUSEUMS
AND GALLERIES OF
PARIS

APA PUBLICATIONS
Part of the Langenscheidt Publishing Group

Editorial

Editor
Cathy Muscat
Design
Klaus Geisler
Picture Editor
Hilary Genin
Picture Research
Susannah Stone
Editorial Director
Brian Bell

Distribution

UK & Ireland
GeoCenter International Ltd
The Viables Centre, Harrow Way
Basingstoke, Hants RG22 4BJ
Fax: (44) 1256-817988

United States
Langenscheidt Publishers, Inc.
46–35 54th Road, Maspeth, NY 11378
Fax: (718) 784-0640

Canada
Prologue Inc.
1650 Lionel Bertrand Blvd., Boisbriand
Québec, Canada J7H 1N7
Tel: (450) 434-0306. Fax: (450) 434-2627

Worldwide
**Apa Publications GmbH & Co.
Verlag KG (Singapore branch)**
38 Joo Koon Road, Singapore 628990
Tel: (65) 6865-1600. Fax: (65) 6861-6438

Printing

Insight Print Services (Pte) Ltd
38 Joo Koon Road, Singapore 628990
Tel: (65) 6865-1600. Fax: (65) 6861-6438

©2002 Apa Publications GmbH & Co.
Verlag KG (Singapore branch)
All Rights Reserved

First Edition 2002

CONTACTING THE EDITORS
Although every effort is made to
provide accurate information, we
live in a fast-changing world and
would appreciate it if readers would
call our attention to any errors or
outdated information that may
occur by writing to:
**Insight Guides, P.O. Box 7910,
London SE1 1WE, England.
Fax: (44 20) 7403-0290.
e-mail:
insight@apaguide.demon.co.uk**

www.insightguides.com

ABOUT THIS BOOK

The museums and galleries of Paris are among the best, and most visited in the world. This book features over 180 of them. With such an overwhelming choice, deciding on which ones to see is the biggest dilemma most visitors have to face. Art lovers have a particularly hard time of it – you could spend a day in the Louvre just making your way from *Venus de Milo* to *Mona Lisa*. All tastes, passions and interests are catered for, from the vast national institutions to the smallest specialist museums: you can take a crash course in modern art at the Pompidou Centre or rocket science at Parc de la Villette; follow the revolutionary trail at the Carnavalet museum; talk to the animals at the Natural History museum; immerse yourself in the life and work of artists from Delacroix to Dalí. Some museums are worth visiting just to see inside the fine, historic buildings they inhabit; others for the sheer eccentricity of their collections.

The purpose of this book is to help to make the choosing easier by giving you a taste of what's on offer. Practical information, such as addresses, telephone numbers and transport details, is given at the beginning of each review, and the location of each museum is shown on a full-colour map. Most reviews end with one or two suggested refreshment stops in the vicinity. A series of introductory features provide additional background on how Paris came to be the repository of so many treasures through the centuries.

For the latest museum news and our monthly exhibition selection, check the special updates page of our website: **www.insightguides.com**.

The writing team

The main contributor to this book was arts journalist and incurable francophile **Natasha Edwards**. She has been editor and art critic of *Time Out Paris* since 1993, but also writes on contemporary art, design and travel for London's *Independent*, *Tate Magazine* and *Condé Nast Traveler*, among other publications. She covered all the major collections and most of the fine art and decorative art museums, and compiled the listings of exhibition venues, photographic galleries and architectural institutions. She also wrote the features on the *Ecole de Paris* and *Contemporary Art*.

American travel writer **Brent Gregston** has been exploring the museums of Paris for four years. He reviewed most of the history and science museums, many of the artists' and writers' museums, and ventured further afield to research the out-of-town chapter.

The third key member of the writing team was **Olivia Snaije**, another American in Paris, who has worked as a freelance journalist both in Paris and New York. She reviewed a number of museums and wrote the essay on *Mitterrand's Grands Projets*.

Other contributors were **Steven Mudge**, whose musical expertise informed the music chapter, art historian **Anthea Snow**, who wrote the essays on *Louis XIV*, *Napoleon's Plundering* and the *Universal Exhibitions*, and Insight Guides editors **Cathy Muscat** and **Clare Peel**.

INSIDE FRONT COVER: St Benedict's disciples, stained glass (Musée du Moyen Age).

OPPOSITE: *Young Women of Provence at the Well* by Paul Signac, 1892 (Musée d'Orsay).

I.M. Pei's Pyramid, entrance to the Louvre.

FEATURES

MAPS

Crispin and Scapin by Daumier, *c.* 1850.

ABOVE: La Grande Arche
de la Défense.
RIGHT: Female figurine
in terracotta from
Mesopotamia or
Northern Syria,
c. 4500 BC.

PARIS MUSEUMS & GALLERIES

Monet's garden at Giverny.

1930s screen goddess Danielle Darrieux.

FOLLOWING PAGES: Details
from *The Poppyfield*, by
Claude Monet, 1873
(Musée d'Orsay);
Liberty Leading the People
by Eugène Delacroix, 1830
(Musée du Louvre);
Mona Lisa by Leonardo
da Vinci, 1503–6
(Musée du Louvre).

LOUIS XIV: PATRON OF THE ARTS

Under Louis XIV the arts were dedicated to *"la gloire"*. Vast sums were spent asserting the power and glory of king and country through art and architecture, music and literature, drama and the decorative arts

"**E**very age has produced its heroes and statesmen… But the thinking man, and what is rarer the man of taste, numbers only four ages in the history of the world; four happy ages when the arts were brought to perfection… The fourth age is that which we call the age of Louis XIV; and it is perhaps of the four the one which most nearly approaches perfection."

In *The Age of Louis XIV*, Voltaire's masterpiece of historical study published in 1751, the king is presented as the natural heir to Alexander the Great and the Roman emperors. During Louis XIV's remarkably long reign, stretching 72 years from 1643 to 1715, he himself encouraged such elevated comparisons, nurturing and fashioning the image of the monarchy through extensive patronage of the arts.

Architects and power brokers

Portrait of Louis XIV in his coronation regalia, 1701, by Hyacinthe Rigaud (Musée du Louvre).

Louis XIV had a passion for architecture and took pains to involve himself personally in any project, meeting his architects and gardeners every day during most of his reign. However, his interest was also a deliberate strategy. As Colbert, the king's finance minister, pointed out, architecture is always equated with power: "Your majesty knows that, in the absence of striking military exploits, nothing more marks the greatness and the spirit of princes than buildings".

From 1661 Louis was tireless in his building and reconstruction projects in Paris, Versailles and the provinces, for which gardens and royal squares (such as the Place des Victoires in Paris) provided the setting and added to the sense of theatre. Paris, and then Versailles, were to be the new Rome, setting the standards for a new classical age. At Louis' service in this endeavour were Jean-Baptiste Colbert (1619–83), who oversaw the vast building programmes, top architects Louis Le Vau (1612–70) and Jules Hardouin-Mansart (1646–1708), the king's master gardener, André Le Nôtre (1613–1700) and painter Charles Lebrun (1619–90). Apart from Versailles, their legacy of landmarks includes the châteaux of Marly, St-Cloud and Sceaux, and the Dôme des Invalides in Paris.

During Colbert's time, the relative importance of improvements in Paris and at Versailles became the subject of an ongoing battle of wills between the finance minister and his monarch. Colbert wanted Louis to reside in the Louvre palace and for Paris to be the seat of government, considering the work on Versailles to be an unwarranted extravagance. He wished to bring the Louvre "to perfection". To this end Charles Lebrun produced the splendid decoration of the new Gallery of Apollo, and the great Italian Baroque sculptor and architect Bernini was invited to Paris in 1665 to work on the architecture. Bernini produced a superb bust of Louis XIV (1665; Versailles) during his stay, but the visit was not a success. Astonishingly arrogant and sensitive to the slightest negative response, Bernini was interested in the big picture, in dramatic effect, while Colbert refused to be distracted from the practicalities of the floorplan and the demands of the French climate. Despite initial agreement from Louis, Bernini's plans were shelved as soon as he departed for Rome, probably on the basis that they were too Italianate. Claude Perrault's design for today's eastern colonnade was adopted instead.

The Portière of Mars from the Gobelins tapestry workshop, 1660, after Charles Lebrun.

Versailles: the centre of power

The conditions for building at Versailles were certainly not auspicious, but what began as a damp and marshy site with a hunting lodge for Louis XIII became, after a series of expansions from 1661 to 1689, one of the greatest statements of royal power and artistic patronage. The additions to Versailles, designed by Le Vau, were known as the "Enveloppe", because they surrounded the old building on three sides.

Louis was involved in every aspect of the palace's design, down to the fine detail of the interiors. He gave the layout a new symmetry and formality, achieving a harmony and proportion parallel to that sought in the architecture. The decoration of the interior was entrusted to Lebrun, a politician as much as an artist, and the key director of the arts under Louis XVI. He established a visual language for the king that was based on classical mythology, which was played out at Versailles – with particular gusto in the salons of War and Peace. The classical past and its mythology were hugely influential as sources of symbolism and allegory in the 17th century, continuing the classical revival of the Renaissance period. Louis XIV's use of Graeco-Roman history and the pagan pantheon as sources of visual and verbal imagery was, therefore, part of a familiar artistic tradition.

Louis adopted the sun as his personal emblem. It was a symbol of power – representing the king as the "planet" around which others orbit in order to survive – and divinity – the embodiment of Apollo, the god of light, poetry and music. It was never subtly applied; the parallel was drawn directly and constantly throughout his reign. In 1665, Louis, who loved to dress up, even appeared in a ballet dressed as "the Sun" . The fact that he was, and still is, referred to as the "Sun King" reflects his success in propagating this image, which was exploited most strongly at Versailles. Here, where courtiers continually circled the king, hoping to stay in favour, he granted official audiences in the Apollo Room (a room also used for music, one of the king's great passions).

Allegory of Louis XIV as patron of the arts by Jean Garnier, 1662 (Musée du Château de Versailles).

In the park, the magnificent Fountain of Apollo represents daybreak, as the sun-chariot is drawn from the sea across the sky. Created in 1671 from a sketch by Lebrun, this gargantuan sculpture makes a definitive statement about Louis' power, reinforced by the Fountain of Latona and the Dragon Fountain. In the former, Latona, mother of Apollo, is avenged against a group of unruly shepherds, who had stirred the water to make it muddy just when she wanted to drink. The shepherds, ridiculed in turn, are transformed into frogs. In the Dragon Fountain, Apollo slays a giant python. Both draw parallels with the rebellious movements that took place between 1648 and 1652 known as the Fronde, and reassert the strength of the king. These challenges to absolutism by a conspiracy of nobles and provincial parliaments had been instrumental in persuading Louis to transfer his court outside the city limits, away from the unruly Parisian mob.

Reflections of glory

The enormous formal gardens (800 hectares/2,000 acres) at Versailles offered numerous opportunities for sculptural invention. The technically skilled Jacques Sarrazin taught many of the park's sculptors, including Lebrun's great ally, François Girardon (1628–1715), who produced work in an increasingly classicising style. Together the sculptures asserted the idea of Versailles as microcosm, with Louis at its centre, incorporating representations of the four elements, the

Mercury on Pegasus, one of the Marly Horses by Antoine Coysevox, 1701–2, in the Louvre.

four seasons – including *Winter*, a superb rendering of Saturn – the four parts of the day, and the four corners of the earth.

In the last decades of the 17th century, Antoine Coysevox (1640–1720) introduced a more Baroque emphasis, as seen in his famous stucco bas-relief in the Salon de la Guerre (the Salon of War). This depicts Louis trampling on his enemies with the flamboyance and energy that is so characteristic of the style. Coysevox produced dozens of ornamental sculptures for the park at Marly (a royal residence built between 1679 and 1686), once again celebrating Louis' triumphs. More than 40 of these are now displayed in the Louvre's Cour Marly *(see page 72)*. His statue of Louis dressed in Roman armour, made for the Paris town hall, hails the king as ruler of the new Classical age that France so wanted to achieve.

Having absorbed more than 5 percent of France's annual income and employed about 25,000 workers on a daily basis, Versailles finally became home to the court in 1682. The palace was a vast theatre where the king took centre stage at the head of a ritualistic and ostentatious culture. It provided the backdrop to his magnificence and symbolised the artistic achievements of his monarchy. While his countrymen might have been loud in its praises, however, foreign visitors found the self-referential décor less tolerable: "he is strutting in every panel and galloping over one's head in every ceiling… I verily believe that there are of him statues and busts, bas reliefs and pictures above two hundred in the house and gardens" (Lord Montague).

The Duc de Saint-Simon, a penetrating observer of court life, commented with typical acerbity: "He liked nobody to be in any way superior to him… This vanity, this unmeasured and unreasonable love of admiration, was his ruin." The portrait of a swaggering Louis XIV (1701; Louvre) by Hyacinthe Rigaud (1659–1743) perfectly captures this sense of hubris through dress and pose *(see page 13)*. One of the period's foremost painters, Rigaud enveloped the king in swathes of ermine, making Louis the epitome of royal absolutism and attracting numerous further commissions from those wishing to be represented with similar grandeur.

Promoting the arts

Despite the self-serving nature of his artistic patronage, Louis was also capable of royal munificence, spending around 800,000 livres a year on works of art made in France to be given as presents. Some of these works were the product of the royal "manufactories," which were established not only as a means of strengthening the economy, but also for the regulation of the decorative arts and the promotion of them in the service of the Crown. Voltaire gives full credit to their achievements: fine cloth, once imported from England and Holland, was now made at Abbeville; silk interwoven with gold and silver thread came from Lyons and Tours; 1,600 lace-makers were engaged, including specialists from Venice and Flanders; glass was made to rival that of Venice; handwoven carpets made at the Savonnerie workshops outdid the craftsmanship of Turkey, while the tapestry factories at Les Gobelins, Beauvais and Aubusson competed with those of Flanders.

At Les Gobelins, founded in Paris in 1667, 800 tapestry-makers brought to life works by the director Charles Lebrun, reproduced the paintings of Poussin, and copied those of Italian masters such as Raphael; the intricately woven ten-piece *History of Scipio* (1688–9), after Jules Romain, hangs in the Louvre. Under Lebrun's guidance, Les Gobelins could decorate and furnish the royal palaces according to set standards and programmes, often using Graeco-Roman themes.

Louis XIV in the costume of the Sun King in the ballet *La Nuit, c.* 1665.

Skilled craftsmen of every kind were employed at the royal workshops, including goldsmiths, embroiderers, and cabinet-makers such as André-Charles Boulle. A specialist in wood, tortoise-shell and brass marquetry, Boulle achieved painterly effects that are extraordinarily fluid and nat-uralistic. He was appointed Ebéniste du Roi (king's cabinet-maker) and undertook royal commissions that included the panelling and floors for the Dauphin's apartments at Versailles. Impor-tantly, in times of hardship when war was draining the country's reserves, decoration could be cre-ated more cheaply from marquetry and embroidery than from silver and other expensive materials.

The Louvre museum testifies to Louis' qualities as an inveterate collector. He was the first king to develop a royal collection, favouring the classical style and Poussin *(see page 67)*, Claude Gellée and Lebrun in particular. Lebrun's four huge canvases depicting the history of Alexander (1661–73; Louvre) on a truly epic scale were well suited to Louis' tastes, with their references to military glory and kingly virtue. Not only did Louis buy the works of contem-poraries, and the contents of their studios, he also acquired the collections of Cardinal Mazarin and the banker Jabach, which included such Renaissance masterpieces as Raphael's *Baltazar Castiglione (c.* 1514–15; Louvre), and the superbly naturalistic *Nicolas Kratzer* (1528; Louvre) by Hans Holbein the Younger.

Colbert was untiring in his patronage of the arts on behalf of his king, and yet he had no great aesthetic interest of his own. His burning motivation was the necessity of the State to control the production of art, as everything else. The corollary of this was that the court should be the arbiter of taste, and that royal patronage should become the greatest influence in French culture, thereby bolstering its own position.

The royal academies

With this desire to control French culture in mind, Louis XIV built on the initiative of Riche-lieu, who had set up the Académie Française for Louis XIII in 1635, and created individual insti-tutions dedicated to specific branches of learning. These academies set standards of taste and allowed for the centralised control of education. The Academy of Painting and Sculpture had been established by Mazarin in 1648, but was reorganised under Colbert in the mid-1660s, with Lebrun becoming director in 1683. In 1663 the Petite Académie was formed (later the Academy of Literature), followed in 1671 by the Royal Academy of Architecture and, in 1672 by the Royal Academy of Music under Lulli. In 1666 the French Academy in Rome was also founded, where 12 students at a time could study the great classical masters at first hand. There was even a pro-posed Royal Academy of Spectacles, for tournaments, fireworks and other pageantry. The role

Le Grand Carrousel, an extravagant celebration orchestrated by King Louis XIV in the courtyard of the Tuileries Palace, to celebrate the birth of the Dauphin in 1662 (Musée du Château de Versailles).

of the academies in the aggrandisement of the monarch was clear. As Louis himself put it to the Petit Académie: "I entrust to you the most precious thing in the world, my *gloire*. I am sure that you will do wonders…". The Observatoire, an austere building designed by Claude Perrault to fit its purpose as home to the newly founded Academy of Sciences (1666), publicly proclaimed Louis as protector of the sciences as much as of the arts.

The Architecture Academy, under Nicolas-François Blondel, aimed to bring this discipline to perfection by adhering to the classical theories of harmony and proportion. The painting academy, in turn, took Poussin's classicism as its model and taught the genres according to a strict hierarchy: history painting was at the top, followed by portraiture, landscapes, genre (or everyday-life painting) and finally the lowliest, still life. The Academy set the pattern for the majority of schools established in the following centuries. Its practice was codified and theory-based, to the extent that in 1698 Lebrun wrote a treatise that aimed, without a trace of irony, to rationalise the expressions of the passions in art. Drawing (rather than colour), composition, perspective and proportion were of primary importance, and students were encouraged to use models from antiquity rather than real life as their basis for study.

Although the academies' restrictive practices seem remarkable in disciplines now valued for their freedom, it should be remembered that their establishment was founded on a concern for standards, for the intellect, and for the production of suitable and tangible reflections of France's prestige. Under Louis XIV, artists acquired a new and distinct status.

Literary and musical genius

To achieve the desired results, research was carried out in the provinces to find sources of talent, and encouragement was given in the form of pensions. By this device, Louis could buy up support for the Crown, ensure his good image for posterity, and limit negative press. A list of suitable men of letters who might act as *"les trompettes du roi"* was therefore drawn up. The quid pro quo basis of these payments did not escape the notice of contemporary writers.

Most of the major figures of the day received state pensions, including Corneille, Racine, Molière and La Fontaine, although some fell out of favour for not falling into line. These names alone are proof that Louis XIV's reign coincided with a great flowering of the literary arts, and the king made full use of his architectural backdrops for the display of their works: the Grotto of Thetis at Versailles was used for a production of the *Malade Imaginaire* by Molière (1622–73) in 1674, and operas were staged in the Marble Courtyard. Louis was rarely content to be just a spectator. He played the guitar and is said to have danced exceptionally well, and performed in several ballets before the court.

Molière playing the role of Caesar in Corneille's *Death of Pompey*, c. 1657 (Musée Carnavalet).

Jean-Baptiste Lulli (1634–87), Surintendant de la Musique from 1661 and founder of the music academy, collaborated with Molière on a series of comedy-ballets, while managing the lavish musical entertainment at the court and creating a new French style of opera. Like their artist contemporaries, Lulli and Philippe Quinault (1635–88) turned to classical mythology for their operas, using the stories to interpret Louis's reign. But their productions, like those of the great 17th-century dramatists, rose above mere encomiums. Lulli's early operas were so well received that Louis named the Palais Royale as the permanent home of opera in France. Molière also remained in high favour, with Louis in full support of his mocking dissection of society, so long as the king was exempt. In 1680, Louis ordered all the French actors in Paris to combine to form a single company, and so established the French national theatre, the Comédie Française.

While royal patronage was nothing new, Louis XIV gave it an entirely new scale, and unprecedented attention to detail. Using theatrical display, as well as the more tangible forms of sculpture, painting and architecture, he created an indelible link between the art of his time and his person. Not only were great things achieved under his rule but, as Voltaire points out, *"c'est lui qui les faisait"* ("it was he who did them").

NAPOLEON'S PLUNDERING

After Napoleon's defeat at Waterloo many stolen masterpieces
were repatriated, but not all the trophies from his European
campaigns found their way back home

N apoleon Bonaparte was just 30 when, in November 1799, he became First Consul and head
of the French Republic. His skill as a politician was matched by his military genius: "He was
passionately keen on war, because he excelled in warfare. He favoured it above all as a
means of rousing the nation and of impressing it…" (Armand Lefèbvre). In his victorious campaigns, paintings, sculptures and other valuable artefacts became the trophies of his conquest and
the tangible proof of French hegemony. The contemporary architect, Quatremère de Quincy, stresses
Napoleon's acquisitiveness on these occasions: he was "devoured by anticipatory lust for the best
things in every country whether masterpieces and precious objects or men of talent and renown."

Despite such determination, the process of acquiring works of art, not to mention the debate
surrounding the legitimacy of such behaviour, made this a policy fraught with complications
that threatened the success of its outcome.

Theft or preservation?

After the Revolution of 1789 it was essential for the royal collections to become the people's
property; the suppression of the churches and the flight of émigrés had also brought works into
public ownership. The new Musée Central des Arts (previously the Louvre palace) opened in
1793 to house these nationalised works of art, offered the ideal venue for Napoleon to carry out
his grand plan of establishing a Universal Gallery in which to display his gains.

Jacques-Louis David's monumental painting of Napoleon crowning his empress Josephine in 1802 (Louvre).

The majority of Napoleon's war trophies were not simply looted at random. His confiscations
were planned in advance and under expert guidance, with their ultimate destination in mind.
Cogent arguments were put forward to justify the acquisitions through military means. In the first
place, France would be able to ensure the best conditions of security and conservation. This same
rationale was applied only a few years later to justify the removal of the Parthenon sculptures
from the Acropolis in Athens, under the guidance of Lord Elgin. Greece, it was felt, did not
benefit from the same standards of conservation as Britain, and the works were therefore at risk
of disappearing entirely unless displayed in London. A number of the works acquired by
Napoleon were in terrible condition, their supports riddled with worm holes and their surfaces
covered with flaking paint.
The French were pioneers in
methods of restoration, so the
conservation argument was
not unfounded.

Secondly, a universal gallery
would be not only vast but also
all-encompassing, bringing
together under one roof works
that illustrated all the different
schools – Italian, Flemish and
Spanish – alongside those from
antiquity. Centuries of art could
now be seen together and
would be available to all. It
would be a collection without
precedent.

On a more self-serving note, France wished to make its art the finest in the world, and this would be all the more possible if the greatest examples from earlier centuries were available to its artists. Louis XIV had established the French Academy in Rome in 1666 for this express purpose, but Napoleon now brought Rome (and elsewhere) to the academies.

"The Republic acquires by its courage what could not be obtained with Louis XIV's immense wealth... Van Dyck and Rubens are en route for Paris and the Flemish school rises en masse to ornament our museums... France possesses an inexhaustible means of increasing human knowledge and perfecting civilisation." (Grégoire, 1794). This educational aim was also a key reason for bringing home Classical sculpture, in keeping with the academic insistence on copying from the antique.

In ideological terms France, as the land of liberty, was seen as the legitimate home of works of art, and as the only soil on which such artefacts could truly flourish. As Barbier, the lieutenant who escorted the first convoy of pictures removed from Belgium in 1794, stated: "Too long these masterpieces have been sullied by the aspect of servitude... These immortal works are now deposited in the homeland of arts and genius, the homeland of liberty, blessed equality and the French republic."

The rhetoric was highly persuasive for contemporaries, but concerns were voiced as early as 1796 about the need to recognise the symbolic value of works within their own country. Such arguments came hard on the heels of the work of the German scholar Johann Winckelmann (1717–68). The first to write a history of art, rather than a history of artists, he emphasised the need to consider art within its own time and its own cultural context, whether geographical, political or artistic. Now, at the time of Napoleon's Italian campaigns, the architect Quatremère de Quincy made a similar plea for the importance of context.

Trophies of war

Ownership, or patrimony, is a vexed question. Rome itself was the home of many Greek artefacts that had not been returned to their original siting after the demise of the Roman Empire. Indeed, those in favour of the acquisitions saw Paris as the heir to Rome and believed that France was doing no more than Italy herself had done. Equally, those opposed to the "plundering" recognised the impossibility of a complete restitution of works, and also that artefacts might well be moved at other times through economic transactions rather than military force. Of particular concern, though, was the risk for the future of making works of art the trophies of war, to be carted to a new location at each victory or defeat.

The deliberate confiscation of art treasures from the defeated countries was at first only tentatively suggested, when the idea was mooted to send informed citizens after the army to gather information and bring back key works. However, the Belgian campaigns of 1794 set the ball rolling. Four Flemish works were displayed in the Louvre less than two months after victory. The gains included the central section of Rubens' profoundly moving *Descent from the Cross* (1614) from Antwerp Cathedral, which had marked the artist out as the greatest painter in northern Europe of his day.

The choice of works confiscated here and in Italy reveals the taste of the time. Rubens and Van Dyck were the popular spoils of the Belgian campaigns; but while Jan van Eyck's *Madonna with Canon van der Paele* (1436; Groeningemuseum, Belgium) and *Adoration of the Lamb* panel (c. 1426–32; St Bavo, Ghent), with their exquisitely rendered detail, were removed, very few other Northern Renaissance works of the 15th century were taken. Equally, in later campaigns, Breughel was considered almost beneath contempt, while Mantegna and Giovanni Bellini, and even Leonardo da Vinci and Michelangelo, were by no means sought after.

The memoirs of the politician Jean Chaptal indicate, rather acerbically, that Napoleon himself had no aesthetic interest in art, and that he went so far as to avoid looking at the exhibits if he

Napoleon and his generals; detail from *The Grenadier* by Edouard Detaille (Musée de l'Armée).

The Marriage Feast at Cana, (c. 1562) by Veronese was one of hundreds of artworks acquired by Napoleon during his Italian campaigns (Musée du Louvre).

was visiting the Louvre. Frédéric Masson, writing at the turn of the 20th century about Napoleon's education, suggests how little the arts in general appealed to him: "No literature; no classical reminiscences whatever; not a word of Latin… no striving after rhythm. No poetry… no novels. But on the other hand history and again history."

Napoleon's motivation lay in the glory of bringing home such trophies of war, and, it is likely, in the comparisons that could be drawn with Rome in parading the booty of Athens. At the end of the first Italian campaigns, in 1798, an ostentatious parade through the streets of Paris marked the occasion with as much pomp and glitz as possible, with exotic beasts, musical entertainment and bombastic speeches, in emulation of the Roman excess.

On the masterpiece trail

For the Italian campaigns, a team of commissioners followed Napoleon's route, selecting paintings, sculptures and other artefacts on the basis of numbers agreed at each victory. The list's specifications included 100 works of art and 500 manuscripts from Rome (1796), and 20 artworks, plus 600 manuscripts from Venice (1797). Despite this apparent control, there were obvious drawbacks to the system. The balance of the collection steadily being acquired not only suffered from the blindspots of the commissioners, but also from the need to stipulate the number of works without proper advance knowledge of them. In addition, some significant pieces held by Renaissance patrons had already been dispersed.

Nevertheless, the focus of attention was placed on Raphael above all others, on Titian and Veronese, and also on Correggio, whose popularity might have stemmed from a sensuous, almost seductive quality that anticipated that of 18th-century French painting. A notable Raphael acquisition, from Milan, was the cartoon for the School of Athens (1509–11), a perfect resolution of High Renaissance principles. The fresco itself, in the Stanza della Segnatura (one of the papal apartments), was impossible to move, since the appropriate technique had yet to be developed.

This was a source of frustration for those wishing to take what they considered to be the epitome of greatness.

From Venice came three great Veronese Feasts. Two of these were returned during the reclamations of 1815, while *The Marriage Feast at Cana* (1562–3), a sumptuous vision of convivial Venetian society, originally in a Benedictine refectory on San Giorgio Maggiore, was considered too delicate to transport a second time and so remained in the Louvre. Other works included Titian's *Martyrdom of St Lawrence* (1548–59) from the Church of the Gesuiti. This painting anticipates the artist's last phase, with a new expressionism, deep shadow and bursts of glaring light, together with dramatic foreshortening.

Florence fell victim to Napoleon's rapaciousness in 1799. Although the Uffizi remained virtually untouched, the Pitti Palace lost such works as Giorgione/Titian's pastoral idyll, the *Concert Champêtre* (1508; Louvre). Meanwhile, the list of gains from Rome read like a roll call of classical sculpture: the *Apollo Belvedere*, the *Laocoön*, the *Belvedere Torso* and the *Dying Gaul* (all of which were later returned).

Showcasing the spoils

With this continual influx, the Musée Central was stuffed with masterpieces. On arrival, works were exhibited in the Salon Carré, to popular acclaim, from where they were transferred to the enormous Grande Galerie. Even this could not provide enough space, however, and soon the overspill was accommodated at Versailles, where the Musée Spécial de L'Ecole Française had been established in 1793. A Galerie des Antiques, for the display of classical artefacts, was opened in 1800 on the ground floor of the Paris museum.

Works of art went to furnish Napoleon's palaces but, more importantly, provincial France also became a beneficiary of this wealth. A museum culture was fostered as widely as possible and with long-lasting effect. In 1800, Napoleon decreed that 15 galleries should be established where it was likely that educational use might be made of the art, distributing more than 800 pictures throughout the various *départements*. The chosen towns included Bordeaux, Marseilles, Dijon and Toulouse. Regional museums that were later independent of France were set up, for instance in Brussels and Geneva. Elsewhere in the empire, Napoleon's brother Louis founded in 1808 what became the Rijksmuseum in Amsterdam. His brother Joseph laid the groundwork for the Prado in Madrid, which opened in 1814, retaining much that might otherwise have been sent to Paris. The Brera in Milan was established in 1803.

Cupid and Psyche (1787–93) by Canova, the leading Neo-classical sculptor who worked for Napoleon (Musée du Louvre).

Also in that year, the Director-General of the Musée Central, Vivant-Denon, proposed that it should be renamed the Musée Napoléon, reflecting both the First Consul's growing status, on the eve of becoming Emperor, and his pride in the institution. Denon's fidelity to Napoleon after his appointment in 1802 lasted right until the crushing defeat in 1815. He accompanied the campaign to Egypt and became the guiding hand in the later acquisitions, systematically attempting during his visit to Italy in 1811–12 to fill gaps in the collection with works by such late medieval and early Renaissance artists as Cimabue, Giotto, Fra Angelico and Fra Filippo Lippi. Works were also brought from Germany and Austria in 1806 and 1807, including a number of paintings by Rembrandt and Watteau. In 1808, Napoleon bought the collection of Prince Borghese, his brother-in-law (including sculptures such as *The Borghese Gladiator*, 1st century BC; Louvre), thus acquiring works by arguably more legitimate means.

Restitution by force

Ultimately, however, the gains were short-lived. A desire for restitution began to be voiced in 1814, and when the Empire fell, in 1815, reclamation began in earnest. Enormous resistance

was mounted, particularly on the part of Vivant-Denon and his assistant Lavallée, but they were eventually coerced by military force and the combined insistence of the allies. In the case of the papal artefacts, the sculptor Canova was sent on a specific mission of recovery.

Most of the confiscations were returned, although many originally housed in churches went on to live in galleries – notably Bellini's San Giobbe Altarpiece (*c.* 1478; Accademia, Venice), minus the architectural frame that had linked its spiritual world to the church interior. The restitution of works in some of the more remote satellite museums, and those on a huge scale, was less straightforward, however. In fact, as many as half the Italian works were retained, including paintings by Bronzino, Botticelli and Ghirlandaio. Early masterpieces, such as Cimabue's *Virgin with Angels* (*c.* 1270) and Fra Angelico's *Coronation of the Virgin* (before 1435), were not considered a priority by the commission in charge of repossessing Tuscan works.

But perhaps the most symbolic of all the restitutions was the return of Venice's four bronze horses (the *quadriga*), the city's highly prized spoils of Constantinople, which had been taken from the basilica of San Marco. These the French had placed equally prominently on top of the Arc du Triomphe du Carrousel, and they were returned together with the Lion of St Mark.

The scale of Napoleon's acquisitions was unprecedented, creating a collection of unimaginable strength, even by today's standards. Although individual circumstances – or the desire to be lenient rather than punitive – meant that anticipated works were not always removed, close to 1,500 works were drawn from foreign schools, and the same number of Classical sculptures, vases and other treasures. This was despite the fact that cities such as Padua, Naples and Vienna escaped almost or totally unscathed and that other countries evaded Napoleon's clutches altogether. After the Peace of Amiens in 1802, visitors from Britain, including the artist J.M.W. Turner, rushed to see and be amazed by the spoils. They caught the museum at one of its finest moments, fulfilling the revolutionaries' ambitious aim that: "Paris must be the European metropolis of the arts" (*La Décade Philosophique*, 1794).

THE UNIVERSAL EXHIBITIONS

"How noble would be a European exhibition, and what a
mine of instruction it would be for all"

France was the first to champion the benefits of regular international exhibitions, and from the second half of the 19th century until their demise just before World War II it was the acknowledged master of these increasingly spectacular events. The French Expositions Universelles vied for over 80 years with Britain's Great Exhibitions and America's World Fairs to present the largest and most prestigious display of products and progress. For six months at a time, the exhibitions brought together some of the largest gatherings ever seen, as millions flocked to be edified and amazed – as well as to buy.

These grand gestures developed gradually, from small and hesitant beginnings in the late 18th century. After the 1789 Revolution, the industrial arts in France were thrown into confusion. The close regulation of the guilds was suppressed and at the same time traditional aristocratic patronage all but disappeared. A new freedom of employment and commerce beckoned, but some fresh stimulus was also necessary – a new relationship had to be nurtured with new consumers.

Entry ticket to the 1889 exhibition.

With the English blockading French ports during the Napoleonic Wars, excess produce was hard to dispose of, while internal political discord called for added reassurance that French industry was still functioning. In response to these pressures, an initial exhibition was held in 1798, with products displayed in the forecourt of the Louvre. The show ran for just four days and was centred around the products of three national factories: Sèvres ceramics, Les Gobelins tapestries and Les Savonneries carpets. Its popularity led at once to more ambitious plans.

Made in France

On 15 October 1798, on the Champs de Mars, where Napoleon was to celebrate his victories, 110 exhibitors gathered under the "Temple of Industry", a portico designed by the great pro-republic artist Jacques-Louis David, to exhibit their latest products and inventions. The eclecticism of future exhibitions was established, as clocks by Breguet and glassware by Le Creusot stood alongside the products of gunsmiths, milliners and typographers, all intent on elevating "the peaceful trophies of industry to the same eminence as the trophies of heroism". The exhibition of French industry had become associated with national identity at the highest level, and with the state's post-revolutionary utopian aims.

Paris celebrating the opening night of the 1889 exhibition, by François Roux (Musée Carnavalet).

To swell the crowds of visitors, there were military parades, fireworks and dancing, as well as numerous unofficial sideshows. This clash of high ideals and popular culture was prophetic and would become a constant cause of concern throughout the 19th century, as the desire to raise standards of production and to educate the public was threatened by the lure of the amusement park. As technology advanced and the Expositions became increasingly flamboyant, however, the possibilities of combining entertainment, advertising and education grew. At the 1900 Exposition, notable exhibits included Le Transsiberien, where spectators could sit in luxurious wagons while a complete panoramic landscape, stretching from Moscow to Peking, unfolded before them, punctuated by stops at the main stations.

Showcasing the latest feats of engineering in the Galerie des Machines.

Such extravagant publicity was a far cry from the principles laid down a century earlier. In 1801 a decree was submitted for a public exposition of French industry to be held annually, making France the first country to establish such a policy. Entry would be competitive, judged first by local officials and then by leading figures in art, science and industry, with awards based on quality or originality. Conté was one of the first to receive a gold medal, for his "artificial crayons", which were hailed as one of the most promising products.

Courbet's controversial paintings, including The Studio (detail), were rejected by the 1855 exhibition selection committee.

By 1806 the number of exhibitors had grown to over 1,400. Despite this strong start, however, the Empire's wars precluded further events for the next 12 years. During the Restoration and July Monarchy, the Expositions – held at four- and then five-year intervals – grew in scale and scope. In 1834 products were divided for the first time into classifications within temporary pavilions built on the place de la Concorde, with machinery separated from chemicals, and textiles from luxury goods. The final national exhibition, in 1849, lasted six months – setting the standard for future international events – with over 4,500 exhibitors on the Champs Elysées.

The iron age

France was the first to recognise the trade benefits of an international exhibition, but it was the enthusiasm of Queen Victoria's husband, Prince Albert, that brought the idea to fruition in London's Great Exhibition of 1851. In 1855, Paris took up the challenge set by Paxton's Crystal Palace by building the Palais de l'Industrie for the city's first Exposition Universelle. The temporary nature of exhibitions favoured innovative buildings and the introduction of new engineering technologies, but as expressions of national identity, the fairs also veered towards traditional architecture and materials imbued with status. And so, after much protesting from the engineers, the iron structure of the Palais was clad in stone. With the 1867 Exposition, however, the tables were turned, as France built an enormous yet beautifully logical structure from ironwork and glass formed into concentric ovals that each contained a separate class of exhibit. Engineering took perhaps its greatest leap in 1889 with the erection of the Eiffel Tower and the Galerie des Machines. The large-span glazed-roof structures of the latter, managed to combine solidity with lightness and grace on a vast scale.

Clash of the Titans

As exhibitions became international, the fine arts took on their key role, as a reflection of the host nation's cultivation and status. At the first Exposition Universelle, in 1855, France immediately asserted herself as the lead nation in terms of artistic activity, with an enormous 5,000-strong section devoted to the arts; half of this was French, including 35 works by Delacroix and 40 by Ingres. But in the midst of the apparently inexhaustible debate between exponents of Romanticism and Neo-classicism, Courbet was treading new ground with his realist painting, which focused on direct experience and the unsentimental depiction of the poor. Considered controversial by the jury, his monumental *Burial at Ornans* and *The Studio* (Musée d'Orsay) were rejected, prompting swift retaliation – he hired his own space and held a solo exhibition within the main site.

Courbet's defiant stand was the first of several in a developing rift at the Expositions between avant-garde and academic art. Manet, whose *Olympia (see page 85)* had received a hostile response at the Salon of 1865, set up his own pavilion at the 1867 Exposition; this was the same year that Cabanel's *Birth of Venus* (Musée d'Orsay), famously described by Zola as fashioned from "a kind of pink and white marzipan", was selected. Increasingly, the works of Millet were also excluded, and the Impressionists were rejected as a group, while the sickly confections of Bouguereau continued to please.

Pissarro was quick to spot the supreme irony of the 1889 Exposition, which championed reactionary art while at the same time celebrating the centenary of the Revolution. It was only in the retrospective art show of 1900 that France's exceptional contribution began to be acknowledged. The Expositions had delivered some of the most impressive displays of art ever seen, and yet the Ecole des Beaux Arts' tight grip on French cultural ascendancy had effectively limited its opportunity for success. In a fitting twist, the Expositions' ethnographic exhibits proved extremely influential for avant-garde art at the turn of the 20th century.

With some countries endeavouring to hold competing exhibitions at the same time, and others boycotting events, regulations were introduced that limited the frequency with which each country could be host. Competition was rife at the Expositions, with military and imperial display to

While Courbet's work was rejected, Cabanel's sentimental *Birth of Venus* (1863) was selected for the 1867 Exposition.

the fore, despite the stated aim that such events should reduce international tension and promote education, trade and progress. Vast sums were spent on these extravagant showcases of national identity, prompting Walter Benjamin to state that merchandise had become the people's fetish.

Industrial arts

The advent of mass production and mass communication had an acute affect on 19th-century French design as it adjusted to new audiences and new technology. Furniture, ceramics, glassware – all the arts as applied to industry – revealed an extreme eclecticism and historicism at the Expositions, with manufacturers scurrying to satisfy all the tastes of a newly affluent market. The infatuation with an enormous range of styles, from Classical to Baroque and Rococo to Gothic, was further galvanised by exploration and colonisation, and by the Expositions themselves, where Western artefacts were juxtaposed with exhibits from Japan, Oceania and Africa. This

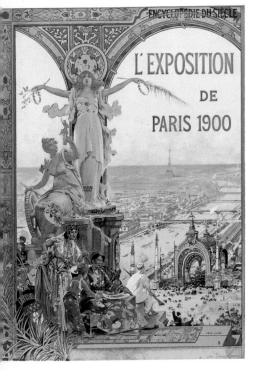

Poster for the 1900 Exposition by Luigi Loir.

dizzying pastiche of styles remained the norm until 1900, when Le Corbusier hailed a "magnificent gesture that would enable people to throw off the hand-me-downs of an outworn culture" – namely 'l'art nouveau'.

Art Nouveau to Art Deco

The 1900 show incited violently opposed reactions: from those who saw Art Nouveau's flowing, organic style with its whiplash lines and imagery drawn from nature as a senseless distortion and debasing of taste, to Le Corbusier's championing of it as a true act of courage. Nevertheless, the huge gathering of Art Nouveau designers, including Guimard, Daum Frères, Charpentier and Majorelle, drew an international audience for the style, with Gallé's superb glassware receiving a Grand Prix. Art Nouveau not only promoted creative freedom above tradition, it offered a unified aesthetic that took in furniture, architectural features, ceramics and wallpaper, with complete interiors that could seduce the Exposition visitor. The style reached its apogee in the 1900 Exposition, leaving a lasting reminder in the graceful metro station entrances designed by Guimard.

In 1925 Paris held an Exposition des Arts Décoratifs et Industriels Modernes, placing the focus specifically on modernity in design and actively discouraging products based on historical styles. The resulting synthesis of exoticism and luxury (including the use of materials such as ebony, lacquer, shagreen and chrome) applied to solid rectilinear forms with bold colours that drew on Fauvist and Cubist art, became known as Art Deco. The 1925 Exposition provided its greatest showcase. A key source of popular design during the 1920s and 1930s, Art Deco exemplified the tension between traditionalism and modernism; its forms were suited to mass-production but its appeal also lay in exclusivity and craftsmanship.

The last show

Elsewhere at the 1925 Exposition, another outlook was becoming apparent. This was concerned with frame rather than surface, with functionality and the eradication of decoration – what was later termed by the American architect Philip Johnson the "International Style". Le Corbusier's Pavilion de l'Esprit combined a fluid treatment of space with a modular form that had great implications for prefabricated housing, although it was only with the final Paris Exposition, in 1937, that Modernism was truly embraced. This final event provided a fitting climax, with 100 hectares (250 acres) of exhibition space, before war finally drew the phenomenon of the Exposition Universelle to a close.

THE ECOLE DE PARIS

At the start of the 20th century, foreign artists and writers flocked to Paris for refuge and inspiration. Their bohemian lifestyle is as much a part of the Parisian myth as the era's legacy of artistic works

Today, the name Ecole de Paris still conjures up the incredible artistic momentum of Paris between the wars, the mood of intellectual ferment, of artistic and literary debate, and the arrival of cocktails, jazz and the tango. It was neither a school or a movement, nor an organised group or association of artists – rather it is an appellation that has come to designate those essentially foreign-born artists who congregated around Montmartre in the first decade of the 20th century, and later, after World War I, in the cafés and studios of Montparnasse.

The term was originally coined by critic André Warnod in 1925 when describing "the magnetic attraction which draws artists from the entire world. Alongside French artists have appeared foreigners who have trained in France and who thus prove the existence of the Ecole de Paris". It was only later that it was used specifically for foreign artists – many but by no means all of them Jewish.

The Lapin Agile, a popular hang-out for Montmartre's Bohemian set, 1928.

Artists' asylum

Paris was an intellectual and cultural magnet. This was a bold city, where academic tradition had been challenged by the Impressionists, Cézanne and the Fauves; a city open to avant-garde currents like Cubism, Expressionism and Dadaism. And as its reputation for free-thinking and artistic innovation spread, Paris also became a magnet for foreign artists in search of refuge or a new beginning, be they Jews escaping the ghetto, Russians fleeing the Revolution or Americans seeking adventure and an escape from Prohibition.

Although not a style, the Ecole de Paris is associated with figuration, not abstraction, marked by a form of expressionism and a certain relationship to the contemporary world, not Surrealism. At its centre were Chagall, Soutine, Modigliani, Foujita, Pascin, Kisling and Van Dongen, but beyond that boundaries become blurred: Picasso, yes (although he's such a massive figure of modern art that he is hard to fix in any school), Juan Gris, and Ossip Zadkine possibly, but not Jacques Lipchitz or Brancusi, nor Max Ernst. More peripheral figures include Michel Kikoïne,

Woman with Blue Eyes by Amedeo Modigliani (Musée d'Art Moderne de la Ville de Paris).

Simon Mondzain, Chana Orloff, Marie Vassilieff, the Chilean Ortiz de Zarate, and Maurice Utrillo, French born but whose drunken lifestyle and attachment to Montmartre make him an eminently suitable candidate. Indeed, sometimes one has the impression that today Ecole de Paris has lost its wider sense and is simply a useful catch-all term for those artists who don't fit neatly into any other group.

(To complicate matters further, the Ecole de Paris is not to be confused with what is often called the Nouvelle Ecole de Paris, a term used to describe postwar artists in Paris who dealt, this time, with a form of abstraction. It included Portuguese Maria-Elena Viera da Silva, Chinese Zou Wou Ki and Russian Serge Poliakoff.)

The exhibition 'L'Ecole de Paris 1904–1929, la part de l'autre' at the Musée d'Art Moderne de la Ville de Paris in 2000/1 took a broader perspective by opening (or reopening) the definition to include all artists of foreign origin who worked in Paris, however briefly, after 1904 (the year Picasso moved into the Bateau Lavoir – *see below*), and by putting the stress on the rapid spread of Cubism. Thus it added to the core list Spanish artist Juan Gris, the Russians Archipenko and Sonia

Delaunay, Czech abstractionist Frantisek Kupka, Dutch painter Piet Mondrian, Lithuanian sculptor Jacques Lipchitz, Mexican muralist Diego Rivera, futurist Gino Severini, dadaist Jean Crotti and surrealist Giorgio de Chirico. It also rediscovered lesser names, such as Polish sculptor Xawery Dunikowski and Swiss painter Alice Bailly, and embraced photographers such as Man Ray, Brassai, Steiglitz, Ilsa Bing and Berenice Abbott. Even this was inevitably a partial, one-sided look at what was going on in Paris: Cubism doesn't make much sense if you look at Picasso and not Braque; and Van Dongen must also be considered in relation to Derain, Matisse and the other Fauves.

A way of life

The Ecole de Paris, though, was as much to do with lifestyle as artistic style. These artists rented studios at the Bateau Lavoir in Montmartre, or at La Ruche, Cité Falguière, Villa Seurat, rue Campagne-Première and countless others around Montparnasse. But exchanges also took place in the cafés and brasseries of Montparnasse, such as Le Select, La Dôme, Le Dingo and the Café de la Rotonde, the glamorous Art

The terrace in L'Estaque, 1908, Georges Braque (Centre Pompidou). Braque's partnership with Picasso, gave birth to Cubism.

Deco brasserie and dancehall La Coupole, which opened in 1927 and whose columns were painted by different artists, in cabarets such as Le Bal Nègre and Le Jockey, and in the notorious lesbian club Le Monocle.

The artists painted each other but also writers, critics, poets like Apollinaire, Blaise Cendrars and Max Jacob, Gertrude Stein and Henry Miller, and dealers like Daniel-Henry Kahnweiller, Ambrose Vollard and Paul Guillaume. Their paintings captured drinkers, dancers and prostitutes, Parisian icons like the Eiffel Tower, and themes like clowns and the circus, which some have interpreted as a typically melancholic outlook.

Excluded from the Ecole de Beaux-Arts as foreigners, many of the artists studied at private art academies such as the Académie de la Grande Chaumière, the Académie Russe and the Académie Matisse (in what is now the Musée Rodin). Most avant-garde of the lot was the Académie Vassilieff, opened by Russian artist Marie Vassilieff in an alley of studios at 21 avenue du Maine in

To My Wife, by Marc Chagall, 1933–4 (Pompidou Centre).

1911 (today preserved as the Musée du Montparnasse, *see page 137*). Here, she dispensed with formal teaching methods in favour of classes given by the pupils themselves. During World War I, she ran a canteen for impoverished artists frequented by Picasso, Braque and Modigliani among others; and in the 1920s she organised celebrated fancy-dress balls such as the Bal Banal and Bal Transmental.

Chagall, Pascin and Foujita

Who then were the key figures of the Ecole de Paris? Born in Vitebsk, later a student in St Petersburg, Marc Chagall (1887–1985) came to Paris for the first time in 1911. He rented a studio at La Ruche and soon became friends with the poets Apollinaire and Blaise Cendrars. His paintings from this period combine his personal, often joyful, mysticism, impregnated by Jewish Hassidic tradition and Russian folklore, and the formal influences of Cubism in joyful paintings of family events and rituals. Chagall returned to Russia in 1914 to marry his beloved wife Bella but came back to Paris in 1923.

Bulgarian Jules Pascin (1885–1930) moved first to Munich and then, in 1905, to Paris. He stands out as a superb draughtsman in nudes and complex erotic genre scenes that reflected his own debauched lifestyle and, despite a love of voluptuous French 18th-century Rococo painters, a style and subject matter that were closer to those of Toulouse-Lautrec's cabaret scenes.

Famed for his once enormously popular, delicate linear paintings of nudes and cats, Japanese artist Tsuguharu Foujita (1886–1968) arrived in Paris in 1913 and later lived alongside Soutine and Modigliani in the Cité Falguière. In the 1920s he lived out a *ménage à trois* with his wife Lucie Badoud, alias the model Youki, and her lover, Surrealist poet Robert Desnos.

> ### To Pay Homage
>
> Work by the "Ecole de Paris" is on show at:
> - Centre Georges Pompidou, see page 55
> - Musée d'Art Moderne de la Ville de Paris, see page 97
> - Musée de Vieux Montmartre, see page 182
> - Musée de l'Orangerie, see page 106
> - Musée d'Art et d'Histoire du Judaisme, see page 119
> - Musée Picasso, see page 90
> - Musée Zadkine, see page 161

Modigliani, Van Dongen and Soutine

From a family of wealthy Italian Jews, Amadeo Modigliani (1884–1920) was one of the artists known as "*les peintres maudits*" (cursed painters) – talented, precocious and suffering from tuberculosis, indulging in drugs and alcohol. Modigliani arrived in Paris in 1902. Early in his career he tried his hand at sculpting, carving primitive, elongated heads directly out of stone, inspired by African art and Brancusi's work. Today, though, he is best known for his elongated, stylised portraits of women, such as Beatrice Hastings and his last, tragic mistress Jeanne Hébuterne, as well as portraits of fellow artists and writers including Soutine and Max Jacob.

The Dutch artist Kees Van Dongen (1877–1968) arrived in France in 1900 and moved into the Bateau Lavoir, which put him in contact with the most avant-garde currents of the time. Although closely associated with Fauvism and later a successful portrait painter, Van Dongen produced work that is marked by a particular sensuality – as in the once-scandalous *La Châle Espagnol* and in the daring regard of the *Saltimbanque au Sein Nu*, which depicts a bare-breasted dancer at the Folies Bergère.

Most clearly representing the expressionist current, Lithuanian painter Chaim Soutine (1893–1943) arrived in Paris in 1913. Although he soon became very successful, his frenzied, thick brushstrokes and distorted outlines, influenced by Van Gogh, the Fauves and, above all, Rembrandt, express a tormented outlook in powerful psychological portraits and landscapes.

Kiki de Montparnasse

Curiously, though, the figure who best epitomises the liberated spirit of artistic Montparnasse was not an artist, but model and muse Kiki de Montparnasse. Born Alice Prin in 1901, she arrived in Paris during World War I, and soon became part of the artistic circle who met at the Café de la Rotonde. Painted by Soutine, Van Dongen, Kisling and Foujita with her characteristic black fringe, she also entered the Surrealist pantheon, as mistress and model of Man Ray; she starred in several of his experimental films and in his photo *Le Violin d'Ingres*. Beautiful, charming, outrageous, Kiki painted, danced, sang lewd songs at Le Jockey and published her memoirs at the age of 28.

Perhaps, then, one should take Ecole de Paris literally, that it is Paris the city, not any particular academy or teacher, that was the inspiration, as place of liberty, cultural melting pot and school of life. By World War II that spirit had passed: Chagall fled to the US (although he returned to the south of France after the war), Modigliani and Pascin were dead and Soutine died after an operation. It was no longer Paris that was the centre of artistic experimentation but the United States.

Kiki de Montparnasse in a Red Jumper and a Blue Scarf, by Moise Kisling (1891–1953).

MITTERRAND'S GRANDS PROJETS

Mitterrand left his mark with his "Great Works" –
eight monumental building projects that in two
decades transformed the city skyline

François Mitterrand, a man of letters and the first Socialist president of France, was elected to office in 1981. Several months later, during his first press conference, Mitterrand defined his plans for the economy and announced that several big cultural projects were underway. This set in motion what was to become the most ambitious building scheme in Paris since the 19th century. Over the next 14 years, Mitterrand personally saw to completion a series of architectural projects that came to be known as the Grands Projets (Great Works), which forever altered the Parisian skyline.

There had been no real policy for Paris as a capital since Haussmann re-organised the city in the mid-1800s. Baron Georges-Eugène Haussmann, the Paris Prefect from 1853 to 1870, carried out Napoleon III's plans to modernise the city with authority and ruthlessness. Inspired by London's infrastructures and architecture, Haussmann's façades and squares echoed the Georgian style of the times. Wide avenues were built for better traffic and crowd control during social uprisings. Entire neighbourhoods were razed, including most of the medieval streets surrounding Notre-Dame cathedral, in order to clean up the city, which still had problems with cholera epidemics and other diseases.

Measuring roughly 100 metres by 100 metres (328 x 328 ft), La Grande Arche at la Défense has the same dimensions as the Cour Carrée at the Louvre.

Ambitious plans

François Mitterrand was far less radical than Baron Haussmann. Nonetheless, using steely determination, extreme political agility and US$6 billion, he embarked on a different mission – to make sure that Paris was anchored to the map as one of the cultural capitals of the world.

During his first term, Mitterrand concentrated on laying the foundations for most of the buildings, including the Ministry of Finance (formerly housed in the Richelieu wing of the Louvre), and

on the restoration of the Louvre. The Grande Arche project at La Défense, a financial and shopping district on the western outskirts of Paris was begun; work also started on the Bastille Opéra and on the Parc de la Villette, with the adjoining Cité des Sciences and Cité de la Musique, located on the site of former slaughterhouses built during Haussmann's times. Buildings such as the Institut du Monde Arabe and the Musée d'Orsay, which had been commissioned by Mitterrand's predecessor, Valéry Giscard-d'Estaing, were also finished.

Mitterrand's second term was devoted mainly to a project that was particularly close his heart – the planning and construction of a new National Library, which would be one of the world's largest.

Accusations of megalomania aside, in a remarkably short time Mitterrand had transformed Paris into a laboratory for contemporary architecture and made the Ministry of Culture more powerful than it had ever been. Several factors contributed to his success.

First, his motivation: "His needs as a man of culture had to be satisfied," said Emile Biasini, who directed the Louvre renovation and was later named secretary of state for the Great Works. "The policy of the Grands Projets was intimately linked to his desire to make cultural activities an integral part of our nation's life, and to bring into the present our great historical heritage."

Second, Mitterrand's ability as a politician allowed him to surround himself with people who would ensure that the Grands Projets did not get mired in political squabbles. Jack Lang, the flamboyant Minister of Culture for most of Mitterrand's tenure, played a very important role in the orchestration of the projects, as well as making cultural events accessible to everyone. Emile Biasini, a man who had the reputation of getting the job done, was also a Gaullist, which smoothed over whatever differences Mitterrand had with Paris's Gaullist mayor at the time – Jacques Chirac. Concurrently, while some opposition was inevitable, the flurry of attention being given to the capital by the President sparked a sort of competitiveness within the mayor's office. "Paris benefited from this political tension," says Parisian architect Antoine Grumbach, who presided on the jury for the competition of the Grande Arche at La Défense.

Finally, Mitterrand had two further advantages that helped ensure his success: he had time on his side – two seven-year terms to be precise – and, unlike Haussmann who expropriated land for his projects, Mitterrand built his Grands Projets on state land, which made administrative procedures much shorter.

Building boom

Competitions for the various projects were constantly under-way. According to law, all public buildings exceeding a cost of US$180,000 had to be open to an architect's competition. Mitterrand, says Grumbach, hated not being able to pick the designs himself. With Biasini's help, he was able to circum-vent the law for one project – the renovation of the Louvre. Biasini had convinced Mitterrand that the Chinese-American architect, I.M. Pei, was the only man for the job. By cultivating a rapport with the Louvre's in-house architect, Georges Duval, Biasini persuaded Duval to hire Pei as an associate.

I.M. Pei's glass and metal pyramid entrance to the Louvre, the subject of tremendous polemic at the time, is today the most successful and universally praised of the Grands Projets, while Mitterrand's pet project, the National Library, known as the TGB (Très Grande Bibliothèque), is one of the least successful.

Mitterrand wanted to build a library that would offer the public, as well as researchers, a veritable world in which the most advanced technology would help them find whatever it was they were looking for. Controversy concerning the library began at once. The intelligentsia were not happy about a library that would be used by academics and the public at the same time. The design itself, by Dominique Perrault, was highly contested, mainly due to concern for the 12 million books, which were to be stocked in four 80-metre (262-ft) high glass towers, where temperature and exposure to light were difficult to regulate. After years of haggling, and a few alterations to the project, the massive National Library finally opened in 1997, in an urban wasteland that is slowly developing into a new neighbourhood.

I.M. Pei's Louvre Pyramid, an architectural icon, second only to the Eiffel Tower.

Decentralisation

From 1984 until Mitterrand's term ended in 1995, new structures were constantly being inau-gurated. Many of the buildings were located on the periphery of the city: the Cité des Sciences and Christian de Portzamparc's Cité de la Musique at La Villette, at the far northern end of Paris; von Spreckelsen's Grande Arche at La Défense, on the northwestern outskirts; the Ministry of Finance and the National Library on the southeastern outskirts.

Parc de la Villette, designed by Bernard Tschumi.

Paris's boundaries had been extended, creating new neighbourhoods and, at the same time, clearly marking the city's confines. Mitterrand also opened up a visual axis, extending the so-called Triumphal Way that runs from the Louvre Pyramid through the Arc du Carrousel in the Tuileries gardens to the Arc de Triomphe, to the Grande Arche at La Défense on the Seine's west bank.

" It was a political gamble, decentralising everything. Did anyone think that people would go all the way to La Villette to listen to concerts? Well, they do." says Grumbach.

And was there a "Mitterrand style"? Bernard Latarjet, an advisor to Mitterrand during that period, thought not. "Mitterrand had limited power in the choice of a project. He liked the Louvre but didn't like the Bastille Opéra at all, which was Jack Lang's choice."

But Antoine Grumbach disagrees. "Mitterrand had a vision of architecture which was pure, simple forms. It reminds me of the schoolbooks we had as children. On the last page there were the multiplication tables and the five primary geometric shapes. It's as if he was inspired by these very forms. Whenever there was a choice, he systematically went towards those forms. He wasn't a baroque man!"

"My criticism is that the buildings are a collection of objects, simply planted there, not urban projects." continues Grumbach. "From an architectural point of view, besides the pyramid, none of the buildings are points of reference."

While they may not be reference points, some of the buildings are a big success with the public: the Louvre, which before the renovation was notoriously run-down, has 6 million visitors a year; the Musée d'Orsay, which had been an abandoned train station, has 2½ million, while crowds of 5½ million a year go to La Villette.

A legacy of landmarks

In a city that has a tremendous concentration of distinctive monuments, Mitterrand's Grands Projets increased the number of landmarks the weary tourist feels compelled to see, and carved out new neighbourhoods for Parisians. Early in this new century, Parisians seem tired out by the political histrionics the buildings provoked, and the exorbitant cost of their upkeep. The only major current project is the development of the Quai Branly area and Musée des Arts Premiers (a museum of "tribal arts"), initiated by Jacques Chirac. Jean Nouvel, the architect who built the Institut du Monde Arabe and the Grand Stade de France in St-Denis, won the competition to develop the Seine-side museum. Due to open in 2004, it will house an important collection of African, Asian, American and Oceanic works of art gathered from other collections – its core formed by the Musée de l'Homme's anthropological collection currently housed in the Palais de Chaillot (see page 193).

The Opéra Bastille, designed by Carlos Ott.

The current Paris council is unlikely to invest huge sums in major building projects. Polls taken during the 2001 mayoral elections showed that Parisians' needs were simple, being more concerned with using taxpayers' money to reduce dog waste and create bicycle lanes. François Mitterrand will go down in history as having forever put his mark on Paris. And the US$6 billion price tag? It is, after all, as Biasini put it, merely the price of a new aircraft carrier.

CONTEMPORARY ART

The appearance of new public venues and commercial galleries has brought a new dynamism to the Paris art scene

Until recently, the main showcases for contemporary art and photography in Paris have been the Centre Pompidou, Musée d'Art Moderne de la Ville de Paris, Fondation Cartier, Centre National de la Photographie and the Maison Européenne de la Photo. In 2002, two new public venues were added to the list: the adventurous Site de Création Contemporaine in the Palais de Tokyo and the smaller Plateau in the 19th *arrondissement*. A third new gallery, the Fondation Pinault in the adjoining suburb of Boulogne-Billancourt, is due to open in 2004.

Two annual prizes – the Prix Ricard presented at the Espace Paul Ricard, and the Prix Marcel Duchamp, awarded by an association of French collectors (ADIAF), the winner of which has an exhibition at the Centre Pompidou – are also gaining recognition. All are signs that there's plenty going on in an art scene that at first sight appears low key, unfocused and elitist compared to the highly energetic and visible New York art scene, and the highly mediatised, clearly defined Brit pack of London's YBA scene, or the powerful market-led arena in Germany.

A global view

Curiously, for a country that is highly chauvinistic on many counts, and where both galleries and artists are suspected of huge levels of public funding, the contemporary art scene in Paris is amazingly open and international. Exhibitions, both in museums/public spaces and in commercial galleries, offer plenty of opportunities for an overview of what is going on all over the world. At any one time you're likely to find shows by artists from across Europe, America and the Far

Martial Raysse's *Turkish Bath* gives a modern twist to Ingres' masterpiece, pictured on page 68.

East – possibly rather more easily than shows of art that have been produced locally. In this climate of international dialogue, many young artists have networks with artists in other countries and exhibitions frequently tour the world.

The gallery circuit

The institutions work in tandem with the commercial galleries *(see page 134)*. Many of these are clustered in the Marais, with older groupings in St-Germain-des-Prés and off the Champs-Elysées, and a nucleus of young galleries with a conceptual bias around rue Louise-Weiss in the 13th *arrondissement*. Unlike museums, where a solo show will usually be a one-off culmination of years of work, galleries build up a relationship with their artists and follow their career in the long-term. They also display the work of young artists often long before they have major museum shows and, in the case of complex installations or videos, help in the production of the work itself, whether it involves airline sponsorship to film in different countries, or teams of assistants. In this sense they function rather like the drapery painters of the grand history painters in the 17th and 18th centuries.

There is also an increasing circuit of alternative spaces – artist-run spaces like Glassbox or independent curators putting on shows in unexpected places, from private flats to Paris's 19th-century covered galleries, shop windows, department stores, hotels or outdoor locations. Just as art has moved beyond the traditional canvas and bronze, you'll find on one hand art that has moved outside the conventional museum and gallery, often in site-specific projects that relate to a particular architectural space or urban context, and, on the other, the sort of massive, public artwork that can only exist in a museum-style environment.

Salons and studios

An overview of contemporary creation can be had at FIAC, held every autumn at Paris-Expo, which generally features around 160 French and international galleries. A more recent arrival, Art Paris, held at the Carrousel du Louvre, is less cutting edge and more geared to private collectors, while the salon Paris Photo has quickly established its place with a successful mix of historic and contemporary, classic and art photography. For an insight into artists' lives, the annual open studio schemes that are organised in many districts of Paris and the suburbs, notably the Bastille, Ménilmontant, Montreuil and the 13th *arrondissement*, let you take a peek at artists' workspaces, although the most successful and known artists rarely participate.

If Paris itself is no longer the artistic magnet it was in the early 20th century, and if the notorious, bohemian entourage has been replaced by a more discreet, rather closed intellectual bubble, the city still exercises an enormous pull on artists from all over the world, whether because of France's human rights record, the availability of grants and studios, or the position of Paris at the centre of Europe. One of the most noticeable contributions in the 1990s was made by Chinese artists, many of whom arrived after the massacre at Tiannanmen Square, with work that often combines all the issues and techniques of contemporary art with elements drawn from Chinese heritage, drawing on ancient myth, rites and medicine.

Seven Virtues and Seven Vices by Bruce Nauman, 1983 (Saatchi Collection, London).

The art

The plurality of current art in its subjects, in its media (painting, photography, installation, video, drawing, sculpture, soundtracks and computers are all equally valid), in its cultural and artistic references, and in its interaction with music, film, fashion, architecture and even science and medicine, can make it hard to get a handle of current production. Indeed, many contemporary artists work in a whole variety of media: Rebecca Bournigault uses video, photography and drawing; Fabrice

Hybert uses painting, ceramics, installation and video; Franck Scurti produces videos, objects and sculptures. Just as occurred throughout the 20th century, there are those artists who take refuge from the outside world, and those whose art reflects and comments on it, those who seek objectivity and those who seek expression. Of course, at any one moment, several generations overlap: artists associated with *Nouveau Réalisme* like Martial Raysse, Arman and Jean-Pierre Raynaud; those associated with minimalism, abstraction and environments like Aurélie Nemours, François Morellet and Daniel Buren; and conceptual artists like Christian Boltanski, Annette Messager, Bertrand Lavier and Sophie Calle, all still exist alongside the rising new generation of artists.

Liza Lou's *Back Yard* installation at the Fondation Cartier, 2001.

The new generation

For many young artists, Marcel Duchamp remains a father figure, but the current scene also owes much to movements like Fluxus, 1970s conceptual art, and to figures like Bruce Nauman, as well as to neo-pop art in its fixation with brand names, consumer products, the media, kitsch and the everyday. Natacha Lesueur who deals with the body, food and media images of women in clever photoworks, is one of many artists using fashion, brands and logos to comment on issues of society, the body, sexuality, identity and social tribes. Alain Séchas' cat figures ape human behaviour, Claude Closky picks out subliminal mathematical series and linguistic and visual codes. But there are also issues of art production itself, and questions of representation, authorship, fact and fiction, documentary and narrative.

Video and installation have added the dimensions of temporality, sound, even smell or temperature, creating environments in which the artwork interacts with the viewer and a specific space. In the installations of Véronique Boudier, decaying food or oozing jelly creeping across a floor may be combined with sound effects and video. The breathtaking installations of Thomas Hirschhorn, composed of aluminium foil, sticky tape and cardboard, treat issues such as capitalism and consumerism, the UN or disease. If, on the one hand, autobiographical content abounds – from the hard-hitting slice-of-life photos of Delphine Kreuter to the wittily self-deprecating videos of Pierrick Sorin – on the other, art poses questions of authorship and personal style: there's an undoubted current of collaborations, cooperatives, artists' networks and shared exhibitions.

Central Paris

0 — 200 m
0 — 200 yds

A **B** **C** **D**

N

1

Rd.-Pl. des
Champs Elysées-
Marcel Dassault
Franklin D.
Roosevelt

Av. Jean Mermoz

Av. Matignon

Av. Gabriel

Place
Beauvau

Rue du Cirque

Rue de l'Elysée

Archevêché
de Paris

Blvd Malesherbes

Rue Tronchet

Rue du Faubourg St Honoré

St-Michael's
English Church

Palais de
l'Elysée

Comédie
Caumartin

Le Musée du
Parfum Fragonard

Chaussée
d'Antin

Musée
de l'Opéra

Ri

Théâtre
Marigny

Av. Gabriel

Ste-Marie
Madeleine

Madeleine

Olympia

Opéra

Pl. Ch.
Garnier

Blvd Haussmann

Blvd des Italien

Av. de Marigny

Espace
Paul Ricard

Blvd de la Madeleine

Blvd des

Capucines

Rue du Quatre Septembre

4 Septembre

2

Church of
Scotland

Place
François 1er

St-Jean
Baptiste

Av. Montaigne

Théâtre R.
Barrault

Av. Franklin-D-Roosevelt

Palais
de la
Décou-
verte

Galeries
Nationales
du Grand
Palais

Grand
Palais

Av. W. Churchill

Petit
Palais

Champs Elysées
Clemenceau

Place
Clemenceau

Av. des Champs Elysées

Espace
Pierre Cardin

Pl. de la
Concorde

Concorde

Rue Royale

Crédit Foncier
de France

Ministère de
la Justice

N. D. de
L'Assomption

Rue St-Florentin

Rue St-Honoré

Rue du Mont Thabor

Rue de la Paix

Place
Vendôme

Honoré

St-Roch

Pyramides

Av. de l'Opéra

Avenue de l'Opéra

Rue Louis le Grand

Bibli-
Natio
Ric

Musée du Cabinet
des Médailles

JARDIN
DU
PALAIS
ROYAL

3

Quai d'Orsay

Rue Surcouf

Rue Jean Nicot

Cours la Reine

Pont
Alexandre III

Pont
des Invalides

Min. des
Affaires
Etrangères

Min. des
Affaires Europ.

Assemblée
Nationale
(Palais Bourbon)

Invalides

Rue de l'Université

Quai

Assemblée
Nationale

← Seine

Pont de la Concorde

Galerie Nationale
du Jeu de Paume

Musée
de l'Orangerie

Terrasse des Feuillants

Rue de Rivoli

JARDIN DES
TUILERIES

Quai des Tuileries

Quai Anatole France

Min. de l'Artisanat
du Commerce et
de la Consommation

Musée de la
Légion d'Honneur et des
Ordres de Chevalerie

Musée d'Orsay

Tuileries

Musée de la Mode et du Textile
Musée des Arts Décoratifs
Musée de la Publicité

Arc de Triomphe
du Carrousel

Place du
Carrousel

Pont du Carrousel

Quai Voltaire

Rue de Lille

Rue de l'Université

Rue de Verneuil

Quai Malaquais

Comédie
Française

Palais
Royal

Palais Roya
Musée du L

Cour Napoléon

Pyramide

Quai du L

Musée N
du Lo

Quai de

4

La Tour
Maubourg

Rue Duvivier

Rue Amélie

Blvd de La Tour Maubourg

Place des
Invalides

Hôtel des
Invalides

Musée
de l'Armée

Musée de l'Ordre
et de la Libération

St-Louis

Eglise
du Dôme

JARDIN DE
L'INTENDANT

Rue Saint Dominique

Min. de
la Défense

Institut
Geographique
National

Varenne

Rue de Grenelle

Rue de Bourgogne

Basilique
Ste-Clotilde

Min. du
Tourisme

Min. de
l'Agriculture et
de la Pêche

Musée
Rodin

Blvd St-Germain

Musée
d'Orsay

Solférino

Rue de Belle-Chasse

R. de l'Université

ST-GERMAIN
DES PRÉS

Rue du Bac

St-Thomas
d'Aquin

Ensb-a
(Ecole Nationale
Sup. des Beaux Arts)

Rue Jacob

Rue de Seine

Université
Paris V

Rue Bonaparte

Musée National
Eugène Delacroix

Rue Mazarine

Quai de

Musée
de la
Monn
de Pa

5

Avenue de Tourville

Ecole
Militaire

Avenue de Breteuil

Avenue Duquesne

Rue d'Estrées

St-François
Xavier

St-François
Xavier

Pl. du Prés
Mithouard

Avenue de Saxe

Rue Masseran

Rue Cal. Bertrand

Rue Ebla

Rue Oudinot

Rue des Invalides

Rue Vaneau

Boulevard des Invalides

Rue Barber de Jouy

Place Vauban

Rue de Varenne

Musée Maillol-
Fondation
Dina Vierny

Boulevard Raspail

Vaneau

Rennes

Rue de Sèvres

Bon
Marché

Sèvres
Babylone

Espace Electra-
Fondation EDF

Rue de Babylone

Rue de Rennes

Rue de Grenelle

St-Germain
des Prés

St-Sulpice

Rue du Four

St-Germain
des Prés

Blvd

Rue de Rennes

Rue du Vieux Colombier

Rue Madame

St-Sulpice

St-Sulpice

QUARTIER

LATIN

Pl. Rue Saint Sulpice

Institut Fra
d'Architec

Place
l'Odé

Odéon

Mabillon

Saint - Ge

6

Séguir

Place
de Breteuil

Blvd Garibaldi

Sèvres
Lecourbe

Rue Bouchut

Pl. Henri
Queuille

Avenue de Breteuil

Rue de

Duroc

Fondation
Dubuffet

Rue du Montparnasse

Blvd du Montparnasse

MONTPARNASSE

Falguière

Rue de Vaugirard

Pasteur

Musée de
la Poste

Musée
Bourdelle

Musée du
Montparnasse

Montparnasse
Bienvenue

Rue de l'Arrivée

Rue de Vaugirard

Place du
18 Juin 1940

Montparnasse
Bienvenue

Tour
Montparnasse

Musée
Ernest Hébert

Rue Saint Placide

St-Placide

Rue de Fleurus

Rue Littré

Rue Notre - Dame - des Champs

N.-D. des
Champs

N. D. des
Champs

Vavin

Musée du
Luxembourg

Petit
Luxembourg

Palais du
Luxembourg
(Sénat)

JARDIN DU

LUXEMBOURG

Rue Guynemer

Rue Auguste Comte

JARDIN
R. CAVELIER-
DE-LA-SALLE

R. Miche-let

Pl
F

Pl

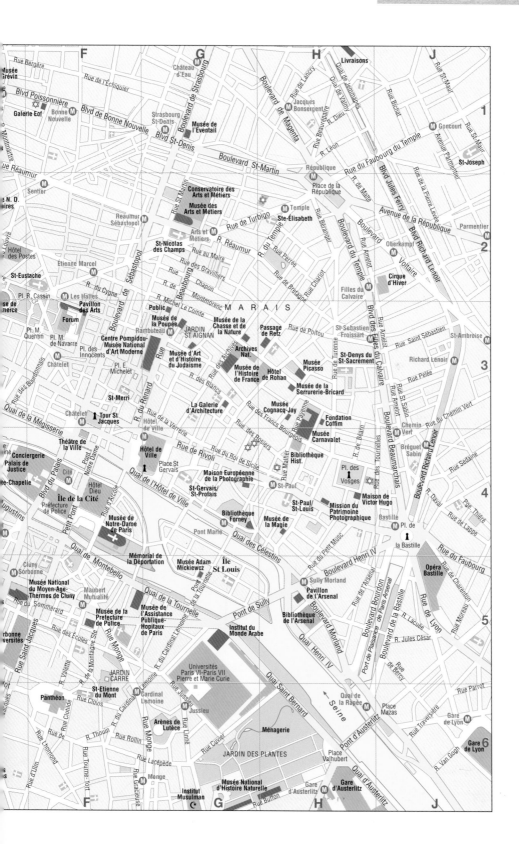

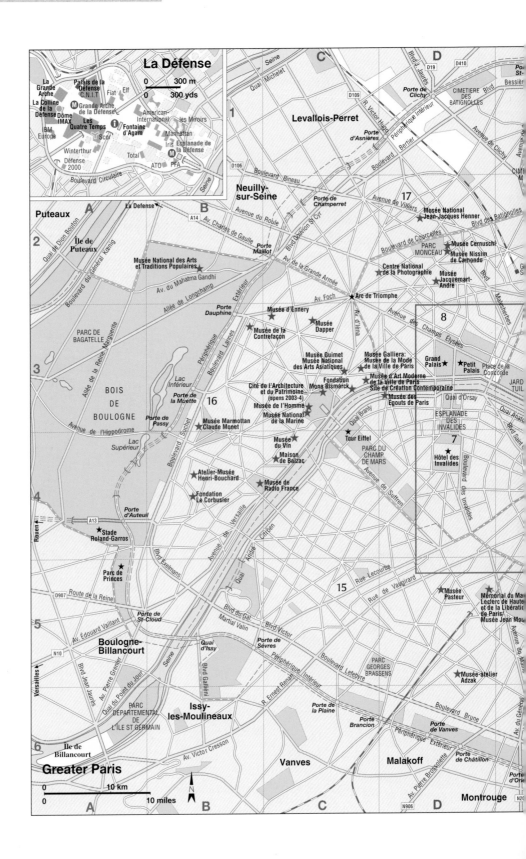

La Défense

0 ____ 300 m
0 ____ 300 yds

La Grande Arche
Palais de la Défense C.N.I.T Fiat Elf
La Colline de la Défense
Dôme
IMAX
BM Europe
Scor
Winterthur
Défense 2000
Grande Arche de la Défense
Les Quatre Temps
Fontaine d'Agam
American-International
les Miroirs
Manhattan
Iris Esplanade de la Défense
Total
ATO PFA

Boulevard Circulaire

Seine

Puteaux

La Défense

A14 Av. Charles de Gaulle

Neuilly-sur-Seine

Levallois-Perret

Quai de Michelet
Seine
R. Victor Hugo
Porte de Clichy
CIMETIERE DES BATIGNOLLES
Boulevard Bineau
Avenue de Villiers
Porte de Champerret
Porte d'Asnières
Boulevard Bertier
Périphérique Intérieur
Avenue de Clichy

17

★ Musée National Jean-Jacques Henner

★ Musée Cernuschi
★ Musée Nissim de Camondo

PARC MONCEAU

Boulevard de Courcelles

Centre National de la Photographie ★

★ Musée Jacquemart-André

Av. de la Grande Armée
Porte Maillot
Blvd Pershing St Cyr
Av. de la Grande Armée
Av. Foch ★ Arc de Triomphe
Avenue des Champs Élysées

8

Île de Puteaux

Quai de Dion Bouton

Boulevard du Général Koenig

2

PARC DE BAGATELLE

BOIS DE BOULOGNE

Allée de la Reine Marguerite

3

Lac Inférieur

16

Porte de la Muette

Lac Supérieur

Avenue de l'Hippodrome

Porte de Passy

Boulevard Suchet

Périphérique

Boulevard Lannes

Porte Dauphine

Allée de Longchamp

Av. du Mahatma Gandhi

★ Musée National des Arts et Traditions Populaires

Extérieur

★ Musée d'Ennery
★ Musée Dapper

★ Musée de la Contrefaçon

Musée Guimet
Musée National des Arts Asiatiques

Musée Galliera: Musée de la Mode de la Ville de Paris

Grand Palais ★ ★ Petit Palais Place de la Concorde

Musée d'Art Moderne de la Ville de Paris Site de Création Contemporaine

Cité de l'Architecture et du Patrimoine (opens 2003-4)

★ Fondation Mona Bismarck

★ Musée de l'Homme

Musée National de la Marine

★ Musée des Egouts de Paris

Quai d'Orsay

JARD TUIL

ESPLANADE DES INVALIDES

7

★ Hôtel des Invalides

★ Musée du Vin

★ Maison de Balzac

★ Tour Eiffel

PARC DU CHAMP DE MARS

Quai Branly

★ Atelier-Musée Henri-Bouchard

★ Fondation Le Corbusier

★ Musée Marmottan Claude Monet

★ Musée de Radio France

4

Porte d'Auteuil

A13

★ Stade Roland-Garros

Avenue de Versailles

Quai André Citroën

Av. de Suffren

Avenue de la Motte-Picquet

Boulevard des Invalides

5

★ Parc des Princes

D907 Route de la Reine

Porte de St-Cloud

Blvd Exelmans

Rue Lecourbe

15

Rue de Vaugirard

★ Musée Pasteur

★ Mémorial du Mal Leclerc de Haute et de la Libération de Paris/ Musée Jean Mou

Boulogne-Billancourt

N10

Av. Édouard Vaillant

Blvd du Gal Martial Valin

Blvd Victor

Quai d'Issy

Porte de Sèvres

Périphérique Intérieur

Boulevard Lefebvre

PARC GEORGES BRASSENS

★ Musée-atelier Adzak

Av. Pierre Grenier

Quai du Point du Jour

Seine

Blvd Galliéni

R. Ernest Renan

Porte de la Plaine

Porte Brancion

Porte de Vanves

Boulevard Brune

6

PARC DEPARTEMENTAL DE L'ÎLE ST GERMAIN

Issy-les-Moulineaux

Périphérique Extérieur

Porte de Châtillon

★ Île de Billancourt

Greater Paris

Av. Victor Cresson

Vanves

Malakoff

Porte d'Or

0 ____ 10 km
0 ____ 10 miles

N

Montrouge

N906 N2

A B C D

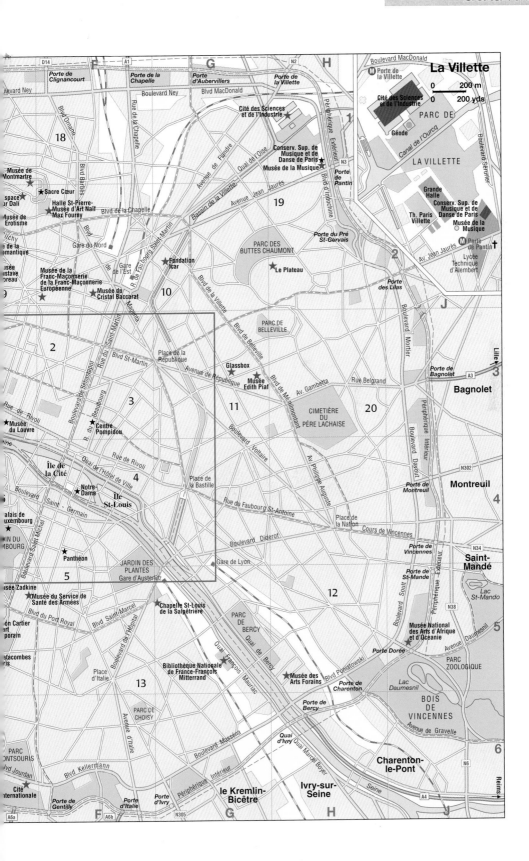

Greater Paris map showing numbered arrondissements and landmarks.

Key labels include:

Porte de Clignancourt, Porte de la Chapelle, Porte d'Aubervilliers, Porte de la Villette, Boulevard MacDonald, La Villette

Cité des Sciences et de l'Industrie, Géode, PARC DE LA VILLETTE, Grande Halle, Conserv. Sup. de Musique et de Danse de Paris, Th. Paris Villette, Musée de la Musique, Porte de Pantin, Lycée Technique d'Alembert

Boulevard Ney, Blvd MacDonald, Rue de la Chapelle, Avenue de Flandre, Quai de l'Oise, Bassin de la Villette, Avenue Jean Jaurès

18, Musée de Montmartre, Sacre Cœur, Halle St-Pierre-Musée d'Art Naïf Max Fourny, Blvd Barbès, Blvd de la Chapelle

Conserv. Sup. de Musique et de Danse de Paris, Musée de la Musique

Musée de l'Erotisme, Musée Gustave Moreau, Musée de la Vie Romantique, Gare du Nord, Gare de l'Est, Musée de la Franc-Maçonnerie de la Franc-Maçonnerie Européenne, Musée du Cristal Baccarat

19, PARC DES BUTTES CHAUMONT, Porte du Pré St-Gervais, Le Plateau, Fondation Icar, Porte des Lilas

10, Blvd de la Villette, PARC DE BELLEVILLE, Blvd de Belleville

2, Place de la République, Blvd St-Martin, Avenue de République, Glassbox, Musée Edith Piaf

Boulevard Mortier, Porte de Bagnolet, Bagnolet, Lille

3, Centre Pompidou, Rue de Rivoli, Rue de Rivoli, Musée du Louvre

11, Av. Gambetta, Rue Belgrand, CIMETIÈRE DU PÈRE LACHAISE, 20, Boulevard Davout, N302

Île de la Cité, Notre-Dame, Île St-Louis, Place de la Bastille, Boulevard Voltaire, Av. Philippe Auguste, Porte de Montreuil, Montreuil

4, Rue du Faubourg St-Antoine, Place de la Nation, Cours de Vincennes, Porte de Vincennes, N34

Palais de Luxembourg, JARDIN DU LUXEMBOURG, Boulevard Saint-Germain, Boulevard Diderot, Gare de Lyon, Porte de St-Mande, Saint-Mandé

5, Panthéon, JARDIN DES PLANTES, Gare d'Austerlitz, Musée Zadkine, Musée du Service de Santé des Armées

12, Lac St-Mando, Musée National des Arts d'Afrique et d'Océanie, Porte Dorée, PARC ZOOLOGIQUE

Chapelle St-Louis de la Salpêtrière, PARC DE BERCY, Blvd du Pont Royal, Blvd Saint-Marcel, Boulevard de l'Hôpital, Fondation Cartier art contemporain

Catacombes de Paris, Bibliothèque Nationale de France-François Mitterrand, Musée des Arts Forains, Blvd Poniatowski, Porte de Charenton, Lac Daumesnil, BOIS DE VINCENNES

13, Place d'Italie, PARC DE CHOISY, Quai François Mauriac, Quai de Bercy, Porte de Bercy

PARC MONTSOURIS, Blvd Jourdan, Cité internationale, Blvd Kellermann, Porte de Gentilly, Porte d'Italie, Porte d'Ivry, Avenue d'Italie, Boulevard Masséna, Quai d'Ivry, Quai Marcel Boyer, Charenton-le-Pont, N6, Reims, Avenue de Gravelle, Avenue Daumesnil

le Kremlin-Bicêtre, Ivry-sur-Seine, Seine, A4, N305, A6a, A6b

0 200 m
0 200 yds

STATE OF THE ART

The museums and galleries of Paris are in a constant state of flux. Across the city, new institutions are being created while old ones are being renovated, breathing new life into an already dynamic cultural scene

Unlike the lottery golden egg that has transformed the system of arts funding in Great Britain, France's museums still rely largely on state or municipal funding – though sponsors are playing an increasingly important role. This dual system provokes a healthy rivalry between the national and municipal museums that helps to nurture the cultural wealth of Paris. The cultural landscape has been further enriched by the ambitions of presidents and politicians keen to leave their mark in the form of arts institutions and architectural landmarks.

The museums of Paris may be the envy of the world, but their top-ranking position is maintained at a price. The running costs of these institutions are astronomical and, despite the millions of tourists that flood through their doors each year, the pinch is still being felt. The Centre Pompidou was given a major facelift for the millennium, but insufficient funds mean the temporary exhibition budget has been cut back. Over at the Louvre, an unfortunate number of departments are closed on a regular schedule every day due to staff shortages. The restoration of the Grand Palais – a grand glass and iron monument built for the 1900 Universal Exhibition – has been dragging on ever since the central gallery was suddenly closed overnight in 1993, and no one seems to have quite decided what to do with the stunning 1920s building (or the crocodiles in the basement) of the Musée National des Arts d'Afrique et d'Océanie.

Nonetheless, the renovation of the Musée Guimet-Arts Asiatiques has been a great success, inciting Parisians as well as tourists to (re)discover this long-neglected museum, and money is still being invested in major refurbishments of long-established museums in an attempt to transform their dusty collections into modern and dynamic attractions. And, it seems, money can be found to create new institutions. The Site de Création Contemporaine at the Palais de Tokyo, opened in 2002, has injected a much-needed burst of vitality into the contemporary art scene, with a radical opening policy (midday to midnight) that should broaden the audience beyond the regular gallery-going public. The new Musée des Arts Premiers (Museum of Tribal Arts), due to open in 2004 in a sparkling Seine-side building by Jean Nouvel, will no doubt become another "must-see" on every visitor's agenda.

However, it is the Louvre, one of France's oldest museums, that has emerged in the 21st century as one of the most forward-looking institutions of all. First opened to the public in 1793, it has managed to survive over two centuries, go high-tech overground and medieval under it, bring in all the user-friendly trappings of escalators, museum guides and restaurants, assuring its place as one of the greatest and most popular museums in the world.

PRECEDING PAGES: *La Fée de l'Electricité* (detail), 1937, by Raoul Dufy (Musée d'Art Moderne de la Ville de Paris); *Ball at the Moulin de la Galette*, 1876, by Auguste Renoir (Musée d'Orsay).
LEFT: The inside-out architecture of Piano and Rogers Pompidou Centre.

The Major
Collections

The acquisitiveness of French monarchs, the victory spoils
of Napoleon and the taste of countless collectors have
combined to assemble in Paris some of the greatest
cultural masterpieces to be found anywhere in the world

Musée Carnavalet

The history of Paris told through paintings, sculptures and *objets d'art*, spread across the rooms and corridors of two grand Marais mansions

Map reference: page 41, H4
23 rue de Sévigné, 3rd
Tel: 01 44 59 58 58
www.paris-france.org/musees/musee_carnavalet
Metro: St-Paul. Bus: 29, 69, 76, 96
Open: Tues–Sat 10am–6pm; closed Mon and public hols. Some rooms closed 12.30–2pm.
Bookshop. Wheelchair access. Library. Research facilities. Tours in English (by appointment).
Admission free.

Courtyard of the Hôtel Carnavalet.

The Musée Carnavalet recounts the history of Paris from its origins as the Gallo-Roman settlement of Lutetia to a modern-day metropolis, as seen through the eyes of contemporary artists. It is spread across a network of intimate rooms in two adjoining city mansions: the Hôtel Carnavalet (16th and 17th centuries), home of Madame de Sévigné from 1677 to 1696, and the Hôtel Le Peletier de St-Fargeau (17th century).

There are over one hundred rooms and galleries to explore. Those with plenty of time can follow the floor plan supplied at the entrance and tour the museum chronologically. If you have only an hour or so to spare it may be more beneficial to target a particular theme, such as the French Revolution or Parisian Life under Louis XIV. Like Paris itself, the Carnavalet can also be a rewarding place for a purposely aimless walk through centuries of Parisian art and décor, misery and grandeur.

The Orangery and Renaissance rooms

The museum has a vast collection of ancient objects unearthed during archaeological digs and construction work. A rotating selection of statuettes, coins, tools, pottery, jewellery and burial items are set out in the former orangery, offering an overview of prehistoric to medieval Paris (the Middle Ages is covered in depth in the Cluny Museum; *see page 78*). These four small galleries are a short prologue to the city's history. The opening act is the Renaissance (rooms 7–10).

The Hôtel Carnavalet was one of the first Renaissance buildings in Paris, and most of the ground floor dates from its construction in 1548. At that time, Paris was essentially a medieval city in the midst of transformation and a hostage to the Wars of Religion between the Protestants and the Catholic League. There are portraits of the scheming Catherine de Medici, her son Henri III, scar-faced Duc de Guise, leader of the League stabbed to death in 1588 under Henri III's orders, and Henri IV mounted on a rearing horse, alongside fragments of the original bronze equestrian statue of him which stood on the Pont Neuf. Two ominous paintings *(Procession de la Ligue dans L'île de la Cité* and *Procession de la Ligue sur la place de Grève)* depict the militant League on parade – with priests wearing cuirasses and shouldering arquebuses – outside the Louvre and in front of the half-built Town Hall.

Peace returned to Paris after the Protestant King Henri IV converted to Catholicism ("Paris is worth a Mass" he famously said) and took control of the city in 1594. Influenced by Italian Renaissance design, he created the symmetrical Place Royale (now Place des Vosges), which became the model for Place des Victoires and Place Vendôme; and the Pont Neuf, the first bridge in Paris without houses.

Louis period styles

Louis XIV (1643–1715) instituted the practice of combining the skills of artists and master craftsmen to make furniture and decorative accessories. As a result, French craftsmanship entered a golden age during the period of absolute monarchy under the next three kings, Louis XIV, XV and XVI. It was not unusual for the aristocracy to make the decoration of their Parisian mansions a lifetime occupation. When many of these homes were destroyed in the 19th century to

LEFT:
Self-Portrait
by Albrecht
Dürer, 1493.

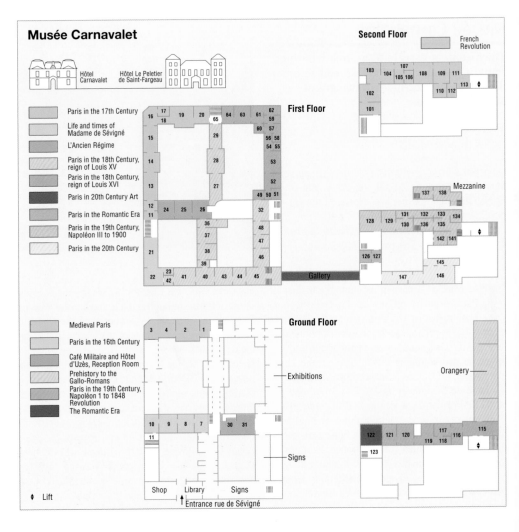

make way for Haussmann's new boulevards, their interiors were moved to the Hôtel Carnavalet, which the Paris Prefect had convinced the city to buy specifically for the purpose of conserving them.

In addition to a new sense of style, Louis XIV also gave the city its first monuments, such as the Dôme church and the Hôtel des Invalides. Architecturally, the Carnavalet owes much to the era of Louis XIV, when it was remodelled and endowed with open staircases, mansard roofs and the formal Classical garden.

Among the period interiors, the drawing-room from the Hôtel Colbert de Villacerf (room 17) serves as a perfect example of 17th-century decorative style with its gilt wood panelling, grotesques, trompe l'oeil, and ceiling painting of *Apollo and the Seasons*. The drawing room and bedroom of the

Hôtel de la Rivière (rooms 19–20) were decorated between 1652 and 1655 for the bishop of Langres by Charles Lebrun, who created or supervised the production of most of the art and decoration commissioned by Louis XIV *(see page 13)*.

The Carnavalet was the home for 20 years of Madame de Sévigné (1626–96), salon hostess and prolific letter-writer, whose writings reveal so much about the life of 17th-century French aristocrats. The Sévigné rooms (21–23), which retain the original wood panelling, are devoted to her life. These contain two charming portraits of her (by Claude Lefèbvre and Robert Nanteuil) above her Chinese lacquered writing desk and portraits of members of her coterie, including one of a young mustachioed Molière in the role of Caesar in Corneille's play *The Death of Pompey (see page 17)*.

The Louis XV style (1723–74) revelled in curves, delicate colours and Rococo ornament. Tastes became more feminine and every piece of furniture acquired a curved leg; artisans used more hand painting and Oriental lacquers. They also incorporated tinted wood, veneer, marquetry and Sèvres porcelain plaques into their designs. Exquisite make-up and gaming tables became standard boudoir accessories.

The Blue Room (room 37) is a piece of Rococo heaven with a playful chorus of furniture, stucco, panelling and objets d'art. The style in its later phase turned more sober, anticipating Neo-classicism, as in the unusual white and gold panelling of the Hôtel d'Uzès Reception Room (room 31), created in 1767. The wall panels depict trees hung with musical instruments and the doors are decorated with symbols of the four corners of the universe.

Like his father, Louis XV kept the royal court at Versailles, but Paris continued to flourish commercially and artistically without him and became the capital of the Enlightenment. In Paris, intellectuals liked to keep each other company in the salons of wealthy, witty women such as Ninon Lenclos and Madame Neckar.

Room 48 recalls the Enlightenment philosophers, writers and encyclopaedists, notably Voltaire, Rousseau and Diderot, in portraits, period furniture and other memorabilia. Voltaire's chair has wooden tables that slide out from either arm – one to hold a book and one to hold pen and paper. The principles of the Enlightenment strongly influenced the Rights of Man and the Citizen (room 104), the revolutionary proclamation which became the preface to the French Constitution.

The portrait of Louis XVI (*Louis XVI en Costume de Sacre*, room 49) by Silfred Duplessis shows him off as an absolute monarch in the manner of Louis XIV. But it is all an illusion; politically, France was moving towards Revolution. Rococo gave way to Neo-classicism under Louis XVI. The discovery of the ancient city of Pompeii had sparked a revival of Graeco-Roman styles. Rooms became smaller, more specialised and more pastel (rooms 52–55); round or oval boudoirs were all the rage and chair legs became straight again.

The Demarteau Room (58) is a brief return to the reign of Louis XV. It is the combined work of Boucher, Fragonard and Huet, fashionable Rococo painters who enjoyed the most prestigious royal decorative commissions. Created in 1765, the wood panelling originally decorated the engraver Demarteau's shop. The paintings wallow in pastoral bliss: three of the doors were painted by Boucher, the fourth (near left) is by Fragonard, who also painted the flowers, while the birds and animals were probably Huet's work.

ABOVE: Louis XVI Salon Bleu.
RIGHT: Claude Lefèbvre's portrait of *Mme de Sévigné*, 1665, whose celebrated letters provide a real insight into the customs and intrigues of Parisian high society in the 17th century.

DECISIVE DATES

300 BC	The Parisii tribe settle on the Ile de la Cité.
52 BC	Romans defeat Gaul and build Lutetia on the same site.
360	Lutetia changes its name to Paris.
485–508	Franks defeat the Romans and make Paris capital of New Frankish kingdom.
1253	Sorbonne University opens.
1453	End of the Hundred Years' War.
1572	St Bartholomew's Day massacre of Protestants.
1682	Louis XIV moves his court to Versailles.
1702	Paris is divided into *arrondissements* (districts).
1789	French Revolution.
1792	Abolition of the monarchy and birth of a Republic.
1804	Napoleon crowned Emperor.
1815	Battle of Waterloo; the monarchy is restored.
1830	Revolution in Paris; constitutional monarchy.
1848	Revolution again; fall of restored monarchy.
1851	Napoleon III becomes Emperor.
1852–70	Haussmann undertakes massive redesign of the city, creating boulevards, sewers and parks.
1870–1	Paris besieged by Prussians; end of Second Empire.
1889	Eiffel Tower built for the Universal Exhibition.
1914–18	World War I.
1925	Art Deco style debuts at Exposition des Arts Décoratifs.
1940	World War II. Paris bombed and occupied by Germans.
1944	Liberation of Paris in August.
1958	Creation of Fifth Republic with de Gaulle as President.
1968	Student riots in the Latin Quarter.
1977	Construction of Pompidou Centre.

The Hope of Happiness dedicated to the Nation. Allegory of the French Revolution, with Louis XVI led by Righteousness and Necker led by Truth (holding the mirror), by Dubois, end 18th century.

Revolutionary Paris

For all the philosophising about equality and human freedom in Paris salons, the majority of Parisians still lived in medieval conditions; during the food shortage of the summer of 1789, 88 percent of a worker's wages went to buy bread.

The Estates General, a kind of parliament representing nobility, clergy and commoners, was called into session for the first time since 1614 to address France's crisis. The Revolution's most talismanic work of art – Jacques-Louis David's *Le Serment du Jeu de Paume (The Tennis Court Oath)* in room 101 – recalls the moment in 1789 when the deputies of the National Assembly, representing the Third Estate (the commoners), met in an indoor tennis court at Versailles, where they swore to establish a new constitution. At the centre of his painting, light shines off the head of Jean Sylvain Bailly commanding the oath while the People look on. Wind-whipped drapery above their heads symbolises the revolutionary tempest. Ironically, David was never able to finish it because protagonists, such as Mirabeau, soon fell into disgrace; Bailly would perish at the guillotine.

Parisians attacked Bastille on 14 July 1789, in search of weapons. The Bastille room (room 102) documents the storming of the fortress-prison, forever after a symbol of the overthrow of tyranny and the reason for France's most important national celebration. There is a scale model of the fortress and several paintings depicting it before and after demolition, including one by Robert Hubert (himself a prisoner during the Terror; see his paintings of prison life in room 107). Among the Bastille memorabilia are the fetters that chained one of the last seven prisoners, and souvenirs supposedly carved out of the rubble.

Before her execution, the Parisian poor were obsessed with Marie Antoinette's callousness and supposed immorality; after her death, she became the focus of a cult-like fascination. The Carnavalet's royal relics (rooms 105–106) include sentimental portraits of her as a widow after Louis XVI was beheaded; a lock of her hair intertwined with that of her supposed lover, the Princess of Lamballe (who was later murdered and beheaded by a mob); her son's tin soldiers; and the spinning-wheel she used in prison. One engraving shows her in court denying the bizarre charge of incest with her son, Louis XVII ("nature forbids a mother even to answer such an accusation"), and another depicts her weeping over the Dauphin as he is led away to save him from "moral and physical degradation".

Ce Tribunal étoit composé de déterminés Révolutionaires, n'ayant aucun idées des formes Judiciaires; clesquels ennivrés de vin et de fumées concluaient par envoyer à la mort tous les prisonniers, qu'on leur amenoient à l'exception d'un petit nombre. Donc en leurs arrivant, donna la chose. S'un d'eux la pipe à la bouche faisoit l'office d'accusateur public; En vain l'accusé voulait prouver son innocence, on lui répondoit ironiquement qu'il avoit raison, qu'il pouvoit sortir; On le conduisoit à la porte où il trouvoit la Mort!

Prison Tribunal of 2 and 3 September, 1792, by Pierre Le Sueur.

The National Convention (room 108) was elected to provide a new constitution for the country after the overthrow of the monarchy, and it governed France during the crucial period of the Revolution, from late 1792 to 1795. It formally abolished the monarchy and established the republic. The second phase of the Convention (June 1793 to July 1794), better known as the Terror, was a period of war and internal rebellion; the revolutionary government fell into the hands of the Committee of Public Safety. After show trials, suspects and their entire families were sent to the guillotine. The Revolution then proceeded to "devour its children", including its most influential leaders Danton, Marat (murdered in his bath by fellow revolutionary Charlotte Corday, who was repelled by his violent excesses) and, ultimately, Robespierre. All are the subjects of paintings in this gallery.

Popular imagery came into its own during the French Revolution. Revolutionary symbols, mottoes, insignias and prints had a profound impact on the collective psyche of a country in which the majority of the population was still illiterate. The gouaches by an obscure artist named Pierre Le Sueur (room 112), taken from a popular illustrated journal, tell the story of the Revolution in colourful tableaux that are alternately funny and grim.

Napoleon's Paris

After a transitional period, known as the Directoire, Napoleon seized power decisively in 1799. He mobilised Parisians to rebuild churches, expand the Louvre, dig the Canal de l'Ourcq for fresh water, construct new quays and erect the Arc de Triomphe.

The new century brought dramatic changes in Parisian interior design. The extravagant ornamentation and asymmetrical motifs of the rococo style gave way to straight lines and geometric patterns. The budding fashion for Roman, Greek and Egyptian motifs became de rigueur. After Napoleon crowned himself emperor, imperial gold-leafed sphinx, wreaths, urns and eagles became ubiquitous.

A painting by Jacques Bertaux, in the Empire room (room 115), meticulously retraces the coronation day procession of Napoleon I as it crossed the Pont Neuf, on 2 December, 1804; Robert Lefèvre's portrait offers a close-up of the upstart emperor. The same room displays Napoleon's horse pistols, dress breastplate in engraved brass, the dress arms of some of his greatest soldiers, a portrait of his mistress Madame Hamelin and his death mask. However, the beautiful Madame Récamier, whose salon attracted some of the most notable political and literary personalities of the day, in a

A Sèvres cup and saucer decorated with emblems of the Revolution, 18th century.

celebrated picture by François Gérard, upstages the Corsican general. Louis-Léopold Boilly, a master of crowd scenes, shows two sides of Napoleon's Paris: a stream of draftees (room 115) on their way to war, and prostitutes working the galleries of the Palais-Royal (room 117). Camille Corot, the master of landscapes from whom the Impressionists would learn much, also painted Paris on rare occasions, as in *Le Pont Saint-Michel* and *Le Quai des Orfèvres* (room 118).

Romantic Paris

The story of revolutionary Paris continues for most of a century after the fall of Napoleon and the restoration of the monarchy. Louis XVIII gave Paris its first pavement, gas lighting and bus lines; however, the city was still an urban maze in the

Society beauty *Juliette Récamier*, by François Gérard, 1805. Her fashionable salon was frequented by the most prominent political and literary figures of her day.

early 19th century, when the barricades went up again in 1830 and 1848. The story of the "Three Glorious Days" of 1830 – the uprising that put an end to Charles X's reign – is told in melodramatic works like Jean-Louis Bézard's *The Fall of the Louvre, July 29, 1830* and Péron's *Transport of Unidentified Cadavers Following the Uprising of July 1830*.

In 1848, France was still ruled by a king, albeit a so-called "Citizen King" (Charles X's cousin, Louis-Philippe), and of a population of 30 million only 200,000 French citizens had voting rights. Another revolution brought down the monarchy for the last time. However, the insurrection was brutally suppressed and Louis-Napoleon Bonaparte, nephew of Napoleon I, came to power. He made himself Emperor in 1852.

All this revolutionary turmoil had a great impact on the sensibilities of artists and writers, at a time when Paris was one of the centres of the Romantic movement in Europe (rooms 122 and 124–125). This section of the museum has many paintings of the key literary and artistic figures of the age including Franz Liszt, Victor Hugo, Théophile Gautier, Lamartine and Eugène Delacroix.

Out with the old, in with the new

The story of "nouveau Paris" begins with the Second Empire. Napoleon III (reigned 1852–70) appointed a lawyer named Haussmann (see portrait attributed to Henri Lehmann in room 128) as Prefect and gave him dictatorial powers. With the help of an army of engineers and architects, Haussmann transformed Paris which, by the time of the Belle Époque, came to be regarded as the most magnificent city in Europe (rooms 128–138). He endowed the city with its symmetrical grid of avenues and boulevards as well as sewers, parks, and clean drinking water. Haussmann never let respect for "vieux Paris" interfere with his plans for "nouveau Paris".

He cleared the Ile de la Cité of virtually every medieval building. Ironically, it was Haussmann who decided, in 1866, to create the Carnavalet museum, and the majority of its period interiors come from buildings demolished during his administration. Devotees of pre-Haussmann Paris included Preservationist societies and writers like Baudelaire and Hugo; they were pitted against modernisers who argued that the city needed a completely new infrastructure and that "vieux Paris" was an unhealthy place to live in ("picturesque but insalubrious" according to one 19th-century guidebook).

Nouveau Paris was to become a city of international exhibitions, starting in 1855 *(see page 24)*. Each one was more lavish than the last, showcasing the wonders of modern industrialisation. The Eiffel Tower was built for the 1889 exhibition. The 1900 fair was the most ambitious of them all, a celebration of mass consumerism that attracted 50 million people from all over the world.

The gift of a magnificent cradle *(Berceau d'apparat)* – the work of goldsmith Froment-Meurice and the steel-and-iron architect Baltard – on the birth of the imperial prince in 1856, marked a high point in Paris's relationship with Napoleon III. The end of the Second Empire came in 1870, when Napoleon, driven by his wife and perhaps the memory of his uncle's military glory, declared war on the Prussians. Within a couple of months the French army was defeated and Napoleon abdicated. The Second Empire became the Third Republic, but within weeks the Prussians lay siege to Paris. The event is chronicled in a strange work by Corot, *Paris Incendié* (room 130).

Paris surrendered and a civil war ensued between the French government, who had ratified a peace treaty with the Prussians, and the republican workers. In March 1871, the Paris Commune was declared, its assembly peopled by workers, artists, writers, teachers, doctors and lawyers. Room 131 has portraits of some of the Commune's leading figures, including the writer Jules Valles by Gustave Courbet and the revolutionary schoolmistress Louise Michel. The insurrection that followed threw Paris into chaos. The burning of the Tuileries is recalled in a painting by Siebe Ten Cate. Ultimately, the uprising was violently crushed by the Versailles government and, in the last weeks of May, thousands of Communards were killed.

Fin de siècle

Paris recovered quickly from revolution and war and, by the end of the century, was the most avant-garde city in Europe. This was the Belle Epoque (rooms 137 and 138), when, after so much hardship and bloodshed, Parisians embraced fun and change. Between 1880 and 1890, the city housed more painters, sculptors, writers, poets, musicians and other creative artists than any other metropolis. Artistic movements were born, cabarets and dance

An argument in the Lobby of the Opera, 1889, by Jean Béraud, whose paintings capture the spirit of the age.

clubs proliferated and café society flourished. Jean Béraud's paintings *(see page 53)* capture the spirit of the age.

According to the "art everywhere" principles of Art Nouveau, everyday objects were worthy of beautiful design and decoration. The Salon du Café de Paris (room 141) is an archetypal Art Nouveau interior by the architect Henri Sauvage. The Czech artist Alphonse Mucha, best known for his Art Nouveau posters, went even further in his design for a jewellery shop (bijouterie Fouquet, room 142) where tendrils of iron flow in undulating lines around peacocks and a seahorse fountain.

LEFT: Art Nouveau interior of Fouquet's jewellery shop on rue Royale, designed by Alfonse Mucha and built in 1900.

The 20th century

The years between the Great War and World War II saw an astonishing variety of artistic expression in Paris. The ballroom from the Hotel de Wendel (room 146), painted by Catalan artist José María Sert y Badia and based on the theme of the Queen of Sheba, dates from the 1920s. Two of the greatest novels of the 20th century were published in Paris in this decade, James Joyce's *Ulysses* and the bulk of *Remembrance of Things Past* by Marcel Proust. The Carnavalet has re-created Proust's cork-lined bedroom (room 147), where he wrote most of the novel's 7,356 pages and later died of pneumonia.

The Galerie de Liaison on the first floor, which connects the two *hôtels*, is the final stage of this stroll through Parisian history. It is hung with paintings of Paris in the 20th century, including works by Utrillo, Picasso and Foujita, alongside visions of Paris and city life by contemporary artists.

FOOD AND DRINK: L'As du Fallafel (34 rue des Rosiers, 3rd; inexpensive): this hectic kosher deli in the heart of the Marais offers assorted Jewish specialities. Camille (24 rue des Francs-Bourgeois, 3rd; tel 01 42 72 20 50; moderate): a popular corner bistro on a lively Marais thoroughfare, with conveniently long serving hours.
See also Musée Picasso, page 92.

RIGHT: *The Allée des Acacias in the Bois de Boulogne by Roger de la Fresnaye, 1908.*

Centre Pompidou – Musée National d'Art Moderne

An unrivalled collection covering the principal art movements of the 20th century, and beyond, displayed in a building that is itself an icon of modern Paris

Map reference: page 41, G3
Place Georges-Pompidou, 4th
Tel: 01 44 78 12 33. www.centrepompidou.fr
Metro: Hôtel de Ville, Rambuteau.
RER: Châtelet-Les-Halles. Bus: 21, 29, 38, 47, 58, 67, 70, 72, 74, 76, 81, 85, 96
Open: Mon, Wed–Sun 11am–9pm; Brancusi Workshop 1–7pm; closed Tues, 1 May
Café and restaurant (see page 58). Bookshop and design shop. Children's gallery and workshops. Guided visits. Audio-guides. Auditorium. Public library. Cinema. Wheelchair access. Admission charge.

The Pompidou Centre opens until 9pm.

France may have been at the forefront of artistic experimentation at the start of the 20th century, but it took a curiously long time to establish a national museum of modern art. When it finally arrived in 1945, the Musée National d'Art Moderne was born out of the fusion of the collections of living French art (then housed in the Musée du Luxembourg) and foreign art (then at the Jeu de Paume). It was a relatively modest affair then, exhibited from 1947 in one wing of the Palais de Tokyo. That all changed with the museum's amalgamation in 1967 with the CNAC (Centre National d'Art Contemporain) and the launch in 1969 by President Georges Pompidou of an international architectural competition for a cultural centre that was to be both museum and centre of creation.

The building

Chosen from 681 entries, the winning project, inaugurated in 1977, put the young Italo-British duo Renzo Piano and Richard Rogers on the international map with their revolutionary high-tech design. At the time highly controversial, the steel and glass structure had a radical inside-out solution. It put the services (colour-coded heating pipes and air-conditioning ducts) and circulation (escalators that snake up the west façade, soon adapted as the logo of the museum) on the exterior, leaving free the space within for floors that could be adapted in different configurations. More than just a visual statement, the architecture also augured a new form of cultural centre. The Musée National d'Art Moderne and temporary exhibition galleries are just one aspect of a multi-discliplinary institution which also contains a large public library (on two floors), performance space, auditorium and cinema, as well as neighbouring avant-garde music institute IRCAM.

The collections

Despite the recent enlargement of the gallery space as part of the millennium refurbishment programme, only a small proportion of the Pompidou's 50,000-strong collection can be seen at any one time. Nonetheless, you can appreciate substantial displays of Cubism and Surrealism, an unrivalled holding of Matisse that stretches from early Fauvism and Classical odalisques to late cut-outs, and whole rooms or sections devoted to such artists as Braque, the Delaunays, Kandinsky and Klein.

Entered on level 4, the collection now begins with the contemporary before going up to the historical on level 5, revealing the huge diversity of the period covered and the change in what is now considered art.

Whereas the historic part of the collection presents a relatively comprehensive trawl through art history, the very nature of contemporary art – much of it large-scale installation and environments or video art and photography – and the eternally expanding collection mean that you won't see a complete survey of recent schools. Rather, the display (which changes substantially each year) presents a rotating selection of key works, recent acquisitions, thematic displays or presentations of individual artists. Thus *Ben's Shop* was not in the rehang of 2001, Dubuffet's *Jardin d'Hiver* remains, and Beuys' *Plight (see page 57)* has returned; meanwhile Pop, Nouvelle Figuration and Arte Povera have been largely replaced by Support-Surface *(see below)* and performance.

Fourth floor: 1960 to the present

Since its latest hang in April 2001, the central aisle focuses on abstraction and minimalism. You can contrast Frank Stella's early, grey, shaped canvas *Mas o Menos*, 1964, with the profusion of dayglo colours, collage and calligraphic scrawls of his more recent *Polombe*, 1994. There are monochromes by Gottfried Honnegger and Alain Charlton, white on white canvases by Robert Ryman, geometrical abstraction by Agnes Martin, François Morellet and Aurélie Nemours, a series of Josef Albers' *Homages to the Square* of the 1950s, felt sculpture by Robert Morris, and minimalist works by Carl André and Donald Judd that established a new relationship between sculpture and space.

A room is devoted to French artist Yves Klein, important both for his work on the monochrome and his relation to art actions. For Klein, the monochrome approached his ideal of pure sensation, especially his canvases using the deep ultramarine pigment that is known as "Klein blue", which he associated with the limitless expanses of sea and sky. In his *Anthropométries,* the female model was covered in blue paint and rolled over the canvas, itself a form of art action or happening and a fusion of the subject and the medium, in which the work was created not by painting but by contact of the body with the canvas.

A large room gives pride of place to Support-Surface. Claude Viallat's large, unstretched painting using his favourite "bean" motif, and his suspended knotted rope, Daniel Dezeuze's *Rouleau Horizontal*, a roll of bamboo fence, and works by Toni Grand and Christian Jacquard, show how this French movement of the late 1960s and early 1970s questioned ideas of pictorial space and the traditional canvas support and materials, yet sought a validity for painting and colour.

Video, happenings, body art and performance in the 1960s and '70s introduced the idea of time, events and the artist him or herself as part of the artwork. Fluxus, the international group that included Yoko Ono, John Cage, George Brecht and Nam June Paik, focused on social and political statements in the Dadaist tradition, and is represented by objects and games. Look out for Robert Filiou's striking *Seven Childlike Uses of Warlike Material*. Performances and videos by Bruce Nauman, Dennis Oppenheim, Wolf Vostell, Michel Journiac, Gine Pane and Japanese group Gutai stress the importance of the body, sexuality and identity.

Blue Homage by Yves Klein, 1960.

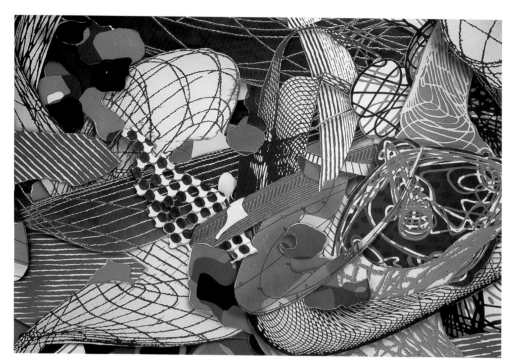

Polombe by
Frank Stella,
1994.

Environments and installations include Jean-Pierre Raynaud's *Container Zéro* (1988), created from his fetish material of white tiles, Absalon's *Habitation*, a prototype living space, and Joseph Beuys' powerful *Plight*, a room covered in rolls of thick felt containing a grand piano. The latter gives an incredible sense of all-enveloping silence, and evokes associations with warmth, insulation, protection, primitivism and sophistication.

Works of the 1990s represent only a fragment of the collection but show some of the diversity of the current art scene. They include photoworks by Jean-Marc Bustamente, Valérie Jouve and Candida Hofer; installations by Giuseppe Penone (including a room entirely covered in bay leaves) and Christian Boltanski; a sound and video installation by Ugo Rondinone; and simulacra by young artists such as Xavier Veilhan and Gabriel Orozco. Video art, soundworks and CD-roms by artists can be seen in a New Media space.

Fifth floor: 1905–60

Laid out over numerous small rooms, suitable for the oils on canvas and small-scale sculptures that dominate the period, the historic part of the collection covers the key movements and tendencies in Europe and the US, bringing out the continuous dia-

logues between abstraction and representation, the objective and the subjective. A selection of key paintings and sculptures (by Picasso, Matisse, Duchamp, Delaunay) runs down the central aisle, while small glass cases in the corridors between rooms present drawings, photographs, documentation and small maquettes. There are also three outdoor sculpture terraces where works by Calder, Ernst and Miró are displayed against a magnificent Parisian backdrop.

Running roughly chronologically, the display starts with the works of two seminal figures of 20th-century painting – Matisse's lyrical *Le Luxe I* and a Picasso study for one of the *Demoiselles d'Avignon* seen as a forerunner of Cubism with its resemblance to an African mask. The selection of work by the Fauves – so-called "savages", originally a derogatory term coined by critic Louis Vauxcelles at the 1905 Salon d'Automne to describe the artists' then-shocking and apparently arbitrary use of pure colour as a means of expression – includes paintings by Derain, Matisse, Vlaminck, Dufy and Marquet. Several works by Georges Braque, from his short Fauve period spent at l'Estaque near Marseille in the winter of 1905–06, show a distinctive, fleeting touch and are an interesting precursor to his better-known Cubist paintings in the succeeding rooms.

In contrast, a room of Matisse's slightly later paintings, including *The Violinist at the Window*, *Portrait of Greta Protzor* and *Interior with Bowl of Goldfish*, painted during World War I, reveal a much more sombre tonality and the use of what was to become a favourite motif, the window, by which he could explore the passage between interior and exterior. As ever, he was interested in the expressive value of colour and the relationship between line and colour, which reached its extreme in the pure colour of his late cut-outs.

Expressionist tendencies in other countries can be seen in paintings by the German artists Emil Nolde and Ernst Ludwig Kirchner, and the Russians Nathalie Gontcharova, Michel Larionov and Marc Chagall, who looked to peasant themes and colourful folk art.

Cubism to Abstraction

Several rooms devoted to Cubism show the influence of tribal art and Cézanne in the new idea of representing multiple reality and three dimensionality on two dimensional canvas. Braque's *Le Viaduc à l'Estaque* shows the influence of Cézanne in both its dominant tonality of greens and ochres and its geometrical structuring of the canvas. From 1909, Braque and Picasso worked together to create a new visual language, reducing the palette to greys and ochres and treating the picture as a series of planes that verges on abstraction while also keeping references to reality in hints of bottles, heads or guitars. From around 1911, they brought

in typography and collage – as in Picasso's *Portrait de Jeune Fille* (1914) in which he combined painting with collage motifs and *trompe l'oeil*. Works by Gaudier-Brescka and Lipchitz, and Henri Laurens' constructions *Tête* and *Bouteille et Verre* (1918), which combined the multi-viewpoint approach of Cubism and painted colour, show the extension of Cubist ideas into sculpture.

Kandinsky's emphasis on the imaginative and subjective can be seen in an important array of his early landscapes and improvisations, including *Avec l'Arc Noir* (1912). Although he kept the occasional references to landscape and folk motifs, Kandinsky developed a form of abstraction based on liberation from subject and perspective, freedom of colour, and the inspiration of music, in a search for the intuitive and what he termed "The Spiritual in Art".

Composition with Two Parrots by Fernand Léger, 1935–39.

In contrast, the objective approach can be seen in Malevich's Suprematism, both in the ultimate reduction of *Black Cross* (1915), and in the later version on plaster (before he returned to a form of Russian folklore in *Man and Horse*, 1933). It is also evident in the development of geometrical abstraction by Piet Mondrian, Moholy-Nagy and Van Doesburg, and in the creations of other artists working with abstraction such as Auguste Herbin, Jean Pougny and Sophie Taeuber-Arp.

After early Cubist paintings, in which he followed the schema of geometric forms but developed a personal system of primary colours, Fernand Léger's large canvases of the 1930s show his interest in both humanity and the mechanical world – as seen in paintings such as *Composition with Two Parrots* and *Les Loisirs*. *Hommage à Jacques-Louis David* shows his rejection of Impressionism for the Neoclassical linearity of David.

The Delaunays explored colour not as an expression of emotion but of the dynamism of modern life, through the vibrations created by juxtaposing certain bands of colour – as seen in Robert Delaunay's *Manège de Cochons* (1921), depicting the colour and movement of a fairground, and Sonia Delaunay's *Prismes Electriques*.

Dada and Surrealism

Represented by works by Arp, Duchamp, Grosz, Hausmann, Man Ray and Picabia, Dada was a revolt against official art and the established order, in favour of the absurd and liberty of expression. The name they chose for their movement was deliberately nonsensical. Emblematic of their idea of anti-art are Raoul Hausmann's *Der Geist unserer Zeit* (*The Spirit of our Time*), an assemblage of wooden head, tape measure, collapsible beaker, etc., and Marcel Duchamp's readymades: *Bicycle Wheel (see page 139)*, *Fountain* and *Bottle Rack* (1913–14), which have been hugely influential on artists ever since, both in the use of found objects and in his questioning of the idea of the author – Duchamp signed the *Urinal Fountain* R. Mutt.

A large holding in Surrealism includes paintings by Miró, Ernst, de Chirico, Magritte, Sima, Dalí, Tanguy, Matta, Lam, Masson, Gorky and Pollack, and sculptures from Giacometti's Surrealist phase. With the emphasis on anti-logic and the Freudian unconscious, the movement took various different strands, such as the dreamworlds, mythologies and visions of Magritte or Dalí; the graphic signs of Miró; or the automatic drawings and frottages of

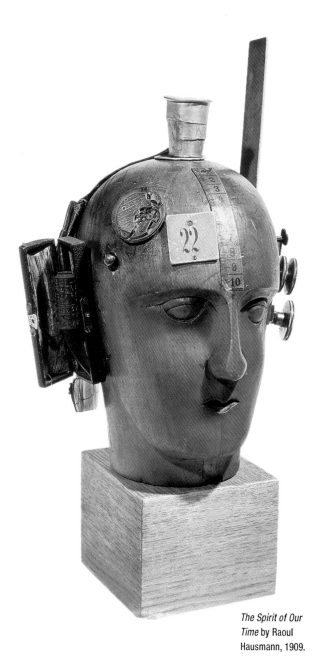

The Spirit of Our Time by Raoul Hausmann, 1909.

Nu de Dos à la Toilette, by Pierre Bonnard, 1931.

Ernst. The fascinating reconstruction of one wall of André Breton's studio in rue Fontaine conveys a sense of Surrealism as an intellectual movement and the diversity of its sources. Here Breton, a poet, artist and writer, met with fellow artists and writers such as Aragon, Eluard and Tanguy. He arranged his collection juxtaposing drawings by Picabia and Miró with American Indian and Oceanic tribal masks, crystals and ritual objects, folk art and curios gleaned from fleamarkets.

Return to figuration

The revival of a form of Classicism in the 1920s and 1930s is seen in portraits by Christian Schad, *Portrait du Comte St-Genois d'Anneaucourt* (1927)

and Otto Dix, *Portrait de la journaliste Sylvia Von Harden* (1926); both earlier associated with Dada, they combined finesse of detail, and techniques inspired by the German Renaissance with an acerbic vision of Berlin society.

The return to figuration in portraiture, still life and the classical nude is also seen in the work of Italian painter Mario Sironi; in Derain's portrait of his wife; Picabia's poetic *Salicis* (1929), with its dreamlike layering of transparent, Botticelli-inspired figures; in Picasso's *Harlequin* (1923), and *La Liseuse* (1920); in Matisse's *Odalisque à la Culotte Rouge* (1921); and in Bonnard's intimist, personal explorations of colour and space in paintings of his wife, Marthe, or his garden in the south of France.

Postwar tendencies

In the postwar period, the distortion of the body by Francis Bacon in his large triptych *Three Figures in a Room* (1964) is presented alongside French "art informel" by Jean Fautrier and the work of Jean Dubuffet, influenced by children's drawings and graffiti. Using found fragments of cloth and fabric, the sculptor Etienne Martin similarly dispensed with traditional structure for a sense of indefiniteness, although he also sculpted in more traditional bronze and wood. *Le Manteau (Demeures 5)* (1962) recalls a shaman or the crucifixion in its form of rags and ropes, but also forms part of a long series that implicitly refers to the home *(demeure)*; the curious *Passementeries*, in clusters of dark netting and bits of brocade, suggest reliquaries or mourning.

Postwar European tendencies in abstract painting include the literature-influenced calligraphic paintings of Alechinsky and Saura, the gestural abstraction of Wols and Degottex, the large black-on-black canvases of Pierre Soulages and the work of artists of the so-called Nouvelle Ecole de Paris of the 1950s – Zao Wou Ki, Jean Bazaine, Serge Poliakoff and Viera da Silva.

A figure who doesn't fit neatly into any movement is the artist Simon Hantai. Influenced by Breton's theory of automatism ("the suspension of the control of reason allowing the release of subconscious imagery"), he began in the 1950s with canvases using writing. He went on to develop his distinctive system of Pliages ("Foldings"), creating lyrical canvases through a complex system of folding and tying them.

World War II saw the pivot of the artistic avant-garde shift across the Atlantic. American abstract painting includes colour-field paintings by Rothko, Barnett Newman, Ellsworth Kelly and Ad Reinhardt, canvases by West Coast painters Joan Mitchell and Sam Francis, and the Abstract Expressionism of Jackson Pollock. After being influenced by Surrealism, Picasso and American Indian sand paintings (traces of which remain in the canvas *The Man-Woman Cuts the Circle*, 1943), Pollock began his first drip paintings in 1947. He used industrial paint and placed the canvas flat on the ground, as a way of renouncing the image for the action and gesture of painting itself.

Design and architecture

Incorporated within the museum, the design and architecture collection allows one not only to follow some of the principal designers of the 20th century but also to see the interaction between fine art and design in movements such as De Stijl and Pop art. Only a small proportion of the collection is on display. This focuses on International Modernism, De Stijl and the Bauhaus (furniture by Eileen Gray, Charlotte Perriand, Alvar Aalto, René Herbst, Gerrit Rietveld, Mies van der Rohe; architectural models and drawings by Le Corbusier and Robert Mallet-Stevens), and on 1950s functionalism (Jean Prouvé, Charles and Ray Eames). The contemporary floor goes from postwar housing, via experimental and utopian architecture of the 1960s and '70s by Archizoom and Superstudio, or the furniture prototypes of Ettore Sottsass, to recent projects by Herzog & De Meuron, Shigero Ban and Daniel Libeskind and by designers such as Jasper Morrison, Marc Newson and Ronan Bouroullec.

Atelier Brancusi

Shortly before he died in 1957, Romanian-born sculptor, Constantin Brancusi, bequeathed to the state the 15th-*arrondissement* studio he had lived in for 30 years. Reconstructed first outside the

Brancusi's studio.

Odalisque in Red Culottes, by Henri Matisse, 1922.

Palais de Tokyo, the studio was rebuilt again in the 1990s, this time outside the Pompidou Centre, with a new outer shell that allows you to see into his living and working spaces while attempting to preserve the authentic clutter as if the artist were still there. For Brancusi, the Atelier provided a total environment where he made no distinction between living, working or displaying his works. As well as sculptures and studies, such as the rough-hewn *Endless Columns*, his streamlined birds and oval heads, Brancusi left all his tools and furniture, including his bed, table and the wooden stools he carved himself, and the photos with which he continuously documented his work.

One of the 16 sculptures in the Stravinsky Fountain outside the Pompidou Centre, designed by Tinguely and Niki de St-Phalle.

*FOOD AND DRINK: With a terrace overlooking the Centre Pompidou, the stylish **Café Beaubourg** (43 rue St-Merri, 4th; tel: 01 48 87 63 96; moderate), designed by Christian de Portzamparc, is a great spot for people-watching over a drink or light meal. **The Quiet Man** (5 rue des Haudriettes, 3rd; tel: 01 48 04 02 77) is a tiny Irish bar offering Guinness and traditional Irish music without the shamrock-laden clichés that riddle many of Paris' Irish pubs. Eccentric tea-room-cum-café, **Le Quincampe** (78 rue Quincampoix, 3rd; tel: 01 40 27 01 45; inexpensive) has an inviting den at the rear and a French/North African-inspired menu.*

Musée National du Louvre

Old master paintings, magnificent antiquities, medieval treasures and objets d'art within a colossal palace: the gargantuan Louvre has something for everybody

Map reference: page 40, E3
Rue de Rivoli, 1st (entrance through Pyramid, Cour Napoléon or Carrousel du Louvre)
Tel: 01 40 20 53 17/recorded info: 01 40 20 51 51
www.louvre.fr
Metro: Palais-Royal. Bus: 21, 27, 39, 68, 69, 95.
Open: Mon, Thur–Sun 9am–6pm; Wed 9am–9.45pm; closed Tues.
Cafés, restaurants. Shops. Audio-guide. Auditorium. Pushchairs. Wheelchair access/hire. Guided tours. Prints and drawings room by appointment. Admission charge.

T he Louvre first opened to the public as a museum on 10 August 1793, a measure voted for by the Legislative Assembly after the French Revolution and commemorated by an inscription on the domed Rotonde d'Apollon. But it was François Mitterrand's Grand Louvre project that doubled the gallery space and made the Louvre one of the most modern and enterprising museums in Paris.

The palace

The Louvre is not simply a palace housing a museum of art. Many of the works are also intimately linked to the palace, with their origins in the royal collections; and here and there you'll find painted ceilings, carved stairways, or chunks of the medieval fortress: a portrait of Louis XIII by Philippe de Champaigne adorns one wall amid

Leonardo da Vinci's enigmatic portrait of *Mona Lisa* (1503–6) was bought by King François I when the artist came to work at his court.

Egyptian pharaohs. There are more stairways and courtyards than you can count, areas of crisp new walls, glazed atria and modern escalators, and other parts where you find yourself amid a Rococo riot of putti, gilding and allegorical ceiling paintings.

The palace had its origins in the defensive fortress built into the city wall by King Philippe Auguste in 1190 and then transformed into a royal residence in the 14th century by Charles V. One result of the Grand Louvre project was the uncovering of sections of medieval curtain wall and moat hidden inside the later palace; however, only one room remains from this period, the Salle St-Louis (underneath the Sully wing), rediscovered by chance in the 1880s, with central supporting column and grotesque heads. It was François I who began pulling down the medieval castle to build his own fine Renaissance palace, a process continued by his successors. Henri IV continued the Cour Carrée and built the gallery along the Seine to join the Louvre to the Tuileries palace. Under Louis XIV, Claude Perrault added the colonnaded eastern front, but the monarch himself lost interest and moved out to

NAVIGATING THE LOUVRE

The sheer extent of the collections can be mind boggling. There are not merely Rembrandts but followers of Rembrandt, portrait busts, kilometres of maiolica plates, countless Aphrodites, innumerable ancient Greek terracottas and legions of Egyptian mummies. While the different collections are colour coded, and there are numerous signs and orientation maps, it's still easy to get lost at times or, as you follow a staircase or turn a corner, to find yourself suddenly transposed from Ancient Greece to Renaissance Italy, France to Mesopotamia.

Note that queues are often shorter if you enter via the Carrousel from rue de Rivoli or directly from Palais-Royal Metro rather than through the Pyramid in the Cour Napoléon. If you

have a museum pass or have bought a ticket in advance (including at the Virgin Megastore inside the Carrousel shopping centre), you can jump queues and also use the additional entrance through the Porte des Lions. It is also quicker to pay with a credit card at the machines rather than waiting to pay at the till. There are fewer visitors for the late-night opening on Wednesday. Tickets are valid for a whole day allowing you to leave and re-enter as you wish.

Be sure to pick up a plan at the desk under the Pyramid. Note that because of staff shortages, not all rooms are open every day. If there's something you particularly want to see, look on the website for the regular schedule of closures or ring to check.

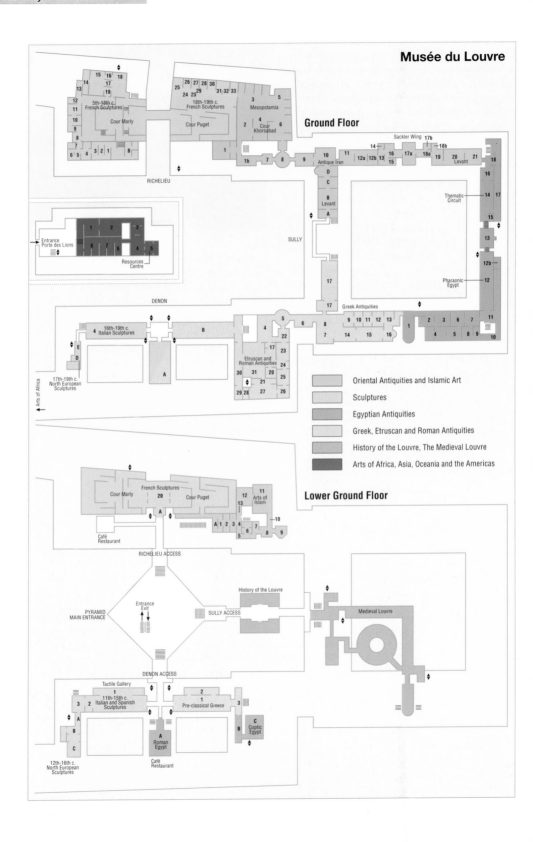

Musée du Louvre

Ground Floor

5th-18th c. French Sculptures
Cour Marly
18th-19th c. French Sculptures
Cour Puget
Mesopotamia
Cour Khorsabad
RICHELIEU
Antique Iran
Sackler Wing
Levant
Thematic Circuit
SULLY
Pharaonic Egypt
Greek Antiquities
DENON
Entrance Porte des Lions
Resources Centre
16th-19th c. Italian Sculptures
Etruscan and Roman Antiquities
17th-19th c. North European Sculptures
Arts of Africa

Oriental Antiquities and Islamic Art

Sculptures

Egyptian Antiquities

Greek, Etruscan and Roman Antiquities

History of the Louvre, The Medieval Louvre

Arts of Africa, Asia, Oceania and the Americas

Lower Ground Floor

French Sculptures
Cour Marly
Cour Puget
Arts of Islam
Café Restaurant
RICHELIEU ACCESS
History of the Louvre
PYRAMID MAIN ENTRANCE
Entrance Exit
SULLY ACCESS
Medieval Louvre
DENON ACCESS
Tactile Gallery
11th-15th c. Italian and Spanish Sculptures
Pre-classical Greece
Coptic Egypt
Roman Egypt
Café Restaurant
12th-16th c. North European Sculptures

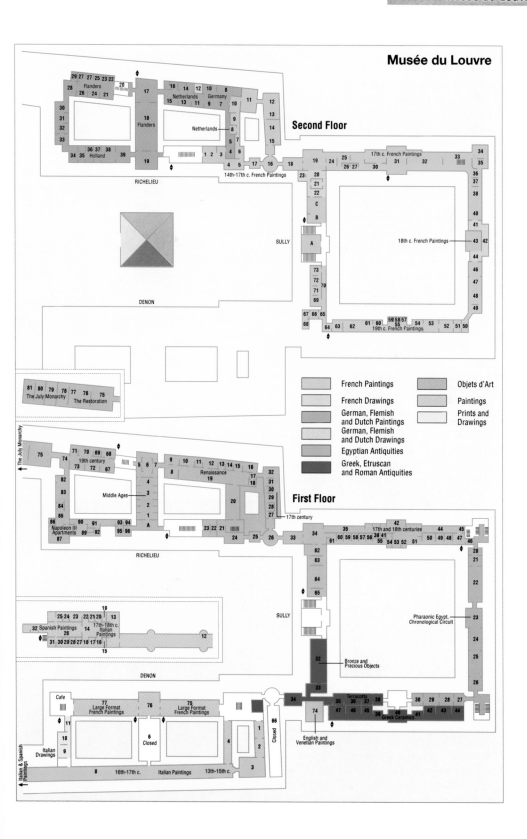

Musée du Louvre

Second Floor

29 27 25 23 22
28 Flanders 26 24 21
20
17
30
31
32
33
18 Flanders
34 35 Holland 36 37 38 39
19

16 14 12 10 8
Netherlands 15 13 11 9 7 Germany 10
11 12
13
14
9 15
Netherlands 8
7
5 4
6
4 3 2 1
4 5 17 16 18
19 24 25 26 27 30 17th c. French Paintings 31 32 33 34 35
14th-17th c. French Paintings 23 20
21
22
C
B
A
36
37
38
40
41
18th c. French Paintings 43 42
44
46
47
48
49

RICHELIEU

SULLY

DENON

73
72
70
71
69
67 66 65
68
64 63 62 61 60 59 58 57 55 54 53 52 51 50
19th c. French Paintings

Legend

French Paintings	Objets d'Art
French Drawings	Paintings
German, Flemish and Dutch Paintings	Prints and Drawings
German, Flemish and Dutch Drawings	
Egyptian Antiquities	
Greek, Etruscan and Roman Antiquities	

First Floor

81 80 79 78 77 76 75
The July Monarchy The Restoration

The July Monarchy

75 74 71 70 69 68
73 72 67
19th century
5 6 7
9 10 11 12 13 14 15 16
8 Renaissance 19
17
18
32
31
30
29
28
27 17th century

4
3
2
1
A
Middle Ages

82
83
84
85
86 90 91 93 94
Napoleon III 89 92 95 96
Apartments 87

23 22 21
24
25 26
33 34
35 42
17th and 18th centuries
38 41 44 45
60 59 58 57 56 55 54 53 52 51 50 49 48 47 46
61
62
63
64
65

RICHELIEU

SULLY

25 24 23 22 21 20 19 13
32 Spanish Paintings 26 14 17th-18th c.
Italian Paintings
31 30 29 28 27 18 17 16 12
15

Pharaonic Egypt, Chronological Circuit 23
24
25
26
20
21
22

DENON

Cafe
77 Large Format French Paintings 76 75 Large Format French Paintings
11
10
9
Italian Drawings
8 16th-17th c. Italian Paintings 13th-15th c.

6 Closed
4
1
2
3
66
Closed

Italian & Spanish Paintings

32 Bronze and Precious Objects
33
34 74 English and Venetian Paintings
35 36 37 38 Terracotta
47 46 45 Greek Ceramics 40 41
30 29 28 27
42 43 44

Versailles. Under Napoleon, Percier and Fontaine added the rue de Rivoli and grand new staircases. However, it was Napoleon III who turned it into pretty much what it is today, completing the Cour Napoléon and extending the Rivoli façade. Even though it was already a museum, the Louvre continued to be used by various government departments until the Ministry of Finance finally moved out reluctantly in 1989.

The most visible feature of the Grand Louvre project is the glass pyramid designed by Sino-American architect I.M. Pei. Opened in 1989, this serves as a new entrance and focus of the underground Carrousel, where the museum has been enriched by an auditorium, shops, restaurants and exhibition spaces used for fashion shows and art fairs. After initial controversy, the Pyramid has become a much-admired part of the Parisian landscape, providing a striking contrast with the carved golden façades of the historic palace.

French painting

(Richelieu wing 2nd floor; Sully wing 2nd floor; Denon wing 1st floor).
French paintings are arranged in an essentially chronological order, from the late Gothic period to the mid-19th century, except for the largest Neoclassical and Romantic paintings which hang in the Grande Galerie. A small section of medieval painting opens with the mid-14th-century *Jean Le Bon* (John the Good), the earliest known independent French portrait. A *Calvary* by Jean de Beaumetz (one of 24 versions painted for monks' cells at the Chartreuse of Champmol, near Dijon), commissioned by the Duke of Burgundy in 1388, and an altarpiece for Champmol by Henri Bellechose point to the flourishing of art in Dijon under the patronage of the Dukes of Burgundy. Several religious works from the Provençal school include the expressive *Pietà de Villeneuve-Lès-Avignon* (*c.* 1455), attributed to Enguerrand Quarton; this features stiffly

posed figures, sensitively painted faces and exotic domes and spires silhouetted against a gold field background. Other Provençal primitive works include the tiny double portrait of *René d'Anjou* and *Jeanne de Laval* by Nicolas Froment, and a *Pietà* by Nice painter Louis Bréa. Look also for the two side panels from an altarpiece showing saints and donors by Jean Hey, also known as the Maître de Moulins.

François I by Jean Clouet (*c.* 1480–1540) marks a turning point in French portraiture, as the influence of the Italian Renaissance began to be felt in France. But portraits were often small, precious items as seen in the room of small 16th-century portraits by his son François Clouet and Dutch-born painter Corneille de Lyon. Mannerist paintings, such as *Diane the Hunter*, *Venus at her Toilet* and Jean Cousin's *Last Judgement*, show the impact of the Italian painters who came to work for François I and the taste for strange, crowded compositions and complex allegories.

The 17th century

Paintings by French Caravaggesques who worked in Rome in the early 17th century and were inspired by the dramatic lighting and realism of Caravaggio,

François I, King of France, attributed to Jean Clouet, *c.* 1530. The Valois king began the transformation of the Louvre from a medieval fortress into a royal residence, and also established the first royal collection of paintings.

Autumn by Nicolas Poussin, *c.* 1640, one in a series of four
paintings illustrating the four seasons through biblical episodes.

include Claude Vignon's *La Chanteuse* (The Singer)
and Valentin de Boulogne's *Concert with Antique
bas-relief* (1622–25). There are even some early
works by Simon Vouet, which are in marked contrast to the even lighting and cool oranges and blues
of his later mythological and religious subjects seen
in the next room. If Philippe de Champaigne's portraits of Louis XIII and Richelieu epitomise his mastery of the official state portrait, there is also his star-
tlingly austere *Ex Voto de 1662*, depicting two
Jansenist nuns at the Abbaye de Port Royal.

The dominant figure of the mid-17th century
was Nicolas Poussin (1594–1665), who spent
much of his career in Rome. His complex mythological scenes and pastorals, with their rigorously
structured compositions and intellectual subtexts,
attracted an aristocratic patronage: over 30 of the
canvases owned by the Louvre came into the collection during the reign of Louis XIV. These
include *The Triumph of Flora, The Rape of the
Sabines,* the more frozen, strictly symmetrical
composition of the *Judgement of Solomon,* and the
late *Four Seasons* painted for Richelieu. The
recently rediscovered altarpiece, *Sainte Françoise
Romaine*, painted in 1657 for Cardinal Rospigliosi,
depicts the obscure 15th-century saint who had
been invoked during the plague that struck Rome
in 1656–57. Claude Lorraine (1600–82) was likewise influenced by Italy, but less by the subject
matter than by the golden Italian light – in his

paintings classical subject matter was merely an
excuse for his interest in landscape and port scenes.

Standing apart are the night scenes of Georges de
la Tour. His haunting religious works *Mary
Magdalene* and *St Joseph Carpenter* seem strikingly modern in their simplified compositions, realist
details and fascination with lighting effects (each is
lit by a single candle). A more worldly side is seen
in the *Card Cheat,* in which a young man succumbs
to the temptations of gaming, wine and luxury.

Official painting was dominated by the grandiose
allegorical style of Charles Lebrun, who also decorated the Louvre and Versailles for Louis XIV *(see
pages 13 and 210)*. His mastery of colossal compositions can be seen in the four giant canvases illustrating the life of Alexander the Great. As official
painter to the king, the analogy in Lebrun's choice
of subject was flatteringly evident, but the complex
battle scenes also show him putting himself in the
lineage of Michelangelo and Leonardo. On a more
human scale, his *Chancellor Séguier* turns the
equestrian portrait into a festive pageant.

The 18th century

The early 18th century is marked by the arrival of
Jean-Antoine Watteau (1684–1721). His works
include the large *Pierrot* (also known as *Gilles*), the
delicate moral scene *Le Faux Pas* and the
Pilgrimage to Cythera, an idealised landscape that
reflects Watteau's background in theatrical decoration – although long known as "Embarkation for
Cythera", the pilgrims are already on the island and
are preparing, reluctantly, to leave.

There are numerous works by Watteau's followers including Pater, Lancret, Gillot and Van Loo.

The Card Cheat by Georges de la Tour, *c.* 1635–40.

RIGHT: *The Bather*, by Ingres, 1808.

BELOW: Fifty years later, Ingres used the same figure in *The Turkish Bath*, 1862, which he completed at the age of 82.

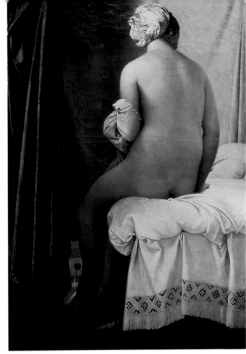

The Louvre's large number of works by Jean Siméon Chardin (1699–1779) includes several of the small still lifes by which the artist raised humble everyday objects to an almost spiritual level. There are several charming portraits, the celebrated *The Skate,* with its hissing cat, and a pastel self-portrait which hangs in the Corridor des Poules, along with other 18th-century pastels.

High Rococo is typified by François Boucher (1703–70) in the sensuality of *L'Odalisque* or the pretty cherubs and clouds in the large square version of *Forge of Vulcan*; but his *Le Déjeuner* (1739) presents an intimate and unsentimental domestic scene, possibly of the artist's family. If Fragonard, pupil of both Boucher and Chardin, is particularly associated with decorative frivolity, his style changed several times. Quite at odds with his reputation for sentimentality are the virtuoso series of *Fantaisies*: these remarkably fresh, quickly executed portraits, dating from around 1750, were intended to capture moods and attitudes rather than any particular likeness.

The 19th century

The end of the 18th and early 19th centuries were marked by the battles between line and colour, the Neo-classical return to classical subjects and heroic values, and the Romantic emphasis on emotion and movement. There was also the impact of (and often artists' involvement in) the French Revolution.

In the Richelieu wing, David's double portrait of a scientist and his wife, the portraits by his numer-ous pupils, including Guérin, Gros, Girodet and Gérard, and Marie-Guillemine Benoist's striking *Portait of a Negress*, show a more intimate aspect of Neo-classicism than the vast, sometimes chilly canvases in the Grande Galerie. There's also an interesting set of Neo-classical landscapes painted on the Grand Tour by Pierre Henri de Valenciennes, as well as Ingres' celebrated *The Bather* of 1808. Inspired by Raphael's *La Fornarina* in the Palazzo Barberini in Rome, this was a figure he re-used more than 50 years later, this time playing a lute, in the circular *Turkish Bath*. Several severe portraits by Chassériau allow one to appreciate the original, and sometimes disturbing vision of this pupil of Ingres. Lining up in the Romantics' corner are works by Delacroix and Géricault, including Géricault's *Study of a Mad Woman* and small horse paintings and richly coloured Orientalist subjects by Delacroix.

The Richelieu gallery ends with the beginning of painting *en plein air* by the Barbizon School painters Daubigny, Theodore Rousseau and Corot, artists also represented at the Musée d'Orsay. Among huge numbers of paintings by Corot are some particularly fine works from his Italian period, such as the *View of Volterra*, and several sensitive portraits.

The Grande Galerie

In the Grande Galerie are the large Neo-classical and Romantic canvases painted for political ends. David's classical subjects in which he uses ancient mythology to extol heroic virtues include *The Oath* of the Horatii (1784) with its strongly symbolic composition, often interpreted as a Republican message (although it was originally commissioned for the crown), and the grand spectacle of the *Intervention of the Sabine Women* (1789), as well as the gigantic *Sacré de Napoléon*, glorifying the new regime, and David's famous *Portrait of Mme Récamier*. Gros' *Napoleon at the Battle of Eylau* shows an almost journalistic recording of the horrors of Napoleon's winter campaign in Russia. Géricault's *Raft of the Medusa* shows his virtuoso handling of human bodies and a vision of suffering based on the real tale of shipwreck and cannibalism that had shocked the public in 1816 (a couple of small preliminary studies are on the second floor).

Delacroix's expressive Romantic approach is seen in his stirring *Liberty Leading the People* (1830) and the *Death of Sardanopolos*, but Romanticism could also descend into sentimental official art as in the pathos of Delaroche's *Napoleon Crossing the Alps* and the *Young Martyr*.

Italian and Spanish painting

(Denon wing, 1st floor)
The Italian department opens with Botticelli's fresh and surprisingly naturalistic portraits of girls in two frescoes painted for the Villa Leman near Florence; their frivolous mood contrasts with the uncompromising starkness of the powerful fresco, *Crucifixion*, by Fra Angelico. In the long gallery don't miss Fra Angelico's *Coronation of the Virgin* (c. 1430–32), painted for San Domenico in Fiesole, near Florence. Note the graphic arrangement of the figures, the way in which blue is used to give rhythm to the composition, and the picture within a picture – the back of the Bishop's cope is decorated with scenes from the life of Christ.

Other early masterpieces include Cimabue's *Virgin and Child* (c. 1270), still showing the influence of Byzantine icons; the greater naturalism of Giotto's *St Francis* (c. 1300); and the gentle and romantic-looking young man by Botticelli. In the *Battle of San Marino* (1430s, of which other panels are in the National Gallery, London, and the Uffizi, Florence), Paolo Uccello combines his fascination with the newly discovered rules of perspective (seen in the foreshortened horses) and a colourful graphic pattern of raised lances.

Mantegna's *Virgin of Victory* (1496, painted for Francesco Gonzaga II) combines the artist's typically classicised figures and a luxurious background of exotic foliage and birds. A more joyous side to

Mantegna is seen in his treatment of mythological subjects (*Mars and Venus*, 1497). A side room contains works of the Sienese school, including Piero della Francesca's heavy-lidded profile portrait *Sigismondo Malatesta* (1451).

Among paintings from the High Renaissance is the *Mona Lisa* (behind glass since being attacked in the 1980s), whose enigmatic smile has been imitated by everyone from Duchamp to cigar advertisers. The painting is so surrounded by crowds that she is hard to look at, but this problem is being addressed with the construction of a special *Mona Lisa* room, due to open in 2003. There are plenty of other works here that merit attention, including Leonardo's *Virgin of the Rocks* and *Virgin with St Anne and John the Baptist*. These, like the *Mona Lisa*, entered the collection under François I, who had invited Leonardo to France at the end of his life. Raphael's *The Virgin and Child with John the Baptist* illustrates the

Virgin and Child in Majesty surrounded by Six Angels, by Cimabue, *c.* 1270, an Early Renaissance masterpiece acquired by Napoleon.

Venus and the Graces Presenting Gifts to a Young Woman, Sandro Botticelli, *c.* 1483. This is one of a pair of frescoes from the Villa Leman near Florence, thought to have been commissioned for a wedding.

sweetness and harmony of Raphael's religious works, but it is his two small paintings *St Michael and the Dragon* and *St George and the Dragon* that are particularly captivating. In Veronese's vast canvas, *The Marriage Feast at Cana (see page 20)*, the biblical subject is treated with a love of worldly splendour that typified mercantile Venice. The painting was cleaned in the early 1990s, bringing out the mastery of composition and richness of colour.

Other Venetian works are displayed in the Salon de Sept Cheminées (alongside the Louvre's small collection of British painting). Among them are the *Concert Champêtre* – long attributed to Giorgione but now considered one of Titian's early works, Titian's striking profile of *François I*, Tintoretto's brooding self-portrait, and Lorenzo Lotto's intense, acid-coloured *Christ Carrying the Cross*.

Italian Mannerist works include the elongated portraits of Bronzino and Salviati, works by Parmigianino, Pontormo, Correggio and Giulio Romano. The wispy forms of *Moses Saved from the Waters* by Nicolas dell' Abate, who worked first in Bologna and later in France for François I, show the distortion of Parmigianino taken to extreme elegance. Also typical of the Mannerist love of the strange are the distinctive fruit, leaf and vegetable heads of the *Four Seasons*, painted by Arcimboldo for Hapsburg Emperor Maximilian II.

Later Italian works include Caravaggio's *Fortune Teller* and *Death of the Virgin*, whose striking natu-

ralism in a biblical scene caused outrage at the time, and paintings by the Carraccis and Guido Reni.

The small Spanish collection is patchy but does include works by 15th-century artist Bernardo Martorell, El Greco's *Christ on the Cross with Donors* and Ribera's *Boy with a Club Foot*. Goya's portrait of *Comtessa del Carpio* is displayed in the Beistegui collection in the Sully wing.

Northern schools

(Richelieu wing, 2nd floor)
Works by Flemish Primitives include Hans Memling's *Virgin and Child with St James and St Domenic*; Roger Van der Weyden's *Annunciation,* in a lovely Flemish interior (*c.* 1435); and the carousing, drunken fools of Hieronymous Bosch's *Ship of Fools*. Look out, too, for Quentin Metsys' *Banker and his Wife* and some wonderful 16th-century fantastical landscapes; and Velvet Breughel's *Battle of Issus*, with its seething mass of figures.

But it is Rubens' *Medicis Cycle*, displayed on its own in the Medicis Gallery that dominates the Flemish collection. The 24 paintings were produced from 1622–25 for Marie de Médicis, widow of Henri IV, for the Palais de Luxembourg in order to glorify herself and Henri IV's military victories. Considered to be largely by the hand of Rubens himself, rather than by his studio, the compositions are a fascinating cocktail of mythological symbolism and history – as in such episodes as *The Instruction of* the Queen by the Three Graces or Triumph at Juliers, where the winged figure of Victory looks over the Queen mounted on a white horse. In a quite different mood is Rubens' tender portrait of his second wife, Hélène Fourment, with two of their children. He also painted her in a more formal full-length portrait in black. Nearby are Van Dyck's portrait of *Charles 1 of England out Hunting* and *James Stuart*, in diaphanous shirt sleeves. Look into the small side rooms, too, for several of Rubens' rapid oil sketches and some fine landscapes by David Teniers the Younger.

The Louvre's Rembrandt collection covers his range of subject matter: the uncompromising *Flayed Ox*; the tender, luminous nude, *Bathsheba at her Bath*; some small, contemplative religious scenes; and three self-portraits. Compare the high tonality and detail of the two early self-portraits from 1633 with the late self-portrait of 1660, which barely emerges from the background.

There are numerous landscapes, interior and genre paintings, including works by de Hooch, Metsu and Van Borch, as well as Vermeer's *Lacemaker* and *Astronomer*. The minute detail and *trompe l'oeil* framing devices makes the output of Leyden-based painter Gerrit Dou (one of Rembrandt's first pupils) stand out, whether it's *The Dutch Housewife,* with her ewers and dead poultry, Dou's self-portrait or *The Trumpet*. In contrast, works from Haarlem were often characterised by their much broader style and use of thin paint, as in Frans Hals' virtuoso *The Fool*, and in the lively, almost monochrome seascapes of Van Goyen. Look out for the exotic landscapes of Franz Post, who visited Brazil in the 1630s.

The German Renaissance collection is hidden away in a series of small rooms and cabinets, but includes a number of important treasures, among them Dürer's *Self Portrait (see page 46),* portraits by Cranach and Holbein's *Anne of Cleves*.

Six new rooms, opened in 2001, show northern European paintings of the 18th and 19th centuries, notably *Tree with Crows* by Caspar David Friedrich and works by a surprising array of Scandinavian artists, including a series of views of Denmark and Norway by Balke, and striking, sober portraits by Eckersberg and Kobke.

The small British collection in the Salle des Sept Cheminées *(see page 70)* includes portraits by Reynolds and Gainsborough, landscapes by Turner, Wright of Derby and Constable, and a Shakespearian scene by Fusseli.

The Astronomer, 1668 (below) and its twin painting, The Geographer (1668–9), were painted by Vermeer to celebrate the progress of science in Europe in the 17th century.

Anne of Cleves by Holbein (1539).

French sculpture

(Richelieu, ground floor, lower-ground floor)

The most dramatic element of the Richelieu wing, which opened in 1993, was the glazing over of two courtyards to create two sculpture courts. Here, monumental French sculpture originally destined for outside can be seen under natural light.

The Cour Marly gathers sculptures commissioned by Louis XIV and Louis XV for the Parc de Marly. Place of honour goes to the *Chevaux de Marly* (1745), Coustou's two rearing horses being restrained by a groom, which are treated in a remarkably naturalistic manner, and to the earlier equestrian pieces by Coysevox. (Copies of the Chevaux de Marly open up the avenue de Champs-Elysées at place de la Concorde.) Other sculptures from the park include allegorical groups by Coustou and Van Cleve of the Seine, Marne, Loire and Loiret rivers, *Neptune* by Coysevox, and statues of Diana's companions.

In the Cour Puget are the four monumental bronze captives by Desjardins, which originally adorned the base of the statue of Louis XIV in place des Victoires, and Pierre Puget's *Milo de Croton*; on the edge of the courtyard look out for the Rococo frieze by Clodion and Puget's relief of *Alexander and Diogenes*.

Adjacent rooms trace the history of French sculpture. Medieval works include Romanesque heads from St-Denis, capitals from Cluny, a powerful, angular 12th-century wooden Christ from Burgundy, Virgins illustrating the different regional schools, and 14th-century figures of Charles V and Jeanne de Bourbon, which were originally on one of the Louvre's gateways. The dramatic, late 15th-century Tomb of Philippe Pot is a masterpiece of the Burgundian School, in which the knight in full armour is borne by eight black-robed, hooded bearers. Three reliefs of nymphs and titans carved by Jean Goujon for the Fontaine des Innocents exemplify French Mannerist art at its most sophisticated.

Look also for Germain Pilon's *Three Graces* on a pedestal by Domenico del Barbione in the Monument du Coeur d'Henri II, and for the 17th-century funerary sculpture by François Anguier. Amid much rather pompous, official 18th-century portraiture and mythological subjects, notice the celebrated nude sculpture of Voltaire by Pigalle.

Italian, Spanish and Northern European sculpture

(Denon, ground floor, lower-ground floor)

Although French sculpture dominates the collection, other European sculpture includes Donatello's painted terracotta relief of the *Virgin and Child*; Michelangelo's *Dying Slave* and *Rebellious Slave*, carved for the tomb of Pope Julius II; the smooth Neo-classicism of Canova, including the swooping *Cupid and Psyche (see page 21)*; and work by Danish artist Thorvaldsen. Note that small Italian Renaissance and Mannerist bronzes are shown in the Decorative Arts galleries.

Decorative arts

(Sully, Richelieu, 1st floor)

Displayed around former state rooms and in reconstructed period interiors, the extensive decorative arts collection is perhaps one of the least-known aspects of the Louvre. Yet it provides a wide-ranging array not just of French decorative arts, but also German Gothic goldwork and Italian Renaissance and Mannerist ceramics and sculpture.

The medieval displays complement those at the Musée du Moyen Age *(see page 78)*, with early medieval and Byzantine ivories, enamel reliquaries from Limoges, Bible covers, Gothic chalices and

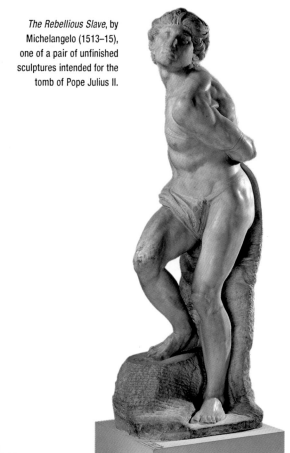

The Rebellious Slave, by Michelangelo (1513–15), one of a pair of unfinished sculptures intended for the tomb of Pope Julius II.

FAR LEFT: Large earthenware dish moulded in relief with reptiles and fish, Bernard Palissy (*c.* 1565).

LEFT: Enamel dish illustrating the capture of Calais by the French in 1558, Léonard Limousin.

jewels. Many of the most precious items came from the Treasure of St-Denis, which belonged to the royal abbey. The abbey was rebuilt by the powerful politician and scholar, Abbot Suger, in the 12th century and was constantly enriched throughout the Middle Ages. Although dispersed and partly destroyed during the Revolution, the finest pieces survived, including the three elaborate cups made for Suger, a crystal vase with gold and enamel mounts, a delicate 10th-century Egyptian rock crystal ewer with Italian gold lid, and the spectacular Egyptian porphyry vase mounted with eagle head and wings. Charlemagne's sword, with intricate gold strapwork and beasts on the hilt, Charlemagne's stirrups, and Charles V's golden sceptre (with a figure of Charlemagne on the top) show how the Capetian

monarchs sought legitimacy through association with Charlemagne and the Holy Roman Empire – a tradition continued in the so-called Crown of Charlemagne made for Napoleon's coronation, which reused antique cameos from a reliquary in the St-Denis treasure.

After the essentially religious nature of the medieval objects, the cultural burgeoning of the Renaissance is reflected in tapestries, carved chests, ceramics and bronzes made for royal and aristocratic patrons. The Brussels tapestry cycle, *Maximilian's Hunt* (1531–3) consists of 12 panels depicting stag and boar hunting and hawking, the twelve months of the year and the signs of the zodiac. Although it is not known for whom they were originally commissioned, the tapestries depict

MUSÉE DES ARTS DÉCORATIFS, MUSÉE DE LA MODE ET DU TEXTILE, MUSÉE DE LA PUBLICITÉ

The museums of decorative arts, fashion and textiles, and advertising are housed in one wing of the Louvre palace *(107 rue de Rivoli; tel: 01 44 55 57 50; www.ucad.fr; open Tues, Thur, Fri 11am–6pm, Wed 11am–9pm, Sat, Sun 10am–6pm, closed Mon)*, but administered independently from the Musée du Louvre, by the Union Centrale des Arts Décoratifs.

The **Decorative Arts Museum** complements the Louvre's Objets d'Art department, but is different in that its collections go right up to the present. It is currently undergoing a major renovation project and only the Medieval and Renaissance departments are open: exhibits include a fine Gothic bedchamber, medieval religious painting, Flemish tapestries, Venetian glass and the reconstruction of an aristocratic Renaissance chamber. Later period rooms are due to reopen in 2003, although the museum continues to have an active programme of temporary exhibitions, often focusing on modern or contemporary designers.

Upstairs, the **Advertising Museum** occupies rooms refurbished by architect Jean Nouvel, who has tried to preserve traces of previous occupants along with urban references in a café and interactive displays. The collection includes some 50,000 posters dating from the end of the 13th century to World War II, and another 50,000 produced since 1950, along with promotional memorabilia, advertising clips and packaging, including works by artists such as Mucha and Toulouse-Lautrec. Only a small proportion of these is ever on view, however, in temporary exhibitions whose subjects have ranged from individual graphic artists to the history of Citroën advertising. Young artists are often invited to create works for the windows, stairway and café.

The **Fashion Museum** changes its display annually to reflect different aspects of the collection, which ranges from rare 17th-century dresses to the very latest designer wear. If the emphasis is on *haute couture* and on the avant-garde designers who changed 20th-century fashion – Dior's New Look, Roger Vivier's shoes, Courrèges, etc. – there are also interesting oddities, such as clothes and shoes made during World War II austerity, and children's clothing.

VENUS DE MILO

Dating probably from the 2nd century BC, the statue with its serene gaze, soft curves and naturalistic drapery rivals the *Mona Lisa* as an icon of female beauty. She was discovered, minus her arms, on the island of Melos in 1820 (a discovery celebrated in the ceiling of room 34 on the first floor) and promptly purchased by the French government for 6,000 francs. The sensuous statue has been identified as Aphrodite, the Greek goddess of love and beauty (Venus being the Roman equivalent), who is often represented half naked, and was probably inspired by the works of Praxiteles. Working in the mid-4th century BC, the Greek sculptor was a forerunner of Hellenistic art and his nude interpretations of youthful gods and goddesses were often copied.

recognisable people and places: the month of March includes Emperor Charles V in red on a horse in the centre and a view of the city of Brussels, while others depict the nearby forest of Soignes. Ceramics include Spanish Hispano-Moresque lustreware, Italian maiolica from Urbino painted with mythological and Biblical subjects, and the naturalistic plates of French 16th-century potter, Bernard Palissy, and his followers.

As well as Palissy's much-imitated oval platters (modelled with snakes, shells and lizards, *see page 73*), a group of ceramic frogs, snakes and other fragments excavated in the Tuileries point to the possible location of Palissy's workshop and a grotto he is supposed to have made for Catherine de Medici. Virtuoso enamels by 16th-century master Léonard Limousin include religious subjects and the superbly rendered portrait of the Connétable Anne de Montmorency. This is in its original ornate frame with grisaille cartouches, very different to the stylised *champlevé* motifs of medieval enamels. Italian bronzes include reliefs by Riccio and small bronze statues by Giambologna and Tacca.

Whole rooms of panelling and furniture, some of it with royal associations, trace the stylistic developments and mastery of the 17th- and 18th-century French cabinetmakers. Numerous pieces by Boulle, dating from the start of the 18th century,

show his characteristic use of tortoiseshell and bronze marquetry; a pair of wardrobes has figures of Socrates and Asparic, another has ormolu mounts of cherubs and hunting attributes. A curiosity is the set of silver furniture made in Augsburg in about 1700. Mid-18th-century Rococo furniture includes Charles Cressent's ormolu and marquetry clock and the "monkey commode" that has ormolu mounts of two children and a monkey on a swing. As well as French 18th-century porcelain from the Vincennes and Sèvres factories, there is faïence from Marseilles, Moustiers, Rouen and Sceaux, including four busts representing the seasons which are a technological *tour de force*.

On the same floor, Napoleon III's apartments, used until the 1980s as reception rooms by the Ministry of Finance, have preserved their period interiors of glittering chandeliers, opulent gilding and crimson velvet.

Greek, Roman & Etruscan antiquities

(Denon, Sully ground floor; Denon lower-ground floor; Sully 1st floor)
Early Greek sculpture is displayed in Denon lower-ground floor, including the Kourus of Actium, a stylised, frontal view of a male torso. Upstairs, the Galerie des Antiques contains a fragment of the Parthenon and Roman copies of classical Greek

Marble relief from a Roman temple, depicting a census and a sacrifice to Mars (*c.* 100 BC).

statues showing the development of the classical canon in different representations of Athena. In the parallel gallery is the mythical *Venus de Milo (see opposite)*. The *Winged Victory of Samothrace*, another top Louvre attraction, stands at the top of the Daru staircase.

Hellenistic sculpture and antique copies are displayed in the impressive Salle des Cariatides, designed by Pierre Lescot for Henri II; the galleried entrance, supported by four giant female caryatids sculpted by Jean Goujon, shows how the Renaissance returned to antiquity for its inspiration. Among the sculptures is *Artemis à la Biche* or the "Diane de Versailles", depicting the Greek goddess of hunting, with one hand touching a small deer and a sheaf of arrows on her back, which has a sense of movement characteristic of Hellenistic sculpture. It was given to Henri II by Pope Paul IV and was originally displayed at Fontainebleau, before being moved to the Grande Galerie at Versailles. Look, also, for the alabaster *Gaulois Blessé*; the small *Three Graces*, symbolic of beauty, the arts and fertility, originally in the Borghese collection; a drunken Bacchus; and the curious *Hermaphrodite Sleeping* – on one side a sensuous woman, on the other a well-endowed man.

There are also substantial collections of Greek red and black painted vases, several rooms of small terracotta figures and anthropomorphic vessels made for cult purposes, toys and theatre masks, and displays of Greek and Roman glass.

Roman antiquities are housed in the sumptuous apartments of Anne of Austria (widow of Louis XIII, mother of Louis XIV), decorated by Louis Le Vau in the 1650s with paintings by Giovanni Francesco Ramanelli and sculptural reliefs by Michel Anguiers. Several portraits of Augustus at different ages show how the idealised sculptural representation of the emperor evolved. Look, also, for the *Sarcophagus des Muses* and the lively relief that once decorated a temple on the Champ de Mars in Rome; this depicts the census of Roman citizens, and a bull, sheep and pig being led to sacrifice. Items from Roman Africa and the Middle East include fragments of mosaic from Algeria, Carthage and Christian Syria. Centrepiece of the impressive Cour de Sphinx is a large mosaic from the Villa Constantine depicting hunting scenes and allegorical figures of the seasons.

Roman bronzes and metalwork are displayed in the Salle des Bronzes and include a 2nd-century Gallo-Roman gilt bronze *Apollo*, numerous small bronze statues and vessels that once belonged to

Red granite sarcophagus of Rameses III engraved with a kneeling figure of the goddess Nephthys, 20th Dynasty (1184–1153 BC).

the royal collection, a small *Eros and Psyche*, bronze mounts from Roman furniture, and silver treasures, among which are finds from a Roman villa on the slopes of Vesuvius (a haul known as the Boscoreale Treasure).

The Etruscan civilisation flourished in central Italy from roughly the 7th century BC until subjugation by Rome in the 1st century AD, producing vases and terracotta vessels, masks and jewellery. The outstanding item is the terracotta *Sarcophagus of the Ceretian Couple* (c. 530–510 BC) sculpted reclining on a sofa at a banquet in a combination of naivety and realistically depicted details of hairstyles and ornaments.

Egyptian antiquities

(Sully ground-floor, 1st floor; Denon lower-ground)
The Egyptian collection spans over 4,000 years from the fourth-millennium BC to the Coptic era (4th–6th centuries AD). Its core originates from the victory spoils of Napoleon's Egyptian campaign of 1798. The collection was subsequently expanded, largely through the efforts of the famous Egyptologist Jean François Champollion (1790–1832), the first person to decipher hieroglyphics. Beyond the pink granite *Giant Sphinx*, insights into Egyptian life and the Nile culture are given through a thematic presentation on the ground floor, followed by a chronological presentation on the first floor. The first themed

rooms are laid out with displays of painted wooden models of boats, sculpted fish and hippopotamuses, household furniture and jewellery, objects related to agriculture and hunting, music and pastimes, and Egyptian art and writing. A highlight is the *Mastaba of Akhethetep* from Saqqara, from *c.* 2,400 BC. A narrow entrance leads into a chamber decorated with painted reliefs showing scenes with oxen, goats, scribes, boats and fish.

The later rooms follow religion and funerary rites. Six small sphinxes originally from Saqqara, and a row of apes from the base of an obelisk at Luxor lead to a large barrel-vaulted hall. This is laid out with sculptures and architectural elements from temples that were conceived as palaces for gods on earth. There are several statues of the lion-headed goddess Sekhmet and the feet from a giant statue of Amenophis III. The rites of mummification and burial were seen as a precursor to resurrection, and their significance is reflected in the massive stone sarcophagi, in the precious mummy cases in which the embalmed bodies were placed, a bandaged mummy and the statues, amulets, jewellery and jars of entrails that accompanied the dead. The sarcophagi are usually carved with narrative friezes, protective figures, and the nocturnal trace of the sun. Embalming was also used for revered animals, and the museum has a large collection of mummified animals including cats, dogs, fish and a crocodile.

On the first floor, the chronological sequence begins with early stone figures including the famous *Seated Scribe* from the Ancient Empire and 3rd-Dynasty standing figures. Middle Empire painted wooden figures include a woman carrying an offering and the very tall figure of governor Hapidjefai. Highlights from the New Empire include the black diorite double statue of *God Arman Protecting Tutankhamen* (1336–27 BC), inscribed stele, gold amulets inlaid with precious stones, painted papyrus scrolls, bronze statues of cat goddess Bastet and the striking "cube statues" – squatting figures of priests and intendants in which the head sits on the almost cubic form of a stylised body covered in hieroglyphics.

The *Seated Scribe* is made from painted limestone and alabaster, with eyes of rock crystal: 5th Dynasty (2500–2350 BC).

Persian *Winged Bull* from Susa, Achaemenid Dynasty, *c.* 500 BC (glazed tiles).

Oriental antiquities & Islamic arts

(Sully, Richelieu 1st floor; Richelieu lower-ground floor)

The Oriental antiquities collection (essentially from the Eastern Mediterranean) may be overshadowed by the Egyptian collection, but it is no less important. For one thing, it holds the oldest item in the Louvre – the 7,000-year-old neolithic statue from Ain Ghezal (on long-term loan from Jordan), discovered in 1985. The flat, frontal statue, made from a type of white gypsum with eyes outlined in bitumen, was probably destined for a ritual. Other highlights include Cypriot terracotta figures and stag-shaped vessels, Mycenaean pots with geometric decoration, carved ivory and chalcolithic vessels from the Negev. There are carved reliefs from Syria and Byblos, where mercantile trading led to the development of the first alphabet by the Phoenicians; note the statue of Osarkon I inscribed with both letters and hieroglyphs. Among the other early reliefs is the stele of *Baal au Foudre* (15th–13th century BC), depicting a figure with a spear, and lively reliefs from the palace of King Kapana. More recent items include the vivid portrait busts from the tombs at Palmyra (3rd–1st century BC) and the stylised male and female heads (5th–4th-century BC) that were carved into sarcophagus lids in the Levant.

But the most spectacular items are the reconstructions of palaces at Susa and Khorsabad. The palace of Persian king Darius I at Susa (in present-day Iran) was constructed in around 510 BC. Its glazed, moulded brick reliefs of lions, gryphons and archers, picked out in pale blue, ochre, white and black glazes, show the striking sense of decoration in the friezes which formed part of the architecture of the palace itself, while a massive column with a double-headed, bull-shaped capital from the royal audience chamber gives some idea of the palace's colossal scale. The display also includes metalwork, statues, ceramics and accounting instruments. The Cour Khorsabad reconstructs a section of the palace of Sargon II from Khorsabad in Mesopotamia (present-day Iraq), which was discovered in 1843 by French consul Paul-Emile Botta (who originally believed it to be Ninevah). Gigantic winged bulls with stylised bearded human heads guard a gateway. The reliefs include a hero mastering a lion and friezes from the throne room depicting warriors and royal servants.

The later Islamic art section covers the decorative arts up to the 19th century. This features glazed earthenware with relief decor of foliage and hunters, calligraphic plates and tiles, Iranian lustreware, Iznik pottery, Syrian metalwork with elaborate silver and copper inlay, enamelled glass mosque lamps, Oriental carpets, navigation instruments and weapons.

Tribal art

In the Pavillon de Sessions, 120 sculptures from Africa, the Pacific, Asia and America – among them painted Fang masks from Gabon, eskimo masks, ancient Mexican ceramic figures and Aztec sculptures – have brought tribal art into the Louvre for the first time. They provide a taster of the forthcoming Musée des Arts Premiers, due to open in 2003–4.

*FOOD AND DRINK: There are numerous places to eat, both inside the museum and in the adjoining Carrousel du Louvre complex. Within the museum, the elegant **Café Richelieu** serves light meals and teas, and there are two further cafés, the **Café Mollien** and **Café Denon**, in the Denon wing. Under the glass pyramid, sandwiches, pastries, and drinks can be bought near the ticket kiosks to the Richelieu wing, while the **Grand Louvre** is a more formal restaurant serving classic French cuisine. In the Carrousel du Louvre, the **Restorama** is a food court offering a variety of cuisines and snacks including Lebanese, Chinese and Tex-Mex, vegetarian food, pizzas and sandwiches. For something more chic, the stylish **Café Marly's** design is a clever mix of contemporary and historic.*

Female figurine in terracotta from Mesopotamia or Northern Syria (*c.* 4500 BC).

Musée du Moyen Age – Thermes de Cluny

A sumptuous collection of medieval tapestries, sculpture and precious artefacts displayed in the authentic setting of Paris' finest Gothic mansion, alongside traces of Roman Paris

Map reference: page 40, E5
Hôtel de Cluny, 6 place Paul-Painlevé, 5th
Tel: 01 53 73 78 00. www.musee-moyenage.fr
Metro: Cluny-La Sorbonne, St-Michel. Bus: 21, 27, 38, 63, 85, 86, 87
Open: Mon, Wed–Sun 9.15am–5.45pm; closed Tues, some public hols.
Shop. Research library. Concerts. Guided tours in English. Admission charge.

Built between 1485 and 1498 as the Parisian residence for the powerful abbots of Cluny, the Hôtel du Cluny provided the perfect setting for fervent medievalist Alexandre du Sommerand, who rented the upper floor to display his collection in the 1830s. This collection formed the basis of the museum – often simply referred to as "Musée Cluny" – created by the state in 1843 and directed by his son Edmond du Sommerand.

Take a walk around the courtyard before you go inside. While the U-shaped plan around an entrance courtyard set the way for later Marais mansions, the polygonal staircase that protrudes from the main façade, the gargoyles and decoration on the arcade and dormer windows are still clearly Gothic. On the staircase, scallop shells (symbol of St Jacques of Compostella) and the Amboise coat of arms refer to Jacques d'Amboise, the abbot of Cluny who built the *hôtel*. Inside, the mansion still has some of its original stone fireplaces and a wonderful Rayonnante Gothic chapel, and retains a domestic scale appropriate for the intricacy and detail that were a feature of the finest medieval craftsmanship. A modern wing has been incorporated seamlessly into the harmonious structure.

The surprisingly diverse collections are arranged in part by genre and in part thematically; textiles, stained glass and architectural fragments are largely

Stained-glass window of St Timothy with the martyrs' palm, Alsatian school (mid-12th century).

downstairs, enamels, metalwork, panel paintings and illuminated manuscripts mostly upstairs, while sculptures, carved chests, ivories and tapestries are scattered throughout the museum. The collection centres essentially on western Europe, but, in addition to some Coptic textiles, there are also a few important Byzantine pieces: the 6th-century ivory of Ariadne, surrounded by nymphs and satyrs, and a 11th/12th-century Byzantine cross.

Perhaps the most unusual feature of the Hôtel de Cluny, however, is that the abbots chose to build over and alongside the most important Roman ruins in Paris – the late 2nd-century Thermes de Lutèce bathing complex. The impressive vaulted frigidarium (cold room) is undergoing structural consolidation, but remains open to the public; it contains Roman fragments excavated in Paris, including pillars carved with reliefs, the frieze from a child's sarcophagus and a statue of Roman emperor Julian the Apostate (361–3 AD), who adopted Lutetia as Imperial Capital for a very short time. Smaller rooms include the tepidarium (warm bath), caldarium (hot bath) and a section of the hypocaust heating system.

Sculpture and architecture

Architectural fragments from the Abbaye de Ste Geneviève and other demolished churches, Romanesque capitals from St-Germain-des-Prés, and statues from St-Denis, the Sainte-Chapelle and Notre-Dame present a remarkable survey of French medieval sculpture and make the museum a memorial to long-disappeared corners of medieval Paris. Fine pieces from other countries include carved alabasters from Nottingham, showing how the same New Testament story would be treated again and again in production-line style; carved capitals from Catalonia; and good examples of Flemish and German wood-carving. A room of cleverly backlit stained glass, representing biblical scenes such as the story of Samson, and other roundels from the Sainte-Chapelle, allows one to appreciate from close up the combination of lively narrative and jewel-like colours.

Most remarkable is the array of sculptures from Notre-Dame showing how sculptural style evolved over the century that the cathedral was being built. The earliest pieces come from the St Anne doorway (c. 1148) in which the elongated column

figures with a tight, linear pattern of narrow drapery folds still form part of the column structure. Contrast these with the fragments of angels blowing trumpets from the Last Judgement tympanum (*c.* 1210–20) and the large apostles and martyrs with their flowing robes from the southern transept of the 1250s. Look out for the rare, free-standing sculpture of Adam that originally stood inside the cathedral.

Most miraculous survivors of all are 21 of the original 28 heads of the Kings of Judah (*c.* 1220). Removed after the Revolution in 1793 because they were associated with monarchy, they were rediscovered by chance, along with many other fragments, during construction of a car park in the 8th *arrondissement* in 1977. Striking in their sober massiveness, the traces of paint on one head can only hint at how colourful the Notre-Dame façade must once have been.

Returning through the 13th-century doorway from the lady chapel of St-Germain-des-Prés (attributed to master mason Pierre de Montreuil and carved with naturalistic foliage that climbs over capitals and between the narrow colonnettes), the next room contains more relics of the oft-rebuilt church of St-Germain-des-Prés. Twelve mid-11th-century Romanesque capitals from the nave are carved in an enormous variety of motifs from interlaced strapwork to a man on a lion, mythical beasts and a Christ in majesty. Look out,

The facade of Notre-Dame was once decorated with statues of the Kings of Judah, traditionally held to represent the Kings of France. The surviving heads are now on display in the museum's sculpture gallery.

also, for the statue (*c.* 1160) of a Prophet with a long twisted beard possibly from St-Pierre de Montmartre, two elegant stylised heads from the façade of St-Denis, figures of apostles originally from the interior of the Sainte-Chapelle and the delicate, curved angel from Poissy.

Upstairs, the display centres on a series of small Virgin and Child sculptures and ornately carved altarpieces, which were a feature of the late medieval period. The *Retable de la Passion* (Altarpiece of the Passion) from Antwerp is a piece of enormous complexity. The top is decorated with polychrome wood scenes of the Crucifixion and the Passion, complete with horsemen clad in the Flemish garb of the day, and at the bottom, scenes of the Annunciation and birth of Christ are framed in Gothic cartouches. Smaller portable altarpieces and a small Virgin, whose chest opens to reveal the Crucifixion, illustrate the emphasis on personal piety.

Among the paintings is a *Pietà* from Tarascon thought to have been painted for Provençal king René, and the curious English *Scenes from the Life of the Virgin* (*c.* 1325) with stylised figures against an embossed, geometrically patterned background.

Tapestries from the *Lady and the Unicorn* cycle (*c.* 1500).
Clockwise from Top Left: *Taste, Sight, To my Sole Desire* and *Smell.*

Tapestries and textiles

Undoubtedly the most famous work in the collection, the *Lady and the Unicorn* tapestry cycle is displayed upstairs in a specially constructed semicircular room. The tapestries, probably designed in Paris and made in Flanders at the end of the 15th century, feature an elegant lady accompanied by a cuddly, smiling lion and a docile-looking unicorn, both of whom carry the pennant of the Le Viste family with its three crescent moons. Five panels depict an allegory of the senses – *Taste*: the lady takes a sweet from a golden cup held by her maid; *Hearing*: she plays a small organ; *Sight*: the unicorn resting its forelegs on the lady's knee looks into a mirror she is holding; *Smell*: the lady weaves a wreath of flowers; *Touch*: she strokes the unicorn's horn. In the enigmatic sixth, the lady stands in front of a small tent on which a banner reads "A Mon Seul Désir" (To My Sole Desire): is she greedily taking the jewels and succumbing to sensual cupidity, or is she virtuously renouncing them and thrusting the jewels back into the casket?

Whatever the meaning, the tapestries are in remarkable condition, and alive with captivating details: rabbits and other animals pop up all over the *mille-fleurs* floral ground while a monkey – nibbling a sweet here, sniffing a rose there – echoes the lady's actions.

If religious artefacts and subjects inevitably dominate the museum (ecclesiastical patronage was the prime means of showing off both wealth and spirituality), the collection of tapestries provides some of the best information about secular life, from warfare to costumes, meal times and the rituals of courtly love. *La Vie Seigneuriale* or Manorial Life, an early 16th-century Dutch tapestry cycle displayed downstairs, depicts all the lordly pastimes of the day: hunting and falconry, a noble reading poetry to his lady love, lovers in a wood and the promenade accompanied by servants carrying platters of fruit. In the background are a wealth of animals and faithfully rendered trees and

THE MEDIEVAL GARDEN

Cluny's medieval garden is not a reproduction of a medieval garden but an imaginative modern evocation of the Middle Ages, taking its inspiration from objects in the collection and evoking the two spheres of the spiritual and the profane that governed the medieval world. It is planted with species depicted in manuscripts, altarpieces and tapestries – mainly herbs and medicinal plants, bushy shrubs and early roses. The naturalism of a wooded glade contrasts with four geometrical formal gardens (kitchen garden, medicinal garden, garden of profane love and a celestial garden symbolising sacred love) and a tiny enclosed field of flowers, as well as canals inspired by medieval cloisters and *mille-fleurs* tapestries. There are plenty of fun details in the toddlers' play area, with springy rabbits, lions and monkeys, and animal footprints in the terracotta-tiled path, ensuring it is a true local park, not an academic exercise.

plants. Another tapestry, displayed among chests, ewers, shoes, wooden combs and other personal effects, vividly depicts the grape harvest.

A room of textiles features several striking fragments from Coptic Egypt, in which motifs such as spotted guinea fowl, lions or curling vines – picked out in contrasting black and white – reflect Byzantine, Islamic and Classical traditions. Other highlights are the 13th-century embroidered silk stocking of Cardinal Armand de Via, and a sumptuous red velvet saddle cloth made for Edward III of England (*c.* 1330) embroidered in gold thread with rampant leopards.

Metalwork and enamels

Ornate gold reliquaries carved like miniature Gothic church spires, three 7th-century golden votive crowns set with cabochon gemstones and crystals, the 11th-century gold altar-front from Basle cathedral, and the delicate golden rose made for the Avignon papacy in 1330 are part of a treasury illustrating the finesse of medieval metalwork. The highlight, though, is the superb collection of Limoges enamels. Italian and later Renaissance enamels from Limoges often made use of transparent colours, but in the 11th to 13th century, the preference was for opaque blues, turquoise and deep, iron red, combined with gilding and smaller areas of white, black, green and yellow in lively and surprisingly bold patterns. Various techniques were used, in particular *champlevé* (where enamel colours fill grooves cut in to metal) and *cloissoné* (filling in with enamel colour an outline made of flattened wire). Often made to house saints' relics, Limoges enamels were valuable objects in their own right. Look out for two small reliquaries depicting the martyrdom of Thomas à Beckett, probably made shortly after his death in 1190, and the stylised Christ in Majesty, which once covered a precious manuscript.

FOOD AND DRINK: Ever-fashionable Latin Quarter brasserie, Balzar (49 rue des Ecoles, 5th; tel: 01 43 54 13 67; moderate) is a pleasant stop for afternoon tea or coffee or a full-blown meal. Steps from the museum, Le Reflet (6 rue Champollion, 5th; tel: 01 43 29 97 27; inexpensive) is a laid back spot for a drink or snack. Le Soufflot Café (16 rue Soufflot, 5th; tel: 01 43 26 57 56; inexpensive), a typical café-brasserie with a large pavement terrace, serves drinks, salads and hot food all day. Or stay in medieval mood at L'Ecurie (2 rue Laplace, 5th; tel 01 46 33 68 49; inexpensive) eating char-grilled steaks in a labyrinth of ancient vaulted cellars.

ABOVE: Gilded, *champlevé* enamel plaque depicting Christ in Majesty (late 12th century).

LEFT: Pair of bronze eagle-shaped brooches, 6th century.

Musée d'Orsay

The national museum of 19th-century art, housed in a converted railway station

Map reference: page 40, C3
62 rue de Lille, 7th
Tel: 01 40 49 48 14. www.musee-orsay.fr
Metro: Solférino. RER: Musée d'Orsay. Bus: 24,
63, 68, 69, 73, 83, 84, 94
Open: Tues, Wed, Fri, Sat 10am–6pm, Thur
10am–9.45pm, Sun 9am–6pm (opens 9am from
20 June to 20 Sept); closed Mon.
Café and restaurant. Bookshop and giftshop.
Wheelchair access and wheelchair and
pushchair hire. Guided visits. Audio-guides.
Lectures and concerts. Multimedia room.
Admission charge (ticket valid for one year).

The skylit sculpture aisle runs the length of the museum along the old railway tracks.

The national museum of 19th-century art found its ideal home in the former Gare d'Orsay, an ornate Beaux Arts train station designed by Victor Laloux. Opened in 1900 to serve passengers to the Exposition Universelle *(see page 26)*, it was built around a metal frame with a long, glass-roofed nave hidden behind an imposing stone façade. But in 1939 it ceased to serve mainline trains as the platforms were too short for modern expresses. In 1977 President Giscard d'Estaing saved the building from demolition and declared that it would be converted into a new national museum. Italian architect Gae Aulenti came up with the design for a skylit, central sculpture aisle along the line of the old tracks, inserting large internal partitions to create a series of rooms on either side. The Musée d'Orsay was finally opened to the public by Mitterrand in 1986.

The museum's collection, which covers the period from 1848 to 1914, is made up of works previously in the Louvre, the Impressionist collection from the Jeu de Paume and earlier works from the Musée National d'Art Moderne. Although best known for the Impressionists, the collection covers all key movements in later 19th-century French art, beginning with the late Romantics and official salon painters *(see page 83)*, and going via Realism, *Sappho*, by Impressionism and Symbol- James Pradier ism to Post-Impressionism (1852). and the Nabis. Seen in the

context of these movements, the Impressionists are better understood. There is evidence both of their continuity with the *plein air* painters who had preceded them, and their radical break with tradition; they rejected the established hierarchy of subject matter with its layers of allegorical meaning and traditional drawing in favour of a canvas built up by colours.

Although overwhelmingly dominated by French painting, over the past few years the Musée d'Orsay has been making an effort to acquire works by key European and American artists from the same period.

The collection also covers the then-new art of photography presented in temporary exhibitions from the work of pioneers like Fox Talbot, Daguerre and Niepce to portraits by Nadar, Muybridge's experiments with movement and photos by artistic amateurs such as Zola and Lewis Carroll.

The sculpture aisle

The central sculpture aisle follows the different currents of Romanticism and Neo-classicism in the mid 19th-century. On the one hand, François Rude's monument *Napoleon Waking up to Immortality*, in which the figure draped over a dead eagle and chains expresses Romantic grandeur, in an allusion to the late emperor. On the other, late Neo-classical exercises by Pradier, Cavelier and Guillaume draw on antique sculpture, while Mercié's *Young David* looks to Donatello and the Renaissance.

Jean-Baptiste Carpeaux, the major figure of Second Empire sculpture, stands out from his more sentimental, idealised and conventional contemporaries Dubois and Falguière, and from the sweetly smiling faces of Carrier-Belleuse. In its sense of musculature and movement, Carpeaux's bronze *Ugolin*, taking a subject from Dante's *Inferno (see also Musée Rodin, page 93)*, shows the influence both of Michelangelo and of Rubens and Flemish painting. At the rear of the sculpture aisle, a model of the opera district inserted under the floor, architectural drawings and a cut-away section model of the Palais Garnier focus on the building that best epitomises extravagant Second Empire architecture *(see page 164)*.

Ground floor paintings

The painting collection begins with Ingres (room 1), whose highly finished style and superb draughtsmanship remained an influence both on official art of the later 19th century and on figures such as Moreau, Puvis de Chavannes and Degas. Although Ingres' key works are in the Louvre, some late paintings, notably *La Source*, are here. His pupil, Amaury Duval, followed Ingres' sense of linearity and purity, though in watered down form, in *L'Annonciation* and the *Portrait of Madame L.*

Room 2 traces the Romantic current of Delacroix, with his swirling 1854 oil sketch, *The Lion Hunt*, full of tumultuous energy and colour. Painterly Delacroix is generally considered the antithesis of linear, classical Ingres, but Chassériau was a rare artist who bridged the divide, seen here in *Le Tépidarium* and the exotic *Chefs de Tribus*. There are plaster copies of Barye's allegorical sculpture groups of *Order*, *Strength*, *War* and *Peace*, which figure on his monument on the Ile St Louis. Also worth singling out is Préault's extraordinary bronze relief, *Ophelia*, with its Romantic espousal of death.

"Art pompier", the official art that found favour at the annual Salons, was dominated by historical and mythological subjects, such as Thomas Couture's *Les Romains de la Décadence*, a grandiose composition inspired by Veronese, and the sugary cupids and powder-blue sky of Cabanel's *Birth of Venus (see page 25)*. The latter canvas, which was bought by Napoleon III after the 1863 Salon, was enormously popular in its day, but later fell from grace. It lingered in the Louvre's storerooms until it was rehabilitated recently, no doubt due to our modern appreciation of kitsch. *The Death of Francesca*, also by Cabanel, and a curious relief by Henri Cross, show the mid-19th-century taste for medievalism, also a feature of the Pre-Raphaelites in Britain.

Crispin and Scapin by painter, sculptor and caricaturist, Honoré Daumier (*c.* 1850).

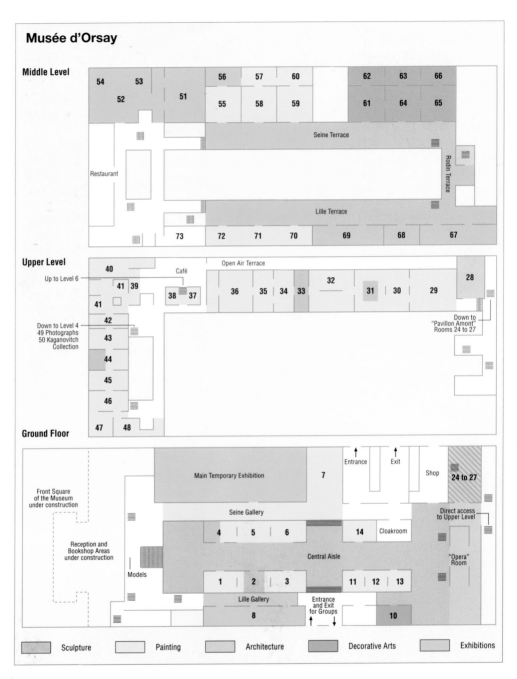

Musée d'Orsay

Middle Level

54 53
52 51
56 57 60
55 58 59
62 63 66
61 64 65

Restaurant

Seine Terrace

Rodin Terrace

Lille Terrace

73 72 71 70 69 68 67

Upper Level

Up to Level 6

40
41 39
41
42
43
44
45
46
47 48

Café

38 37

Open Air Terrace

36 35 34 33

32

31 30 29

28

Down to Level 4
49 Photographs
50 Kaganovitch
Collection

Down to
"Pavillon Amont"
Rooms 24 to 27

Ground Floor

Front Square
of the Museum
under construction

Main Temporary Exhibition

7

Entrance   Exit

Shop   24 to 27

Seine Gallery

Direct access
to Upper Level

Reception and
Bookshop Areas
under construction

4 5 6

14   Cloakroom

"Opera"
Room

Models

Central Aisle

1 2 3

11 12 13

Lille Gallery

8

Entrance
and Exit
for Groups

10

| Sculpture | | Painting | | Architecture | | Decorative Arts | | Exhibitions |

In his day, Daumier (room 4) was best known for his biting cartoons published in journals such as *Charivari*, but today he is recognised for his originality as a sculptor and painter. The 24 painted clay heads, *Célébrités du Juste Milieu*, which represent prominent politicians and magistrates and illustrate universal virtues and vices, combine highly tactile modelling and mordant satire. In his paintings, Daumier transposes the virtuoso draughtsmanship of his caricatures into thin, fluid oils with dramatic lighting, a limited palette and great emotive and narrative force. He found his sources in both literature and daily life. *Don Quixote and the Dead Donkey* (part of a series originally intended for Daubigny's

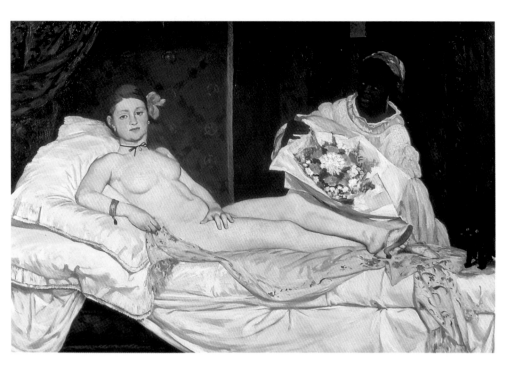

Manet's *Olympia* was received with as much hostility at the 1865 Exposition Universelle as his now celebrated *Déjeuner sur l'Herbe* (also in the museum) had been two years earlier, at the famous Salon des Refusés.

house at Auvers-sur-Oise), *The Washerwoman*, the dramatic *The Thieves and the Donkey*, and the fantastic expressions of *Crispin et Scapin (see page 83)* show why he is often considered a bridge between Romanticism and Realism.

Rather than using grand subject matter, the Barbizon School (room 6) extolled the virtues of nature, rural life and painting in the open air in a way that anticipated the work of the Impressionists. There are late landscapes by Théodore Rousseau and Corot, and Daubigny's atmospheric *Winter*, which shows his light, almost impressionist handling. Millet was more concerned with giving a spiritual and moral value to peasant labour in paintings such as *Shepherdess with her Flock*, *The Haymakers' Rest* and *Angelus*. Puvis de Chavannes' panels *Vigilance*, *Histoire*, *La Toilette*, and the curious *Poor Fisherman* (room 11), capture the appearance of Italian frescoes, although they are painted in oil as the artist sought a return to religious significance and to give a new moral impetus to academic painting.

Also downstairs (rooms 13 and 14) are pre-1870 works by artists who were later at the forefront of the Impressionist movement. Among them are Degas'

portraits of his sister *Thérèse de Gas* and other family members and the history painting *Semivamis Construisant Babylone* strongly marked by Giotto and the Italian Renaissance.

Manet's *Olympia* caused a scandal when presented at the 1865 Salon. Although it stands in the long tradition of Titian's *Venus of Urbino* and Goya's *Maja*, the nude staring brazenly out of the canvas as her black servant hands her a bouquet of flowers was interpreted by moral society as a prostitute (as was the woman in *Déjeuner sur l'Herbe*, which hangs upstairs), and criticised for her lack of modesty.

Pauvre Pêcheur (The Poor Fisherman) by influential symbolist painter, Puvis de Chavannes (1881).

*L'Arlesienne
(Madame Ginoux)* by
Vincent van Gogh
(1888).

Upper level

Escalators lead up to the upper floor – the Galerie des Hauteurs – which contains the wealth of the museum's Impressionist and Post-Impressionist paintings. The first room (29) is dominated by Manet's controversial masterpiece *Déjeuner sur l'Herbe*. It was the talking point of the 1863 Salon des Réfusés, both for the brutality of its technique and for its depiction of a nude woman accompanied by two fully-clothed men. For Manet, the subject was "a modern Giorgione", a new take on the Giorgione/Titian *Concert Champêtre* in the Louvre *(see page 70)* typical of his references to the old masters. Other works in the donation include Fantin-Latour's *Homage to Delacroix*, Monet's *Poppyfield (see pages 6–7)* and several works by Sisley. In the next room, other early Impressionist works include Caillebotte's *The Floor Scrapers*, Berthe Morisot's tender *Cradle* and Whistler's exercise in grey and black, *The Artist's Mother*.

Degas was not so much an Impressionist in technique – he continued to work in his studio from preliminary studies rather than adhere to the original Impressionist idea of painting in the open air – but in his interest in modern life. Whether backstage at Palais Garnier, at the racecourse, in the café of *L'Absinthe* or portraying gentlemen near the Bourse, Degas' paintings (room 31) show his fascination with unusual viewpoints and his distinctive way of cutting off the image – a stylistic trait influenced by Japanese woodcuts. There is also a case full of Degas' small bronze sculptures of dancers. Degas' pastels exhibited further on (rooms 37, 38) include several scenes of dancers and *The Tub*.

Manet, likewise, often worked on urban life, also in his studio, although his *Sur la Plage* took a subject previously treated by Monet. The superb *Portrait of Berthe Morisot*, artist and sister-in-law, divides the face into two broad areas of light and dark, while *Asparagus* and *Lemon* are typical of the tiny, brilliant still lifes that he often painted as gifts.

Monet and Renoir (rooms 32, 34, 39) were the two artists who, in the 1870s, stuck closest to the Impressionist ideal of pure colour and modelling through light. Monet's *Le Déjeuner* (1873) focuses on the domesticity of a garden table and his son

Jean, while *La Gare St-Lazare* and *Coal Barges being Unloaded* reflect his fascination with the bustle of Paris streets and *quais* and the excitement of steam trains.

Van Gogh (room 35) sought expression through both colour and the brushstrokes themselves, as in the uneasy, blue *Self-Portrait* with its agitated, swirling strokes. *The Siesta* was painted while he was interned in 1889 in the asylum at St-Rémy. It is based on a drawing by Millet, an artist he rated alongside Michelangelo "for the very reason" as he wrote to his brother Theo in 1885, "that they do not paint things as they are, traced in a dry analytical way... but as they feel them." *The Bedroom at Arles* and *The Arlésienne* were painted at Arles, where he discovered the intense hot colours of the south, while *The Church at Auvers* and *Portrait of Dr Gachet* were produced at Auvers-sur-Oise shortly before his death.

Cézanne (room 36) originally exhibited with the Impressionists, but differed from them in his search for fundamental underlying structure. His early portraits of fellow artist *Achille Emperaire* and *Uncle Dominique as a Lawyer* used thick paint applied with a palette knife. Later works show his research into ordering nature on canvas, influenced both by the rationality of Poussin and the landscape around his native city Aix-en-Provence – seen here in landscapes, the *Card Players*, the still life *Apples and Oranges* and in several studies of *Bathers*, in which the figures are as much a part of the structure of the canvas as the trees and rocks.

Two large panels by Toulouse-Lautrec were painted for a booth at the Foire du Trône fairground, commissioned in 1895 by celebrated Moulin Rouge dancer La Goulue; they depict Lautrec's favourite models, dancers and personalities.

LEFT: *L'Absinthe* by Edgar Degas (*c.* 1875–76).

ABOVE: *The Card Players* by Paul Cézanne (1890–95).

Tahitian Women on a Beach by Paul Gauguin (1891).

If the Impressionists were interested in surface, atmosphere and appearance, Odilon Redon was obsessed, like the other Symbolists, with an underlying reality, the fantastical and with dreamworlds: in 1879 he published an album of lithographs called *Dans le Rêve* – In the Dream. A room of his mystical, often tormented drawings includes *Eve, The Shell, Apollo's Chariot, The Buddha*, with its almost electric colours, and the spiritual *Le Sacré Coeur*. Other pastels include the intense works of Lucien Lévy-Dhurmer, works by Roussel, Denis and Hungarian artist Rippi-Romeri, Mucha's *The Abyss*, and Mondrian's early *Depart pour la Pêche*.

The Breton village of Pont-Aven was first visited by Gauguin in 1886, and here he was to find his mature style alongside his young protégés Bernard and Sérusier. Paintings like Bernard's *Bathers with Red Cow*, the Breton women of Sérusier's *The Downpour* and Gauguin's *Portrait of the Artist with Yellow Christ*, sought to express moods and emotions as the artists abandoned perspective and naturalistic representation for *cloisonnisme* – flat blocks of colour outlined with rhythmic black contours – that prefigures the Nabis movement *(see page 89)*.

Gauguin's later works painted in the Pacific (room 44) pointed to his rejection of modern Western civilisation and his championing of primitivism, both in his lifestyle and idealisation of the island women and in his use of colour, stylised forms and pattern – as seen in paintings such as *The White Horse* and *Tahitian Women* or in his primitivist carved door panels from his house "La Maison de Jouir".

Middle level

The opulent Salle des Fêtes, once the station hotel's grand reception room (which has conserved its garlands of chandeliers and lavish mouldings) houses academic marble sculpture and also Fantin-Latour's famous group portraits, depicting his artistic and literary contemporaries: *Table Corner* (Verlaine, Rimbaud, etc) and *A Studio in the Batignolles Quarter* (Manet, Zola, Renoir *et al*).

To the side, several rooms (rooms 70–72) feature the Nabis painters Vuillard, Bonnard and Denis. The movement, founded in 1888, took its name from the Hebrew for "prophet", as they sought a return to spiritual meaning in painting. Influenced by the Pont-Aven School, by Japanese prints and by medieval stained glass, they juxtaposed blocks of colour. Look out for Vuillard's *In Bed*, an extraordinary, flat composition of angular blocks of various shades of brown, and the set of big decorative panels, *Public Gardens*, with its graphic pattern of light falling on gravel paths.

Bonnard often focused on intimate domestic scenes as in *The Dressing Gown* with its dominating pattern, *La Femme au Chat* and *La Toilette*, while his *Portrait of the Bernheim Brothers* is characteristic of his distinctive palette. Smaller paintings by the Nabis are on the top level, and include Maurice Denis' exquisite *Sunlight on the Terrace*, Bonnard's *White Cat* and Vuillard's *Portrait of Félix Vallotton* and *Profile of a Woman in a Hat*.

Decorative arts

The decorative arts galleries on the ground and mezzanine levels parallel developments in fine art and also reflect the rise of mechanical, manufactured production. The main highlight downstairs is the elaborate wardrobe made by Diehl and Brandoly for the Exposition Universelle of 1867, its bronze mounts beautifully carved by Emmanuel Frémiet (1824–1910) with charging Merovingian warriors in a chariot drawn by oxen. Sèvres vases with appliqué relief decoration, and revivals in Renaissance techniques of painted enamel, bring out 19th-century eclecticism.

On the mezzanine, a fine collection of Art Nouveau decorative arts includes furniture and silverware by Henri Van der Velde, the Nenuphar (waterlily) bed and bedside cabinet by Majorelle, a leading figure of the Nancy school, drawings and furniture by Guimard, metalwork by Paul Follet and Jean Durand, and a wood-panelled salon by Alexandre Charpentier.

*FOOD AND DRINK: Within the museum itself there is a splendid **Belle Epoque restaurant** (tel: 01 45 49 47 05; moderate) on the middle level, which serves lunch and tea. The **Café des Hauteurs**, behind the glass station clock on the upper level, serves salads, light meals and cakes all day, and above that (misleadingly called the "mezzanine") is a small self-service sandwich and snack bar.*

Le Bistrot de Paris (33 rue de Lille, 7th; tel: 01 42 61 15 84; inexpensive) is a good-value bistro where food is served in a prettily revamped Art Deco setting.

ABOVE: *In Bed* by Edouard Vuillard (1891).

RIGHT: *Nenuphar bed* by Louis Majorelle (1905–09).

This melancholic *Self-Portrait* (1901) was painted during Picasso's so-called Blue Period.

Musée National Picasso

The artist's personal collection, donated to the French state in lieu of death duties, and now housed in a grand Marais mansion

Map reference: page 41, H3
Hôtel Salé, 5 rue de Thorigny, 3rd
Tel: 01 42 71 25 21
Metro: St Paul, Chemin-Vert. Bus: 20, 29, 65
Open: Mon, Wed–Sun 9.30am–5.30pm (until
6pm Apr–Oct); closed Tues
Café. Bookshop. Wheelchair access.
Admission charge.

One of Picasso's particularities was the number of works, from all periods of his long and extremely prolific career, that he always kept around him, despite his frequent house and studio moves, occasionally even buying back works he regretted having sold.

This remarkable gallery displays a large proportion of Picasso's personal collection, donated to the state by his family in lieu of inheritance tax. His paintings, drawings, ceramics, sculptures, collages and manuscripts are laid out in chronological order, covering every stage of his life and work. All Picasso's works, but particularly his paintings, ooze life, humour and, above all, sex in a career that can never be separated from his personal life, his children and his various wives and lovers.

The Hôtel Salé

With its gracious, curved, entrance courtyard, watched over by sphinxes, and grandiose cherub-adorned stairhall, the Hôtel Salé is one of the finest mansions in the Marais. It was built 1656–59 by Jean Boulier for the wealthy tax collector, Pierre Aubert de Fontenay. He was responsible for collecting the *gabelle* or salt tax, hence the hotel's nickname "salty". However, not long after he had moved in, Fontenay was forced to leave due to his involvement in the trumped-up scandal surrounding Louis XIV's minister Fouquet *(see page 208).*

For a while, the house served as the Venetian embassy, but after the Revolution, it went through various incarnations, first as a school, then a wrought-iron workshop and technical college, until it was finally renovated and reopened as the Picasso museum in 1985 (a small display in the old chapel shows archive prints and photos, including ones of the chemistry labs that once stood in the courtyard).

The early years

The visit begins on the first floor, at the top of the magnificent carved Baroque stairway, with some of his early works (this period is better represented in the Picasso Museum in Barcelona). These include the *Portrait of a Woman* and the arresting, tense *Self-Portrait*, 1901, from his "blue period"; it is often interpreted as his melancholic early days in Paris, but perhaps it was also inspired by Symbolist works such as Puvis de Chavannes' near monochrome murals in the Pantheon. With their thick paint and burning colours, two slightly earlier paintings, the *Death of Casagemas* and *Portrait of Victor Cocquot* (both 1901) are more obviously influenced by Van Gogh and Toulouse-Lautrec.

Several studies from 1906–07 for the *Demoiselles d'Avignon* (1907; now in the Museum of Modern Art, New York), which prefigured Cubism in its revolutionary use of space, are displayed alongside African and Oceanic masks and carvings from Picasso's own collection of tribal art. Look at the deliberate "primitivism" in the face of the *Seated Nude*, as well as the fantastic economy of line and colour in *Head and Shoulders*, or similar reduction to the essential in the pink *Self-Portrait* painted in autumn 1906. The *Demoiselles* also paid reference to Cézanne's bathers, and the influence of Cézanne is even more apparent in his early green and ochre landscape. This paves the way for Cubism's radical new way of expressing volume on a two-dimensional plane as Picasso and Braque broke with the rules of perspective and modelling through light and shadow. Among Picasso's exercises in full-blown Cubism is the fine *Man with a Mandolin* (1911) in which the picture is broken up into small fragments. Later, he began to reintroduce representational elements, as in *Man with a Pipe* (1914), where the portrait incorporates a piece of wallpaper and the stencilled word "Journal". Picasso also experimented with the Cubist idea of multiple perspectives in a fascinating series of 3D tin and card reliefs and painted "constructions" of violins, bottles and guitars. These presage the continual dialogue between two and three dimensions, painting and sculpture in his work.

Styles and themes

Picasso's career is often divided into stylistic periods, but the vast body of his work defies classification. He produced works in different styles during the same period, as he experimented with realism, pointillisme, and so on. For example, *Portrait of Olga* (his first wife), painted in 1917, is both classical and innovative in its composition, combining a conventional pose with an unconventional lack of perspective and unfinished elements. *Pierrot as*

Harlequin (1924), and the mythological themes in the *Flute of Pan* (1925) are highlights of what is considered Picasso's return to classicism.

An adjacent room displays a selection of fluent, pencil line portraits dating from 1920 to 1922 of composers Satie, Stravinsky and de Falla, with whom Picasso had collaborated on stage sets, and Leon Bakst, designer for Diaghalev's *Ballets Russes*.

Although never officially a Surrealist, evidence of Picasso's links with the movement is seen in such compositions as *Grand Nu Assis* (1929) with her extraordinary sprawling limbs and sense of abandon; in *Nu Sur Fond Blanc* (1928), all teeth and sexual organs; or in the spiky metal construction *Project for a Monument to Apollinaire*, made in memory of the avant-garde poet and art critic.

Bathers are a recurring theme, whether in the delightful *Two Women Running Along the Beach* (1922) and other small studies in his realist style; the small *Bather Opening a Cabin* (1928); or in the large canvas *The Swimmer* (1929), in which the body is reduced to a pink shape on blue.

A glass case contains several of the curious sand-covered tableaux-reliefs incorporating collaged objects which Picasso produced at Juan-les-Pins in August 1930; this was at much the same time as

The Bathers (1918). Swimming and bathing are a recurring theme in Picasso's work, recalling summers spent on the Riviera and in Normandy.

André Masson was producing sand paintings in Antibes (another sign of Picasso's affinities with the Surrealist movement).

Mediterranean culture also emerges in his recourse to Greek mythology, or in the bull-fighting references to his native Spain, whether in complex etchings or the bull's head sculpture made from a recuperated bicycle seat and handlebars.

Picasso's women

ABOVE: *Portrait of Dora Maar* (1937), Picasso's muse and mistress.

RIGHT: Bronze sculpture of *La Femme à la Poussette* (1950).

In 1927, Picasso met Marie-Thérèse Walter, who was to serve as model for numerous paintings and sculptures produced at Boisgeloup, the artist's house in Normandy – notably as the ideal female form in his *Large Head* sculpture, in drypoint etchings, and in the painting *La Lecture*. Contrast Picasso's portrait of the blonde, curvaceous Marie-Thérèse (1937), painted in soft greens and purples, with the far more angular, spiky form, sharp red fingernails and vibrant colours of his portrait of Dora Maar, painted in the same year: two different styles associated with two different women: gentle Marie-Thérèse he lived with in Normandy and the Riviera; Dora Maar, photographer and artist, in arty, intellectual St-Germain-des-Prés.

Another key work of this productive middle period is the unusual *Two Girls at their Toilet* (1938), a vast wallpaper collage originally intended to be the cartoon for a tapestry.

Sculpture and ceramics

One of the outstanding aspects of the collection is the sculpture, including key works such as the *Woman with Pram*, *Goat* and *Girl on a Swing*. Picasso used an incredible variety of techniques and materials, from plaster and bronze to carved wood and found objects – *Ape*'s head is made from a toy car, the *Girl on a Swing* from cast wicker baskets and shoes, and the *Woman with Outstretched Arms* from a painted tin sheet. A small cellar room is devoted to Picasso's ceramics, including imaginative painted platters and curvaceous anthropomorphic vases.

Late works and collected works

The series of *Déjeuner sur l'Herbe* (1961) in which he reworks the theme of Manet's painting, and *Le Buffet à Vauvenargues* (1959–60) showing the dark tonality of Spanish painting and the influence of Velázquez, are a reminder also of Picasso's continual return to earlier masters. Picasso's last paintings were long considered a splashy and crude

decline, but they have been rehabilitated increasingly as proof of the painter's continuing energy and inventiveness right up to his death in 1973. Towards the end of his life he concentrated on the themes of the painter and his model, matadors and guitarists, the family and old age. Picasso was also a collector, and examples of tribal art are dotted around the museum, while one room contains canvases by Cézanne, Matisse, Modigliani, Braque and Derain.

FOOD AND DRINK: Apparement Café (18 rue des Coutures-St-Gervais, 3rd; tel 01 48 87 12 22; inexpensive): a comfortable place for salads or a drink, laid out like a flat and filled with an eccentric array of bric à brac. Chez Omar (47 rue de Bretagne, 3rd; tel: 01 42 72 36 26; inexpensive): one of Paris' best-loved North African restaurants, appreciated as much for the atmosphere as for the couscous and grills. See also Musée Carnavalet page 54.

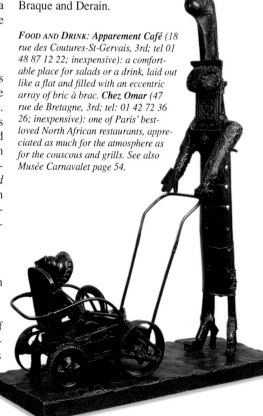

Musée National Rodin

Sculptures and studies by Auguste Rodin, displayed around the beautiful 18th-century house and gardens where the artist lived from 1908

Map reference: page 40, B4
77 rue de Varenne, 17th
Tel: 01 44 18 61 10/recorded information 01 44
18 61 11. www.musee-rodin.fr
Metro: Varenne. Bus: 69, 82, 87, 92
Open: Apr–Sept Tues–Sun 9.30am–5.45pm,
Oct–Mar Tues–Sun 9.30am–4.45pm; closed Mon.
Café. Bookshop. Audio-guides. Archives and
library (by appointment). Admission charge.

The Thinker, 1880, a motif Rodin developed from the unfinished Gates of Hell doorway.

Today, Rodin's work is considered a bridge between Classical 19th-century sculpture influenced by antiquity and the Renaissance, and the sculpture of the 20th century. He was born in 1840 into a modest family in the Latin Quarter. He studied drawing and maths at the "Petite Ecole" but failed to get into the Ecole des Beaux-Arts. Instead, he was forced to earn his living as an ornamentalist, working as assistant to Eugène Carrière-Belleuse and the Belgian sculptor Antoine-Joseph van Rasborough, both in Paris and Brussels. Then a visit to Italy in 1876, where he discovered Michelangelo. transformed his career. The resulting sculpture, *The Age of Bronze*, scandalised the 1877 Salon, where critics found it so naturalistic that they believed Rodin had cast it directly from a live model. But no publicity is bad publicity, and it marked the beginning of his notoriety, leading to his first major commission, the never-completed *Gates of Hell*.

By 1900, Rodin was a successful artist, honoured with a pavilion by Pont de l'Alma for the Exposition Universelle, where he exhibited hundreds of his small groups. He was an artist of his time, allied to Symbolism and, in his search for naturalism, to his Impressionist contemporaries. But he was also an innovator, as he pared back his compositions and cut out extraneous detail, or combined and fragmented figures to maximise expression.

The gardens

It's a good idea to start with the garden, where bronze casts of several of Rodin's major works are displayed amid large lawns, hedged enclosures, pools, mature trees and conical topiaried yews, providing a context for the studies and smaller works around the house. Admire the force of the *Burghers of Calais*, with the evocative gestures of the different figures and the strength of their outsize hands and feet. In contrast, the bronze has a delicacy and almost viscous, flowing quality in the incredibly complex *Gates of Hell* as nude figures emerge at all angles and in contrasting scales from the rocky, tempestuous background. There are over 180 figures, some of which, like the *Three Shades*, *Ugolino* and *The Thinker*, are used independently elsewhere. Inspired by Ghiberti's Baptistry doors in Florence, and taking as their source Dante's *Inferno*, the gates were originally commissioned in 1880 for a museum of decorative arts. This was never built, but Rodin continued to work on the idea and re-use different figures in varying combinations and sizes for the rest of his life.

Then there's the craggy figure of Balzac and the large version of *The Thinker*, originally displayed in place du Panthéon and moved here in 1922 (when Rodin had fallen out of fashion). Among the sculptures behind the house are individual Burgher figures, *Ugolino* and the squatting female caryatids from the *Gates of Hell*.

A side pavilion contains numerous marble portrait busts, *La Source*, *Ariane* and other studies in which figures emerge from the block of stone.

The Hôtel Biron

Built 1728–32 by Jean Aubert for the Peyrenc family, the Hôtel Biron was variously used for public balls, as a cardinal's residence, by the Russian ambassador and by a religious community before becoming home to numerous artists and writers at the start of the 20th century. Rodin himself moved here in 1908 and campaigned to save the house when it was threatened with demolition. The French government bought the mansion and in return Rodin agreed to leave all his collections to the state.

These included hundreds of sculptures and drawings, and his collections of furniture, antiquities and Impressionist paintings, all of which formed the basis of the Rodin museum, which opened in 1919. The carved Rococo panelling in the two circular drawing rooms has recently been restored and two of François Lemoyne's overdoor paintings of mythological scenes have been returned to the house, giving some idea of its original decoration.

Ground floor

Beyond an arcaded entrance hall, a large salon overlooking the gardens contains some of the artist's collection of antique Greek and Roman statues, alongside his own large *St John the Baptist* and the later *Walking Man*, in which Rodin used the same pose to maximise its power through gesture rather than conventional iconography. There is also a copy of Rembrandt's *Bathsheba* and Rodin's late, bronze torso, which the former may well have inspired.

Chronologically, the visit starts to the left of the bookshop with an early portrait by Rodin of Reverand Eymard, from 1863, small landscape oil paintings of Belgium and early busts. *The Idyll d'Ixelles* and delicately modelled terracotta *Young Girl in a Floral Hat* show Rodin conforming to the detailed, prettiness of the day, influenced by Carpeaux and the 18th-century sculptor Clodion. Later rooms form a marked contrast, as Rodin alternated projects for official monuments with constant reworkings of groups of figures, in which he played with balance, movement and scale, the support, gravity and anti-gravity.

In the *Hand of God* (1902) a woman is curled up within a gigantic hand that emerges from a block of marble, evoking God as creator and protector. Here, Rodin played with scale and the contrast between the smoothly finished marble figure and the rough-hewn, chisel-marked block – themes later visited in different mood in the *Hand of the Devil* (upstairs). In *Adam and Eve*, *Paolo et Francesca* – a subject from Dante's *Inferno* of adulterous medieval lovers condemned to eternal damnation – and its successor *The*

Fugit Amor, a sculpture in bronze (1887).

Kiss, Rodin explored the formal and expressive possibilities of the couple; others, like *Eve and the Serpent* and the *Centauress*, are complex allegories. Rodin also continued to sculpt portrait busts, receiving the patronage of avant-garde aristocrats such as Anna de Noailles and Lady Sackville-West.

Camille Claudel

One room contains several sculptures by Rodin's much younger pupil, model and mistress, Camille Claudel (herself depicted in a portrait head by Rodin), who he met in 1883. These show both Claudel's emotional sensibility and her place within the Art Nouveau aesthetic of the time, notably in the group *L'Age Mûr* and in *The Wave*, in which three tiny female figures in bronze are dwarfed by a green onyx wave. Rodin, however, was never going to leave his common-law wife Rose Beuret and finally broke up with Claudel in 1898. She showed increasing sings of paranoia, reflected perhaps in the tortured figure of Clotho (upstairs), and was committed to an asylum in 1913.

First floor

Upstairs, the collection is particularly interesting for showing how Rodin developed his major commissions. Groups and assemblages using figures from the *Gates of Hell* include *Ugolino*, *Fugit Amor*, as well as the *Three Shades* on the stairway, in which three identical figures are seen from different angles. A whole room of studies for the *Burghers of Calais* includes small clay and plaster head and hand studies, the individual small-scale figures, and maquettes reworking the composition: these show how Rodin's idea evolved from the initial group on a traditional plinth, and a group with a swooping, winged angel, to the free-standing figures of the final sculpture.

Studies of Balzac show how Rodin's idea for the monument developed from a paunchy nude and Balzac in a frock coat – based on contemporary portraits of the writer who had died in 1850 – to the dramatic, cloaked final figure, in which Rodin no longer seeks to express physical likeness but the essence of the author's creative powers. The sculpture so shocked the Société des Beaux-Arts when unveiled at the 1898 Salon that it was turned down and only finally cast and installed on boulevard Raspail in 1939.

Elsewhere, Rodin explores the theme of emergence as figures come out of rocks, waves or from within antique Greek vases. One of the strangest

The Kiss, 1886, depicts Paolo and Francesca, the ill-fated lovers from Dante's Inferno.

works is *Le Sommeil* (Sleep), built up in plaster, wax, clay, paper and nails, which later served as a model for at least two marbles.

Towards the end of his life, Rodin became interested in dance (as were numerous artists of the time), inspired by modern dance pioneer Isadora Duncan, by touring Cambodian dancers and by the arrival of the Ballets Russes in Paris. There are some terrific terracotta figures of Nijinsky that capture the suppleness of the dancer's movements.

Rodin's collection

Hanging around the museum are the paintings that Rodin acquired during his life, including works by his contemporaries Monet and Renoir, Van Gogh's *The Mowers* and *Portrait of Père Tanguy*, and Edvard Munch's painting of Rodin's *The Thinker* in the gardens.

FOOD AND DRINK: *The Café du Musée Rodin is an idyllic café in the museum gardens.* La Pagode *(57bis rue de Babylone, 7th; tel 01 45 55 48 48; inexpensive), nearby, is an exotic Japanese tea room in a Japanese cinema built in 1895. For more substantial fare there are a number of good restaurants around the Invalides area.* L'Esplanade *(52 rue Fabert, 7th; tel 01 47 07 38 80; moderate) is a fashionable Costes restaurant decorated with tongue-in-cheek military references to Les Invalides by Jacques Garcia. Classic French cuisine is meticulously prepared at* Tante Marguerite *(5 rue de Bourgogne, 7th; tel: 01 45 51 79 42; expensive), the Paris offshoot of top Burgundian chef Bernard Loiseau.*

You don't have to visit the Louvre to see Rembrandt and Rubens, nor are Monet and Matisse confined to the Orsay and Pompidou. If you delve into the city's lesser-known art collections, you'll find many surprises – and fewer crowds

Musée d'Art Moderne de la Ville de Paris

A coherent survey of 20th-century art, in particular as it relates to the city of Paris, with strong holdings of the Fauves, Ecole de Paris and conceptual art from the 1970s

Map reference: page 42, C3
Palais de Tokyo, 11 av du Président-Wilson, 16th
Tel: 01 53 67 40 00
www.paris-france.org/musees
Metro: Alma-Marceau, Iéna
Bus: 32, 42, 63, 72, 80, 82, 92
Open: Tues–Fri 10am–5.30pm, Sat, Sun 10am–6.45pm; closed Mon, public hols.
Café. Shop. Admission free.

The monumental Palais de Tokyo was originally built as the Electricity Pavilion for the 1937 Exposition Universelle, but the long-term plan was to convert it into two museums. One wing was intended to hold the post-1905 part of the municipal art collection, which could no longer fit into the Petit Palais; the other wing (now the Site de Création Contemporaine, *see page 137*) was planned for the national collection of modern art, which was divided at that time between the Musée du Luxembourg and the Jeu de Paume.

But World War II intervened, after which the space was mostly used for temporary salons; the Musée d'Art Moderne de la Ville de Paris didn't open until 1961. Then, in 1977, the core collection of French and international art was given a new home at the Pompidou Centre *(see pages 55–62)*. The municipal collection of modern art that remained in the Palais de Tokyo has since been augmented by donations and purchases. While the emphasis at the Centre Pompidou is on international art, here the focus is on French artists and foreign émigrés who worked in Paris.

1905–60

Raoul Dufy's vast *La Fée Electricité* (The Electricity Fairy, *see pages 36–7*), displayed in an oval room, serves as a reminder of the building's original purpose. It's a typically lively Dufy composition, although here the artist depicts scientific progress and famous scientists, including Pierre and Marie Curie, Faraday and Ampère, rather than his more familar sailing boats and promenaders.

After two introductory contemporary works – Ange Leccia's giant video projection *Le Mer* of 1992 and Tania Mourad's gleaming white, domed *Meditation Room* – the presentation takes a largely chronological route, with useful introductory texts (in French) before each room. The collection starts with the Fauve and Cubist movements that shocked early 20th-century audiences, along with a small array of African or "primitive" art that was highly influential on artists of that period. In parallel, works such as *La Clownesse*, in pastel and watercolour, present the individualistic and pessimistic vision of Georges Rouault. The boldness of André Derain's 1906 *Personnages Assis dans l'Herbe* (Three Figures Seated on Grass), with broad blocks of viridian green and ochre and half of one head a swathe of bright red, is typical of the Fauves' search for expression through colour; the same can be seen in Vlaminck's landscapes and Matisse's *Pastorale* (1906). There are Cubist portraits and still lifes by Picasso, Braque and Gris, the main protagonists of the movement, and Cubist sculpture by Lipchitz.

Room 2 focuses on the Cubist heritage of Cézanne, carried on by Albert Gleizes, Jean Metzinger, André Lhote and Léopold Survage, who reinterpreted Cézanne's palette, geometrical impulses and allegorial subject matter for a more narrative style than the analytical Cubism of Picasso and Braque. Don't miss the small *Cabinet de Peinture*, a work created *in situ* in 1989 by Franco-Italian artist Niele Toroni using his trademark brushstroke motif, in which the act of painting is an interaction with architectural space.

Three Figures Seated on Grass by André Derain (1906).

Nu dans le Bain,
Pierre Bonnard (1937).

In room 3, the anarchic, anti-establishment spirit of Dada is represented by Kurt Schwitters' collages, the more abstract tendency of Jean Crotti (brother-in-law of Marcel Duchamp) and fine works by Francis Picabia, showing both his light-hearted aspect in the collage *Vase of Flowers* and, in others, a more classical, allegorical style. Alongside Surrealist works by André Masson, Giorgio de Chirico and Max Ernst, Romanian-born Victor Brauner's *Conglomeros*, a sinuous sculpture of three entwined figures who merge at the head, stands out.

Works by Robert Delaunay and Fernand Léger in room 4 show how each developed a style distinctive from Cubism. Delaunay's *L'Equipe de Cardiff* (The Cardiff Team, 1912–13) illustrates not only Orphism – the theory of colour and optics developed by Delaunay and his wife Sonia – but also his love of contemporary life. The painting had at its source photographs from a newspaper story, posters and texts, while the background features other symbols of modernity of its time, such as a plane, a giant Ferris wheel and the Eiffel Tower. The modern machine age features, too, in Léger's *Les Disques*, painted in 1918, in which his geometrical forms are symbolic of wheels and cogs.

Non-figurative art between the wars (room 5) includes the geometrical abstraction of Franz Kupka, Jean Dubuffet's wood relief made out of bits of bark, and reliefs and sculptures by Hans Arp. There's a large group of works by Jean Fautrier, whose abstract paintings and plaster heads are haunted by suggestions of the body and skin. While they veer towards monochrome, many of Fautrier's canvases play with texture, using thin oil paint over a papier mâché or stucco base.

The collection is particularly rich in figurative art of the 1920s and 1930s (room 6) by Bonnard, Dufy, Matisse and numerous representatives of the so-called Ecole de Paris, the foreign artists who settled in Paris between the wars in a ferment of artistic and intellectual exchange *(see pages 27–9)*. Look out for Soutine's *Femme à la Robe Bleu* (Woman in a Blue Dress) with its intense colour and swirling brushstrokes, portraits by Modigliani and Van Dongen, and sculpture by Zadkine. Two superb paintings by Bonnard, *Le Jardin* and *Nu dans le Bain* (Nude in the Bath) show his use of dense bands of pattern and highly personal colour combinations.

1960 and later

The postwar section addresses abstraction in Hantai's "pliages" *(see page 61)*, Lucio Fontana's slashed canvases and Pierre Soulages's gestural paintings of the 1960s (room 7). It also features works by the artists associated with Support-Surface in the early 1970s (room 10), notably Claude Viallat's *Filet Polychrome* (1970–1), a painted rope net, and Daniel Dezeuze's grid in painted wood, all of which show the artists' rejection of the traditional canvas support and materials of painting.

Representational art continues with Nouveau Réalisme – the French branch of Pop art (room 8) – and Nouvelle Figuration (room 9). The fluorescent colours and neon of Martial Raysse, the torn poster work *Boulevard de la Chapelle* by Jacques Villeglé, the car compression by Franck César, and the assemblage of Renault car wings by Arman show how the Nouveau Réalistes were interested in popular imagery and consumer objects; however, these artists were more prone to destroying and tearing than simple appropriating, in the style of their counterparts, the US and British Pop artists.

Nouvelle Figuration is used to describe figurative artists including Jacques Monory, Hervé Télémaque, Valerio Adami and Erro, who were influenced by cartoon images and pop culture in the late 1960s and early 1970s. Also in this section is a small room (room 11) devoted to Italian Arte Povera.

A strong selection of 1970s' conceptual art (room 12), concerned with methodology, narrative and process in works involving text, photos, maps and plans, features Richard Long's *St Just Line*, photoworks by Annette Messager and Gilbert & George, Paul-Armand Gette's interesting *La Plage Eté... 1973,* with its combination of botanical observation and photo-journalism, and the obsession with memory that characterises Christian Boltanski's work.

The final rooms deal with the disparate tendencies of the late 20th century, including installation, sculpture, painting, photography and video. Recent acquisitions from the 1990s include a giant Louise Bourgeois bronze spider, works by Richter, Hains, Lavier, Mylayne and Bustamente, and changing presentations of videos by artists such as Rosemarie Trockel, Rebecca Bournigault and Pierre Huyghe.

Salle de Matisse

In a special basement room two versions of Matisse's *La Danse*, the giant mural commissioned in 1930 for the Barnes Foundation in Philadelphia, show how Matisse dealt with the composition for a specific architectural space. The first, *Danse Inachevée* (Unfinished Dance) of 1931, which was rediscovered only in 1992 after having been rolled up and hidden away in an attic, reused figures from earlier paintings *La Joie de Vivre* and *La Danse Chtchoukine* but with an increased number of dancers. In the second version, *La Danse de Paris* (begun in 1931 but completed in 1933 after *La Danse Barnes*), Matisse found the solution of using large paper cut-outs (auguring the technique he used increasingly at the end of his life) and simplifying the figures to a rhythm of half cut-off forms against a bold graphic background.

Temporary exhibitions

The museum is particularly well known for its temporary exhibitions. These range from survey shows of different currents of modern art often viewed from an original perspective, such as the Fauves and the Ecole de Paris, and monographic retrospectives on artists including Alexander Calder, Mark Rothko and Niele Toroni, to its adventurous exhibitions programme featuring young international artists.

LEFT: *Spider* by Louise Bourgeois (1995).

FAR LEFT: *La Mariée Devissée* (The Undone Bride), by Jean Crotti (1921).

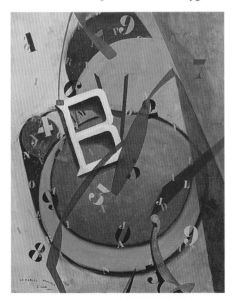

FOOD AND DRINK: Café de l'Art Moderne: the museum's own café is a popular spot for lunch or Sunday brunch with tables outside on the terrace when it's fine. La Fermette Marbeuf 1900 (5 rue Marbeuf, 8th; tel 01 53 23 08 00; moderate): classic French cooking in a grand Art Nouveau conservatory setting. La Maison Blanche (15 av Montaigne, 8th; tel 01 47 23 55 99; expensive): the restaurant built above the Théâtre des Champs-Elysées has been taken over by the talented Pourcel twins from Montpellier, with modern Mediterranean-slanted cooking to match the chic contemporary décor, artful lighting and superb views.

Musée Cognacq-Jay

Paintings, furniture and *objets d'art* of the 18th century, displayed in authentic panelled rooms of a restored *hôtel particulier*

Map reference: page 41, H3
8 rue Elzévir, 3rd
Tel: 01 40 27 07 21. www.mairie-paris.fr/musees
Metro: St-Paul, Chemin-Vert. Bus: 29, 69, 76, 96
Open: Tues–Sun 10am–5.40pm; closed Mon
Admission free.

The art and antiques amassed by Ernest Cognacq, who founded La Samaritaine department store in 1870, and his wife Marie-Louise Jay, reflect the interest in 18th-century refinement and humanity of this pair of enlightened collectors. The museum opened originally in 1929, next to one of Cognacq's stores on the boulevard des Capucines, but it transferred in 1986 to the newly restored Hôtel Donon in the Marais, built in the 1580s for Médéric de Donon, controller general of the king's buildings under Henri III.

The collection is displayed over a succession of salons and small rooms or "cabinets", which are furnished to give the feel of a private house. Some have their original panelling, while others feature period panelling acquired by the Cognacq-Jays from other houses. There are examples of both the Rococo style, with its assymetrical cartouches and carved floral and rocaille motifs, and the more geometrical Neo-classical style that dominated the 18th century.

Drawings and paintings

The visit starts with a lovely Chardin oil of a young man in tricorne hat playing cards, which is indicative of the quality of many of the works here.

The Kiss by Jean-Baptiste Pater (1695–1736), a follower of Watteau's style.

The first room focuses on works on paper, and the lighting is dim to conserve the fragile drawings. Works in the collection are shown in rotation every six to eight months, to limit their exposure. Among the most notable drawings are a tricolour chalk of a *Siren* by François Boucher, and drawings by Fragonard, Watteau, Ingres and Prud'hon. In a small adjoining room is a delicate painting of Gilles by Watteau. The finely carved wood-panelling in this room dates from 1760.

The large salon next door contains portraits by Jean-Marc Nattier, Fragonard and Sir Joshua Reynolds. The so-called "Louis XIV" room is fitted with two carved period doors, and shows that the Cognacq-Jays also had an eye for quality when it came to earlier periods: Rembrandt's *Balaam and the Donkey* (1626) showing a much brighter palette than that used in the artist's mature works, and a tiny, dramatically lit, stormy landscape with a gnarled oak tree by Jacob van Ruisdael. Also in the same room are two scenes of Venice by Canaletto, a particularly bravura Fragonard of a young man in a hat, a Tiepolo oil sketch of Cleopatra (a study for a larger work now in the National Gallery of Melbourne), and a tiny Chardin still life, showing how he could invest something as homely as a copper pot and couple of onions with an almost spiritual quality.

Portraiture, however, dominates the collection, including two pastels by Quentin de la Tour, the leading pastellist of the 18th century. His own acute self-portrait and the serene portrait of *La Présidente de Rieux en Habit de Bal* (The President of Rieux in Evening Dress) have a highly finished style that approaches that of oil painting, but with a softness that appealed to 18th-century tastes. The Cognacq-Jays' acquisitions also extended, unusually for the time in France, to English portraiture: including paintings by Sir Joshua Reynolds and Thomas Lawrence and a portrait of Miss Power by pastellist John Russell.

The Cognacq-Jays showed a love of scenes of bourgeois daily life, including two oils on copper by Nicolas-René Jollain and several gouaches by Swedish-born Niklas Lafrensen. More austere in mood are the Neo-classical paintings of Hubert Robert, set amid the antiquities of ancient Rome. Only occasionally did their taste verge on the cloyingly sentimental – in a set of paintings by Jean-Baptiste Greuze and in the wide-eyed and rather sinister *Petit Garçon au Polichinelle* (Little Boy and his Punchinello), attributed to Marguerite

Gérard, which hangs in a blue-and-white panelled room amid children's portraits and childhood scenes. Also upstairs, look out for the small "cabinet" containing several tiny sparkling paintings by Francesco Guardi, with his more fleeting, impressionistic vision of the Venetian lagoon.

Furniture and *objets d'art*

The furniture collection reflects the refinement and craftsmanship of French artisans of the period. Among the highlights are a large Boulle-style bureau, Louis XV chairs with Beauvais tapestry backs, fine clocks, and a pair of parquetry commodes. Ceramics include early Meissen porcelain figures by master modeller Kaendler, early Sèvres porcelain and examples of imported Chinese celadon ware in European gilt-bronze mounts.

A long gallery contains portrait miniatures and decorative accessories, including tiny enamel cigarette cases, snuffboxes and pillboxes, eyeglasses and elaborate novelty watches.

FOOD AND DRINK: Camille (24 rue des Francs-Bourgeois, 3rd; tel: 01 42 72 20 50; moderate): a useful Marais address, serving French bistro favourites from noon to midnight. See also Musée Picasso and Musée Carnavalet.

Portrait of Joanna Lloyd of Maryland (c. 1775) by Sir Joshua Reynolds (Musée Cognacq-Jay).

Musée Jacquemart-André

The grand entrance of the 19th-century Hôtel André, home to the Musée Jacquemart-André.

An exceptional collection of Italian Renaissance masterpieces and 17th- and 18th-century fine and decorative art, presented in an opulent 19th-century setting

Map reference: page 42, D2
158 bd Haussmann, 8th
Tel: 01 45 62 11 59
www.musee-jacquemart-andre.com
Metro: Miromesnil, St-Philippe-du-Roule, St-Augustin. Bus: 22, 28, 43, 52, 54, 80, 83, 84, 93
Open: daily 10am–6pm
Café. Shop. Audio-guide in English.
Admission charge

The sumptuous Hôtel André was built by Henri Parent in 1869–75 for the collector Edouard André (son of a wealthy banking family), at a time when this area of smart western Paris was first being developed. In 1881, André married society portrait painter Nélie Jacquemart, who hung up her paintbrushes to accompany her husband as he travelled Italy and the Orient or scoured salerooms.

The Musée Jacquemart-André is often described as a miniature Louvre or the Parisian version of New York's Frick collection, and part of its appeal is to be able to see the works that the couple amassed in the setting for which they were originally intended. The grand colonnaded entrance, spacious reception rooms, lavish painted ceilings and chic gentleman's smoking room, plus a set of smaller apartments for daily use, give a vision of the affluent lifestyle of the haute-bourgeoisie under the Second Empire.

The salons and library

Much of the ground floor reflects the Jacquemart-Andrés' taste for the 18th century. In the Salon des Peintures, paintings include Chardin's *Attributes of the Sciences* and *Attributes of the Arts*, Boucher's mythological fantasy, the oval *Sommeil de Venus* (Venus Sleeping), and a lovely portrait of the Marquise d'Antin by Jean-Marc Nattier, court painter to Louis XV. Even if Nattier's paintings always seem to have identical expressions and peaches-and-cream complexions, this is him at his best, revelling in his subject's gentle prettiness and her luscious satin robes.

Next door, the splendid Grand Salon, with Rococo panelling, was designed with an ingenious hydraulic device that enabled the space to be enlarged for receptions. As well as Beauvais tapestries, the Salon des Tapisseries contains Chinese porcelain and fine French 18th-century furniture, including a set of Louis XV armchairs and a parquetry secretaire by Joseph. The Boudoir is devoted to later 18th-century, Neo-classical furniture and portraits including works by Elisabeth Vigée-Lebrun, Prud'hon and David's *Comte Français de Nantes* wearing sumptuously rendered ceremonial robes.

In the former library are works of the Dutch and Flemish schools, including portraits in the broadly painted style of Haarlem by Franz Hals and Judith Leyster and a small Van Ruysdael landscape. These hang alongside Dutch marquetry furniture and a case of Egyptian antique souvenirs. There are three paintings by Rembrandt showing his early realist portrait style, his later, more atmospheric, psychological vision in the portrait of *Dr Tholinx*, and the small but striking *Pilgrims at Emmaeus*.

The Winter Garden

Perhaps the most unexpected room in the house is the Jardin d'Hiver, or Winter Garden, with its marble floor and columns, marble busts, lush plants and a spectacular double-revolution marble staircase that leads up to a balustraded oval gallery. Downstairs, just off this room, a small smoking room (Fumoir) creates a masculine ambience with North African inlaid tables, red velvet upholstery, Chinese and Japanese carpets and English portraits by Beechey, Reynolds, Lawrence and Hoppner.

At the top of the Winter Garden staircase admire the fresco of the *Reception of Henri III in Venice by Federigo Contarino* painted in 1745 by Tiepolo for the Villa Contarini and acquired by the Andrés on their travels. The restored fresco depicts the king, accompanied by his servant and hunting dog, being greeted by the doge under a limpid blue sky; several women observe the scene from the balcony in two accompanying *trompe l'oeil* pendants. Another fresco by Tiepolo can be seen on the ceiling of the former dining room, which is now the museum's restaurant and tearoom.

St George and the Dragon (*c.* 1439–40) by Paolo Uccello.

The Italian Collection

Upstairs, the area originally intended to be Nélie's studio became the Jaquemart-Andrés' "Italian museum" – an exceptional collection of Renaissance paintings, Luca della Robbia terracotta reliefs and architectural details. Among the highlights are portraits of the Virgin by Botticelli and Botticini and, in the harder-edged, more decorative style of Raphael's teacher Perugino, Mantegna's *Madonna with Three Saints* and the grisaille *Ecce Homo*.

From the Venetian school, look out for the two small predellas (long, narrow painted or sculpted strips from the bottom of an altarpiece) by Carlo Crivelli, the daringly simplified *Virgin and Child* by Giovanni Bellini and *Ambassade Hippolyte, Queen of the Amazons* by Vittore Carpaccio, showing the artist's fascination with narrative and decorative detail. However, the most adorable painting has to be Paolo Uccello's small *St George and the Dragon*, in which a winsome, snake-like dragon is being speared by the brave knight, as a waif-like damsel in distress looks on; the landscape of fields and castle walls in the background show Uccello's fondness for playing with perspective.

FOOD AND DRINK: Café Jacquemart-André (open 11.30am– 5.30pm): the mansion's former dining room, with Brussels tapestries on the walls and a ceiling by Tiepolo, provides an elegant setting for quiches and salads at lunch and cakes and ice creams for tea.

Musée Maillol – Fondation Dina Vierny

Maillol's sculpture set alongside other modern and contemporary art amassed by his model and muse, Dina Vierny

Map reference: page 40, C4
59–61 rue de Grenelle, 7th
Tel: 01 42 22 59 58. www.museemaillol.com
Open: Mon, Wed–Sun 11am–6pm; closed Tues
Metro: Rue du Bac. Bus: 63, 68, 69, 83, 84
Café. Shop. Wheelchair access. Admission charge.

Dina Vierny was introduced to French sculptor Aristide Maillol in 1934, when she was 15 and he was 73; for the next 10 years (until Maillol's death) she was his principal model. In 1995, she opened this museum in the 18th-century Hôtel Bouchardon (named after Edmé Bouchardon, who sculpted the *Four Seasons* foun-

tain at the entrance). The collection begins downstairs with Maillol's large bronzes of *La Rivière* and the *Three Graces*, as well as a re-creation of the artist's studio. Scattered over the two upper floors are numerous other bronzes, including the seated nude *Mediterranean*, *Harmony*, the *Four Seasons*, *Pomona* and *L'Ile de France*, as well as terracottas and large chalk drawings that served as preliminary studies for sculptures.

La Nuit, bronze sculpture by Aristide Maillol (1902).

The artist's figures are allegories, rather than portraits, and are all variants on the long-bodied, wide-hipped ideal of womanhood and nature (Maillol rarely sculpted male figures). Considered among the leading sculptors of the early 20th century (although with few true successors), he emerges as a curiously self-sufficient figure, who persistently examined the same themes in his search for purity and harmony. This was a very different approach from Rodin's research into psychological depth, the Cubist experimentation with form and the Surrealist dream-inspired creations of his contemporaries.

Influenced by classical sculpture, but with a simplification that also perhaps suggests cycladic art, the smoothly finished surface, warm patina, and rounded forms of Maillol's work appear calm and undramatic yet they have a surprisingly powerful presence in their poise and limpid serenity.

Arts and crafts

Although Maillol is best known as a sculptor, the museum also shows him as painter and designer. He was interested in the revival of craftsmanship and the decorative arts, and the collection includes woodcuts, tapestries inspired by medieval tapestries

Two Young Girls (1891), an early symbolist work by Maillol that is strongly influenced by Gauguin and the Nabis.

at the Musée du Cluny *(see page 80)*, ceramics – notably a lovely blue-and-white faïence fountain – and some curious anthropomorphic oil lamps.

Maillol studied painting originally and there are examples of his work in this genre on show. After he rejected both the Impressionists and the academic style of his teacher Couture, his early Symbolist canvases, such as *Les Deux Jeunes Filles* (1891), are strongly influenced by the Nabis and Paul Gauguin; here, he used flat blocks of colour, serpentine lines, profiled figures and decorative foliage in curious contrast to the volume and solidity of his sculpture. Maillol's late voluptuous nudes of Vierny – he returned to painting towards the end of his life – are more closely allied to his sculpture, as in *Le Grand Nu Jaune*, 1943 (in part a homage to Gauguin), and in double studies of Vierny, in which he played with mirror images of the body.

Vierny's collection

The museum is also well worth the visit for the work by other artists in Vierny's collection, including both those she sat for and those she has championed in the St-Germain gallery that she opened after Maillol's death. There are the Gauguin woodcuts and ceramics that influenced Maillol in the 1880s, and paintings by Nabis members Pierre Bonnard and Maurice Denis. A whole room of drawings by Matisse includes studies of Vierny, self-portraits, bewitchingly simple line drawings and chiaroscuro charcoal odalisques. There are also Degas's charcoal *Danseuses* and drawings by Picasso, Suzanne Valadon, Ecole de Paris artists Foujita and Pascin and a winsome *Spider* by Odilon Redon. Other works include pieces by the colourful naive artists Camille Bourbois and Séraphine, the jigsaw-like geometrical abstraction of Serge Poliakoff, a whole series of drawings by Kandinsky, compositions and reliefs by Jean Pougny and rare multiples and "ready-mades" by Surrealists Marcel Duchamp and Jacques Duchamp-Villon.

Since the 1960s, Vierny has supported contemporary Russian artists, such as Eric Boulatov and Ilya Kabakov whose installation, *Communal Kitchen*, is in the basement. This piece, with its suspended kitchen utensils and sounds of a communal kitchen under the Soviet regime, combines social comment and a powerful psychological atmosphere.

The museum also puts on consistently good temporary exhibitions, which have featured works by Vallotton, Bonnard, Basquiat, Haring, Diego Rivera and Frida Kahlo, among others, and often reveal rarely seen works from private collections.

Vierny has donated casts of several of Maillol's bronzes to the state. These are shown in the Jardin du Carrousel (Louvre end) of the Jardin des Tuileries.

*FOOD AND DRINK: **Le Nemrod** (51 rue du Cherche-Midi, 6th; tel: 01 45 48 17 05; inexpensive): a busy café-cum-bistro where you can pause for a coffee or settle down for a three-course meal. **L'Oeillade** (10 rue St-Simon, 7th; tel: 01 42 22 01 60; moderate): simple seasonal cooking, cheeky pictures and a chic clientele.*

ABOVE: The Impressionist Movement took its name from Claude Monet's ground-breaking *Impression, Soleil Levant* (c. 1873).

LEFT: *Rue de Paris; temps de pluie* (Rue de Paris in the rain) by Gustave Caillebotte (1877).

Musée Marmottan

Temple to the Impressionist Claude Monet

Map reference: page 42, B3
2 rue Louis-Boilly, 16th
Tel: 01 42 24 07 02. www.marmottan.com
Metro: La Muette. Bus: PC1, 22, 32, 52, 63
Open: Tues–Sun 10am–6pm; closed Mon
Shop. Admission charge.

The Musée Marmottan, set in a mansion in smart western Paris, gives an unrivalled overview of the whole of the career of Claude Monet (1840–1926). Major paintings are accompanied by sketchbooks, the artist's palette, accounts, notes, photos and other personal effects and a set of small portraits of the artist's children.

Major works

Among the fine collection of Monet's paintings is *Impression, Soleil Levant* (Impression, Sunrise), the canvas that gave the Impressionist Movement its name. The piece, painted *c.* 1873, was shown at an exhibition held in 1874 in the studio of the photographer Nadar on boulevard des Capucines, alongside works in the same style by Monet, Cézanne, Degas, Sisley, Morisot, Renoir and Boudin. *Impression, Soleil Levant* was rejected by the official Salon, and a scathing critic coined the term "Impressionism".

Other works include Monet's misty view of the Houses of Parliament in London, a facade of Rouen cathedral from the 1890s and an early beach scene at Trouville. *Pont de l'Europe* and *Gare St Lazare* reflect Monet's fascination with trains and steam and show how Impressionism was as much about depicting modern, urban life as it was about technique. Above all, however, it is the group of late paintings, left to the museum by Monet's youngest son Michel, that is particularly outstanding and a reminder that Monet continued to paint well into the 20th century, 50 years after his first Impressionist works.

Exhibited in a special basement room, the set of square canvases of *Nymphéas* (Waterlilies), of 1916–19, are almost luminous, viridian green and electric blue exercises in colour, inspired by the waterlilies, watery reflections and weeping willows of Monet's Japanese garden at Giverny (*see page 200*). Bold colour exercises painted with broad brushstrokes, these late *Nymphéas* – and the long, horizontal *Glycines*, which is related to the paintings in the Musée de l'Orangerie (*see pages 106–7*) – are a long way from the more delicate luminosity of Monet's earlier period.

These later works show how the artist had moved away from conventional ideas of composition and his earlier interest in capturing transient light and climatic effects towards all-over canvases without any obvious top or bottom and which simply evoke vegetation and watery reflections. In contrast, in the even later series of the Japanese Bridge of 1923–4, characterised by deep red and green pigments and thick, impasto paint, the artist seems intent almost on cutting out the light.

Monet's contemporaries

Thanks to other donations, Marmottan has a representative collection of Monet's fellow Impressionists and Realist contemporaries. Highlights include Caillebotte's *Rue de Paris*, several works by Pissarro and Guillaumin, Renoir's *Girl in a White Hat*, a pastel portrait of Manet, a small Manet portrait of Berthe Morisot, *plein-air* paintings by Boudin and Raffaeli, and an unusual Gauguin of a bowl of vibrant red flowers. Symbolist and Nabis works include the atmospheric monochrome paintings of Eugène Carrière and Maurice Denis's *Maternity*. A recent donation of paintings and pastels by Berthe Morisot is characterised by her affectionate portraits of children.

Empire furniture and medieval art

The superb First Empire furniture on show reflects the connoisseurship of Paul Marmottan, whose collection was the original basis of the museum. The style is distinguished by its elegant streamlined forms and motifs inspired by Napoleon's Egyptian campaign of 1798, replete with caryatids, mummies, winged sphinxes and eagles. Look out for the mahogany *bateau-lit* with bronze Egyptian head mounts, which was used by Napoleon in Bordeaux, a massive mahogany desk supported on winged lions, and several grand bronze chandeliers and candelabras. In the pretty circular salon on the ground floor, don't miss the geographical clock in Sèvres biscuit porcelain (1813–21). The head at the top rotates on the hour, and 12 roundels on the enamel dial enable the viewer to determine when it is midday around the world.

The medieval artworks amassed by Paul Marmottan's father Jules form an interesting counterpoint to Monet's paintings. The collection includes Gothic furniture and wood carvings, a Virgin by Mabuse, a Crucifixion by Bouts and the 16th-century Burgundian tapestry cycle, *Life of St Suzanne*, joined more recently by the Wildenstein donation of illuminated manuscripts.

Food and Drink: La Gare (19 chaussée de la Muette, 16th; tel: 01 42 15 15 31; moderate): restaurant and bar in a stylishly converted railway station. Tables are set along erstwhile platforms and tracks, and there are numerous train references.

Musée de l'Orangerie

Thanks to two exceptional bequests, the Orangerie is home to a superb collection of late 19th- and early 20th-century art

Map reference: page 40, C2
Jardin des Tuileries, 1st
Tel: 01 42 97 48 16
Metro: Concorde. Bus 42, 72, 73, 84, 94
Closed for renovation until 2003.

Expected to reopen in 2003 after total renovation, the Orangerie, along with its twin the Jeu de Paume, is all that remains of the former Palais des Tuileries, burnt down during the Paris Commune of 1871. Upstairs is the Walter-Guillaume collection of Post-Impressionist and Ecole de Paris paintings, which was left to the state in 1977. This body of artworks was put together by the dealer Paul Guillaume, who championed Derain, Soutine and Utrillo, among others; following Guillaume's death it was expanded by his widow Domenica, and her second husband Jean Walter. Several works by Soutine include his distorted, expressionist landscapes, still lifes modelled on Rembrandt, and *Le Petit Pâtissier* (The Little Chef, 1922–4), one of a series capturing

The highlight of the Musée de l'Orangerie is Monet's late waterlily series, *Nymphéas* (1914–18) bequeathed by the artist to the state in the spirit of peace.

Musée du Petit Palais

Best known as a major exhibition centre, the Petit Palais also has an important permanent collection of 19th-century art

Map reference: page 40, B2
Av Winston-Churchill, 8th
Tel: 01 42 65 12 73. www.mairie-paris.fr/musees
Metro: Champs-Elysées-Clemenceau. Bus: 42, 73, 83, 93
Closed for renovation until 2003. Telephone or consult website for up-to-date information.

Currently undergoing renovation, the Petit Palais, like its counterpart the Grand Palais, was built for the Universal Exhibition of 1900. Designed by Charles Girault, the Petit Palais is more intimate in style than its bigger brother, with lots of pretty neo-rococo details and painted ceilings. At the centre is a semi-circular garden surrounded by a covered arcade in polychrome marble.

Although best known for well-presented temporary exhibitions, the Petit Palais is also home to the eclectic municipal collection of art that takes in ancient Greek vases and antique sculpture, Italian Renaissance paintings and maiolica, French furniture, objets d'art and painting. However, the main interest lies in the collection of 19th-century French art that includes history paintings by Gros and Couture, an equestrian study by Géricault, sculpture studies by Carpeaux, Courbet's erotic *Le Sommeil*, studies for a monument to Labour by Dalou, numerous maquettes for public sculptures around Paris, and works by the Barbizon School and the Impressionists.

FOOD AND DRINK: See Musée de l'Orangerie, left.

ordinary people; in this piece, the form of the white cook's uniform is as central to the characterisation as the face. There is a finely balanced still life by Cézanne and works by Renoir, Picasso, Utrillo, and Le Douannier Rousseau, as well as portraits of Paul Guillaume by Modigliani, Derain and Van Dongen. After renovation, the paintings will be shown alongside furniture and decorative objects from the same period.

The highlight, though, is the unforgettable and extraordinarily fresh series of waterlilies by Claude Monet, conceived especially for two curved oval rooms downstairs. Donated by the artist to the state in 1918 (although they were installed only in 1927, after the artist's death), the eight vast curved panels hover between abstraction and decoration.

FOOD AND DRINK: L'Ardoise (28 rue du Mont-Thabor, 1st; tel: 01 49 26 90 04, inexpensive): good-value, carefully prepared modern French dishes and classics in a simple, unadorned bistro. Angelina's (226 rue de Rivoli, 1st; tel: 01 42 60 82 00, inexpensive to moderate): the archetypal French tearoom, for ladies who lunch. Dame Tartine (Jardin des Tuileries, 1st; tel: 01 47 03 94 84, inexpensive): just a short walk away in the pleasant setting of the Tuileries gardens.

Sarah Bernhardt (1876) by Georges Clairin (Musée du Petit Palais).

Decorative and Folk Art

Tools and trinkets, locks and keys, crystal and porcelain, dolls, dresses and dog baskets – take your pick of these rich and varied collections for an insight into city and country life across the social spectrum

Musée des Arts Décoratifs

An extension of the Louvre's rich collection of furniture and *objets d'art*

Map reference: page 40, D2
Palais du Louvre, 107, rue de Rivoli, 1st
Tel: 01 44 55 57 50; www.ucad.fr
Metro: Palais-Royal. Bus: 21, 27, 39, 68, 69, 95.
Open: Tues, Thurs, Fri 11am–6pm, Wed 11am–
9pm, Sat, Sun 10am–6pm; closed Mon.
Partially closed for refurbishment.
Admission charge.

Sharing the northwest wing of the Louvre with the Museum of Fashion and Textiles and the Museum of Advertising, the Museum of Decorative Arts forms part of the Louvre collection, but is administered separately by the Union Centrale des Arts Décoratifs. It offers a visual history of interior design, each room being a snapshot of the period it represents. Exhibits range from medieval tapestries and extravagant Empire furniture to 20th-century designs, including a wonderful Art Nouveau bedroom by Hector Guimard. Currently, only the newly renovated Medieval and Renaissance galleries are open. The remaining period rooms are being refurbished and will not reopen until 2003. *For more information on all three museums in the building see box on page 73.*

F*OOD AND* D*RINK: see Musée du Louvre, page 77.*

Musée des Arts et Traditions Populaires

Rural life in France illustrated with tools, costumes, furniture and folk art

Map reference: page 42, B2
6 av du Mahatma Gandhi, 16th
Tel: 01 44 17 60 00. www.mairie-paris.fr/musees
Metro: Les Sablons. Bus: 73, 244
Open: Wed–Mon 9.30am–5.15pm; closed Tues.
Wheelchair access. Admission charge.

The museum of French folk art and tradition is set in a grim-looking building on the edge of the Bois de Boulogne. The core collection was gathered in the 1930s and 40s by ethnographer Georges-Henri Rivière, whose objective was to document life in rural France before industrialisa-

The Tree of Love, wood engraving (1828).

tion and preserve what was rapidly being lost. Although you can sense the ambition and enthusiasm that Rivière must have felt about his project at the time, today's museum is glaringly outdated. Indeed, the newspaper *Le Monde* described it as being in a comatose state. The Ministry of Culture recently announced its decision to move the museum to Marseille in 2008, and it's unlikely that any improvements will be made in the interim.

Despite its dark and dingy layout, the museum has many interesting and unusual artefacts. The ground floor, where the collections are housed, is dark and windowless but the exhibits themselves are brightly lit. The space is divided into sections, beginning with agriculture, fishing, wine-making, and other trades. Eighteenth-century silver wine cups and straw baskets for holding grapes after picking are exhibited alongside old millstones and instruments for making flour and bread.

We learn that croissants were first made to commemorate the lifting of the siege of Vienna by the Turks in 1693. The costume of a shepherd on stilts illustrates an amusing yet practical tradition from Les Landes, a densely forested region of southwest France where shepherds walked on stilts in order to keep a better eye on their flocks and be able to cross swamps.

One room re-traces the stages of typical rural life in the 18th and 19th centuries, from birth to marriage to death. The customs, feasts and rituals are illustrated with displays of typical decorations, costumes and food. Look out for the 18th-century mar-

O*PPOSITE*:
Spring by Art Nouveau poster artist, Eugène Grasset (Musée des Arts Décoratifs).

riage proposal chair from Macon. According to a local tradition, if a woman sat down in the chair after receiving a proposal of marriage this meant "yes", but if she wasn't interested she would remain standing. Various objects used in religious ceremonies to mark special wedding anniversaries are displayed alongside bizarre funeral wreaths framed with the deceased's hair.

The section on superstitious and occult practices is particularly fascinating. There are spooky effigies, engravings depicting a witch's sabbath and reproductions of the tarot cards designed by Edmond, the 19th-century clairvoyant whose advice was sought by the likes of Napoleon III and Victor Hugo.

In the last section of the museum, finely crafted household items – from carved tobacco boxes and cake moulds to painted pots and embroidered belts and bonnets – are displayed alongside musical instruments, puppets and games. Among the highlights here are the *Arbre à Sabots*, a lovely sculpture of a tree carved by a clog-maker and decorated with clogs and birds, and the collection of simple but captivating engravings from the 15th to the 19th century.

Those with children in tow may want to visit the adjoining Jardin d'Acclimatation. Within this amusement park is the **Musée en Herbe** (Mon–Fri, Sun 10am–6pm, Sat 2–6pm), which has temporary exhibitions and children's activity workshops.

FOOD AND DRINK: For a quick bite, a variety of over-priced snacks can be found in the Jardin d'Acclimatation. Further along in the Bois de Boulogne L'Auberge du Bonheur (carrefour de Longchamp, 16th; tel: 01 42 24 10 17; moderate) serves simple French fare.

Déjeuner de Chasse (Hunt Picnic) by Nicolas Lancret's entourage (18th century).

Musée de la Chasse et de la Nature

Paintings, animal trophies, weapons and other decorative objects inspired by the aristocratic sport of hunting

Map reference: page 41, G3
Hôtel de Guénégaud, 60 rue des Archives, 3rd.
Tel: 01 53 01 92 40
Metro: Hôtel de Ville, Rambuteau. Bus: 29, 75.
Open: Tues–Sun 11am–6pm; closed Mon, public hols. Admission charge.

This museum, like its name, puts hunting *(la chasse)* rather than nature to the fore – wildlife, when it comes in at all, is safely dead. The collection is spread over three floors of a fine Marais mansion, which was built in 1651 by one of Louis XIV's favourite architects, François Mansart, for one of his councillors, François de Guénégaud.

Skilful oil studies of squirrels, gamebirds, dogs, deer and lions by Alexandre-François Desportes (1661–1743), France's first great *animalier* painter, occupy the first room and the stairway. On the first floor is a collection of ornate hunting rifles dating from the 16th to the 19th century. The next floor up, a distinctly animal-scented room makes a dramatic transition to big game. The walls and floor are crammed with animal trophies: the stuffed bodies, mounted heads, tusks and skins of antelope, a bison, lion, tiger, rhino and even a pair of gorillas. Next door, a polar bear looms rather incongruously alongside an antler chandelier and antler-backed chairs, a Sèvres porcelain lunch service (decorated with hunting scenes), given by Louis XVIII to the Duc de Berry, a 16th-century Austrian marquetry chest and an Italian Renaissance painting of *Diana the Huntress*.

The quality of the *objets d'art* gives some idea of the social importance of hunting, as the subject crops up on ornate biscuit porcelain groups, wild boar tureens, and German carved ivory and silver tankards. Indeed, hunting and game scenes found their way onto everything from andirons to clocks and console tables. Among the many fine paintings are hunting scenes by Carle Vernet and Alfred de Dreux, still lives by Chardin and Oudry, and works by Desportes painted for the royal hunting châteaux. Look out for his affectionate painting of *Blonde and Diane*, two of Louis XIV's favourite hunting dogs, commissioned for the Château de Marly, which shows how these prized possessions were on their way to becoming pets.

FOOD AND DRINK: Le Bouquet des Archives (31 rue des Archives, 4th; tel: 01 42 7 08 49; inexpensive): friendly, colourful corner café adorned with modern art and pot plants that does a roaring lunchtime trade in salads and generous plats du jour.

Musée du Cristal Baccarat

A collection of over 1,000 precious articles made by one-time purveyors of fine crystal to the imperial courts of Europe

Map reference: page 43, F2
30bis rue du Paradis, 10th
Tel: 01 47 70 64 30
Metro: Poissonnière, Gare de l'Est. Bus: 32, 38, 39, 47, 48
Open: Mon–Sat 10am–6pm; closed Sun.
Shop. Admission charge.

One of a pair of finely engraved vases made for the 1867 Universal Exhibition.

The Baccarat museum traces the history of the influential crystal manufacturer. It adjoins the original showroom, which opened in 1832 in a street that has long been a focus of the glass and porcelain wholesale trade. The sparkling collection is exhibited in authentic glass cases on polished wooden counters. The display follows the evolution of styles and decorative techniques: blown and moulded glass from the 1830s; coloured agate ware from the 1840s; translucent white opal ware with ornate floral motifs from the 1850s; objects inspired by the fashion for the Orient in the 1870s; delicately engraved or enamalled chalices from the early 20th century; chunky cut glass from the 1930s through to sculptural 1970s pieces.

Grandiose, show-off items of doubtful taste but indisputable technical brilliance made for various World Fairs testify to the confidence of 19th-century industrialists. Among the outsized pieces are two vases cased in ruby crystal and beautifully engraved with allegories of earth and water exhibited at the Exposition Universelle of 1867 and the giant pair of candelabra made for Tsar Nicolas II in 1896.

The most notable contribution to Baccarat's design repertoire was made by Georges Chevalier (1894–1987), who joined the company in 1916. He introduced geometrical Art Deco motifs and brought both verve and refinement to the designs – as in the beautiful Jets d'Eau service engraved with fountain motifs, and in the simple streamlining of his 1951 Guyanmer service.

Baccarat also excels in the production of perfume flasks for leading fashion houses and perfumiers. Among the most successful designs are Dalí's *La Roy Soleil* for Elsa Schiaparelli in 1945 and the more recent design for Dior's *J'Adore* launched in 2000.

Much of the fun, though, comes in seeing who once drank from Baccarat glasses. Two large showcases are devoted to glasses made for assorted heads of state, monarchs

Baccarat Goldfish Vase, 1878.

and emperors – from a service ordered by Louis-Philippe in honour of Queen Victoria's visit in 1840 to pieces made for the King of Egypt, the Shah of Iran, the Maharajah of Baroda, Franklin D. Roosevelt and Henry Ford II, as well as for the French president and various government ministers.

Outside the historic collection, the commercial showroom displays several lines that have been in more or less continual production, as well as the latest Baccarat designs.

Food and Drink: Brasserie Flo (7 cour des Petites-Ecuries, 10th; tel: 01 47 70 13 59; moderate): the original component of the Flo brasserie group still has the feel of an Alsatian tavern and is a fun place for shellfish, grills or choucroute *and decadent desserts.*

Musée de l'Eventail

Fans and the dying art of fan-making

Map reference: page 41, G1
3rd floor, 2 bd de Strasbourg, 10th
Tel: 01 42 08 90 20
Metro: Strasbourg St-Denis. Bus: 20, 38, 39, 47.
Open: Mon–Wed 2–6pm; closed Thur–Sun and Aug. Shop. Admission charge.

For centuries, the fan was an essential accessory for the high-society woman, as finely crafted (and costly) as a precious piece of jewellery. Fan-making remained an important industry in France until World War I, after which fans went out of fashion and the craft began to disappear. This small private museum doubles as the workshop of France's last active fan-maker, Anne Hoguet, who is keeping the family tradition alive by making and restoring fans.

The entrance corridor introduces the three principal types of fan – the simple "screen fan", which has origins going back to Ancient Egypt and China, the "*brisé* fan" with overlapping struts, and the "folding fan". Beyond the shop, the first room contains tools, presses and the materials used for the "sticks", such as ivory, bone, wood, horn, mother-of-pearl and Plexiglass. The second room is devoted to the "leaves", typically in organza, silk, paper, vellum or lace, and decorated using anything from paint to sequins. The third room, where numerous fans are displayed, was the firm's original showroom and retains its 1893 neo-Renaissance décor with carved walnut fittings and chimneypiece.

The earliest fans here date from the 18th century. The one depicting Apollo and the Muses Paying Homage to Perseus (*c.* 1750) is a particularly fine example and gives an idea of the degree of refinement that could be attained: its tortoiseshell sticks are decorated with mother-of-pearl inlay and gilding and the mythological scene is painted on swan skin. But the majority of fans date from the 19th and early 20th centuries, when fan production was at its peak in France, with some fine examples from other countries such as China, Spain and Madagascar.

The 20th-century collection includes advertising fans for department stores Printemps and Bon Marché, and the Café de Paris, a 1920s fan in Bakelite with guinea fowl feathers, and more recent designer commissions, such as the glittery scissor creation for Karl Lagerfeld.

Food and Drink: Le Reveil du Xème (35 rue du Château d'Eau, 10th; tel: 01 42 41 77 59; inexpensive): a busy local wine bar which serves excellent lunches or cheese and charcuterie *all day, along with assorted Beaujolais crus.*

The rare bird, by Anne Hoguet (2000).

Musée de la Mode et du Costume (Galliera)

Bi-annual exhibitions held in a duchess's palace give an airing to selected items from one of Europe's richest costume collections

Map reference: page 42, C3
10 av Pierre-Ier-de-Serbie, 16th
Tel: 01 56 52 86 00
www.paris-france.org/musees
Metro: Alma-Marceau, Iena. RER: Pont de l'Alma. Bus: 32, 42, 63, 72, 80, 82, 92.
Open: Tues–Sun 10am–6pm during temporary exhibitions only; closed Mon and public hols.
Library (access by appt.). Admission charge.

Velvet evening dress (1887), lithograph by Gustave Janet.

The imposing Palais Galliera, which stands on the north side of the Avenue President Wilson on the approach to the Trocadero, is hard to miss. The mansion was built at the end of the 19th century for the Italian Duchess of Galliera to house her art collection. Although inspired by the Italian Renaissance, the iron structure that supports the freestone building, made in Gustave Eiffel's workshop, was very much of its time. The philanthropic Duchess bequeathed her palace to the city of Paris, and in 1977 it was converted into a fashion museum.

Apart from the costumes selected for display, the majority of the 10,000-piece collection is now kept in a large atelier in the 11th *arrondissement*, with controlled temperature and ventilation and an on-site workshop for repairs and general care. First and Second Empire fashions are well represented, and donations by the likes of Baroness Guy de Rothschild and Princess Grace of Monaco have enriched the 20th-century collection.

Costumes are shown in temporary shows, of which two are held per year. (The museum closes for about a month between exhibitions, so be sure to check it's open before going.) While its mission is to show fashion and costumes in an historical context, the museum also promotes new talents and designers, thereby running into some competition from the Musée de la Mode et du Textile *(see opposite)*. Past shows have included "Evening gowns through the ages", "Givenchy", "The History of Jeans", "Marriage", "Fashion and Revolution" and "Children's Fashions".

Conferences and workshops are held for adults and children on themes related to the ongoing exhibition, and visits and conferences can be arranged in English on request. A library with over 5,500 volumes on the subject of fashion and costumes (some in English) is open to the public by appointment.

*FOOD AND DRINK: For a lively atmosphere and a large selection of decent Italian food, try **Balilli** (rue Freycinet, 16th; tel: 01 47 20 50 52; moderate).*

Musée de la Mode et du Textile

The city's second fashion museum rotates its couture collection in annual exhibitions

Map reference: page 40, D2
Palais du Louvre, 107, rue de Rivoli, 1st
Tel: 01 44 55 57 50. www.ucad.fr
Metro: Palais-Royal. Bus: 21, 27, 39, 68, 69, 95.
Open: Tues, Thurs, Fri 11am–6pm, Wed 11am–9pm, Sat, Sun 10am–6pm; closed Mon.
Admission charge.

The Louvre's *haute couture* collection, spanning the 17th to the 20th centuries, is displayed in rotation. The annual exhibitions are stylishly mounted and imaginatively themed. For example, the 2001–2 exhibition *Jouer la Lumière* demonstrated through lavish displays how textiles and clothes interact with, and are transformed by, light. The focus of the 2002 exhibition is on "designer superstars", to be followed in 2003 by an exhibition on Jackie Kennedy. *For more information, see page 73.*

LEFT: Elegant woman's desk inlaid with panels of Sèvres porcelain, attributed to Martin Carlin (*c.* 1739–85).

RIGHT: Two panels from a folding screen decorated with a tapestry of birds, flowers and fruit from the Savonnerie workshop (18th century).

Musée Nissim de Camondo

A connoisseur's collection of 18th-century decorative arts in a stately mansion modelled on Versaille's Petit Trianon

Map reference: page 42, D2
63 rue de Monceau, 8th
Tel: 01 53 89 06 50. www.ucad.fr
Metro: Villiers. Bus: 30, 84, 94
Open: Wed–Sun 10am–5pm; closed Mon, Tues, public hols. Admission charge.

The Camondos were a wealthy Jewish banking family from Constantinople who settled in Paris in the late 19th century. In 1910, Comte Moïse de Camondo inherited two houses overlooking the Parc Monceau. He promptly destroyed them and set about building this stately home modelled on the Petit Trianon at Versailles. The family moved in at the outbreak of World War I and lived here in a style quite out of its time.

The count had a passion for the 18th century and filled his new house with period furniture and decorative arts, completing the illusion with the fine panelling that lines several of the rooms. In 1935, Moïse de Camondo bequeathed both the mansion and the collection to the state, his purpose being to preserve "the finest examples I have been able to assemble of this decorative art which was one of the glories of France." He also requested that the museum be named after his son Nissim, who had died in aerial combat in World War I.

Preserved much as Moïse left it, the house reveals a connoisseur's taste for the 18th century in all its refinement, and sometimes unexpected colour: loudly patterned Italian marble fountains, Aubusson tapestries, Savonnerie carpets, Sèvres porcelain and fine marquetry furniture from the century's very best cabinetmakers, including Oeben, Reisener, Weisweiler and Leleu.

On the stairs, ormolu-mounted Chinese porcelain and corner cabinets inset with panels of Japanese lacquer reflect the 18th-century taste for the Orient.

The grand salons

The main reception rooms are upstairs on the Upper Ground Floor – so-called because this level gives out on to the formal gardens at the rear. In the impressive Grand Salon, a fine portrait by Elisabeth Vigée-Lebrun hangs above a chest of drawers by Reisener decorated with both geometrical parquetry and floral marquetry. There is a set of chairs upholstered with Aubusson tapestry panels and a small lady's desk inset with Sèvres porcelain plaques. The white and gold panelling came from a *hôtel particuler* in rue Royale.

The main highlight is the Salon de Huet, a circular room overlooking the gardens, so-called because of the pastoral scenes painted by Jean-Baptiste Huet *(see page 49)* that are set into the panelling. The exquisite roll-top desk (*c.* 1760) is by Oeben, its inventor, who also made a similar one for Louis XV at Versailles. In the palatial dining room, note the ornately carved gilt barometer and two glass cases containing silver tureens and wine coolers, which

were commissioned from Roettiers in 1770–71 by Catherine the Great of Russia for her lover, Count Orloff. Off to the side is a small room designed specifically for the display of porcelain (and where Moïse de Camondo apparently dined when alone). Here you'll find the famous Buffon service, in soft-paste Sèvres porcelain, depicting different species illustrated in the Comte de Buffon's *Natural History of Birds* (published 1770), and two smaller sets of Meissen hardpaste porcelain dating from the 1750s, also decorated with birds.

Upstairs, downstairs

The first floor relates more to the private life of the Camondos. Rooms are more crowded and the furniture less opulent. In the Blue Drawing Room is a pair of wide, deep-seated armchairs intended for women wearing voluminous dresses, a day bed and a *duchesse brisée* – a type of chaise-longue composed of armchair and stool. Nissim de Camondo's bedroom has a set of hunting scenes by Alfred de Dreux. Next to the all-tiled, all mod-cons (for the period) bathroom, the dressing room presents photographs, letters and documents, including a picture of Béatrice, daughter of Moïse de Camondo, who died with her two daughters at Auschwitz.

Before leaving, visit the service areas on the lower ground floor. The massive kitchen and roasting ranges, copper pans, scullery, chef's office and servants' dining room conjure images of life "below stairs" in the early 20th century.

FOOD AND DRINK: see Musée Cernuschi, page 127.

Le Musée du Parfum Fragonard

Collection of perfume flasks and perfumiers tools from Ancient Egypt to the 20th century, spread across two small museums

Map reference: page 40, D1
9 rue Scribe, 2nd. Tel: 01 47 42 04 56.
39, bd des Capucines, 2nd. Tel: 01 42 60 37 14.
www.fragonard.com
Metro: Opéra. Bus: 22, 52, 53, 66
Open: Mon–Sat 9am–5.30pm,
from April–Oct open Sun 9.30am–4.30pm.
Shop. Admission charge.

D irectly across the street from the Opéra Garnier *(see page 164)*, the rue Scribe museum is housed in a beautifully restored 19th-century town house complete with ornate mouldings and ceiling frescoes. Illustrations of Mediterranean plants and flowers from botanical books (17th–19th century) cover the walls along a staircase leading up to the first floor. A heady fragrance permeates the air in the first room, which focuses on techniques for extracting and distilling perfume. Blown-glass Florentine flasks (18th-century) used to separate oil from water after distillation, copper stills and beaters are exhibited. While this first room has signs that are both in French and English, English is forgotten from the second room onwards, so it's worth picking up the translated information leaflets provided at the front desk.

Rooms II and III are dedicated to the history of perfume. Ancient Egyptian containers for kohl in alabaster are exhibited, as well as tiny terracotta flasks from Ancient Greece and beautiful miniature ceramic perfume flasks from Carthage (6th–3rd century AD). The simplicity of the amber Roman flasks and bronze and glass Islamic bottles contrasts sharply with the extravagance of Louis XVI's perfume "fountain", made of Chinese porcelain covered

Fragrant 19th-century interior of the Fragonard perfume museum.

with gold, and other elaborate flasks. Fragrance boxes from the 17th century known as *vinaigrettes* held small sponges that were soaked with aromatic vinegar to help revive women prone to fainting fits brought on by tight corsets. A luxurious travel set given by the Duc de Berry to his first wife, the Englishwoman Amy Brown, reminds us how much the concept of travel has changed. The set contains about 60 items in mother of pearl, porcelain, vermeil and crystal, including candle-holders, a teapot and cups, sugar tongs and a make-up mortar.

The tour winds up cleverly in the shop, which is very well stocked with enticing soaps, bath salts, perfume and scented candles at factory prices.

Boulevard des Capucines

The second museum is located in the Théâtre des Capucines, a 20th-century building where Arletty, the legendary Parisian actress and music-hall singer of the 1930s and 1940s began her career. Less charming than the museum on the rue Scribe, its collection of intricate 17th-century perfume flasks from Germany and Holland is interesting nonetheless. Some are in lapis lazuli and gold, others in amethyst, crystal and gold. A 19th-century crystal flask from Bohemia doubles up as a lorgnette designed for evenings at the opera. Another amusing Viennese flask from the same period is in the shape of a knight in armour, fashioned in crystal and gold.

In the early 20th century, perfume companies discovered the importance of packaging, display and advertising, which resulted in close collaboration between perfumiers and glassmakers such as Baccarat *(see page 111)* and Lalique, and graphic artists such as Mucha. Schiaparelli's 1939 "Sleeping" perfume appeared in a Baccarat crystal bottle in the shape of a candle and flame.

The last object in the museum is a perfume organ – a wooden display case containing 300 or so bottles used by perfumiers during the creation of a new scent. The visit ends, as in the rue Scribe museum, in the gift shop.

*FOOD AND DRINK: **Restaurant Opéra** (in the Grand Hotel, 5 place de l'Opéra, 2nd; tel: 01 40 07 30 10; moderate): serves good contemporary French cuisine in a beautiful setting, with mouldings by Garnier, who designed the Opéra next door. For a change of scene, **Le Maroc** (9 rue Danielle Casanova, 1st; tel: 01 42 61 48 83; moderate) provides a welcoming atmosphere, good tagines and couscous among North African décor. See also Musée de l'Opéra, page 164.*

Musée de la Poupée

Two centuries of French dolls

Map reference: page 41, G3
Impasse Berthaud, 3rd
Tel: 01 42 72 73 11
Metro: Rambuteau. Bus: 29, 38, 47
Open: Tues–Sun 10am–6pm, closed Mon, public hols. Admission charge.

Established by an Italian father-and-son team of self-confessed doll fanatics, this small museum is for like-minded enthusiasts of any age. Four rooms lined with 40 display cases trace the evolution of French *poupées*, beginning with the fragile porcelain dolls of the Second Empire – ringleted ladies in tailored dresses that were more showpieces than playthings. The so-called "Golden Age of the Baby", around the turn of the 20th cen-

tury, brought with it a new generation of dolls with more child-like faces, while the introduction of new materials, notably celluloid, gave them the added advantage of being unbreakable. The last cases are devoted to the plastic mannequin dolls of the 1950s and 1960s and the type of implausibly leggy Barbie doll clone still coveted by little girls the world over.

Each doll-filled case is dressed as lovingly as a French shop window and the real pleasure of the museum lies not so much in the dolls themselves as in the detail: a lace-covered parasol, a finely embroidered dress, the doll's own doll, worn and well-loved teddies, miniature toys and furniture. Look out for the dolls' prams and cradles lined up on top of the display cabinets, which can easily be missed. The last room is used for temporary exhibitions and next door is a well-stocked doll shop and hospital.

FOOD AND DRINK: Le Hangar (12 impasse Berthaud, 3rd; tel: 01 42 74 55 44; moderate): serves carefully prepared French cooking in an airy converted industrial space.

Musée de la Serrurerie – Bricard

A collection of locks and keys shows this rarely considered architectural feature to be the object of fine craftsmanship

Map reference: page 41, H3
1 rue de la Perle, 3rd
Tel: 01 42 77 79 62
Metro: St-Paul, Chemin Vert. Bus: 29
Open: Mon–Fri 2–5pm; closed Sat, Sun, part Aug, public hols. Admission charge.

This privately owned lock museum is housed in the vaulted cellars of the elegant Hôtel Libéral-Bruand, built by the architect of Les Invalides for himself in 1685. The upper floors house the offices of Société Bricard, which still manufactures locks in the north of France today. Keys and locks dominate the museum, but the display also takes in door knobs, *targettes* (latches) and other curiosities of the blacksmith's art, from decorative liturgical plaques to harness trappings and early surgical instruments.

The earliest items are Roman and Carolingian keys, including several *clefs bagues* – keys in the form of a ring, typically used to open small coffers. There are simple medieval keys and double-ended *passe-partout* or skeleton keys. Only a few items are labelled (in French), but it is possible to appreciate the decorative finery of many of these objects, as motifs kept apace with the style of the day from medieval Gothic to Rococo scrolls and the acanthus leaves of the First Empire to gorgons and engraved scenes from La Fontaine's fables.

One of the finest items is the ornately decorated Italian lock adorned with *repoussé* classical figures and military trophies from a 16th-century wedding chest. Many of the items had prestigious origins: there's a Neo-classical lock designed for the apartments of Marie-Antoinette, locks from the Tuileries palace and Château de Sceaux – both destroyed in the Paris Commune – and an eagle-headed Russian imperial key belonging to Tsar Nicolas I. Curiosities include the 18th-century, lion-headed Serrure Preistale – burglars beware: its teeth would descend to bite the hands of would-be thieves – and a Serrure Pistolet that fired off warning shots if tampered with.

FOOD AND DRINK: see Musée Picasso, page 92, and Musée Cognacq-Jay, page 101.

World Art and Culture

These outstanding collections of art and sculpture from across the globe are the combined legacy of France's former colonies, the efforts of her archaeologists and the collecting mania of her wealthy philanthropists

Musée d'Art et d'Histoire du Judaïsme

Paris' Jewish museum places a rich array of art, artefacts and documents in the context of Jewish communities and religious celebrations

Map reference: page 41, G3
Hôtel de St-Aignan, 71 rue du Temple, 3rd.
Tel: 01 53 01 86 60. www.mahj.org
Metro: Rambuteau, Hôtel de Ville. RER:
Châtelet-Les Halles. Bus: 29, 38, 47, 75.
Open: Mon–Fri 11am–6pm, Sun 10am–6pm;
closed Sat, Jewish hols.
Café. Bookshop. Audio-guide. Auditorium.
Wheelchair access. Admission charge.

LEFT: Hanukkah lamp in chased and engraved silver (late 17th century).

OPPOSITE: Death of Buddha, his cremation and division of his remains from the Parinirvana (detail), Tibet, 18th century (Musée Guimet).

Opened in 1998 in a restored Marais mansion, the Musée d'Art et d'Histoire du Judaïsme has given Paris' Jewish community a prestigious showcase on quite a different scale to the old Musée d'Art Juif in Montmartre, which it replaced. The original collection has been substantially enlarged by the Strauss-Rothschild collection previously in storage at the Musée National du Moyen Age and by new donations, loans and acquisitions, and the museum is now allied to a programme of concerts, films and temporary exhibitions.

The imposing Marais mansion was built in 1650 for the Comte d'Avaux by the architect Pierre Le Muet. After the French Revolution, it became first a town hall, then from 1842 was converted into a warren of workshops. By the end of the 19th century, many of the inhabitants were Jewish refugees from the pogroms in Eastern Europe. The building was acquired by the city of Paris in 1962 and has been beautifully restored. You enter through the majestic *cour d'honneur*, with crisp Corinthian pilasters and an armorial borne by winged gryphons. A few other remnants inside – the unusual oval gallery over the top of the staircase, traces of frescoes in window bays and in the café – hint at the mansion's former splendour.

Symbols of Judaism

The museum's emphasis is on fine craftsmanship as well as religious practice. Note that although the main explanatory text for each section is in English as well as French, individual labels are in French only, although an optional English-language audio-guide is included with the entry ticket.

An introductory room on the first floor explains the museum's guiding principle "to explore Judaism's transmission in the different environments in which communities developed". Murals of Hebrew texts and a Torah scroll signify the importance of the word and scholarship. Portraits of Jewish people, a 17th-century hannukah candelabra from Frankfurt, Torah finials from Shanghai in the form of pagodas, and a carved relief of Jerusalem from Odessa representing the dream of the promised land show both how Jewish faith and rituals were maintained throughout its history of migrations and diaspora, and how it adapted stylistically to local forms. The head sculpted by Chana Orloff in 1920 points to the dichotomy between the artist as individual as well as member of a community.

From here, a geographical and thematic route begins with Jews in medieval France before the wave of expulsions first by Philippe Auguste in 1188, then by Philippe IV (The Fair) in 1306, and then, most decisively, by Charles VI, whose edict of 1394 expelled all Jews from France. Among the scarce reminders of this community are fragments of 13th-century Hebrew gravestones excavated in the Latin Quarter and a rare iron hannukah lamp from Lyon. Equally rare are the handful of Spanish objects predating the expulsion of Jews from Spain in 1492 by Catholic monarchs Ferdinand and Isabela. However, Italian Jewry from the Renaissance to the 18th century is well represented with Italian synagogue furniture, including a 15th-century, Renaissance

RIGHT: Jewish woman
and her daughter,
Tunisia. Late 19th-
century albumen print.

OPPOSITE LEFT:
"Dreyfus is
Innocent"
poster, produced
in 1898, the
same year that
Emile Zola
published
J'Accuse.

carved and inlaid Ark cupboard from Modena, a gilt Baroque circumcision throne, and two lively paintings of *A Jewish Wedding* and *A Circumcision* by 18th-century Verona artist Marco Marcuola. A vitrine of knives and other items used in the ceremony of circumcision and an ornate silk bar mitzvah cap and tunic embroidered with silver thread show the importance attributed to these ritual items and the museum's method of looking at different communities through various ceremonies or aspects of Judaism. Stages in Jewish life continue with a display of ornate Italian illuminated marriage deeds, wedding rings and belts.

Hannukah lamps from all over Europe and North Africa, representing different styles and periods, include ornate *repoussé* Baroque silverware and filigree work. Printed books and engravings mark the importance of printing, especially in Amsterdam – "the meeting point of two diasporas" to which many Sephardic Jews from the Iberian peninsula and Ashkenazic Jews from Eastern Europe had fled.

The Ashkenazic traditions of Germany and Eastern Europe are represented most notably by a lovely wooden *sukkah* cabin from Austria or southern Germany painted with picturesque scenes, animals and floral motifs. Alongside a collection of models and archive photos of the vanished synagogues of Poland hangs Samuel Hirswenberg's powerful painting *The Jewish Cemetery* of women searching amid falling gravestones, which captures the feeling of torment among the Jewish community during the Eastern European pogroms that began in the 1880s.

Upstairs, the rise of "court Jews" – powerful Jewish families such as the Oppenheimers and

Rothschilds – as advisors and bankers to the courts of Germany and Austria, is reflected in some of the luxurious items they owned, such as prayer shawls, and jewelled Torah crowns and cases. Other exhibits are devoted to the costumes and jewellery of the Sephardic Jews of North Africa and Constantinople.

The next section returns to France, focusing on the Jewish communities – in Alsace-Lorraine, between Bordeaux and Bayonne, and in the ghettoes of Provence – and their emancipation following the Revolution. Items include a Torah scroll and embroidered caps from Carpentras, souvenirs of the Jewish community in rural Alsace, and popular imagery of Jews typified by woodcuts from Epinal of the *Wandering Jew*.

The opening of professions to Jews brought many of them to the city where they could freely pursue commercial, industrial, academic and even military careers. An engraving of the first synagogue built in Paris in 1822 and a series of paintings of Jewish notables reflect the growth of Jewish communities that followed emancipation.

The Dreyfus Case

The museum has an archive of more than 3,000 documents relating to the Dreyfus case, in which Jewish army officer Alfred Dreyfus was wrongly accused and condemned of spying. Those chosen for display show how the case polarised French society: a copy of "*J'Accuse*", Emile Zola's impassioned defence of Dreyfus that hit the headlines of *L'Aurore* in January 1898, "Dreyfus is Innocent" posters and moving letters from his wife are exhibited alongside his deportation order to Devil's Island (French Guiana) and anti-semitic cartoons.

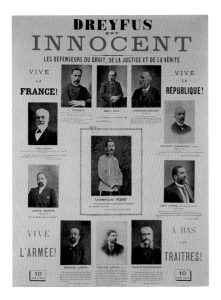

LEFT: *Snakes and Emus* painted on plywood by Nym Bunduk (1907–74), Australia.

Jewish art

The final section of the museum deals with the contribution of Jewish artists to the early 20th century avant-garde, starting with fine book illustrations and ending with a room devoted to the Ecole de Paris *(see page 27)*. A *Mother and Child* by Chana Orloff, paintings by Modigliani, the haunting expressionist oils of Soutine and canvases by Chagall with their characteristic mix of Jewish motifs and Russian folklore reflect the large number of Jewish artists who flocked to Paris in the early 20th century. The mezzanine gallery is used for temporary displays commemorating artists who died in the Holocaust.

The Marais Jews

The museum has been criticised for ignoring the Holocaust, preferring to focus on Jewish history and culture as a whole. While this is an obvious omission, the museum has instead chosen to bring a more personal and human face to the Holocaust. The pre-war Jewish community in the Marais district is presented through photos of their bakeries, restaurants and clothing workshops and in a powerfully understated installation by French artist Christian Boltanski, himself Jewish, whose work often deals with issues of memory.

Plaques set into the wall of a small courtyard façade, visible through a glass wall, record the name, place of origin and occupation of all the Jews who were living in the Hôtel St-Aignan in 1939, 12 of whom died in concentration camps.

FOOD AND DRINK: Chez Marianne (2 rue des Hospitaliers-St-Gervais, 4th; tel: 01 42 72 18 86; inexpensive): a convivial, perpetually busy address for Central European and Middle Eastern Jewish delicacies. Not kosher.

Musée des Arts d'Afrique et d'Océanie

An exceptional collection of African and Oceanic Art, with the added bonus of a well-stocked tropical aquarium

Map reference: page 43, J5
293 av Daumesnil, 12th
Tel: 01 44 74 84 80. www.musee-afriqueoceanie.fr
Metro: Porte Dorée. Bus: PC, 46, 87
Open: Mon, Tues–Sun 10am–5.30pm.
Book and gift shops. Wheelchair access.
Admission charge.

This extraordinary collection has helped inspire yet another *grand projet* in Paris: the Musée des Arts Premiers on quai Branly, due to open in 2004. According to Jacques Chirac, who initiated the project, a new museum is needed "to give the arts of Africa, the Americas, South Pacific and Asia their rightful place in the museological institutions of France". It would be hard to argue that the present location of the museum is "the right place." Somewhat off the beaten track at the eastern end of Paris, by the entrance to the Parc des Vincennes, the building was erected for the 1931 Exposition Coloniale at the height of the colonial era. The structure is an Art Deco fantasy, whose bas-reliefs outside and murals within celebrate France's claim to colonial supremacy in Africa and Southeast Asia.

The museum is currently divided into four main sections: African art, Art of the Maghreb (North Africa) and South Pacific Arts, with a large tropical aquarium in the basement.

Les Arts d'Océanie

Works from the Pacific region occupy the ground floor. The collection of Aboriginal bark paintings from northern Australia is one of the richest in Europe. A human serpent vies for attention with the strange myths depicted in the *Cérémonie Funérarie*, a scene that used to appear on the Australian dollar bill. Complementing these ancient tribal works is a collection of contemporary paintings by Aborigines from Alice Springs. These are characterised by their geometric patterns which, in the tradition of the artists' forefathers, represent mythical beings.

Art from the Pacific islands includes a flute mask from Papua New Guinea (a power object that women were not allowed to look at), a funeral stele from Irian Jaya that symbolises the soul's state of suspension between heaven and earth, and, most impressive of all, the finely tuned vertical tambours carved by the Vanuatu tribes that were used for dancing and drum-relayed messaging.

Les Arts d'Afrique

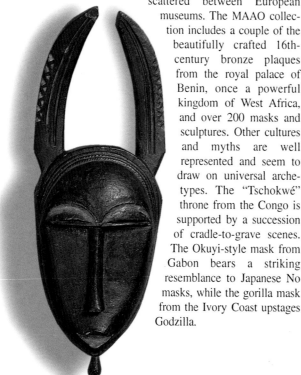

Baoulé horned mask (19th–20th century), Ivory Coast.

The variety of forms in the first-floor galleries reflect the vastness of the African continent; Nigeria alone is twice the size of France, and nearly 300 languages and dialects are spoken there. It has arguably the most important artistic tradition in sub-Saharan Africa, although much of it is now scattered between European museums. The MAAO collection includes a couple of the beautifully crafted 16th-century bronze plaques from the royal palace of Benin, once a powerful kingdom of West Africa, and over 200 masks and sculptures. Other cultures and myths are well represented and seem to draw on universal archetypes. The "Tschokwé" throne from the Congo is supported by a succession of cradle-to-grave scenes. The Okuyi-style mask from Gabon bears a striking resemblance to Japanese No masks, while the gorilla mask from the Ivory Coast upstages Godzilla.

One of the highlights of the African gallery is the group of 53 ritual masks and statuettes from the grasslands of Cameroon, a legacy of Pierre Harter, a doctor who became one of the world's experts on Central African art.

Maghreb

The pottery, tiles, carpets, swords, and jewellery in this section come from the Maghreb, the area of North Africa once officially designated part of "greater France". The squat polychrome pottery with its abstract palms influenced the designs of 19th-century cashmere scarves and the painting of Eugène Delacroix. The Berber water jugs combine the ancient form of a Greek amphora with bronze-age geometric patterns. The exquisite wedding jewellery on display once doubled as a woman's dowry and protection against the evil eye. Look out for the Ottoman brooch and tiara made with diamonds and white gold.

Aquarium

Three thousand fish swim around the museum's murky basement aquariums, providing surreal bursts of colour. They represent 300 species and need 300,000 litres (66,000 gallons) of constantly filtered water. There are piranhas, electric eels, blow fish, angel fish and clown fish, and even a pair of hapless crocodiles confined to a 13-sq metre (140-sq ft) terrarium. The Nautilus pompilius is a close cousin of the extinct ammonite whose 400 million year-old fossils are found all over the planet.

FOOD AND DRINK: La Flambée (4 rue Taine, 12th; tel: 01 43 43 21 80; moderate): regional cooking from the southwest of France (duck, foie gras, cassoulet, etc.) served around a wood fire.

MASKS

Many of the exhibits from Africa and the South Pacific are masks that once played a role in initiation and fertility rites or funerals. These masks take almost any form, from the grotesque to the geometric, from stark caricature to expressive realism. They not only symbolised ancestral spirits but also embodied them in mysterious ways, requiring a system of taboos to protect the wearer and spectator from their magical powers. They were often carved by adult males working in secret. The artists used almost any kind of material for decoration, including human hair, animal teeth and bones, nails or shells. Normally, a mask was not a simple face but part of a whole bodysuit of dried leaves or vegetable fibres that rustled in accompaniment to the dancer's movements.

Sandstone pediment carved with a scene from the *Mahabharata* depicting the demons Sounda and Oupasounda fighting over a celestial nymph (11th century), Khmer period, Cambodia.

Musée des Arts Asiatiques – Guimet

The museum of Asian art has treasures that span the Orient; the Buddhist sculptures from the Cambodian civilisation of Angkor are the jewel in its crown

Map reference: page 42, C3
6 place d'Iéna, 16th
Tel: 01 56 52 53 00. www.museeguimet.fr
Metro: Iéna. Bus: 32, 63, 82
Open: daily 10am–6pm.
Restaurant/tea room. Book and gift shop.
Audio-guide. Auditorium. Guided visits.
Wheelchair access. Library and photo archives.
Admission charge.

Reopened in 2001 after five years of renovation, the long dusty Musée Guimet has come back enlarged and rejuvenated with spacious day-lit galleries that give its collections a new visibility. The national museum of Asian art was based, originally, around the collection bequeathed by Emile Guimet, a wealthy 19th-century industrialist and voyager from Lyon, whose museum of world religions first opened in this classical revival building in 1889.

His collection was later augmented by the Oriental collections from the Louvre and by subsequent acquisitions and donations. These often reflect both France's colonial history and the work of French archaeologists, most notably in their findings of Cambodian sculpture, Chinese paintings from Dunhuang and the Treasure of Begram from Afghanistan.

Arranged geographically, the new galleries (designed by the father-and-son architectural partnership of Henri and Bruno Gaudin) favour natural lighting and uncluttered spaces. The freestanding works are displayed on sober, minimalist concrete plinths and there's an easy flow between rooms. The downstairs galleries focus on India and Southeast Asia, while the upper floors feature the art of China, Japan, Korea, Nepal, Tibet and central Asia. The museum is more than simply a voyage to the Far East; in its pan-Asian coverage it also communicates a sense of the flow of civilisations, religions and influences, such as the migration of Hinduism and Buddhism from India and the spread of ceramic techniques from China, that a visit to just one country rarely conveys.

Note that an audioguide in English is included in the entrance ticket (you have to leave your passport as security), which gives the background to selected key works, but you may find that the same texts in the small Pocket Guide, available in the bookshop, are easier to use.

Cambodia

In the double-height central gallery at the heart of the museum, masterpieces from the medieval Khmer kingdom make up the finest collection of Khmer art outside Cambodia. Hinduism and later, Buddhism were introduced to Cambodia from India bringing in the panoply of gods such as Shiva, Vishnu, Brahma and Ganesh. Cambodia soon developed its own distinctive and refined style characterised by superbly poised, elongated figures with serene, beatific smiles. An indication of the scale of the temple complexes at Angkor is given by the late 12th-century *Giant's Way*, which dominates the entrance to the gallery. It was once part of a massive balustrade at the entrance to the Preah Khan temple complex. Two chunky *devas* – benevolent demi-goddesses – hold a seven-headed cobra, guardian of the monument and symbol of prosperity, whose body originally snaked along for 200 metres. Amid an array of smaller sculptures that includes narrow-waisted goddesses, beautiful Shiva heads with curling lips and long-lobed ears, Skanda astride a peacock and horse-headed god Vajmukha, look out for the 7th-century *Harihara*. This striking statue combines the figure of Shiva on the right (with his tall chignon, third eye and wild cat's skin hanging from his waist), and Vishnu, on the left, bearing a disc and mitre.

In the adjoining gallery is a kneeling statue of Jayarajadevi, depicted as Buddhist deity Tara. Javarajadevi was the first wife of king Jayavarman VII, in whose reign (1181–1218) Buddhism became the state religion and Cambodian art flourished.

In contrast to the graceful simplicity of the single statues, the collection of bas-reliefs from temple lintels and tympanums are rich with detail and folklore. These intricate carvings tell complicated tales involving deities, demons and nymphs, serpents and elephant-headed lions.

Gilded bronze statue of Queen Maya giving birth to Gautama Siddartha, the North Indian prince who became the Buddha (18th century), Nepal.

The rest of Southeast Asia

Rooms leading off the central gallery show how Hinduism and Buddhism also permeated the rest of southeast Asia. There are bronze Buddhas and decorated chests from Thailand, examples of the intricate Burmese style, sophisticated and particularly ornate bronze votive sculptures and temple fragments from Java, and a fine collection of Chanda statuary from coastal south and central Vietnam. Look out for the large statue of Shiva sitting on a lotus leaf with a snake entwined around his chest.

Standing apart stylistically is the art of northern Vietnam, an area ruled for a long time by China. The Chinese influence is apparent in the blue and white glazed altar candlesticks, pale green celadon ware, glazed stoneware, polychrome wood figures, roof ornaments and the group of terracotta reliquaries in the form of pagoda-like towers.

India

The small but high-quality Indian collection spans over 2,000 years, with examples of the principle styles of ancient and medieval art from across the subcontinent. Contrast the northern Indian stone sculptures from the Kushan and Gupta periods (1st–6th centuries) with the sensual sculptures of southern India, in which the celebration of the body is reflected in the use of Chola bronze casting. This fine art produced the voluptuous dancing form of *Nataraja* – the cosmic dance of Shiva, representing the eternal cycle of birth, life and death. Highlights on the ground floor include lively reliefs and sculptures from the classically influenced Amaravati School of Andra Pradesh, rare 4th-century reliefs from Kashmir, and a red sandstone statue of serpent king *Nagaraja* – a superb 2nd-century example of the Mathura style of Uttar Pradesh.

Later Indian craftsmanship is on view on the first floor, where the Jean and Krishna Rebord collection is displayed. The mixture of Moghul jewellery, embroidered and painted fabrics, mother-of-pearl caskets and bejewelled daggers provide a glimpse of secular rather than religious artistry. A series of miniatures (16th–19th centuries) evokes the India of Mughal emperors, Rajput princes and sultans of the Deccan.

China

Chinese antiquities and Buddhist art are displayed on the first floor. The earliest items are the mysterious jade discs that probably served in some sort of fertility rite, along with clay pots and an array of

FAR LEFT: Glazed ceramic horse, Tang dynasty (618–906), China.

LEFT: *Two Women under an Umbrella* by Eizan Kikugawa (1787–1867), Japan.

Shang dynasty bronze vessels from the 12th and 11th centuries BC. The three-legged pots, vases and wine containers are covered in geometric patterns and often have handles in the form of stylised beaks or animal heads. An unmissable item is the exceptionally large bronze pot in the form of an elephant.

Funerary figures from the Tang Dynasty, including sinuous ladies with elaborate hairstyles, musicians, dancers, ladies-in-waiting, servants, horsemen and camels, show the importance of burial rituals in ancient China. These animated figurines made of terracotta were placed in tombs along with paintings and other objects to accompany the dead into the next life – a practice that died out with the rise of Buddhism. They tell us a lot about the lifestyle and social standing of the tombs' occupants. Look out for the set of female polo players on galloping horses that provide evidence of the new aristocratic pastime introduced from India.

Succeeding galleries deal with the arrival of Buddhism in China. Among the numerous meditating Buddha, terracotta heads and reliefs, look out for the Buddha with 1,000 arms and 1,000 eyes.

Another fascinating exhibit is the collection of items gleaned from the hundreds of cave sanctuaries that pepper the cliffs around Dunhuang, in northern China, which were discovered by French archaeologist Paul Pelliot at the beginning of the 20th century. These include two warlike celestial kings in painted wood and several fragile paintings (displayed in rotation) on silk and paper.

Later Chinese art displayed on the second floor gives a panorama of Chinese ceramics and lacquerware. Celadon ware, with its characteristic pale green glaze, often with an incised decoration of fish or foliage, and early white porcelain and black monochrome ware show the early emphasis on refined silhouettes and perfect finishes. The later blue and white porcelain of the Ming and Qing dynasties put the emphasis on decoration, often with fantastical dragon motifs or landscape scenes.

On the third floor, Qing dynasty porcelain shows how a thick, overglaze enamel pink was introduced for the European export market, in so-called "pink chrysanthemum" ware. At the top of the museum, the rotunda gallery contains examples of lacquerware, notably a huge 12-fold lacquer screen decorated with cranes, clouds and pine trees.

Afghanistan and Pakistan

Central to this section is the 1st-century Treasure of Begram, from the ancient Afghan capital north of Kabul. The finds unearthed here in 1937 by Hackin all pointed to a thriving international trade along the Silk Route. Among the precious objects were blown-glass vessels in the form of fish and vases from Alexandria, carved ivories from India, Chinese lacquer and Graeco-Roman bronzes.

Further evidence of the region's place at a cultural crossroads is provided in sculpture. Hellenistic influences can be seen in the classical drapery of the Gandhara-style reliefs from Pakistan and the lovely, Apollo-like *Genie with Flowers*. Don't miss the Buddhist stupas from Hadda, smooth white-domed structures covered in stucco decorated with rows of small figures along the sides.

Tibet and Nepal

Finely detailed fabric paintings of mandalas (circular designs depicting the universe) and scenes from the life of Buddha, metalwork and religious ritual items reflect the distinctive Tantric form of Buddhism that evolved in Tibet and Nepal. Small gilt metal statues encrusted with jewels reveal a

marked predeliction for depicting deities in their grimacing, most terrifying incarnations. Other ritual items include the bejewelled hat of a Buddhist official, tridents and a rare iron baton topped with a carved ivory skull. Known as the Yamadanda, the baton is a symbol of the Tantric god Yama, king of the underworld and judge of the dead.

Japan

Highlights of the Japanese collection are the holdings of Buddhist sculptures from the Nara period (710–794) and paintings and graphic arts from the Edo period (1603–1868), including the remarkable *Portraits of 36 Immortal Poets*, and 19th-century woodcuts by Hokusai. Other items include ancient, primitive terracotta figures, inlaid lacquer incense boxes and writing sets showing various decorating techniques and favourite motifs of chrysanthemums, landscapes and herons, No theatre masks and swords. Japanese ceramics include raku stoneware, Imari porcelain and the earthenware of late 17th-century master Ogata Kenzan.

Korea

Celadon ware, small bronzes, theatrical masks and furniture displayed on the second floor (although you should also look at the two roughly hewn, 17th-century tomb guardians in the entrance lobby) show how Korea developed its own distinctive art forms, whether in an abstract style of decoration or the bright colours and caricaturist style used in paintings.

FOOD AND DRINK: The basement restaurant/tea room at the museum, Le Salon des Porcelaines (tel: 01 47 23 58 03; inexpensive) features a pan-Oriental menu at lunch and French pastries for tea. At Brasserie de la Poste (54 rue de Longchamp; tel: 01 47 55 01 31; moderate), the oysters, steaks and other brasserie standards are unexceptional but the beautifully preserved 1920s Art Deco interior is a treat.

THE BUDDHIST PANTHEON

Just around the corner from the Guimet is a little-known annexe to the museum known as the Pantheon Bouddhique. It houses Emile Guimet's collection of Chinese and Japanese Buddhist art, much of which he brought back from his journey to Japan in 1876. The bulk of the collection is made up of figures of the Buddha in his many forms. Guimet, a humanist, wanted to reconstruct the Buddhist pantheon through paintings and sculptures, his ultimate aim being to communicate a message of peace during a period of great unrest in Europe. Entrance is free and the Japanese garden is open in fine weather.

Musée Cernuschi

An impressive collection of Chinese and Japanese art amassed by a wealthy philanthropist and displayed in his Neoclassical mansion

Map reference: page 42, D2
7 av Velasquez, 17th
Tel: 01 45 63 50 75
www.paris-france.org/musees
Metro: Villiers, Monceau. Bus: 30, 94
Closed for renovation until 2004.

The former mansion of 19th-century banker and philanthropist, Henri Cernuschi (1820–96), houses his collection of East Asian art and still has the feel of a private and slightly dusty home (though the ongoing renovations should spruce it up). It is situated at the eastern entrance of the Parc Monceau, an immaculately tended park bordered by 19th-century mansions and apartment buildings. The permanent collection is on the ground floor while the first floor is used for temporary exhibitions.

Henri (born Enrico, in Milan) Cernuschi was a republican and fervent supporter of Garibaldi who came to France to escape the turmoil of pre-unified Italy. He began seriously to build up his art collection while travelling around the world in the 1870s, this time escaping the turmoil incurred by the Paris Commune uprising. With plenty of money to spend on the ancient artworks that so enthralled him, he returned from China and Japan with a shipload of acquisitions. Twelve years later he announced that he would bequeath his mansion and collection to the city of Paris in return for it having taken him in as a political refugee. The museum has since continued acquiring art, primarily from ancient China.

Among the oldest objects in the collection are a group of terracotta vases in swirling colours with geometric patterns and shapes dating back to 2800 BC. The museum's collection of bronze vases from the Shang and Zhou dynasties (1500–1050 BC and 1050–221 BC respectively) is considered particularly rare because of its exceptional quality. Dominating the ground floor display is a huge, perfectly preserved water basin (*c.* 5th century BC).

The Cernuschi's star attraction is a 12th-century BC vessel (late Shang dynasty), known as *The Tigress*. The bronze jug, elaborately fashioned in the shape of an open-jawed wild cat, was probably used to serve alcohol in ritual ceremonies.

A large stone lintel decorated with mythical animals is representative of the Han dynasty (AD 206–220), as are the little figurines made of terracotta and wood. It was customary in China to bury small statues of people and animals with their dead to ward off evil spirits *(see page 125)*.

In contrast to these miniature figures are five towering Buddhist statues from the 5th to 7th century and the magnificent bronze *Meguro Buddha* – the largest piece that Cernuschi brought back from Tokyo and given a room to itself.

Another of the museums masterpieces is an 8th-century painted scroll *Horses and Grooms* attributed to Han Kan, a court artist and the greatest horse painter of his time. Other highlights include a collection of Chinese celadon porcelain from the 13th century, beautifully exhibited in glass cases along with red and black lacquer bowls and trays.

This little-known museum is generally not overcrowded and the atmosphere is so serene that it makes for a very pleasant and relaxing experience.

FOOD AND DRINK: Among the many bistros in the area Le Bistrot d'à Côté *(16 av de Villiers, 17th; tel: 01 47 63 25 61) is one of the best: Nouvelle French cuisine but plentiful helpings; their* chocolat à l'ancienne *dessert is famous.*

Painted screen (detail), lacquered wood, K'ang-hi period (late 17th century).

Bangwa commemorative statue of a princess, 19th century, Cameroon.

Musée Dapper

Sub-Saharan African art

Map reference: page 42, C3
35 rue Paul Valéry, 16th
Tel: 01 45 00 01 50. www.mairie-paris.fr/musees
Metro: Victor Hugo. Bus: 52
Open: Tues–Sat 11am–7pm
Café. Bookshop. Performance space. Wheelchair access. Guided tours (with advance reservation). Admission charge.

A private, non-profit organisation, the Dapper Foundation is a "dynamic museum" whose mission is to preserve African art and make it better known to the world. Its major collection of sub-Saharan art forms the nucleus of two exhibitions each year. They are displayed in a 16th-

arrondissement mansion built by Charles Plumet and remodelled in 2000.

A visit to any of the Dapper's exhibitions is always enlightening and will help to explain why Braque and Picasso were so profoundly influenced by African art. The works in its collection were created by great sculptors, whose names remain unknown. Many of them are masks traditionally used in African ceremonies: fertility or initiation rites, religious or funeral celebrations, as well as theatre and farce.

The Dapper's permanent collection is something of a mystery since it is never on display in its entirety. Perhaps its most famous possession is the Bangwa statue that the French call the "Mona Lisa of Primitive Art," made famous by a Man Ray photograph taken in 1930. It was purchased for US$29,000 in 1966 and sold to the Dapper for $3.1 million in 1990, showing how the commercial value of African art has recently begun to approach Western levels.

Food and Drink: The Café Dapper in the museum serves snacks and light meals, some of them African. Nearby, Le Petit Rétro (5 rue Mesnil, 16th; tel: 01 44 05 06 05; moderate) is an intimate bistro with a sense of perfectionism, particularly in its blackboard specials.

Above Right: One of a pair of porcelain statuettes, Edo period (1603–1867), Japan.
Below: Carved wooden reliquary figure, Gabon.

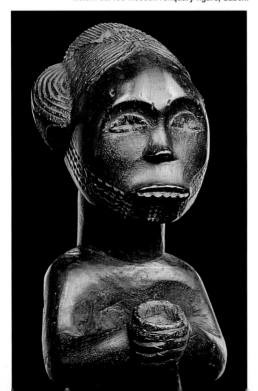

Musée d'Ennery

A pot pourri of Oriental objects displayed in a lavish Second Empire mansion

Map reference: page 42, C3
59 av Foch, 16th
Tel: 01 45 53 57 96
Metro: Porte Dauphine. Bus: 33, 82
Temporarily closed for renovation work. Call Musée Guimet for details (tel: 01 56 52 53 00).

The Musée d'Ennery is an endearing museum, both because of the history behind the extraordinary collection and the fact that it remains displayed more or less as it was (in accordance with a clause in the owners' will) when Adolphe and Clemence d'Ennery lived there.

Adolphe d'Ennery was a popular 19th-century playwright who, among other things, adapted Jules Verne novels for the stage. His wife, Clemence, following a generalised growing interest in Asia, began to collect Far Eastern artefacts without knowing much about what she was buying. Art dealers soon caught on to the enthusiastic collector, and very quickly Clemence d'Ennery amassed over 7,000 objects, buying both original pieces and sometimes entire stocks. She kept her artefacts in beautifully designed showcases, some even inlaid with mother of pearl.

The Ennery mansion, which dates from the Second Empire (1852–70), stands on the imposing Avenue Foch. It has a handsome entrance from

Shadow and light: the steel and glass prisms of the Arab Institute façade open and close according to the movements of the sun.

which a black and red marble staircase leads up to the museum. A series of small rooms open on to a long gallery, crammed with showcases and objects on the wall. Seventeenth-century trunks made for Portuguese explorers by Chinese artisans, 19th-century Chinese tobacco flasks, and bronze, jade and crystal objects and ornaments all vie for space.

The museum is best known for its collection of Japanese *netsukes* – decorative accessories used to fasten small objects like a purse or pouch for tobacco or medicines to a sash or belt. They were carved in either wood, bone or ivory, and the material and decoration was an indication of the owner's place in society at the time. *Netsukes* became very popular during the Edo period (17th–mid-19th century) and the d'Ennery collection spans the three centuries.

The second half of the gallery is lined with Japanese masks from the 11th to the 13th centuries. Life-size lacquered wooden animals from China keep company a mummified monkey's head sitting in a glass case. An important collection of Japanese chimeras, painted blue, green and red, are displayed alongside Japanese and Chinese lacquered boxes in the shape of animals.

One showcase displays the journals and notebooks that Mme d'Ennery used for her research. The combination of her painstakingly detailed inventories with the eclectic nature of the objects that she purchased encapsulates the *fin-de-siècle* fascination with the Orient.

Food and Drink: See Musée Dapper, page 128, and Musée de la Contrefaçon, page 171.

L'Institut du Monde Arabe

A cultural centre and museum of Arab-Islamic art and civilisation housed in Jean Nouvel's stunning high-tech building

Map reference: page 41, G5
1 rue des Fosses-St-Bernard, 5th
Tel: 01 40 51 38 38. www.imarabe.org
Metro: Jussieu, Cardinal Lemoine, Sully-Morland. Bus: 24, 63, 67, 86, 87, 89.
Open: Tues–Sun 10am–6pm
Restaurant, café and tea room. Shop. Library.
Wheelchair access. Admission charge.

The striking building on the banks of the Seine, a blend of modern Western and traditional Arab architectural styles, is symbolic of the institute's *raison d'être* – to create links and establish a deeper cultural understanding between the Western and Islamic worlds. It was with this aim in mind that the project for the Institut du Monde Arabe (IMA) was launched in 1980 by President Giscard d'Estaing in collaboration with 19 Arab countries.

The architect Jean Nouvel's design for the institute, which opened in 1987, contributed greatly to the public's initial interest in the centre. This is one of the most successful buildings erected in Paris since the early 1980s. It stands on the site of a former 12th-century monastery and a 16th-century wine storehouse, and enjoys a commanding position overlooking the Seine and Ile St-Louis,

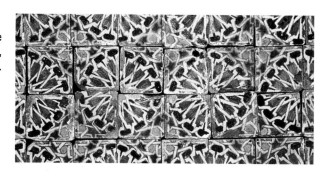

Painted tiles (late 18th century), Tunisia.

Jussieu University and, further west, Notre-Dame cathedral. The northern side of the high-tech steel and glass building is gently curved while the southern façade is a flat patterned wall of gleaming symmetry that recalls traditional Arab lattice-work. Nouvel's complex geometrical patterns are, in fact, variously dimensioned metallic diaphragms, which, in a feat of technology, operate like light-sensitive camera lenses to control the brightness of light penetrating the interior. The result is a high-tech interpretation of the essence of Arab architecture. The interior, with its interplay of light and shadow, is as striking as the exterior. The icing on the cake is the rooftop terrace, from which the panoramic view of Paris is superb.

While the IMA's architecture was a success from the start, the centre teetered on the verge of bankruptcy during the mid-1990s, due mainly to lack of contributions from some member countries unable to keep up with payments – the institute is funded 60 percent by the French Foreign Ministry and 40 percent by Arab states. Once the cash-flow problem was resolved, IMA was able to pick itself up and is now firmly established as one of the world's leading Arab cultural and intellectual centres.

The museum's permanent collection, which includes long-term loans from museums in the various member countries, is spread over the 4th, 6th and 7th floors. (Signs are in French only.)

Early Arabia

The chronological tour starts on the 7th floor, which is devoted to pre-Islamic objects spanning 4,000 years, beginning with a display of prehistoric tools and followed by elegant terracotta amphorae, Punic oil burners and cuneiform tablets. Look out for the tiny fragments of painted ostrich egg found in Carthage (4th–3rd centuries BC) – eggs were considered a symbol of life

"Carolingian" astrolabe (10th century), Spain.

and were often used in funerary rites in Egypt and Mesopotamia. Other highlights from the pre-Islamic period include the imposing series of stone funerary busts from Palmyra (2nd-century AD), and a beautiful, finely restored mosaic from a Christian church in Tunisia, which depicts a deer in shades of terracotta and yellow, with symbols of the cross as a centerpiece.

The first Muslim dynasties

The first centuries of Islam are the focus of the second section, on the 6th floor, which is also partly dedicated to the Institute's temporary exhibitions *(see below)*. In the permanent collection, the first two Muslim dynasties, the Umayyads (661–750) and the Abbasids (750–1258), are represented by inscribed silver coins, paintings and painted objects in ceramic. An excellent collection of mathematical and scientific instruments reminds us of the Arab world's dominance in maths and science during the Middle Ages.

There's an impressive number of intricately decorated astrolabes. The astrolabe, considered "the principal instrument of medieval astronomy", was perfected by the Arabs at the beginning of the 6th century and was used as a navigational aid throughout the Middle and Far East until the 19th century. The 6th-floor circuit ends with a display of rare textile fragments, mostly dating from the 9th and 10th centuries and featuring intricate floral, animal and figurative motifs.

The spread of Islam

The third section is on the 4th floor, which gives you access to the peaceful, plant-filled interior courtyard that Nouvel designed in the tradition of the *ryad*, or patio. This part of the collection covers the dynasties in the Arab-Islamic world from the 9th to the 19th centuries, when the search for the aesthetic was present in all things, whether in crafts, book illustrations, or carpets.

Much of the floor features an excellent and, if you understand French, highly informative display of rugs and carpets. With the spread of Islam throughout Syria, Egypt, Iran and Central Asia, the art of carpet-weaving flourished in these regions. Carpets were central to the interior décor of tents and palaces alike. They covered many items of furniture, were used as decorative hangings and also played an important role in religious life. More than 20 words exist in Arabic to describe different rugs and carpets, many of which are exhibited here, from prayer mats and kilims to tribal carpets.

Also on the 4th floor is the Institut's small but dazzling jewellery collection. Most of the jewels come from Tunisia under the Ottoman Empire, when it was the norm for jewellers to sell gold, silver and precious stones to women who then fashioned their own necklaces or hairpieces.

Cultural events

In addition to the permanent collection, one large temporary exhibition a year is organised, usually running from autumn to spring. The shows are often, but not always, centered around a particular country, such as the Sudan or Yemen. Important exhibitions on individuals, such as Delacroix's travels in North Africa, Matisse in Morocco, and the 12th-century politician and military leader, Saladin, have all been hugely successful.

The IMA has a lively cinematic centre, which shows films on theme cycles every two months, ranging from the subject of love in Egyptian film to Tunisian cinema. Every two years the Arab Cinema Biennale is held here, with features and documentaries in competition. Also on a two-year schedule is the Arab Book Fair, which brings together major Arab and European publishers with an interest in the Arab world.

Books play a major role at IMA, which has a library on the 3rd floor containing 65,000 works in Arabic, French, English and Spanish. Arab newspapers and magazines are available for consultation.

Turkish prayer mat (18th century).

*FOOD AND DRINK: Enjoy good North African cuisine and a panoramic view from the top-floor restaurant of the Institut, **Le Ziryab** (tel: 01 53 10 10 20; expensive). Also on the 9th floor is **Le Moucharabieh** (tel: 01 53 10 10 20; moderate), a cafeteria with variations on the fare served at the Ziryab at much lower prices. **Le Café Littéraire**, at ground level (inexpensive), is a lovely salon de thé, with Hamman-style décor (a profusion of gold and comfortable cushions to sink into) and a laid-back atmosphere.*

Exhibition Galleries

A full listing of art spaces in Paris where temporary exhibitions are held. Venues include galleries devoted exclusively to temporary shows, artist-run spaces, cultural centres and commercial galleries

I f major blockbuster shows tend to appear at the Grand Palais *(see page 135)* or in major museums, notably the Centre Pompidou *(see pages 55–62)* and the Musée d'Art Moderne de la Ville de Paris *(see pages 97–9)*, there's no shortage of other venues around Paris that put on temporary exhibitions. There is much for all tastes, from big names at Fondation Cartier and the Jeu de Paume, and more staid, historical exhibitions at Fondation Mona Bismarck, to the artist-run spaces that tend to concentrate on young artists.

Look out, also, for exhibitions in the town halls of the different *arrondissements,* or for occasional outside sculpture shows in elegant place Vendôme, the Palais Royal gardens, or along the Champs-Elysées, as well as for the happenings and installations that sometimes crop up in more unusual places. Some of the more unexpected venues have included the DIY section of the BHV department store, private apartments and even a hairdresser's salon. Note that the temporary exhibition venues listed here are only open when an exhibition is running.

Jean Nouvel's high-tech glass and steel Cartier Foundation.

Temporary exhibition spaces

Bibliothèque Forney

Map reference: page 41, G4
Hôtel de Sens, 1 rue du Figuier, 4th
Tel: 01 42 78 14 60
Metro: Pont-Marie. Bus: 96
Open: Tues–Fri 1.30–8pm, Sat 10am–8pm.
Bookshop. Admission charge.
Poster, illustration and design shows are mounted by this library, which specialises in the decorative and graphic arts. It is housed in the Gothic townhouse built for the Archbishops of Sens in 1475 and given a fancifully picturesque restoration.

Bibliothèque Nationale de France – François Mitterrand

Map reference: page 43, G5
11 quai François-Mauriac, 13th
Tel: 01 53 79 59 59. www.bnf.fr
Metro: Bibliothèque, Quai de la Gare. Bus: 62, 89.
Open: Tues–Sat 10am–7pm, Sun noon–6pm; closed two weeks Sept. Admission charge.
The final and most costly of President Mitterrand's *grands projets,* Dominique Perrault's gargantuan library has been plagued by constant strikes and technical problems since opening in 1996. However, it is still worth braving for varied, scholarly shows

that present aspects of its collections of prints, artists' books, manuscripts and photography. Past subjects range from globes and the history of writing to prints by contemporary Spanish artist Antoni Tapiès.

Bibliothèque Nationale de France – Richelieu

Map reference: page 40, E2
58 rue de Richelieu, 2nd
Tel: 01 47 03 81 26. www.bnf.fr
Metro: Bourse, Pyramides. Bus: 74, 85
Open: Tues–Sun 10am–7pm; closed two weeks Sept. Admission charge.
France's old national library was formerly the private mansion of Cardinal Mazarine, and some of his original murals remain in the Galeries Mansart and Mazarine – these halls are now used for presentations of prints, drawings, photographs and manuscripts from the library collection. Shows of contemporary artists' work are mounted in an additional space, Le Crypte, created in the cellars in 2001.

Chapelle St-Louis de la Salpêtrière

Map reference: page 43, G5
47 bd de l'Hôpital, 13th
Tel: 01 42 16 04 24
Metro: Gare d'Austerlitz, St Marcel
Bus: 24, 57, 61, 63, 89, 91
Open: daily 8.30am–6.30pm
Wheelchair access. Admission free.
With its central dome and radiating naves, the imposing architecture of Libéral Bruand's austere

OPPOSITE:
La Dame
Blanche
by Pierre
Antoniucci
(1993).

17th-century chapel provides a challenging but surprisingly effective space for contemporary art, notably installations. Although still functioning as a chapel in one of Paris' largest teaching hospitals, it is used each year by major international artists (Kawamata, Kapoor, Kiefer, Holzer among others) as part of the multi-disciplinary Festival d'Automne; occasional one-off events are also staged here.

Couvent des Cordeliers

Map reference: page 41, E5
15 rue de l'Ecole-de-Médicine, 6th
Tel: 01 40 46 05 47
Metro: Odéon. Bus: 63, 86, 87
Open: Tues–Sun 11am–7pm. Admission charge.
This large hall was once the refectory of a medieval convent, later an important meeting place for revolutionaries. It is now part of the medical school and used for eclectic exhibitions of contemporary art, including light and video installations, African artists and a solo show by French artist, Arman.

Ecole Nationale Supérieure des Beaux-Arts (Ensb-a)

Map reference: page 40, D4
13 quai Malaquais, 6th
Tel: 01 47 03 50 00. www.ensba.fr
Metro: St-Germain-des-Prés. Bus: 24, 27
Open: Tues–Sun 1–7pm; closed Mon.
Admission charge.
The annual pick of recent graduates at France's most prestigious art school is an opportunity to pick out future names of the French art scene. Exhibitions are also put on of works from the ENSB-A's own collection of Old Master drawings and prints, including large holdings of Italian artists and works by Géricault, or group shows of contemporary art.

Espace Electra/Fondation EDF

Map reference: page 40, C5
6 rue Récamier, 7th
Tel: 01 53 63 23 45
Metro: Sèvres-Babylone. Bus: 63, 68, 84, 87, 94.
Open: Tues–Sun noon–7pm; closed Aug.
Admission charge.
Owned by the French state electricity board, this converted electricity sub-station is used for eclectic, mainly contemporary, exhibitions that have covered subjects ranging from contemporary Latin American art, James Turrell and garden designer Gilles Clément to ancient Chinese archaeology.

Espace Paul Ricard

Map reference: page 40, C1
9 rue Royale, 8th
Tel: 01 53 30 88 00. www.espacepaulricard.com
Metro: Concorde, Madeleine. Bus: 42, 72, 73, 84, 94. Open: Mon–Fri 10am–7pm.
Admission charge.
The gallery belonging to French drinks company Pernod-Ricard is particularly committed to promoting young artists through its annual Prix Ricard; an award that is fast gaining international recognition. Other exhibitions have featured young international artists in a wide range of media or aspects of contemporary design.

Photographic collage of perspectives in relief, by Agathe Durand, at Espace Electra.

Fondation Cartier pour l'art contemporain

Map reference: page 43, E5
261 bd Raspail, 14th
Tel: 01 42 18 56 72. www.fondation.cartier.fr
Metro: Raspail. RER: Denfert-Rochereau. Bus: 68.
Open: Tues, Wed, Fri–Sun noon–8pm, Thurs
noon–10pm. Admission charge.

The Fondation Cartier, which moved from the Paris suburbs to Jean Nouvel's high-tech glass and steel building in the early 1990s, has become one of the French capital's leading venues for contemporary art and photography. Nouvel's design plays with ideas of transparency, with a façade conceived as a series of parallel planes; these planes are built around a listed cedar tree (planted by the writer Chateaubriand), which makes it hard to say where the building (two levels of exhibition space and the offices of Cartier jewellers) starts and ends. Outside is a garden designed by artist Lothar Baumgarten.

Monographic shows by artists and photographers have featured Noboyushi Araki, Seydou Keita, William Eggleston, Pierrick Sorin, Panamerenko, Alain Sechas and the cutting-edge clothes of Issey Miyake. Imaginative summer shows tend to mix art from different cultures and periods and have taken such themes as Love, Birds or the Desert. On Thursday evenings (Sept–June), the Soirées Nomades feature concerts, videos and performance art.

Fondation Coffim

Map reference: page 41, H3
46 rue de Sévigné, 3rd
Tel: 01 44 78 60 00. www.fondation-coffim.com
Metro: St Paul. Bus: 29
Open: Mon–Fri 10am–6pm, Sat 2–6pm; closed
Aug. Admission free.

Now established in a former print workshop in the Marais, Coffim shows contemporary figurative painting and also awards an annual prize.

Fondation Icar

Map reference: page 43, G2
159 quai de Valmy, 10th
Tel: 01 53 26 36 61
Metro: Colonel Fabien, Château Landon.
Open: Wed–Sun 1–7pm. Admission charge.

At the back of a cobbled courtyard off the Canal St-Martin, a stunning former industrial space has been converted by a Dutch artist into a striking three-storey wood and glass studio-gallery. It now belongs to the American-funded Icar, which puts on occa-

Hommage au Douanier Rousseau, by Robert Combas (1996), Fondation Coffim.

sional exhibitions along with a programme of music and lectures. Past shows have concentrated on major figures of American conceptual art: John Coplans, Dennis Oppenheim and Vito Acconci.

Fondation Mona Bismarck

Map reference: page 42, C3
34 av de New-York, 16th
Tel: 01 47 23 38 88
Metro: Alma-Marceau. Bus: 72
Open: Tues–Sat 10.30am–6.30pm; closed Aug.
Admission free.

A *hôtel particulier* in western Paris provides a chic setting for high-quality, but never radical, exhibitions, often with works on loan from prestigious foreign collections. Past shows have ranged from French equestrian painters to North American folk art.

Galeries Nationales du Grand Palais

Map reference: page 40, A2
3 av du Général-Eisenhower, 8th
Tel: 01 44 13 17 17. www.rmn.fr
Metro: Champs-Elysées-Clemenceau
Bus: 42, 73, 83, 93
Open: Mon, Thurs–Sun 10am–8pm, Wed
10am–10pm. Admission charge.

Paris' main venue for blockbuster exhibitions was originally built for the Exposition Universelle of 1900, and is a fine example of the eclecticism of the period – not surprisingly, perhaps, since several different architects and sculptors worked on its design. Inside, the sinuous metal stairway shows the influence of the Art Nouveau fashion, but the heavily sculpted stone façade remains firmly within official,

Henry Moore's bronze *Reclining Figure* (1951) in the sculpture-filled Tuileries gardens.

monumental Beaux-Arts orthodoxy. The Grand Palais was subsequently used for Salons, except for an interlude during World War II, when German tanks were stored here. Since 1971 it has been used for prestigious art exhibitions put on by the Réunion des Musées Nationaux, including archaeological and decorative arts collections and major monographic art shows that have featured, among others, Poussin, Picasso, Man Ray, Signac and Moreau.

Currently, exhibitions are held only in two spaces opening onto avenue Général-Eisenhower, since the spectacular glass-roofed grand hall opening onto avenue Winston-Churchill was closed suddenly in 1993, when part of the metal vault collapsed. After being left to abandon for several years, costly restoration work has finally started and is expected to be completed by late 2005. The avenue Franklin D. Roosevelt wing houses the Palais de la Découverte science museum *(see page 194).*

Halle St-Pierre – Musée d'Art Naïf Max Fourny

Map reference: page 43, F2
2 rue Ronsard, 18th
Tel: 01 42 58 72 89. www.hallesaintpierre.org
Metro: Anvers, Barbès Rochechouart
Open: daily 10am–6pm; closed Aug.
Café. Bookshop. Children's workshops.
Admission charge.
This former covered market provides a showcase for Art Brut and naive art – the idiosyncratic works produced by self-taught artists, many of them from humble backgrounds or in psychiatric hospitals. Only 12 paintings from the permanent collection are currently on view, although there are plans for expansion.

Jeu de Paume

Map reference: page 40, C2
1 place de la Concorde, 1st
Tel: 01 47 03 12 50. www.rmn.fr
Metro: Concorde. Bus: 42, 72, 73, 84, 94.
Open: Tues noon–9.30pm, Wed–Fri noon–7pm, Sat, Sun 10am–7pm.
Café. Bookshop. Cinema. Wheelchair access.
Admission charge.
When the Impressionist museum moved from here to the Musée d'Orsay *(see pages 82–9),* the former royal "real tennis court of the Tuileries palace was redesigned by architect Antoine Stinco to house contemporary art. The two-storey space is particularly suited to installation and sculpture. Shows have included prominent figures of French art from the 1960s to 1980s, such as Arman and César, as well as video artist/film maker Chantal Ackermann, Spanish painter Miguel Barcelo, American architect Richard Meier and Spanish sculptor Chillida. Look also in the Tuileries gardens, where, thanks to an initiative by sculptor Alain Kirili, works by sculptors including Dubuffet, Moore and Ernst are displayed.

Musée-atelier Adzak

Map reference: page 42, D5
3 rue Jonquoy, 14th
Tel: 01 45 43 06 98
Metro: Plaisance. Bus: 62
Opening times vary. Admission free.
The house and studio built by the late British conceptual artist Roy Adzak in the 1960s is now used for small exhibitions by mainly foreign artists. It is known for its short solo exhibitions and an annual group print show.

Musée du Luxembourg

Map reference: page 40, D5
19 rue de Vaugirard, 6th
Tel: 01 42 34 25 95
Metro: St-Sulpice. RER: Luxembourg. Bus: 84, 89.
Open: daily 11am–5pm. Admission charge.
The Musée du Luxembourg, next to the Palais du Luxembourg, was the first public gallery in France when, from 1750–80, paintings from the royal collection were put on view to the public two days a week. In the 19th century, the gallery was used to display works by living artists acquired by the state, until it was superseded by the creation of the Musée National d'Art Moderne *(see pages 55–62)* in 1945. Now run by the Senate and national museums, it is used for temporary art exhibitions, most of which cover historical topics.

Musée du Montparnasse

Map reference: page 40, B6
21 av du Maine, 15th
Tel: 01 42 22 91 96
Metro: Montparnasse-Bienvenüe, Falguière
Bus: 28, 89, 92
Open: Wed–Sun 1–7pm. Admission charge.
In one of the small alleys of artists' studios that previously littered Montparnasse, this small museum was once the studio and innovative art school run by Russian avant-garde artist Marie Vassilieff. Exhibitions focus on different aspects of Montparnasse's artistic heritage, through photos and archive material as well as paintings, and also sometimes attempt to establish a continuity with the artists who still work in the area today.

Passage de Retz

Map reference: page 41, H3
9 rue Charlot, 3rd
Tel: 01 48 04 37 99
Metro: Filles du Calvaire, St-Sébastien-Froissart
Open: Tues–Sun 10am–7pm
Café. Bookshop. Partial wheelchair access.
Admission charge.
Occupying a wing of a Marais mansion, renovated after a chequered history as a toy factory, the Passage de Retz puts on shows of contemporary art and design, including such topics as narcissism and self-portraiture and designer plastic. The sleek, colourful little café was designed by Christian Biecher.

Pavillon des Arts

Map reference: page 41, F3
101 rue Rambuteau, 1st
Tel: 01 42 33 82 50
Metro: Les Halles. RER: Châtelet-Les Halles
Open: Tues–Sun 11.30am–6.30pm
Wheelchair access. Admission charge.
Administered by the City of Paris, this gallery on the side of Les Halles shopping centre hosts varied exhibitions, principally of painting and photography.

Site de Création Contemporaine

Map reference: page 42, C3
Palais de Tokyo, 2 rue de la Manutention, 16th
Tel: 01 47 23 54 01. www.palaisdetokyo.com
Metro: Alma-Marceau, Iéna. Bus: 32, 42, 63, 72, 80, 82, 92. Open: Tues–Sun noon–midnight; closed Mon. Bar and restaurant. Bookshop. Shop. Admission charge.

Camelot (2001) by Philippe Mayaux, part of the Lost Supermarket exhibition at Espace Paul Ricard.

Housed in the opposite wing of the imposing 1930s' Palais de Tokyo to the Musée d'Art Moderne de la Ville de Paris *(see pages 97–9)*, this state-funded venture, which opened in 2002, is intended to serve as a sort of laboratory for current art production. An adventurous, multi-disciplinary programme focuses on young artists through exhibitions, performances and workshops. The minimalist interior provides the setting for several shows simultaneously; these last anything from a few days to six months.

Artist-run spaces

Galerie Eof

Map reference: page 41, F1
15 rue St-Fiacre, 2nd
Tel: 01 53 40 72 22
Metro: Bonne-Nouvelle
Opening times vary.
This artist-run space mounts a range of exhibitions, from solo shows by individual painters to multimedia collaborations with other organisations.

Glassbox

Map reference: page 43, G3
113bis rue Oberkampf, 11th
Tel: 01 43 38 02 82
Metro: Parmentier, Oberkampf
Open: Fri, Sat 2–7pm.
A small but very active underground space founded by a group of artists in 1997. The group often works in collaboration with other artists' collectives from around Europe.

Livraisons

Map reference: page 41, H1
55 rue Bichat, 10th
Tel: 01 60 97 18 71
Metro: République
Open: Thurs–Sun 2–7pm. Wheelchair access.
The five artists and an architect who opened this space in 2000 hold varied exhibitions and events.

Le Plateau

Map reference: page 43, H2
Corner of rue du Plateau and rue Carducci, 19th
Tel: 01 42 65 43 93
Metro: Buttes Chaumont, Botzaris. Bus: 26, 60.
This contemporary art space opened in spring 2002 as a result both of a campaign by various associations in the 19th *arrondissement* to open an arts centre integrated in the local community, and of a search for an exhibition space within Paris for the FRAC (Fonds Régional d'Art Contemporain) d'Ile de France. Exhibitions of works from the FRAC collection alternate with artist-curated shows and projects with local artists' groups; shows are complemented by cinema screenings and occasional performing arts.

Public

Map reference: page 41, G3
4 impasse Beaubourg, 3rd
Metro: Rambuteau, Hôtel de Ville
Small gallery specialising in short video seasons.

"Ming" 3, Moments de l'Installation (1999) by James Turrell, courtesy Galerie Almine Rech.

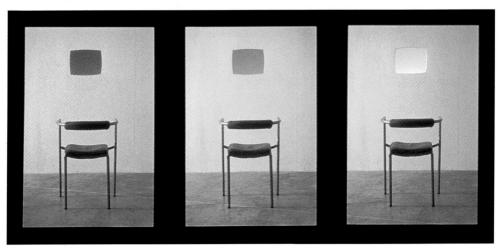

Foreign Cultural Centres

Many of Paris' foreign cultural centres put on regular exhibitions. Ring for up-to-date information or look in *Pariscope*, a weekly listings magazine that also has a section in English.

Centre Culturel Calouste Gulbenkian

Map reference: page 42, C3
51 av d'Iéna, 16th. Tel: 01 53 23 93 93
Metro: Iéna
Portuguese cultural centre.

Centre Culturel Suédois

Map reference: page 41, H3
11 rue Payenne, 3rd. Tel: 01 44 78 80 20
Metro: St Paul, Chemin Vert. Bus: 29, 69, 76, 96.
Another pretty mansion in the Marais, with a commitment to introducing the work of Swedish artists.

Centre Culturel Suisse

Map reference: page 41, H3
32–8 rue des Francs-Bourgeois, 3rd
Tel: 01 42 71 38 38
Metro: Hôtel de Ville, St Paul
Adventurous shows featuring young Swiss artists, particularly good on video art and installation.

Centre Wallonie-Bruxelles

Map reference: page 41, F3
127 rue St-Martin, 4th. Tel: 01 53 01 96 96
Metro: Hôtel de Ville. RER: Châtelet-Les Halles.
The centre of French-speaking Belgium, putting on both art shows and screenings of short films.

Goethe Institut

Map reference: page 42, C3
17 av d'Iéna, 16th. Tel: 01 44 43 92 30
Metro: Iéna
German cultural centre.

Institut Finlandais

Map reference: page 41, F5
60 rue des Ecoles, 5th. Tel: 01 40 51 89 09.
Metro: Cluny-La Sorbonne
Active multi-disciplinary centre that regularly features design and craft as well as fine art.

Institut Néerlandais

Map reference: page 40, C3
121 rue de Lille, 7th. Tel: 01 53 59 12 40
Metro: Solférino

Bicycle Wheel (1963) by Marcel Duchamp, father figure to many young artists.

Renowned for its exhibitions on topics ranging from old masters to contemporary art, design and fashion.

Maison de l'Amérique Latine

Map reference: page 40, C3
217 bd St-Germain, 7th. Tel: 01 49 54 75 00.
Metro: Solférino
Shows in this elegant 18th-century *hôtel particulier* cover the whole of Latin America and works from Pre-Columbian sculpture to recent photography.

Maison de la Culture du Japon

Map reference: page 42, C3
101bis, quai Branly
Tel: 01 44 37 95 00. www.mcjp.asso.fr
Metro: Bir-Hakeim, Champ de Mars-Tour Eiffel.
A wide range of themed exhibitions from ancient ceramics to contemporary Japanese artists are put on in a striking building by British architects, Armstrong Associates.

Commercial Galleries

Paris has several hundred galleries, some of which are eagerly followed by local art circles, others that simply let out space to whoever wants to put on a show. There are particular concentrations in the Marais (3rd/4th), the Bastille (11th), around the Champs-Elysées (8th), in St-Germain (5th) and in the 13th *arrondissement*. The following is a pick of 25 galleries that are worth watching out for, ranging from heavyweights featuring international names to small galleries nurturing young artists. Note that most galleries close from mid-July to mid-September (*see also Photography, page 143, for galleries specialising in photo art.*)

Air de Paris

32 rue Louise-Weiss, 13th; tel: 01 44 23 02 77; www.airdeparis.com; Tues–Fri 2–7pm, Sat 11am–7pm.
New conceptual art from a stable of young international artists is presented in often amusing, if sometimes rather incomprehensible, exhibitions.

Chez Valentin

9 rue St-Gilles, 3rd; tel: 01 48 87 42 55; Tues–Sat 2.30–7pm. Metro: Chemin Vert.
This Marais gallery focuses primarily on young French artists, notably the videos and installations of Véronique Boudier.

Galerie Louis Carré et Cie

10 av de Messine, 8th; tel: 01 45 62 57 07; Mon–Sat 10am–12.30pm, 1.30–6.30pm. Metro: Miromesnil.

This long-established gallery features nouvelle figuration painter, Hervé di Rosa, and sculptor Hervé Télémaque, alongside a stock of works by modern masters such as Dufy, Delaunay and Léger.

Galerie Cent 8

108 rue Vieille-du-Temple; 3rd/13 rue de Saintonge, 3rd; tel: 01 4 74 53 57; Tues–Fri 10.30am–1pm, 2.30–7pm, Sat 10.30am–7pm. Metro: Filles du Calvaire.
This gallery, founded at the end of the 1990s, puts on interesting shows in two exhibition spaces. As well as international names such as Christine Borland and Rémy Zaugg, look out for the drawing/text/film work of Valérie Mrejen.

Galerie Chantal Crousel

40 rue Quincampoix, 4th; tel: 01 42 77 38 87; www.crousel.com; Tues–Sat 11am–7pm. Metro: Rambuteau, RER: Châtelet-Les Halles.
The Crousel gallery was founded in the Beaubourg area over 20 years ago. It mixes big names, such as Tony Cragg and Mona Hatoum, with some of the hottest names of the new generation working with video and installation. This includes the socially/politically committed work of Paris residents Thomas Hirschhorn and Anri Sala.

Liliane et Michel Durand-Dessert

28 rue de Lappe, 11th; tel: 01 48 06 92 23; Tues–Sat 11am–7pm. Metro: Bastille.
An impressive industrial space showcasing Italian Arte Povera, French conceptual art and international photographers.

Galerie Jennifer Flay

20 rue Louise-Weiss, 13th; tel: 01 44 06 73 60; Tues–Sat 2–7pm. Metro: Chevaleret.
This New Zealand-run gallery in the Louise cluster is one of the best places for keeping track of trends in France, the UK and the US, taking in photography, video, installation and a batch of interesting painters.

Galerie de France

54 rue de la Verrerie, 4th; tel: 01 42 74 38 00; Tues–Sat 11am–7pm. Metro: Hôtel de Ville.
A long-established gallery, which cleverly mixes works by early 20th-century and Surrealist masters with an eclectic set of contemporary artists.

Marian Goodman Gallery

79 rue du Temple, 3rd; tel: 01 48 04 70 52; Tues–Sat 11am–7pm. Metro: Rambuteau.
The elegant Paris offshoot of the long-established New York gallery features international artists like Thomas Struth, Lothar Baumgarten, William Kentridge and Steve McQueen.

Galerie Karsten Greve

5 rue Debelleyme, 3rd; tel: 01 42 77 19 37; www.artnet.com/kgreve; Tues–Sat 11am–7pm. Metro: Filles du Calvaire, St Paul.
The Marais outlet for Cologne gallerist Karsten Greve concentrates on big international names like Louise Bourgeois, Cy Twombly and John Chamberlain.

Galerie Alain Gutharc

47 rue de Lappe, 11th; tel: 01 47 00 32 10; Tues–Fri 2–7pm, Sat 11am–1pm, 2–7pm. Metro: Bastille.
A Bastille-based gallery with an eye for picking out young French

talents, many of them female, such as Delphine Kreuter and Antoinette Ohanassian.

Galerie Ghislaine Hussenot

5bis rue des Haudriettes, 3rd; tel: 01 48 87 60 81; Tues–Sat 11am–1pm, 2–7pm. Metro: Rambuteau.

A well-respected gallery specialising in conceptual and neo-conceptual artists. Look out for star names On Kawara, Vanessa Beecroft and Mike Kelley.

Galerie Yvon Lambert

108 rue Vieille-du-Temple, 3rd; tel: 01 42 71 09 33; Tues–Sat 10am–1pm, 2.30–7pm. Metro: Filles du Calvaire.

A powerhouse among French galleries, Lambert has cleverly kept up with trends, latching on to young installation and video artists, such as Douglas Gordon and Keo Jeong-A, alongside US giants such as Jenny Holzer and Andrès Serrano.

Galerie Lelong

13 rue de Téhéran, 8th; tel: 01 45 63 13 19; Tues–Fri 10.30am–6pm, Sat 2–6.30pm. Metro: Miromesnil.

An upmarket gallery guaranteeing a no-risk agenda of big-name artists, such as Hockney, Bacon and Kounellis.

Galerie Jérôme de Noirmont

38 av Matignon, 8th; tel: 01 42 89 89 00; www.denoirmont.com; Mon–Sat 10am–1pm, 2.30–7pm. Metro: Miromesnil.

This relatively new gallery near the Elysée Palace has quickly established a reputation with well-presented shows of flamboyant artists, including Penck, Pierre et Gilles, Shirin Neshat and Jeff Koons.

Galerie Emmanuel Perrotin

5 and 30 rue Louise-Weiss, 13th; tel: 01 42 16 79 79; www.galerieperrotin.com; Tues–Sat 11am–7pm. Metro: Chevaleret.

Perrotin features the young Japanese avant-garde, along with a number of young European artists working with photography and installation, and a few established French names.

Gilles Peyroulet et Cie

75 & 80 rue Quincampoix, 3rd; tel: 01 42 78 85 11; Tues–Sat 2–7pm. Metro: Rambuteau, RER: Châtelet-Les Halles.

Works by photographic-based artists alternate with experimental contemporary designers and modern design classics.

Galerie Almine Rech

24 rue Louise-Weiss, 13th; tel: 01 45 83 71 90; www.galeriealminerech.com; Tues–Sat 11am–7pm. Metro: Chevaleret.

Almine Rech often features photography/video or works on paper by artists such as Ugo Rondinone and young French discovery Rebecca Bournigault.

Galerie Denise René

196 bd St-Germain, 7th; tel: 01 42 22 77 57; www.deniserene.com; Tues–Fri 10am–1pm, 2–7pm, Sat 11am–1pm, 2–7pm. Metro: St-Germain-des-Prés, Rue du Bac.

René is a veteran of the St-Germain scene and remains the reference for kinetic and Op art.

Galerie Thaddaeus Ropac

7 rue Debelleyme, 3rd; tel: 01 42 72 99 00; www.ropac.net; Tues–Sat 10am–7pm. Metro: Sébastien-Froissart, St Paul.

American Pop, neo-Pop and neo-Geo feature alongside photo artists and conceptual artists like Kabakov and Gilbert & George.

Galerie Daniel Templon

30 rue Beaubourg, 3rd; tel: 01 42 72 14 10; Mon–Sat 10am–7pm. Metro: Rambuteau.

One of Paris' best-known galleries, Templon features mainly French and US painters, including French painters Jean-Michel Alberola, Vincent Corpet and eternally young Raymond Hains.

Galerie Georges-Philippe et Nathalie Vallois

36 rue de Seine, 6th; tel: 01 46 34 61 07; Tues–Sat 10.30am–1pm, 2–7pm. Metro: Mabillon, Odéon.

One of the most adventurous galleries in the increasingly staid St-Germain district, which supports young artists Alain Bublex and Gilles Barbier.

Galerie Anne de Villepoix

48 rue de Montmorency, 3rd; tel: 01 42 78 32 24; Tues–Sat 11am–7pm. Metro: Rambuteau, RER: Châtelet-Les Halles.

Recently moved to a spacious building near the Centre Pompidou, this gallery hosts anything from first shows by young hopefuls to the mixed-media installations of Fabrice Hybert and veterans like Suzanne Laffont and John Coplans.

Galerie Anton Weller

57 rue de Bretagne, 3rd; tel: 01 42 72 05 62; Tues–Sat 2–7pm. Metro: Temple, Arts et Métiers.

A place to discover young artists dealing with issues including sexuality, the art market and art diffusion.

Photography

The photographer Edward Steichen once said, "The mission of photography is to explain man to man and each man to himself." A tall order, but one that these galleries and institutions are on a constant quest to fulfil

Sacred Homes,
by Zwelethu
Mthethwa
(1999).

Centre National de la Photographie

Thematic and monographic shows of mostly contemporary art photography

Map reference: page 42, D2
Hôtel Salomon de Rothschild, 11 rue Berryer, 8th.
Tel: 01 53 76 12 32. www.cnp-photographie.com
Metro: Charles de Gaulle-Etoile, George V.
Bus: 22, 43, 52, 83
Open: Mon, Wed–Sun noon–7pm; closed Tues.
Café, shop. Admission charge.

Paris has numerous photography institutions and archive collections but no single place where you can see a comprehensive permanent display of photography. Instead, the main venues all concentrate on temporary exhibitions. There are also changing photographic selections at Musée d'Orsay *(see pages 82–9)* and the Centre Pompidou *(see pages 55–62)*. Other temporary exhibition spaces that regularly feature photographers include the Fondation Cartier *(see page 135)* and the Bibliothèque Nationale de France *(see page 133)*.

Today, photography encompasses everything from the work of purists who still believe that photography means black-and-white prints on paper, to the new directions currently being explored in electronic art and new technology. Subjects covered by exhibitions might range from the work of historic pioneers or social documentary by photographers who work only in the one medium, to contemporary artists for whom photography is simply one medium among others.

Every two years, Paris goes photo crazy for the Mois de la Photo (Photography Month, next in November 2002), run by the Maison Européenne de la Photographie. The event sees historic and contemporary photography exhibitions in museums, commercial galleries and cultural centres around the city, usually selected according to a number of set themes. The wide appeal of photography is well illustrated by the success of the annual Paris-Photo Salon in the Carrousel du Louvre *(see pages 63–77)*. First held in 1997, the show offers a mix of historic, contemporary, art and documentary photography, from about 100 international galleries. Look out, also, for the annual World Press Photo Prize at the same venue.

Housed in part of a 19th-century *hôtel particulier* that once belonged to the Rothschild family, the National Photography Centre (CNP) puts on a wide variety of thematic and monographic shows. Under the direction of Regis Durand, the CNP has shifted its approach from covering both historic and contemporary photographers to an emphasis on current art photography, which reflects the breakdown of barriers between art and photography. This takes in installation and video as well as pure photography, although occasional shows deal with documentary and fashion topics.

The international ambit is broad but has numbered many of today's hippest international talents – from British artist Sam Taylor-Wood and France's Jean-Marc Bustamente to Russia's Boris Mikhailov, Germany's Thomas Ruff, Australia's Tracey Moffat and Japan's Mariko Mori. The "Atelier" section in the cellars – designed, like the café, by experimental Marseille architeçt Rudi Ricciotti – is used for shorter shows by young artists, including work in video and new media.

*FOOD AND DRINK: **Les Lieux:** the centre's own café, notable for its slick design by Rudi Ricciotti, does Mediterranean-style food from noon–6pm (Tues until 3.30pm). On warm days, you can enjoy outdoor dining on the terrace, which looks onto the hôtel gardens.*

LEFT: Danielle Darrieux, captured in 1938 by movie photographer Raymond Voinquel.

LEFT: *Le Jardin Niwa*, an installation by Keiichi Tahara at the Maison Européenne de la Photographie (2001/2).

RIGHT: *Chez Mondrian* (1926) and *View from the Eiffel Tower* (1929), both photographed by Hungary's André Kertesz.

Maison Européenne de la Photographie

Historic and contemporary art photography and photo-documentary exhibitions

Map reference: page 41, C2
5–7 rue de Fourcy, 4th
Tel: 01 44 78 75 00. www.mep-fr.org
Metro: St Paul, Pont-Marie. Bus: 67, 69, 76, 96.
Open: Wed–Sun 11am–8pm; closed Mon, Tues.
Café. Bookshop. Auditorium, Library and video library. Wheelchair access. Admission charge.

Opened in 1996 in the restored Hôtel Hénault de Cantorbe and a daringly minimalist modern extension, this municipally funded institution has galleries spread over several floors and is usually used for three or four shows at a time. The centre has shown major historic figures such as Boubat, Cartier-Bresson, Weegee and William Klein; documentary photographers including Raymond Depardon and Sebastião Salgado; and contemporary art-fashion crossover names such as Bettina Rheims and Ines Van Laemsварde.

Although it has featured art-world figures, notably kitsch duo Pierre et Gilles, this gallery generally takes a more strictly photographic stance than the CNP *(see previous entry)*. The cellars are used for more experimental and multimedia works. Interesting related film series are screened in the auditorium, and the centre organises the biennial Mois de la Photo *(see previous page)*.

FOOD AND DRINK: Rouge George (8 rue St-Paul, 4th; tel: 01 48 04 75 89): this delightful wine bar is all exposed stone and beams. It serves hot dishes, terrines and plenty of good wines.

Mission du Patrimoine Photographique

Monographic and themed shows of historic photography, mounted in a Marais mansion

Map reference: page 41, H4
Hôtel de Sully, 62 rue St-Antoine, 4th
Tel: 01 42 74 47 75. www.patrimoine-photo.org
Metro: Bastille, St Paul. Bus: 69, 76
Open: Tues–Sun 10am–6.30pm; closed Mon.
Archives (at 19 rue Réaumur, by appointment).
Admission charge.

Historic photography shows, often organised in association with other institutions and collections such as the Royal Photographic Society and the Smithsonian Institute, are put on in a small gallery inside one of the most beautiful mansions in the Marais. Past exhibitions have ranged from shows dedicated to notable photographers, from socialites Cecil Beaton and Jacques-Henri Lartigue to press veteran W. Eugene Smith, to themes including the Egyptian pyramids, crime photography and the Spanish Civil War. The Patrimoine Photographique also arranges touring exhibitions and administers photographic estates left to the state, including those of André Kertesz, Roger Parry and Sam Lévin, and the archives of Studio Harcourt.

The rest of the Hôtel de Sully is closed to the public, but the courtyard is a lovely place to sit and contemplate, and it gives access at the back to the Place des Vosges.

FOOD AND DRINK: L'Osteria (10 rue de Sévigné, 4th; tel: 01 42 71 37 08; expensive): so discreet that it's easy to miss it from the street, but the pasta and risottos are some of the best – if pricey – Italian food in Paris. See also left.

Commercial galleries

Many contemporary galleries also exhibit photographic works *(see pages 140–1)*, as does FNAC, the main French music and books chain.

A l'Image du Grenier sur l'Eau

45 rue des Francs-Bourgeois, 4th
tel: 01 42 71 02 31; www.photos-site.com
Classic 19th- and early 20th-century photography.

Galerie 213

213 bd Raspail, 14th; tel: 01 43 22 83 23;
www.galerie213.com
Marion de Beaupré exhibits contemporary photographers often with fashion links.

La Chambre Claire

14 rue St-Sulpice, 6th; tel: 01 46 34 04 31;
www.chambreclaire.com
Photography bookshop that also puts on shows.

Galerie Agathe Gaillard

3 rue Pont-Louis-Philippe, 4th; tel: 01 42 77 38 24
Specialising in classic photographers.

Galerie Baudoin-Lebon

38 rue Ste-Croix-de-la-Bretonnerie, 4th
tel: 01 42 72 09 10. www.baudoin-lebon.com
Mainly contemporary art photography.

Galerie Camera Obscura

12 rue Ernest-Cresson, 14th
tel: 01 45 45 67 08
Classic documentary photography.

Galerie F+A Paviot

57 rue Ste-Anne, 2nd; tel: 01 42 60 10 01
Historic to contemporary photography; strong on the Surrealists.

Galerie Kamel Mennour

60 rue Mazarine, 6th; tel: 01 56 24 03 63;
www.galeriemennour.com
St-Germain's Mennour exhibits big-name contemporaries, including Peter Beard, Larry Clark and Helmut Newton.

Galerie Michèle Chomette

24 rue Beaubourg, 3rd; tel: 01 42 78 05 62
Contemporary and historic photographers.

Galerie Patricia Dorfmann

61 rue de la Verrerie, 4th; tel: 01 42 77 55 41
Contemporary artists who work with photography.

Hypnos

52 rue de l'Université, 7th; tel: 01 45 44 99
71; www.hypnos-photo.com
Pioneers from the 19th and early 20th centuries.

Magnum Print Room

19 rue Hégésippe-Moreau, 18th;
tel: 01 53 42 50 00
Gallery and database for photos from the celebrated agency.

Vu, la Galerie

2 rue Jules-Cousin, 4th; tel: 01 53 01 85 85
International photographers who are represented by Agence Vu.

Architecture

When it comes to architecture, Paris is a city where innovation and conservation are pursued with equal vigour. These institutions celebrate its landmarks and the architects who created them

Cité de l'Architecture et du Patrimoine

Architecture from the Romanesque period to the present day

Map reference: page 42, C3
Palais de Chaillot, pl du Trocadéro, 16th
Tel: 01 44 05 39 10.
Metro: Trocadéro. Bus: 22, 30, 63
Library. Lectures, conferences. Open 2003/4.

Elegant, Neo-classical symmetry at the Palais de Chaillot.

The City of Architecture and Heritage opens in 2003–4 in the renovated east wing of the Palais de Chaillot: a result of the amalgamation and expansion of the former Musée des Monuments Français and the current Institut Français d'Architecture *(see page 148)*. The new institution promises to be not just a museum but a centre of research and debate, with an avowed mission to serve both professional architects and planners and the public.

The museum divides into two sections, one covering the classical and medieval periods and the other the modern and contemporary ones. The Galerie Médiéval et Classique, on the ground floor, gathers the plaster casts, vintage photographs and drawings of the former Musée des Monuments Français in a distinctly 19th-century tour around some of France's greatest architectural treasures.

This part of the museum was founded as the Musée de Sculpture Comparée (Museum of Comparative Sculpture) in 1879, under the impetus of Gothic Revivalist Viollet-le-Duc (notable for his work on Notre-Dame). It houses life-size casts of monuments that showcase the 19th-century mastery of plaster casting; such casts were originally intended to demonstrate the supremacy of the Gothic style and to offer models to architects and artists. Among the highlights in this section are Romanesque doorways from the cathedrals in Vézélay and Saintes, sculpted Gothic portals from Chartres and Amiens, and Renaissance fountains.

OTHER NOTABLE COLLECTIONS

There are substantial collections of architectural drawings and maquettes in the Musée d'Orsay *(see page 83)* and in the Pompidou Centre *(see page 61)*, which are displayed within the museums on a rotating basis. Regular monographic shows on architects such as Renzo Piano and Jean Nouvel are held at the Centre Pompidou.

The Galerie Moderne et Contemporaine, on the second floor, brings the collection up to the present with drawings, photographs and architectural models. In contrast to the chronological presentation on the ground floor, the exhibits on this level are arranged according to six main themes, including "the architecture of the town", tracing architecture's relation to the urban landscape, "building architecture", on the technical aspects of construction, and "metaphors and figures", taking in key movements and figures.

A separate gallery on the first floor deals with recent projects, while temporary exhibition galleries cover architectural heritage and current issues.

FOOD AND DRINK: Le Totem, situated inside the Palais de Chaillot. For details, see Musée de l'Homme, page 194.

Cité Internationale

A collegiate-style complex showcasing notable international architectural styles

Map reference: page 43, E6
Espace Architecture, 19 bd Jourdan, 14th
Tel: 01 44 16 64 00. www.ciup.fr
RER: Cité Universitaire. Bus: 21, 67, 88, PC1.
Open: Wed, Sat, Sun 1–6pm

Photographs, models and archive films introduce the architecture and ideas behind the Cité Internationale, an inter-war initiative modelled on the Oxbridge collegiate university system to provide residential accommodation for foreign students in a spacious landscaped setting. The buildings were

LEFT: Iconic industrial design and exceptional views at the Centre Pompidou.

RIGHT: Le Corbusier, the dapper father of Modernist design.

FAR RIGHT: An example of his work: the Villa Savoye, in Poissy.

designed to reflect their parent nation and range from the international modernism of Le Corbusier's "Swiss Pavilion" *(visits possible; tel: 01 44 16 10 16 for details)* and Dudok's De Stijl-style "Collège Néerlandais" to a neo-ethnic Cambodian house. Other examples include a Swedish house and Claude Parent's 1960s' brutalist Fondation Avicenne.

FOOD AND DRINK: Treat yourself to a classic meal in the 18th-century **Pavillon Montsouris** *(20, rue Gazan, 14th; Tel: 01 45 88 38 52; expensive), overlooking the Parc Montsouris. In fine weather the park's a lovely picnic spot.*

Fondation Le Corbusier

A fine example of the work of Modern Movement architect, Le Corbusier

Map reference: page 42, B4
Villa La Roche, 10 square du Dr-Blanche, 16th
Tel: 01 42 88 41 53
www.fondationlecorbusier.asso.fr Metro: Jasmin
Open: Mon–Thurs 10am–12.30pm, 1.30–6pm,
Fri 10am–12.30pm, 1.30am–5pm; closed Aug.
Admission charge.

This house, designed by Le Corbusier (born Charles-Edouard Jeanneret-Gris, 1887–1965) in 1923–25 for Swiss banker and art collector Raoul La Roche, offers a fascinating opportunity to visit a building by this visionary architect who has been so widely copied and misinterpreted, often with disastrous results. Here, Le Corbusier put many of his ideas into practice, including pilotis (stilts), roof

terraces and strip windows, creating a masterful play of volume and spaces. Although the exterior is the white of cliché, the interior shows the architect's use of colour, full of muted greens, sludge browns, pinks and blues. The house showcases the Modernist master's furniture designs and his Purist paintings and drawings. The adjoining Villa Jeanneret, designed for Le Corbusier's brother, houses the Foundation's library, which includes most of his archives.

One of the finest examples of the architect's purist design is the **Villa Savoye** built in 1929 in a suburb of Paris *(82 rue Villiers, Poissy; RER Poissy, then a 15-min walk; tel: 01 41 12 02 90)*. This building, essentially a block on pilotis with curvaceous walls for counterbalance, is both beautiful and functional.

Institut Français d'Architecture

The country's national architectural insti- tute, home to changing exhibitions on 20th- and 21st-century architects and their work

Map reference: page 40, E5
6 rue de Tournon, 6th
Tel: 01 46 33 90 36
Metro: Odéon. RER: Luxembourg. Bus: 84, 86, 87, 89. Open: Tues–Sun 12.30–7pm; closed Mon. Partial wheelchair access. Admission free.

The Institut Français d'Architecture (IFA) is housed in part of the Hôtel de Brancas, a *hôtel particulier* (private townhouse) dating from 1540 but transformed in the 17th century, with striking allegorical female figures of Justice and Prudence over the street entrance. The exhibitions held here examine 20th- and 21st-century architects or aspects of the built environment, with an emphasis on modernist pioneers and current projects, along with an active programme of debates and lectures. The IFA will eventually close down when the Cité de l'Architecture *(see page 147)* opens in 2003–4.

FOOD AND DRINK: Les Editeurs (4 carrefour de l'Odéon, 6th; tel: 01 43 26 67 76; inexpensive): comfortable café recently revamped with plush armchairs and bookshelves, in reference to the St-Germain publishing tradition. Stop for tea, an apéritif or a brasserie-style meal.

Pavillon de l'Arsenal

A showcase for Parisian architecture and urban design

Map reference: page 41, H5
21 bd Morland, 4th
Tel: 01 42 76 33 97. www.pavillon-arsenal.com
Metro: Sully-Morland. Bus: 86, 87
Open: Tues–Sat 10.30am–6.30pm,
Sun 11am–7pm; closed Mon
Bookshop. Guided tours. Lectures. Library
(by appt.). Wheelchair access. Admission free.

Contained in a striking iron-framed building constructed in the 1870s by a wealthy wood merchant to display his collection of paintings, the city-run Pavillon focuses on Parisian architecture. The permanent exhibition, "Paris, la ville et ses projets", traces the historic development of the city as it spread in roughly concentric rings outward, from a small settlement in medieval times to Haussmann's reorganised city, and its more recent expansion west to La Défense. Urbanism and architecture are examined through a combination of vintage models and excellent colour photographs of recent projects, along with a 50-sq. m (540-sq. ft) model of the city.

Exhibitions include monographic shows, explorations of urbanism and architecture in Paris and other metropolises, and shows focusing on themes such as theatres, hidden courtyards and the use of wood. There are also small displays showing the work of young architects and competition designs.

FOOD AND DRINK: Le Vin des Pyrénées (25 rue Beautrellis, 4th; tel: 01 42 72 64 94; inexpensive): funky old wine merchant's-turned-bistro adorned with flea-market treasures. The food mixes classics and inventions.

NOTABLE MUSEUM ARCHITECTURE

Musée du Louvre: Royal palace and art collection, with sculpted Renaissance and Baroque façades, monumental staircases, medieval fragments and the 20th-century intervention of I.M. Pei's glass pyramid. *See page 63.*

Musée du Moyen-Age: Housed in Roman baths and the Gothic mansion of the abbots of Cluny. *See page 78.*

Musée Picasso: Elegant, well-restored 17th-century mansion built for one of Louis XIV's tax collectors. *See page 90.*

Musée de l'Histoire de France – Archives Nationaux: Grandiose early 18th-century Marais mansion with some of the finest Rococo interiors in Paris. *See page 175.*

Musée de l'Armée: Grand classical architecture designed on a geometrical plan by Libéral-Bruand in the 1670s as a military hospital for the Sun King. *See page 167.*

Musée Jacquemart-André: Opulent, eclectic style of a 19th-century *haute-bourgeois* mansion. *See page 101.*

Musée d'Orsay: Pompous Belle Époque railway architecture, given an inspired conversion in the 1980s. *See page 82.*

Musée des Arts d'Afrique et d'Océanie: Modernist classical revival of 1931 for the colonial exhibition, with Art Deco rooms by Jacques-Emile Ruhlmann. *See page 121.*

Centre Pompidou: High-tech icon by Renzo Piano and Richard Rogers with exposed services and flexible floors. *See page 55.*

Institut du Monde Arabe: Jean Nouvel's design marries high-tech glass and steel with Arabic references. *See page 129.*

Modern Western architecture meets traditional Moorish design at Jean Nouvel's Institut du Monde Arabe.

Artists and Writers

Paris has long been a magnet to artists and writers. The museums in this chapter, mostly housed in their former homes and studios, celebrate their life and work

Maison de Balzac

Reveals the life and times of literary giant, Honoré de Balzac, author of *La Comédie Humaine*, a masterpiece of French literature

Map reference: page 42, C4
47 rue Raynouard, 16th
Tel: 01 42 24 56 38. www.mairie-paris.fr/musees
Metro: La Muette or Passy. Bus: 32, 52, 72
Open: Tues–Sat 10am–5.40pm; closed public hols.
Bookshop. Research facilities/library.
Admission free.

Honoré de Balzac (1799–1850), French school, 19th century.

Honoré de Balzac (1799–1850), the self-styled "quill and ink galley slave", lived here in secret for seven years, from 1840 to 1847, working day and night on correcting and completing *La Comédie Humaine*. This vast body of work, made up of 91 novels and stories peopled with thousands of interconnected characters across the social spectrum, constitutes one of the great masterpieces of French literature.

Pursued by creditors, Balzac escaped to the quiet riverside village of Passy, on the outskirts of Paris, where he rented the house under the assumed name of Monsieur Breugnol (the name of one of the characters in his novels). Set in a leafy garden, the little villa was nicely secluded and had the added advantage of an escape route via rue Berton, a cobbled lane accessible through the back door.

Balzac's modest study, lit by the glow of stained-glass windows, is now a shrine to the prolific novelist. A double-chinned bust watches over his chair and table, of which he wrote: "I possessed it for ten years, it saw all of my misery, wiped away all of my tears, knew all of my projects, heard all of my thoughts." Two galley sheets smothered in corrections written in Balzac's vigorous hand, along with his monogrammed coffeepot, are a reminder of his nightly marathons. Balzac's superhuman capacity for work was fuelled by more than imagination. He drank about forty cups of coffee a day to get him through the long nights of writing.

The Madame Hanska room, all draped in red, is graced by a portrait of the wealthy Russian widow who teased Balzac for 18 years with the prospect of marriage and instant credit relief. She became his wife just five months before his death in 1850, at the early age of 51. Balzac's most prized possession – a jewelled cane that he had made to order from a lead-

ing Parisian goldsmith – lies in its own glass case. It became his "power object", symbolising the gifted insomniac's idiosyncrasy and inspiring a decade's worth of cartoons and satire in Parisian journals.

Down some very steep stairs is a room of archive photographs revealing Passy as a village idyll in the days before 19th-century property developers moved in. Balzac appreciated its tranquillity. "I really need a quiet house, wedged between courtyard and garden, nicely decorated, for this is the nest, the shell, the secure envelope of my life!"

Balzac's literary universe is squeezed into another small room: a genealogical chart outlines the hundreds of characters of his *œuvre*, and their carved wooden figurines line the walls. Finally, there is a windowless room crammed full of Balzac busts, most of them by artists of his day. (Rodin's sculpture of Balzac, wrapped in the cloak he liked to wear when writing, can be seen in the Rodin Museum, *see page 95*.) The house is the seat of the Balzac Studies Group and of the Balzac Society of Friends, with a reference library of 5,000 volumes.

*Food and Drink: Nearby, rue de l'Annonciation offers perhaps the most convincing take on "real" English tea in Paris at **Somerset Place** (no. 9); cuisine du terroir is available at a moderate price at the **Bistro des Vignes** (at the corner of rue Jean-Bologne; tel: 01 45 27 76 64) and satisfying sandwiches and salads at **Tarte Julie** (no. 14).*

Left: *The Flautist by Jean-Jacques Henner.*

plaster torso and a half-size maquette are on display here. Other themes, such as children, sports or medals, are treated in temporary displays in the entrance corridor. Subsequently left behind by avant-garde currents, Bouchard is hardly a major figure of French art, but his studio is run with much dedication by his son and daughter-in-law and gives an atmospheric vision of an artist's life.

FOOD AND DRINK: There are a number of eateries along avenue Mozart. See also Musée Marmotton page 106.

Musée Bourdelle

Modernist sculpture in an original Montparnasse studio

Map reference: page 40, B6
16–18 rue Antoine-Bourdelle, 15th
Tel: 01 49 54 73 73. www.mairie-paris.fr/musees
Metro: Montparnasse-Bienvenüe, Falguière.
Bus: 28, 48, 82, 89, 91, 92, 95
Open: Tues–Sun 10am–5.40pm; closed Mon.
Admission free.

Skylit studio of Henri Bouchard (1875–1960).

Musée Henri Bouchard

Former studio of a prolific sculptor, crammed with his sculptures, sketches and tools

Map reference: page 42, B4
25 rue de l'Yvette, 16th
Tel: 01 46 47 63 46
www.musee-bouchard.com
Metro: Jasmin
Open: Wed, Sat 2–7pm; closed Mon, Tue, Thur, Fri, Sun and 16–31 Mar, 16–30 June, 16–30 Sept, 16–31 Dec. Admission charge.

In 1924, Henri Bouchard (1875–1960) bought a house with an adjoining plot of land in the 16th *arrondissement* (then rather more avant-garde and artistic than its bourgeois image suggests today), where he built his studio and lived and worked until his death in 1960. Today, the lofty, skylit studio is crammed with sculptures, displayed amid a dusty clutter of tools, maquettes, sketchbooks and moulds.

Bouchard's career went through many distinct stylistic phases. His early works of girls and peasants were clearly defined and characteristic of late 19th-century realism. From around 1907–09 he found a new, simplified, stylised aesthetic, and produced sculptures on a larger scale, often idealising workers, as in *The Breton Fisherman*. This led to the much more linear style of the 1920s and '30s, as seen in his numerous war memorials around France, in the tympanum and interior sculptures he produced for the Eglise St-Jean-de-Chaillot or, in his best-known work, the monumental *Apollo* for the Palais de Chaillot, of which the

Spread over the former apartment and studio of Antoine Bourdelle (1861–1929), and two later extensions, the Musée Bourdelle traces the career of the Modernist sculptor, while giving a flavour of the old artistic mood of Montparnasse. After studying at the Ecole des Beaux-Arts under Falguière, whose style he found too academic, Bourdelle worked from 1893 to 1904 as a marble carver for Rodin. His early works show the influence of his master, but he subsequently broke away from Rodin's realism and expressionism in order to follow a highly stylised, deliberately epic reworking of classical sculpture.

The museum is built around a garden in which several of Bourdelle's bronzes stand, including his youthful sculpture of *Adam*; *Hercules the Archer*; the robust *Penelope*; casts of the giant horse from his monument to Argentine independence hero, General Alvear, and of the four allegorical figures of *Force*, *Eloquence*, *Liberty* and *Victory* from its base.

The monument to General Alvear, in Buenos Aires, occupied 10 years of Bourdelle's life, and the full-scale plaster sculpture of the mounted equestrian statue, which draws on Roman and Renaissance models, dominates the big sculpture gallery. Bourdelle's sculpture is often described as architec-

Bourdelle's bronze statue of Hannibal as a boy with an eagle, representing the Carthaginian general's first victory (1885).

Rodin with tempestuous, flowing beard and in his numerous studies of Beethoven. For Bourdelle, the great Romantic composer seems to have embodied all the different aspects of creativity, rather as Balzac did for Rodin. He continued to produce busts, paintings and sketches of Beethoven for over 30 years, portraying him with wild unruly hair, draped, tragic, in meditation or as Bacchus. A further room displays Bourdelle's own collection of Greek and Etruscan terracottas, medieval statuary, as well as paintings by Marseille artist Monticelli.

A new wing, designed by Christian de Portzamparc, opened in 1992, and contains temporary exhibition galleries. Also on permanent display here are the bronzes and maquettes for his war memorial at Montauban and his monument to the Polish poet Adam Mickiewicz *(see page 158)*.

Bourdelle lived in the apartment from 1884 to 1918 (he later moved to another apartment nearby, but held on to the studio) and it still has his furniture, stove, father's woodworking bench and portraits of his parents, wives and children. At the rear, amid overgrown gardens, is Bourdelle's studio and the adjoining studio of Eugène Carrière. The Symbolist's monochrome paintings of maternity and childhood influenced Bourdelle's own paintings and early sculptures, which have similar smiling expressions and sense of emergence. These two workshops form part of a rare surviving alley of studios, of the sort that littered Montparnasse in the early 20th century, where Bourdelle's neighbours included Jules Dalou, and, briefly, Chagall.

*FOOD AND DRINK: One of many Breton restaurants in the area, **Ti-Jos** (30 rue Delambre, 14th; tel: 01 43 22 57 69; inexpensive) serves sweet and savoury pancakes, washed down with cider served in earthenware bowls.*

tural, a characteristic particularly evident in the four figures on the plinth of the Alvear monument and in the gigantic, spear-bearing evocation of *La France*, which suggest not only the inspiration of antiquity but also the column figures of medieval cathedrals.

The grand gallery also contains various versions of *Hercules the Archer*, in which Bourdelle pared back the head in a series of austere planes to symbolise the Greek hero's strength and courage. If the monumental works are frozen and portentous, the reliefs for the façade of the Théâtre des Champs-Elysées, which opened on avenue Montaigne in 1913, are carved with surprising verve: notably *The Muses*, in which the running figures in flowing drapes were inspired by the dancer Isadora Duncan, whose naturalism in movement and dress had revolutionised modern dance at the beginning of the century.

The galleries upstairs focus on small sculptures, including heads and groups of musicians, as well as Bourdelle's occasional paintings, and the Art Deco furniture of his son-in-law, Michel Dufet. Although Bourdelle carried out portrait commissions, his concept of the great artist is best expressed in his busts of Carpeaux, of Rembrandt young and old, of

Relief carved for the façade of the Théâtre des Champs-Elysées (1912–13).

Espace Salvador Dalí

A *Dalicatessan* of minor works and other surreal snippets

Map reference: page 42, E2
11 rue Poulbot, Espace Montmartre, 18th
Tel: 01 42 64 40 10
Metro: Abbesses. Bus: 54, 80
Open: daily 10am–6pm.
Restaurant/Café. Bookshop. Guided tours
(advance reservations). Wheelchair access.
Admission charge.

This museum/gallery is an effort to cash in (admission is almost as high as at the Louvre) on the mediocre work that Dalí cranked out in his old age. The "classics" of the young Dalí, the hero of Montmartre and Montparnasse who helped give birth to Surrealism in the 1920s, are not here (except in reproduction). However, many of the themes are the same, and the Dalí cosmology – God, genitalia, death, ants, melted clocks and "space elephants" – are abundantly represented in 330 minor works, mostly illustrations and sculpture. It is all illuminated by moving spotlights, while Dalí's recorded voice echos through the air-conditioned basement between interludes of New Age muzak.

There are illustrations for *Don Quixote, Alice in Wonderland*, and the *Adventures of Pantagruel* (in a comic style that mimics Hieronymous Bosch). The sketches for the *Holy Grail*, in particular, demonstrate Dalí's ever-powerful draughtsmanship and flair for the expressive line.

The texts are gratingly pretentious. The space elephant (with stork's legs and a pyramid on its back) "is a famous Dalínian concept created to illustrate the great Master's vision of the future." The quotes from Dalí are more entertaining. "With video-cassettes," he assures us, "the world will become a monumental garbage dump in which everyone will be able to make their own pseudo-artistic rubbish."

FOOD AND DRINK: Moulin Vins (6 rue Burq, 18th; moderate). Parisians come here for that Montmartre feeling, particularly after 10pm. Besides drinking wine by the glass or jug you can snack on charcuterie, cheese and salad or steak or rabbit. See also Musée du Vieux Montmartre, page 182.

Musée Eugène Delacroix

Last home and studio of the inspirational Romantic painter

Map reference: page 40, D4
6 rue de Furstenberg, 6th
Tel: 01 44 41 86 50. www.mairie-paris.fr/musees
www.paris-tourism.com/museums/delacroix
Metro: St-Germain-des-Prés. Bus: 39, 48, 63, 70, 86, 95, 96
Open: Mon, Wed–Sun 9.30am–5.15pm; closed Tues and public hols.
Bookshop. Admission charge.

Hidden in a courtyard just off idyllic place Furstenberg is this little gem of a museum where France's leading Romantic artist Eugène Delacroix (1798–1863) spent the last years of his life. The distinctive style of Delacroix is marked by his use of vivid colour (Cézanne called him "the palette of France") and exotic, often violent subject matter. He is best known for his monumental works, notably *Death of Sardanapalus* (1827) and *Liberty Leading the People* (1830, *see pages 8–9*), but is also celebrated for his paintings of Morocco, which he visited in 1832, his animal compositions and watercolours.

His last great works were executed while he lived in this apartment. Delacroix moved here to be near the church of St-Sulpice, where he wrestled for the last ten years of his life with the subject of Good and Evil in a series of large frescoes *(see opposite)*. Although there are no major works in the museum

Jacob Wrestling with the Angel (detail), one of three huge frescoes by Delacroix in the church of St-Sulpice.

Studies of North African architecture and figures from Delacroix's sketch book.

Fondation Dubuffet

Personal collection of the Art Brut artist, displayed in a three-storey mansion

Map reference: page 40, B6
137 rue de Sèvres, 6th
Tel: 01 47 34 12 63
www.dubuffetfondation.com
Metro: Duroc. Bus: 28, 39, 70, 82, 87, 89, 92.
Open: Mon–Fri 2–7pm, closed Sat, Sun, Aug.
Admission charge.

(these are housed in the Louvre, *see pages 68–69, and the Musée d'Orsay, see page 83)*, there are several fine small paintings, including a portrait of the novelist George Sand, self-portraits and sketches from his formative journey to North Africa. Personal odds and ends, such as letters from friends, including the poet Charles Baudelaire, and, in the studio, brushes and a palette with neatly arranged teardrops of paint, add to the sense of intimacy. Much of the museum, however, is devoted to exhibitions related to the artist's work, each lasting around three months.

St-Sulpice

While you're in the area, it's worth making the short (five-minute) walk to St-Sulpice (open daily, 8am–7pm, tel: 01 46 33 21 78, admission free), the church fondly referred to by Delacroix as "my chapel". To get there, cross over the boulevard St-Germain and walk south towards place St-Sulpice, which is dominated on its eastern side by Jean-Baptiste Servandoni's twin-towered Italianesque masterpiece. Delacroix's massive oil-and-wax frescoes can be found in the Chapelle des Saints Anges (Chapel of the Holy Angels) at the back of the church. On the ceiling of the side chapel is *The Archangel Michael Defeating the Devil*, on the right-hand side (as you look into the chapel) is *Héliodore Chased from the Temple*, and on the left is *Jacob Wrestling with the Angel*. He completed these paintings in 1861, just two years before his death.

*FOOD AND DRINK: There's no café in the museum, but you can picnic in the delightful shaded garden laid out with chairs and tables. The nearby boulevard St-Germain has plenty of eating options, but the **Café de la Mairie** (8 place St-Sulpice, 6th; tel: 01 43 26 67 82; inexpensive), overlooking the fountains on the square, is not so disturbed by traffic. It serves standard, good-value brasserie fare and a variety of sandwiches.*

Jean Dubuffet (1901–85) established this foundation himself on order to ensure the proper administration of the paintings, sculptural maquettes and enormous number of works on paper that he left. The body of his work is divided between this 19th-century house and his former workshops outside Paris in the Val de Marne, where Dubuffet built the Closerie Falbala (phone number as above).

Dubuffet worked in different cycles that showed his rejection of the accepted canons of beauty, his exploration of new, often poor materials and his appreciation of both children's and naive art, as he refused to distinguish between abstraction and representation. The collection includes early gouaches, ink drawings, collages in such diverse materials as soil, butterfly wings and wood, cartoon-style townscapes and portraits of friends. Also of interest are the small-scale maquettes from the *Hourloupe* series (sometimes later realised as large-scale sculptures), in which the artist created a parallel world complete with characters, everyday objects, plants and buildings.

As well as lending works to external exhibitions, the Fondation puts on small temporary shows which deal with different themes or series.

FOOD AND DRINK: see Musée Ernest Hébert page 156.

The Triumpher (1973) by Jean Dubuffet.

Musée Ernest Hébert

Paintings and memorabilia of society portrait painter, Ernest Hébert

Map reference: page 40, C5
85, rue du Cherche-Midi, 6th
Tel: 01 42 22 23 82
Metro: Sèvres-Babylone, St-Placide, Vaneau, Duroc. Bus: 39, 70, 82, 84, 89, 92, 94, 95, 96.
Open: Mon, Wed–Fri 12.30–6pm, Sat–Sun and public hols 2–6pm; closed Tues.
Bookshop. Admission charge.

Nestled among the chic boutiques of the 6th *arrondissement*, this is a charming museum set in an archetypal 18th-century town house, with time-capsule interiors where you can browse through the personal bric-à-brac of wealthy society painter, Ernest Hébert (1817–1908). Like his cousin, the novelist Stendhal, Hébert was passionately in love with Italy and lived there for many years. There is a lot more of Italy on the walls than France. Despite his talents, Hébert missed all the avant-garde boats, though traces of Impressionism can be detected in his later works. The best of his paintings include portraits of children – *Le Petit Brigand* and *Le Petit Violoneux Endormi* (The Sleeping Fiddler) – and of sensuous women like *Rosa Nera à la Fontaine* and the *Comtesse Pastré*.

FOOD AND DRINK: There's an ordinary café on the opposite corner, but for something more substantial, **Le Cherche Midi** *down the street (no 22; tel: 01 45 48 27 44; moderate) serves good Italian food, albeit in cramped conditions.*

The Young Huntress, by Ernest Hébert.

The Flautist, by Jean-Jacques Henner, a study for his pastoral painting, *The Eclogue.*

Musée Jean-Jacques Henner

Four floors of paintings by Belle Époque artist, Jean-Jacques Henner

Map reference: page 42, D2
43 av de Villiers, 17th
Tel: 01 47 63 42 73
Metro: Malesherbes. Bus: 30, 31, 94
Open: Tues–Sun 10am–noon and 2–5pm.
Bookshop. Guided tours (advance reservation). Admission charge.

Jean-Jacques Henner (1829–1905) is the most decorated artist in French history: he received the Légion d'Honneur and, just before his death, was promoted to *commandeur*. Today, he remains an interesting case study in the aesthetic values of the Belle Époque. This museum offers a complete retrospective from youthful self-portraits to the last, incomplete painting in the Alsatian painter's œuvre. His signature work was of young women, often cast as nymphs, whose "pale flesh seems to have captured the last caresses of the light", in the words of a smitten Belle Époque critic. His other themes are, unsurprisingly, Alsatian *(Young Alsatian Girl holding a Basket of Fruit, She is Waiting)* and Italian.

Like his contemporary, Ernest Hébert, Henner was an Italophile – he won the Prix de Rome in 1858 – and drew inspiration from the works of Correggio and Giorgione. More information on his life and times can be gleaned from the letters and documents on display. (The museum was being refurbished at time of writing, so ring to check that it's open.)

FOOD AND DRINK: Le Dôme de Villiers (4, av de Villiers; tel: 01 43 87 28 68; inexpensive) is a lively café, bustling with office workers by day and theatregoers by night.

Maison de Victor Hugo

Paris home of a literary genius and dedicated family man

Map reference: page 41, H4
6 place des Vosges, 4th
Tel: 01 42 72 10 16. www.mairie-paris.fr/musees
Metro: Bastille, St Paul. Bus: 69, 76
Open: Tues–Sun 10am–5.40pm; closed Mon,
public hols. Shop. Admission free.

The house at 44 rue du Cherche-Midi, by André Dignimont: Victor and Adèle Hugo's first marital home.

Tucked away in the corner of the place des Vosges – one of the most beautiful squares in Paris – is the Hôtel de Rohan-Guémenée, where Victor Hugo (1802–85) wrote many of his works, including a large part of *Les Misérables*. He rented an apartment on the second floor, where he lived with his wife Adèle and their children from 1832 to 1848, before fleeing after the 1848 revolution to Guernsey (where he spent the next 15 years in voluntary exile). Hugo's Parisian salon drew many great luminaries of the day. "In that old Louis XIII *hôtel*... the king of modern poetry reigned for 15 years, surrounded by his devoted courtiers, who were full of admiration for the master," wrote Eugène de Mirecourt, one among many literary regulars which also included Balzac, Lamartine, Mérimée and Dumas.

The rooms on the second floor trace the story of Hugo's life, which he himself divided into three stages: "before exile, during exile, and after exile". The first rooms are hung with portraits and sketches of his family. His seafaring grandfather, octant in hand; his father, General Hugo, who after a brilliant military career retired to become a man of letters; his mother, who gave her children a liberal education, and his brothers Abel and Eugène. Informal sketches, drawings and paintings of Hugo, his wife Adèle, whom he married in 1822, and their young children by Louis Boulanger and Achille Devéria – who also illustrated Hugo's works – portray Hugo as a devoted family man. The painting of the poet with his young son, Victor, by Auguste de Châtillon, is full of tenderness. But of all the children it is his elder daughter, Léopoldine, who is given most prominence. Her death by drowning at the age of 19, with her husband of just a few months, was one of the great tragedies of Hugo's life. Perhaps the most moving of the "Didine" memorabilia is the sketch of her reading by her mother (1837), framed by Hugo after her death

FAR LEFT: Contemporary caricature of Hugo "la plus forte tête romantique".

LEFT: Portrait of Hugo's mistress, Juliette Drouet, by Charles Voillemot.

with a piece of the dress that she wore for de Chatillon's portrait, *Léopoldine au Livre d'heures*.

The other woman in Hugo's life was Juliette Drouet, depicted as a young woman in a portrait by Voillemot. Hugo met the actress in 1833 and she remained his lover, secretary and critic for fifty years, even following him into exile. The Chinese Room is a recreation of the décor that Hugo designed for the house they shared in Guernsey.

Hugo was renowned for his love of antiques and bric-à-brac, and the rest of the museum's display is made up of furniture, books and mementos of his life, alongside his own pen-and-ink drawings and the photographs he took in exile.

The rooms on the first floor are used for temporary exhibitions, usually based on the theme of Hugo's novels and drama.

*FOOD AND DRINK: Diagonally opposite the museum, **Ma Bourgogne** (19 place des Vosges, 4th; tel: 01 42 78 44 64, moderate) is the most atmospheric bistro on the square, with wooden tables set out under the arcades. The salads are good and steak tartare is a speciality of the house.*

Musée Adam Mickiewcz

Polish artists and writers in Paris

Map reference: page 41, G5
6 quai d'Orléans 4th
Tel: 01 55 42 83 83
Metro: Pont-Marie. Bus: 24, 63, 67
Bookshop. Research facilities/library.
Closed for restoration, reopening in late 2002.

Adam Mickiewcz was the author of *Pan Tadeusz*, the most venerated poem in the Polish literary canon. Many Poles can recite stanzas from it, and a recent film adaptation drew an audience of 10 million Poles, including the Pope. The museum was created by the poet's eldest son in 1903. When Adam Mickiewcz was writing in Paris in the mid-19th century, Poland had been rubbed off the political map by its more powerful neighbours. This collection of paintings, books, maps and documents tells the story of remarkable Polish emigrés in France in the 19th and 20th centuries. Among the exhibits is the expressive death mask of Frédéric Chopin.

*FOOD AND DRINK: **Brasserie de L'Ile St-Louis** (55 quai de Bourbon, 4th; tel: 01 43 54 02 59, moderate). Reliable Alsatian food, choucroute, etc., with a superb view of Notre-Dame's flying buttresses.*

Musée Gustave Moreau

Overflowing with fantastical paintings and drawings that the symbolist painter bequeathed to the state

Map reference: page 43, E2
14 rue de la Rochefoucauld, 9th
Tel: 01 48 74 38 50
Metro: Trinité, St-Georges. Bus: 26, 32, 43, 67, 68, 74
Open: Mon, Wed 11am–5.15pm, Thur–Sun 10am–12.45pm, 2–5.15pm; closed Tues. Admission charge.

The Musée Moreau has to be the most excessive and most fascinating of all Paris' artists museums, perhaps because the artist conceived it himself. He had the special double-storey studio constructed on top of the partially demolished family home, and left to the state the hundreds of oil paintings and literally thousands of drawings and goauches that now fill every centimetre of space.

On the first floor you can see the cramped apartment where Moreau lived with his parents, arranged symbolically in their memory by the artist, with their furniture, family portraits and photographs, Italian maiolica and Palissy plates, and drawings and prints by artists that Moreau admired (including a Rembrandt etching and drawings by Poussin and Chassériau). Its ever-so-proper 19th-

Moreau's *The Unicorn* was inspired by the *Lady and the Unicorn* tapestry series in the Musée de Cluny.

Far Left: *Jupiter and Semélé* (1896).

Left: *The Apparition (Salome)*, 1874.

century respectability is in startling contrast to the outpouring of paint and colour and the fantastic, mystical worlds upstairs, compounding the impression of an artist torn between strait-laced repression and an extraordinarily fertile imagination. Curiously for a figure who was something of a recluse, Moreau was also a talented teacher; his pupils included Henri Matisse and Albert Marquet, as well as Georges Roualt, who became the museum's first curator.

On the second floor, the lower level of the studio is hung with large, mostly unfinished canvases; there's a case of the small, red wax studies, in which he occasionally tried out his compositions in 3D form, and thousands of his drawings, compositional sketches, figure studies and copies after the masters, which can be pulled out on shutters from the wall.

A brilliant colourist and meticulous draughtsman, Moreau reworked themes from mythology and the Bible in a highly personal pantheon. He often combined areas of obsessively rendered detail – in bejewelled costumes, imaginary architecture and exotic bestiaries, inspired by medieval and Renaissance paintings, and by the Mogul miniatures and Hindu sculpture he saw in Paris museums – with other areas of sweeping, broadly painted colour. *The Argonauts* depicts the return of Jason – who, for Moreau, symbolised "proud and graceful youth" – at the prow of a hieratic, pyramidal composition. *Le Fleur Mystique* again forms a pyramidal, almost glaringly phallic composition, with the Virgin Mary sitting on a giant lily, symbol of purity. *Les*

Chimères, described by Moreau as a "Satanic Decameron", is laden with fantastical landscapes inhabited by angels, winged beasts and a surging mass of female figures symbolising female caprice, the unconscious being and diabolical seduction.

A spiral staircase leads to the top floor, where the highly finished version of *Jupiter et Semélé* can be compared with a broadly executed oil sketch and a variant on the composition, which dramatically juxtaposes the tiny figure of Semélé "climbing towards the divine", with the giant figure of Jupiter. Look also through the brilliant gouaches and the racks of small oil studies, which range from looming figures and compositional sketches to almost abstract colour compositions.

In the second room, dominated by a large copy of Carpaccio's *St George and the Dragon*, are studies of *Bathsheba*, *Europa* and the graceful pastoral *Les Licornes* (*The Unicorns*), reflecting Moreau's admiration for the *Lady and the Unicorn* tapestries in the Musée du Cluny *(see page 80)*. In the ominous *L'Apparition*, Moreau has chosen not the conventional image of victorious Salome, with the head of John the Baptist on a plate, but the episode when she is demanding him from Herod. It is the recurring theme of Salome that best epitomises Moreau's vision of woman: powerful, lascivious, manipulative, beautiful and, usually, fateful.

FOOD AND DRINK: Tea Follies (6 place Gustave-Tourdouze, 9th; tel: 01 42 80 08 44): an arty tea room with a retro vibe on a lovely peaceful square not far from the museum. Salads and light meals at lunch, scones and cakes at tea.

Musée de la Vie Romantique

Memories of George Sand and a taste of Romantic Paris

Map reference: page 43, E2
16 rue Chaptal, 9th
Tel: 01 48 74 95 38. www.mairie-paris.fr/musees
Metro: St-Georges, Pigalle. Bus: 74, 67
Open: Tues–Sat 10am–5.50pm; closed public
hols. Teashop. Bookshop. Guided tours (with
advance reservations). Admission free.

A few blocks from sleazy Pigalle there is a forgotten corner of Paris that was known to George Sand and Chopin in the middle of the 19th century as "New Athens", after its close-knit community of artists, composers and writers. A stroll through the streets and passageways of this atmospheric *quartier* is the perfect prelude to a visit to one of the city's most enchanting museums.

At the end of a narrow lane off rue Chaptal stands the former home and garden of painter Ary Scheffer. He settled in the Italianate house in 1830 and added a pair of studios, using one as a salon in which to receive the artistic and intellectual élite of Paris. The ground floor is a shrine to the Baronne Aurore Dupin, aka George Sand (1804–76), one of France's first feminists. She did not actually live here, but was a frequent guest and has taken it over posthumously. The museum is now devoted to the novelist, her family and her intellectual circle of friends.

The arrangement of the George Sand rooms, tastefully decorated with portraits, furniture, drawings, jewels and manuscripts, was inspired by the writer's own descriptions of the period. The result is an evocative rather than informative display. Two paintings by Delacroix, *Lélia* and *L'Education de la Vierge*, stand out. Other odds and ends relate to her friends: Flaubert, Delacroix, Liszt, Rossini, Lamartine, Russian novelist Turgenev and, of course, her lover Chopin. The works of Scheffer, an archetypal romantic tortured by self-doubt, are on show upstairs. His historical and religious pictures, though full of drama, often seem like weak imitations of Delacroix's masterpieces.

Across the courtyard are the studios where Ary Scheffer worked and partied from 1830 to 1858. They are used for temporary exhibitions (normally included with the price of admission).

FOOD AND DRINK: The museum has a lovely garden, open to the public for tea among the roses and wisteria. La Petite Sirène de Copenhague (47 rue Notre-Dame de la Lorette, 9th; tel: 01 45 26 66 66; moderate) is a cosy French-Danish restaurant with old-fashioned banquettes, white-starched tablecloths and just six main courses, all excellent.

Caricature of George Sand in the company of her lover, Chopin, and other illustrious friends.

CIMITIÈRE PÈRE LACHAISE

Set on the top of a hill in the 20th *arrondissement*, east of the city, is the Père Lachaise cemetery – an outdoor museum of sorts, scattered as it is with famous graves, mausoleums and funerary sculptures. The list of literary, musical, artistic and political luminaries buried here is indeed impressive, and it remains the city's most sought-after resting place.

But the cemetery has not always been so fashionable. It was named after Louis XIV's confessor, Père Lachaise, who owned the land when it was occupied by a retirement home for old priests. It was Napoleon's idea to create a new cemetery here, and he requisitioned the land in 1803. Initially, the people of Paris were reluctant to be buried here as it was in an unfashionable district far from the city centre. Attitudes soon changed after Napoleon cannily transferred the remains of Molière and La Fontaine, with much pomp and ceremony, to the new cemetery. Soon everyone who was anyone wanted a plot here, and its boundaries had to be extended several times.

Famous graves

The resulting list of residents is impressive indeed. It includes Delacroix *(see page 154)*, Chopin *(see page 160)*, Rossini, Bizet, Colette, Victor Hugo *(see page 157)*, Balzac *(see page 151)*, Apollinaire, Marcel Proust *(see page 54)*, Gerturde Stein, Sarah Bernhardt and Oscar Wilde, the latter under a fittingly inscrutable sphinx by Jacob Epstein.

Among the celebrities of more recent times at rest here are Edith Piaf *(see page 165)*, Yves Montand, Simone Signoret, and Jim Morrison (of the Doors), whose graffitti-covered grave is the most visited spot.

At the end of the 19th century, The Columbarium was built here to house funerary urns. Isadora Duncan is among the many celebrities whose ashes are housed here.

The Communards' shrine

The cemetery was also the site of the last battle of the Paris Commune against French troops from Versailles, on 27 May 1871. At dawn the next day, the remaining Communards were lined up against a wall and shot. They were buried in a ditch where they fell. The spot is now marked by the Mur des Fédérés (Federalists' Wall), which has become a socialist shrine. Nearby are monuments to both World Wars.

Finding Your Way

Père Lachaise cemetery is laid out like a miniature town, with cobbled streets, each with a name, lined with tombstones and mausoleums instead of houses. You can pick up a map pinpointing the more famous graves at the entrance. The main entrance to the cemetery (open daily 8am–7.30pm, admission free) is on boulevard de Ménilmontant.

Musée Zadkine

Cubist sculpture among the trees

Map reference: page 43, E5
100bis, rue d'Assas, 6th.
Tel: 01 43 26 91 90. www.mairie-paris.fr/musees
Metro: Notre-Dame des Champs, Vavin,
Port-Royal. Bus: 38, 58, 83, 91
Open: Tues–Sun 10am–5.30pm; closed public
hols. Guided tours (with advance reservation).
Wheelchair access. Admission free.

The Musée Zadkine is a small oasis of greenery in the heart of Paris. That was its attraction for cubist sculptor, Ossip Zadkine (1890–1967), who spent much of his artistic career working in the garden atelier. The Russian sculptor was one of many foreign artists who flocked to Paris in the early 20th century *(see Ecole de Paris, page 27)*.

More than 100 sculptures and numerous sketches are exhibited in the house and garden. Arranged chronologically, they represent the materials he worked with (wood, clay, stone and bronze) and his creative "periods" – primitivism, cubism, abstractionism. Some of his most celebrated figures are here: *Tête Héroïque* (1908), *Torse d'Ephèbe* (1920), *Grand Vénus Cariatide* (1919), *Femme à l'Eventail* (1923) and *La Naissance de Vénus* (1950), along with models for his masterpiece, the *Monument à la Ville Détruite*, erected in the Dutch port of Rotterdam in 1947.

FOOD AND DRINK: Wadja (10 rue de la Grande-Chaumière, 6th; tel: 01 46 33 02 02). This pretty Montparnasse bistro used to be a hangout for impoverished artists but today culinary standards have soared. There's a superb-value daily market menu and a well-chosen list of wines.

Some of the sculptures on display in the charming Zadkine museum.

Music

The modern Cité de la Musique, the plush Musée de l'Opéra and the cosy Musée Edith Piaf make up a fine trio of musical museums. Together, they share a vast repertoire of instruments, paintings, stage sets, scores and memorabilia

Cité de la Musique

Up-to-the-minute technology put to the service of one of the world's great collections of musical instruments

Map reference: page 43, H2
Cité de la Musique, 221 ave Jean-Jaurès, 19th.
Tel: 01 44 84 45 00. www.cite-musique.fr
Metro: Porte de Pantin. Bus: PC2, PC3, 75.
Open: Tues–Sat noon–6pm, Sun 10am–6pm.
Shop. Audio-guides in English. Guided group
tours by reservation only (tel: 01 44 84 46 46).
Wheelchair access. Library. Admission charge.

The Cité de la Musique, high-tech home of the Musée de la Musique.

To the northeast of Paris, on a site once occupied by the city's main abattoir and cattle market, is the sprawling arts and science complex of La Villette. The transformation of the 55-hectare (136-acre) area into a huge park, dominated by the Cité des Sciences et de l'Industrie at one end and the Cité de la Musique at the other, was one of former French president François Mitterrand's most successful *grands projets (see page 30).*

The area has been sensitively regenerated – the lessons of the planning fiasco at Les Halles, where all ten wrought-iron halls of the historic produce market were demolished, having been learnt. Designer Christian de Portzamparc arranged the modern buildings of the City of Music around the original 19th-century iron and glass market hall, which stands on the main concourse between the Music Conservatoire and the museum/concert hall.

Although the music museum has a collection of over 4,500 musical instruments, 900 of which are on display, the emphasis is on live performance and living traditions, rather than a fastidiously documented collection of ancient instruments. An aural back-up to the exhibits is provided in the form of an audio-guide, available in several languages. As you wander towards a showcase, "sound pockets" activate the infrared headset. You can listen to a recording of the displayed instrument, followed by an informative commentary. (This is a good idea but can be frustrating if you have insufficient time to listen to each commentary in full.)

Instruments through the ages

The impressive collection of instruments on display is mostly organised by century and therein by theme – from the Italian Baroque and the music of Versailles (17th century), to opera, the Parisian Salons and public concerts (18th century), and romantic orchestra, grand opera, lyric drama and World Fairs (19th century). There are also sections on musical notation in the West and World Music, plus temporary exhibition spaces.

Many of the instruments are works of art in their own right, notably several gleaming 17th-century trumpets by Johann Wilhelm Has, one of the most renowned brass instrument makers; a fine collection of lavishly decorated pianofortes by celebrated firms such as Erard & Frère; several violins by Stradivarius, including the 1708 Cremona "Davidoff"; and the quirkily shaped, experimental stringed instruments by Jean-Baptiste Vuillaume. Also on show are instruments that reputedly belonged to composers, including Fauré, Berlioz and Chopin, as well as numerous portraits of these and other musicians. Other rarities include a full Javanese Gamelan orchestra, which inspired the composer Debussy when he first heard it at the 1889 Paris International Exhibition.

The area of the museum dedicated to the 20th century is currently being reorganised in order to accommodate a whole new section, which is due to open at the end of 2002. Instruments from the first half of the century will be integrated into the existing exhibition, while a new display space, known as Espace 21, will be dedicated to contemporary music from the 1950s onwards.

Model venues

Also of note in the Musée de la Musique are the models of the Paris Opéra, Bayreuth Festspielhaus and the concert hall that once stood at the Trocadéro – a grandiose venue for Berlioz's *Symphonie Fantastique*. These are beautifully constructed and help to provide an accessible exploration of the history of Western classical music and concert venues. For

LEFT: The opulent auditorium inside Charles Garnier's Paris Opéra.

those with a relatively good grasp of French, touch-screen computers dotted throughout the museum provide further historical background.

In addition, the museum has its own mini auditorium, where students or professors from the Conservatoire give occasional ad hoc concerts using historical instruments. If you don't want to leave the opportunity of hearing live music to chance, the guided tours include live performances on their itineraries. At certain times, experts are at hand to explain the mysteries of some of the more unusual instruments, such as the Ondes Martinot, which was invented in 1928 and much used by Messiaen, and was a forerunner of electronic music.

*FOOD AND DRINK: Just outside the museum, the **Café de la Musique** (place Fontaine aux Lions, 19th; tel: 01 48 03 15 91; moderate) offers appealing cocktails and light meals in a trendy atmosphere, and there's a large terrace overlooking the former marketplace. If you want a full meal, the nearby **Au Boeuf Couronné** (188 av Jean-Jaurès, 19th; tel: 01 42 39 44 44; moderate) serves up groaning platters of rare steak accompanied by* pommes de terre soufflées. *A real whiff of old Paris.*

Musée de l'Opéra

A spectacular setting for a collection of scores, portraits, costumes and sets from the world's biggest opera stage

Map reference: page 40, D1
Palais Garnier, 1 pl de l'Opéra, 9th
Tel: 01 40 01 24 93. www.opera-de-paris.fr
Metro: Opéra. Bus: 68, 21, 27, 95, 22, 52, 53, 66, 81
Open: daily 10am–4.30pm
Shop. Admission charge.

Rehearsals permitting, tickets for viewing the museum of the Opéra de Paris also include a visit to the now-restored opera house. Architect Charles Garnier was commissioned in 1860 by Napoleon III to build an opera house for the imperial capital, and his lavish designs, ranging from the Classical to the Baroque, were wholly in tune with the pomp and opulence that characterised the Second Empire. Ironically, it took 15 years to complete the project, by which time the Empire had collapsed and Napoleon III had died. Apparently, Garnier had to face the indignity of paying for his ticket on opening night. Some statistics give an idea of the scale of the Opéra: it has 1,991 seats, 334 boxes, 1,606 doors, 7,593 keys, 450 fireplaces and 6,319 steps. Beneath the building is an underground lake, which inspired the setting for Leroux's *Phantom of the Opera*.

On the front façade, the graceful sculpture of *La Danse* by Jean-Baptiste Carpeaux *(see page 83)* stands out from the statues of the great composers of the 19th century. The original is now in the Musée d'Orsay, but the copy by Paul Belmondo (father of actor, Jean-Paul Belmondo) is a faithful reproduction.

Inside the Palais Garnier

The profusion of marble and gilt that decorates the interior of the opera house is almost oppressive in its excess, but the glamour of the building's various foyers is undeniable, providing the ideal setting for the élite to show off their cultural and style credentials. The grand marble staircase, which leads to the stalls and most expensive boxes, was conceived by Garnier as the ultimate celebrity catwalk. "Everything is designed so that the parade of spectators who climb the stairs become themselves a show."

The five-tiered auditorium, which is dripping in red velvet and gilt, is dominated by a six-ton chandelier, which famously crashed down on the audience during a performance of Gounod's *Faust* in 1896. The painted ceiling of the auditorium, executed by Marc Chagall in 1964, covers the original painted work, *Les Heures du Jour et de la Nuit* (*The Hours of Day and Night*), by Lenepveu, which is still intact underneath.

FAR LEFT: Part of the elaborate gilded ceiling mosaic in the Palais Garnier's foyer.

LEFT: Marc Chagall's wonderfully incongruous painted ceiling in the Garnier auditorium.

The museum

The museum is set on two floors within the opera house, in a wing of the theatre originally conceived as the Pavillon de l'Empereur. The ground floor is generally used for temporary exhibitions, often linked with new productions. The museum and library proper contain scores and documentation concerning all the operas and ballets performed at the institution since its foundation in 1669. More visually appealing are the models of ancient stage sets, original costumes and the musicians' portrait gallery, including a portrait of *Richard Wagner* by Renoir, for which the composer was apparently reluctant to sit.

Among the artists' memorabilia are a pair of Nijinsky's ballet shoes and souvenirs of Diaghilev, donated by the late dancer Serge Lifar. The dance tradition at the Palais Garnier is historically strong and, with the appearance of the Opéra Bastille in 1989, it is now the principal stage in Paris for ballet.

FOOD AND DRINK: A pause for coffee or a drink at Garnier's **Café de la Paix** *(12 bd des Capucines, 9th; tel: 01 40 07 30 20; expensive), overlooking the Opéra, still has a certain expense-account chic, but for something stronger try* **Harry's Bar** *(5 rue Daunou, 2nd; tel: 01 42 61 71 14; moderate), which serves the driest dry martinis in town. For a classical French meal with a listed interior,* **Au Petit Riche** *(25 rue le Peltier, 9th; tel: 01 47 70 68 68; moderate) is popular.*

Musée Edith Piaf

Touching tribute to the diminutive queen of French *chanson*

Map reference: page 43, G3
5 rue Crespin-du-Gast, 11th
Tel: 01 43 55 52 72
Metro: Ménilmontant. Bus: 96
Open: Mon–Thurs 1–6pm (by appointment only); closed Sept. Shop. Admission: donation.

If any French popular artist can be said to have iconic status, it must be Edith Piaf. Born in 1915 in the working-class district of Belleville, she scraped a living from an early age, singing in the streets, local cafés and bars, until she was discovered by a nightclub impresario who put her on stage. This tiny museum run by Les Amis d'Edith Piaf is a loving tribute to the "little sparrow".

First to be conquered is the "viewing by appointment" system, which involves telephoning a couple of days in advance and being given entry codes for

The "little sparrow", Edith Piaf.

the building. However, die-hard fans will consider it worth the trouble. The collection of memorabilia is lovingly displayed in two rooms of a private apartment, within walking distance of Père Lachaise cemetery, where Piaf is buried. Posters, photographs and golden discs chart the life of the singer/songwriter from near-blind street urchin to international recording star, through drug-ravaged illness and disastrous relationships, to her tragically early death in 1963. She left a legacy of over 200 recordings.

To accompany the visit, you will be treated to recordings of her singing – a voice of such melancholic intensity as to render other exhibits of secondary interest. The tiny shoes, little black dress and life-size cardboard cut-out are the most moving exhibits, underlining just how remarkable the strength and range of Piaf's voice were given her diminutive size.

Piaf was also a well-known actress and starred in several films produced by the late Marcel Blistène, whose wife made a sculpture of the singer for the museum. Entrance is free but donations are welcome.

FOOD AND DRINK: The café **Le Soleil** *(136 bd de Ménilmontant, 20th; tel: 01 46 36 47 44; inexpensive) has one of the best people-watching terraces in the city, and the characterful* **Chez Jean** *(38 rue Boyer, 20th; tel: 01 47 97 44 58; inexpensive) is a good-value eating/drinking place.*

Explore Parisian history from every angle. Inspect Napoleon's army or investigate the Paris police; uncover the worlds of freemasons and forgers; enter the murky depths of the catacombs; or simply enjoy the fun of the fair

Musée de l'Armée

Louis XIV's hospital for wounded soldiers now houses Napoleon's tomb and a vast military museum

Map reference: page 40, A4
Hôtel des Invalides, 6 place Vauban, 7th
Tel: 01 44 42 38 77
www.invalides.org
Metro: Invalides, Latour-Maubourg, Varenne, St Francois Xavier
Bus: 28, 49, 63, 69, 82, 83, 87, 92
Open: daily, winter (Oct 1–Mar 31) 10am–5pm, summer (Apr 1–Sept 30) 10am–6pm.
Café. Wheelchair access. Research facilities/ library. Tour groups in English (advance reservations only). Admission charge.

The gleaming dome of the Hôtel des Invalides is a masterpiece of French Classical architecture and one of Paris' most prominent landmarks. Behind it is a remarkable 17th-century set of buildings commissioned in 1676 by Louis XIV to provide accommodation and hospital care for wounded soldiers. It also served as the royal arsenal, and it was from here, in 1789, that revolutionaries commandeered 30,000 rifles for the storming of the Bastille. Napoleon, whose wars kept the hospital full, restored the institution to its former glory, making the church a necropolis and regilding its dome. His monumental tomb is now housed in the Eglise du Dôme, while the Army Museum occupies the wings.

The catalogue of weapons begins with the Stone Age and ends with Hiroshima. To grasp the sheer scope of the place, it is helpful to remember that it is a series of museums within a museum, combining the former collections of the Artillery Museum and the Historical Military Museum with the French royal trove of arms and armour; a collection of scale replicas of artillery from Roman to modern times, a wing devoted to World War II and the Occupation, and a separate small museum of military honours.

Napoleon's tomb

In 1840 Napoleon's body was returned to the city from St Helena with much pomp and ceremony, and eventually laid to rest in the crypt of L'Eglise du Dôme (Dome Church). The emperor's mausoleum is fittingly overblown. His remains lie inside six coffins, one inside the other. The last giant coffin, made of oak, is elevated on a base of green granite and surrounded by 12 damsels representing his 12 military campaigns. The museum's director is still officially the "Keeper of the Emperor's tomb."

The armoury

The Musée de l'Armée is spread across either side of the Cour d'Honneur (ticket includes entrance to the tomb and museum). The medieval armoury – the arsenal – on the ground floor of the west wing is a shiny vision of knightly accoutrements, with helmets, cuirasses, thigh-pieces, spears, shields, maces, swords and pikes. They are arranged on wooden shelves as they would have been seen by knights suiting up for a joust in the Middle Ages. In the middle is François I's armour, worn by a mannequin, and its stuffed horse. This wing also has a rare collection of Oriental feudal weapons and armour. Pride of place goes to a Turkish helmet large enough to fit over a turban, and a wall of samurai swords.

The Turenne gallery, occupying the ground floor of the east side – the soldiers' old dining hall – displays

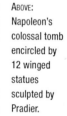

ABOVE: Napoleon's colossal tomb encircled by 12 winged statues sculpted by Pradier.

LEFT: Helmet with gryphon in embossed, engraved and gilded iron (*c.* 1545–1550).

FAR LEFT: *Napoleon on the Imperial Throne in Ceremonial Dress* by Ingres (*c.* 1804).

the flags, trophies and standards that men followed into war through the centuries. The oldest one (1619), at the entrance, is a flag sent to Grison, an allied principality, sporting a lion on its hind legs and the Latin motto "if God (i.e. the King of France) is with us, who can stand against us?"

The rooms on the second floor are arranged in chronological order: those devoted to the monarchy are followed by Napoleon's Italian and Egyptian campaigns, and room after room celebrating victories – Austerlitz, Jena, Borodino – and eventual defeat at Waterloo. The Army Museum is rarely crowded, but tourists and French schoolkids compete for elbow room around certain power objects of the nation's history, particularly in the Boulogne room, which contains Napoleon's coronation saddle, the sword that he wore at Austerlitz, his Légion d'Honneur sash, his signature grey overcoat and battered hat.

The humble drawing room, where he spent the last days of his life on St Helena, has been reconstructed with its original pair of fold-up beds. He died on one of them (probably of arsenic poisoning). Two remarkable portraits of Napoleon represent the high and low points of his megalomaniac career: *Napoleon on the Imperial Throne*, by Ingres (1804), and a painting by Delaroche, *Napoleon I in Fontainebleau*, after his first abdication (1814).

The world at war

The story of World War I is introduced with a fashion parade of uniforms, from those of the very first casualties to the gold-embroidered attire of generals Joffre, Pétain and Foch and the uniforms of

Verdun by Félix Vallotton (1917).

Americans and Commonwealth soldiers. One of the 2,300 French taxis used to transport French soldiers to the Front is a reminder as to just how close the Germans came to Paris in 1914. The collection of weapons includes a scale model of *Big Bertha*, a Taube airplane shot down in the war, and a 1917 Renault tank. A confusing set of models of the battlefield of Verdun doesn't quite make history's most terrible battle come alive. In an eerie semi-abstract painting of Verdun by Félix Vallotton (1865–1925), the landscape itself seems to be in mechanised conflict while clouds of poison gas have effaced the last soldiers.

The World War II section reopened in 2000 in renovated galleries and now exhibits about 1,000 objects and documents. The first rooms are something of a shrine to Charles de Gaulle, complete with his tank commander's leather jacket, first editions of his books and recordings of his speeches. There are on-screen encounters with members of the French resistance and display cases of anti-semitic propaganda. It makes heavy use of archival footage: in room after room, the great turning points of the war are replayed every five minutes. Sometimes they are juxtaposed to great effect – the battles of El Alamein, Stalingrad and Guadalcanal are shown at once on three adjoining screens.

Musée des Plans-Reliefs

The fourth floor displays a collection of scale models of French cities inside illuminated glass cases. Created between the 16th and 18th centuries, and astonishingly precise, these models of fortified cities were classified as military secrets. Many show the star-shaped ramparts created by Vauban, Louis XIV's military architect. St-Tropez, Brest, Strasbourg, Bordeaux, Metz and Mont St-Michel are revealed in miniature, street by street and house by house as they existed before the Revolution. The oldest model is of Perpignan (1686).

Musée de l'Ordre et de la Libération

In a separate wing (and for an additional fee), this museum commemorates the 1,036 soldiers honoured with the Ordre de la Libération medal created by General de Gaulle. The collection has expanded to include general exhibits about the Resistance and the deportations during German occupation. There are displays of clandestine paraphernalia, uniforms of the Free French forces, and photos from concentration camps and of the wartime struggle in French colonies in West and North Africa.

Such beautifully decorated carousels were the work of specialised artists.

FOOD AND DRINK: The market street of rue Cler, just a few blocks away, is a foodie's paradise. There are shops devoted to cheese, bread, wine, charcuterie and chocolate, and opportunities for a lunch at **Café du Marché** *or* **La Crêperie** *(both no. 9) or* **Tarte Julie** *(no. 6). See also Musée Rodin, page 95, and Musée des Egouts, page 172.*

Musée des Arts Forains

All the fun of the fair

Map reference: page 43, H5
Les Pavillons de Bercy
53 av des Terroirs de France, 12th
Tel: 01 43 40 16 22/01 43 40 16 15
www.pavillons-de-bercy.com
Metro: Cour St-Emilion. Bus: 24, 62
Open by appointment only for groups of 15 or more. Wheelchair access. Admission charge.

The main drawback of this museum is having to reserve for a group in order to visit. Otherwise, part of the fun is getting there – the fully automated metro line 14, Meteor, goes straight to the newly developed neighbourhood of Bercy, the so-called "New Left Bank".

The museum's artefacts are the result of life-long collecting by Jean-Paul Favand, an antiques dealer, who in 1996 was able to acquire the Pavillons de Bercy (an 18th-century wine depot) to house his collection. His desire to re-create a fairground as a poetic universe, rather than a technological one, has resulted in a gleaming museum, with 19th-century carousels, amusement stalls, organs, stage sets and other attractions that not only function, but are pure works of art.

During the 19th century, specialised artists primarily from France, Switzerland, Belgium and Britain, worked on carousels, reproducing Baroque, Louis XV or Art Nouveau styles that are all represented in the collection. The 1897 bicycle carousel (riders must pedal to make the carousel turn!) was a joint British and Belgian production. Exotic carousel creatures hang from a wall, casting mysterious shadows. Nearby is a set of German swings with beautifully painted backdrops of Venice. In another section, a magnificent Art Deco organ and other mechanical instruments are featured alongside fairground games and mechanical figures.

FOOD AND DRINK: On the Cour St-Emilion, the **Vinéa Café** *(26–28 Cour St-Emilion, 12th; tel: 01 44 74 09 09; moderate) is a modern brasserie, at its most pleasant during the summer months when the terrace can be used. Next door, at* **Nicolas** *(24 Cour St-Emilion; tel: 01 43 40 12 11; moderate), part of the wine store chain, you can have a glass of any wine from their cellar to accompany your dinner. Good cheese platters, nice atmosphere.*

From Top to Bottom: *René de Birague* by Germain Pilon, 16th century; *Cecilia of Gonzaga* (recto) and a *Unicorn* (verso) by Pisanello,15th century.

Cabinet des Monnaies et Médailles

A hoard of medals, medallions and antiquities housed within the hallowed walls of the old Bibliothèque Nationale

Map reference: page 40, E2
Bibliothèque Nationale Richelieu,
58 rue de Richelieu, 2nd
Tel: 01 47 03 83 30
Metro: Bourse. Bus: 39 and 48
Open: Mon–Fri 1–5.45pm, Sat
1–4.45pm, Sun noon–6pm; closed one
week in Sept, public hols.
Shop. Partial wheelchair access.
Group reservations (tel: 01 47 03 83 34).
Admission charge.

Tucked away on the first floor of the Bibliothèque Nationale Richelieu, which has become something of an anachronism since the opening of the vast new François Mitterrand library on the banks of the Seine *(see page 31)*, this museum doggedly continues its traditional role. The old library had been home to every book published in France since 1500, until most of the collection, one of the biggest in the world, was rehoused in the massive new premises at Tolbiac in 1996. The Richelieu library has kept the specialised departments of prints, drawings, maps, music and original manuscripts, whose contents are aired during temporary exhibitions *(for information about the exhibition spaces in both libraries, see page 133).* As you walk the corridors of the venerable institution, it is worth taking a discreet glance into the magnificent reading room designed by Henri Labrouste in 1863.

The museum's permanent collection is downstairs. The selection of coins and medals on display provide a panoramic view of world coinage and include some of the earliest known examples. Among the medals are the outstanding Renaissance works of court painter Pisanello (1395–1455), who was also a celebrated medallist.

Of more universal appeal are the antiquities in the collection, which includes Graeco-Roman sculpture and silverware, as well as vases and the exceptionally large Augustus Cameo. Curiosities include Dagobert's throne, on which the kings of France were crowned, and Charlemagne's chess set.

Food and Drink: For a stylish designer crowd head for Willi's Wine Bar (15 rue des Petits Champs, 1st; tel: 01 42 96 37 86; moderate), but for a more wholesome French experience, the brasserie Gallopin (40 rue Notre-Dame-des-Victoires, 2nd; tel: 01 42 36 45 38; moderate) is a better bet.

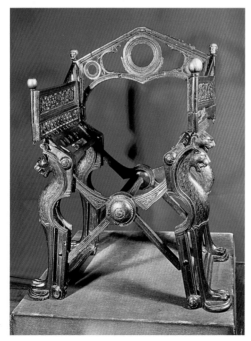

King Dagobert's throne (7th century).

Les Catacombes de Paris

The neatly stacked bones of six million Parisians – not for the faint-hearted

Map reference: page 43, E5
1 place Denfert-Rochereau
Tel: 01 43 22 47 63
Metro, RER: Denfert-Rochereau. Bus: 38, 68.
Open: Tues 11am–4pm, Wed–Sun 9am–4pm;
closed Mon. Admission charge.

The unassuming entrance to the Paris catacombs is through a small pavilion on the large place Denfert-Rochereau. A spiral stairway (90 steps) descends 20 metres (66 ft) underground into an exhibition area that presents a history of the

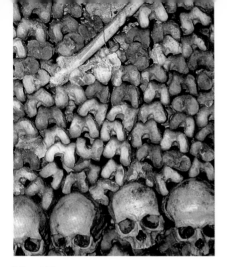

Spine-chilling entrance to the catacombs.

reflect upon man's destiny. Not everyone has felt squeamish about fraterninsing with the dead. Wild parties used to be thrown here before the Revolution, and during World War II the catacombs were the headquarters of the French resistance.

*FOOD AND DRINK: Just off av General Leclerc is the rue Daguerre, a pedestrian street filled with cafés, including **La Chope Daguerre** (17 rue Daguerre, 14th; tel: 01 43 22 76 59; moderate) for honest café fare and a terrace for people-watching, and **Enzo** (59 rue Daguerre; tel: 01 43 21 66 66; inexpensive), a good, if cramped, Italian trattoria.*

catacombs accompanied by photographs. Unlike the catacombs of ancient Rome, which were specifically excavated for use as a Christian cemetery, the Paris catacombs were the result of a sanitation campaign at the end of the 18th century. The Cemetery of the Innocents, in what is now the Les Halles area, had been home to the dead of the city centre's 20 parishes since Merovingian times.

Overcrowding and the stench finally persuaded city officials to move the remains to the hollowed-out galleries of what had been limestone quarries used to build Paris. The gruesome task of transferring bones and bodies began in 1786 and continued on a regular basis throughout the 19th century. In 1810, Héricart de Thury, the General Inspector of Quarries under Napoleon I, improved the layout adding 800 metres (2,600 ft) of galleries, and putting in headstones, crosses and inscriptions.

Low-ceilinged tunnels leading to the ossuary are marked with signs indicating the streets above. A black line on the ceiling, which helped 19th-century visitors find their way before electricity was installed, remains. The entrance, when you finally reach it, is flanked by black and white painted pillars. The chilling inscription over the doorway, "ARRÊTE, C'EST ICI L'EMPIRE DE LA MORT" (Stop, you are entering the empire of death), adds to the general ghoulishness. Take a torch – and someone to hold your hand.

The bones are so neatly stacked that you might be forgiven for thinking they were organised by compulsively tidy workmen. Walls of decoratively arranged femurs and tibias interspaced with skulls line the passageways, and stone plaques indicate the cemetery of origin and the date that the remains were transferred. Throughout the galleries, various plaques in French and Latin reproduce texts that

Musée de la Contrefaçon

A quirky collection of fakes and forgeries

Map reference: page 42, B3
16 rue de la Faisanderie, 16th
Tel: 01 45 01 51 11
Metro: Porte Dauphine. Bus: 52, PC
Open: Tues–Sun 2–5.30pm; closed Mon and public hols. Bookshop. Guided tours (by reservation only). Admission charge.

Fearless fakes (designated by red labels) of designer clothes, purses and perfumes are on view in this elegant townhouse at the edge of the Bois du Boulogne – all displayed next to the real thing (green labels). The oldest known fake is the stopper of a Roman amphora which claims, falsely, that the wine in the amphora is from Sicily rather than Marseille. From Cartier watches to oil pumps, 500-franc notes to Barbie dolls, nothing is sacred. Even the humble Bic razor is a gleam in the counterfeiter's eye. All of the fakes in the museum have been successfully passed off as real. Many of them are really just cheap imitations that appropriate a name and/or logo such as the counterfeit Greek Cointreau (or ex-Yugoslavia's Cointreau), or the Game Child that looks exactly like a Game Boy.

The museum is amusing to look at but serious in intent. It is funded by the French manufacturers' union, the aim of which is to raise awareness of the problem. It notes that half of all French businesses have been the object of some form of counterfeit-related fraud and that the phenomenon threatens jobs in France and the safety of consumers.

*FOOD AND DRINK: **Oum El Banine** (16bis rue Dufrenoy, 16th; tel: 01 45 04 91 22; moderate). Serves Moroccan haute cuisine. Pigeon pastilla, lamb baked in a clay oven, couscous and tagines are all formidable.*

Musée des Egouts de Paris

The sights and smells of the Paris sewer – an underground museum full of surprising facts about waste and water

Map reference: page 42, D3
Pont de l'Alma, opposite 93 quai d'Orsay, 7th
Tel: 01 53 68 27 81. www.mairie-paris.fr/musees
Metro: Alma-Marceau. RER: Pont de l'Alma
Bus: 42, 63, 89, 92
Open: Sat–Wed 11am–5pm May 1–Sept 30,
11am–4pm Oct 1–Apr 30; closed for 3 weeks in
Jan. Shop. Admission charge.

Paris, which grew from a population of 250,000 in the 16th century to 1 million in 1845, was one of Europe's foulest-smelling cities until engineer Eugène Belgrand and Baron Haussmann, Prefect of the Seine under Napoleon III, created a new network which provided the framework for the existing sewer *(égout)*. Construction began in 1857 and within two decades 600 km (373 miles) of sewers had been built. Today, the vast network of tunnels covers 2,100 km (1,305 miles). It follows the exact route of the streets and boulevards above ground and is even marked with the corresponding street names, making it easier for the crews of sewer workers to find their way around.

Once you have come to terms with the idea that a museum devoted to a sewer system might be a bit smelly (it is, but not unbearably so) and claustrophobic, a tour of the city's underworld is a surprisingly entertaining experience. The entrance to the museum is next to the Pont l'Alma, on the left bank of the river in a very chic part of town. Corridors lead down into a universe that has become a reference point for modern cities. Huge water mains overhead line the stone corridors, and great iron dredging and cleaning contraptions, such as the "machine gun" and "flusher trolley", are exhibited. A series of passages leads you to the Galerie Belgrand, an exhibition space with sewage water flowing underfoot.

Panels hanging from the centre of the gallery explain the history of waste management, in English and French, starting with the Roman settlement of Lutetia, with a population of 6,000. Victor Hugo's descriptions of the sewers in *Les Misérables* are of real historical value – one of Hugo's close acquaintances worked on the sewer system. Models of dredgers in plexiglass boxes hanging from cables are interspersed between the panels.

You learn, among other things, what happens every time you have a shower or flush the toilet. Apparently, there is one rat for every human inhabitant above ground. They reduce solid waste by 50 percent but are a real hazard to the sewer workers.

The detailed information about today's computerised system will be of interest to the more technically minded. There is also a display of objects recovered by sewer workers over the years and, to end your visit, a slide show is given in the room next to the gift shop.

Inspecting the cables and pipes of the sewer system beneath Place du Châtelet (photo 1960).

*FOOD AND DRINK: Restaurants in the immediate area are expensive and it's worth walking to rue St-Dominique, where there are a few traditional, moderately priced restaurants, and shops and bakeries galore. **Thoumieux** (79 rue St-Dominique, 7th; tel: 01 47 05 49 75; moderate) serves good traditional French fare, including cassoulet. During the summer, terrace seating at the bistro **La Fontaine de Mars** (129 rue St-Dominique, 7th; tel: 01 47 05 46 44; moderate) is very pleasant. Expect traditional staples like snail and black pudding (boudin), and good wine from the Cahors region.*

One of the quirkier installations in the museum of erotic art.

Musée de la Franc-Maçonnerie

The arcane world of French freemasonry

Map reference: page 42, F2
16 rue Cadet, 9th
Tel: 01 45 23 20 92
Metro: Cadet. Bus: 74
Open: Tues–Sat 2–6pm; closed Mon, Sun, public hols. Shop. Wheelchair access. Guided tours and groups by appointment. Admission charge.

Musée de l'Erotisme

Erotic art from Pigalle to Peru

Map reference: page 42, E2
72 blvd de Clichy, 18th
Tel: 01 42 58 28 73
Metro: Blanche. Bus: 30, 54, 74, 80, 95
Open: daily 10am–2am
Shop. Admission charge.

The erotic museum is not a sex shop in disguise but a serious (well, semi-serious) collection of erotic art, with 2,000-plus objects ranging from the precious to the tasteless. Indeed, the museum has received support from the local administration and tries hard be an art gallery of sorts. Marble stairs link seven floors and everything is precision-lit.

The objects on display are from all over the world: African fertility fetishes, titillating Thai terracottas, phallic votives, X-rated films from the silent era, contorted illustrations from the *Kama Sutra*, and a diverse collection of painting, sculpture and photographs from the sacred to the profane. The Japanese *netsuke* are a star attraction as are the depictions of gay Aztec men and Hindu temple friezes of acrobatic couplings.

It is striking how much of the erotic art is non-Western. But Paris does finally assert itself in exhibits and photos from 19th-century brothels. Of particular interest are some monotypes of brothel life by Edgar Dégas, depicting, among other things, *L'Arrivée d'une Habitué* (The Arrival of a Regular).

The museum organises two exhibitions of contemporary erotic art a year.

FOOD AND DRINK: see Espace Salvador Dali, page 154, and Musée de la Vie Romantique, page 160.

A short visit to this museum in the French Masonic Lodge (Le Grand Orient de France) might shed some light on the esoteric world of freemasonry. Documents trace the history of "the Order" in France and explain masonic symbolism and grades (in French). The origins of freemasonry are traced to the medieval stonemasons' guilds, but somewhere between 1550 and 1700 it began to attract intellectuals and philosophers. Lafayette was a dedicated freemason, as were Napoleon's brother, Joseph, and 19th-century politicos, Léon Gambetta and Jules Ferry.

French freemasons have been do-gooders more often than not, and they tried to save Paris from bloodshed during the Commune uprising in 1871. Their pacifism and secrecy made them sinister to the Nazis, who persecuted them. A document records the 1877 decision to drop the requirement that freemasons believe in God and the immortality of the soul (roughly replaced by "absolute freedom of conscience and human solidarity"). If you speak French, you can even attend a meeting, by arrangement, as a non-initiate.

BELOW: Freemason's snuffbox; ceremonial reception of new "masters" to the lodge.

FOOD AND DRINK: see Musée Grévin, page 174.

Assemblée de Francs-Maçons pour la réception des Maîtres

Larger than life jazz legend, Louis Armstrong.

Musée Grévin

The world's oldest waxworks gallery

Map reference: page 41, E1
10 bd Montmartre, 9th
Tel: 01 47 70 85 05. www.musee-grevin.com
Metro: Cadet, Gds Boulevards. Bus: 39, 42, 48, 49.
Open: daily 10am–7pm
Book and gift shop. Wheelchair access.
Admission charge.

The Grévin Museum came into being when journalist Arthur Meyer asked Alfred Grévin, a draughtsman and caricaturist, to produce figures of celebrities in wax. At that time there were no filmed or photographic reports and the Grévin display became known as a "plastic newspaper".

The century-old waxworks gallery enjoys a sumptuous setting. The lavish confection of Louis XIV and Venetian rococo, rosewood and marble was designed in 1882. The staircase by Rives is an architectural gem. Following its extensive renovation programme (at a cost of 8 million euros), the museum now prefers to call itself a "cultural entertainment site". A wax figure of Ernest Hemingway (1899–1961), drink in hand, is one of 80 new faces. French football heroes, Zidane and Barthez, also get star billing, as well as the improbably endowed computer game heroine, Lara Croft.

However, real-life French actress Sophie Marceau refused to sit for the museum ("You can melt… and you're in the dark all the time.").

The figures in wax are lifelike enough to distract you from their celebrity status since no one can help noticing Napoleon's double chin, Clark Gable's blackheads or Gandhi's scabrous knee. The new faces, though welcome, don't upstage the older wax figures of France's grisly, glorious history, which suffer through medieval plagues and tortures, philosophise in a salon, build barricades and prepare to die on the guillotine.

*Food and Drink: **Chartier** (7 rue du Faubourg-Montmartre, 9th; tel: 01 47 70 86 29; inexpensive). Cheap and cheerful old brasserie that attracts students and tourists, where the surly waiters famously tot up the bill on the paper tablecloths.*

It may not be as popular as Madame Tussaud's, but the Musée Grevin was the waxworks pioneer.

Musée de l'Histoire de France

Highlights from the national archives in rococo rooms

Map reference: page 41, G3
Hôtel de Soubise, 60 rue des Archives, 3rd
Tel: 01 40 27 60 96
www.archivesnationales.culture.gouv.fr/chan
Metro: Hôtel de Ville, Rambuteau. Bus: 29, 75
Open: Mon, Wed–Fri 10am–5.45pm, Sat, Sun
1.45–5.45pm; closed Tues, public hols.
Concerts. Guided tours. Admission charge.

The national archives and museum of French history are housed in an 18th-century mansion in the heart of the Marais.

Rising at the end of a grandiose arcaded *cour d'honneur*, the Hôtel de Soubise was built for the Prince de Soubise in the early 18th century and became the home of the newly created Archives Nationaux shortly after the French Revolution. The museum was founded by Napoleon III in 1867 and is currently being renovated with a view to a new presentation focusing on the different interpretations of French history by various historians and writers.

In the meantime, a selection from the national archives, which possesses documents from the 7th century to the present, are displayed in roughly chronological order, covering not just political events and ground-breaking decrees, but also the sort of incident that builds up an idea of the social issues of the time: on the one hand, a circular sent out by Louis IX in 1226 inviting the barons to his coronation in Reims and the founding charter of the Sorbonne; on the other, a document recording the discovery of an abandoned child in 1676, together with the ribbon that had been tied round his leg, and an *ordonnance* about the use of umbrellas. Official decrees are set in context with hand-drawn maps, fashion plates and popular prints, as well as curiosities such as a poster announcing an eclipse or the glove worn by the man who tried to assassinate Louis XV. Documents relating to the Wars of Religion and the French Revolution are displayed with patriotic postcards from World War I and a Jew's yellow star from World War II.

All explanations (and, of course, documents) are in French, so you need a fairly good reading knowledge of the language to appreciate the subtleties, but the museum is also worth visiting to see the rococo interiors. These were decorated in the 1730s by the best painters and craftsmen of the day, on the occasion of the marriage of Prince and Princesse de Soubise. Downstairs, the prince's apartments are relatively restrained, though the oval salon has remarkable plaster allegorical reliefs of poetry, justice, music, etc. Upstairs, the princess's apartments are a glittery feast of rocaille motifs, gilding, stucco reliefs and painted overdoors by Boucher, Van Loo, Natoire and Trémolières, especially the Chambre de Parade de la Princesse and the light-filled oval salon, which has gilded putti and canvases by Natoire depicting the misadventures of Psyche.

Food and Drink: Le Bouquet des Archives (31 rue des Archives, 4th; tel: 01 42 72 08 49; inexpensive) is a friendly, colourful corner café adorned with modern art and pot plants and does a roaring lunchtime trade in salads and generous plats du jour. See also Musée Carnavalet, page 54, and Musée Picasso, page 92.

Musée de la Légion d'Honneur

Fine portraiture and elaborate chains of honour in a Marais mansion

Map reference: page 40, C3
2 rue de la Légion d'Honneur, 7th
Tel: 01 40 62 84 25
Metro: Solférino. RER: Musée d'Orsay. Bus: 24,
73, 68. Open: Tues–Sun 11am–5pm; closed Mon
and public hols.
Shop. Groups by prior arrangement.
Admission charge.

Just opposite the entrance to the Orsay museum is one of the capital's most under-visited museums. It is housed in the east wing of the lavishly decorated Hotel de Salm, worth visiting just to see the spectacular rotunda overlooking the Seine.

The Légion d'Honneur was instituted in 1802 by Napoleon, whose fine portrait by Antoine-Jean Gros is one of the highlights of the museum. The idea was to restore to post-revolutionary France an honours system worthy of the country. The painting by Jean-Baptiste Debret of the first presentation by Napoleon at les Invalides looks a regal event at odds with the republican ethos behind such an accolade. Earlier orders of merit are also explored, dating from the first French order, L'Ordre de St Louis, which was established by Louis XIV in 1693.

The luxurious costumes of these early ceremonial events are on display beside paintings depicting the investitures, with particularly fine canvases by Van Loo and Pierre-Hubert Subleyras, dating from the first half of the 18th century. More recent times are movingly invoked by a gallery dedicated to World War I, featuring medals and artists' representations of heroic courage. The museum is being fully modernised for the 2002 bicentenary of the Légion d'Honneur.

FOOD AND DRINK: Ignoring the tourist-orientated cafés that surround the Musée d'Orsay, head off for an elegant drink at the fashionable **Hotel Le Montalembert** *(3 rue de Montalembert, 7th; tel: 01 45 49 69 49; expensive), or a fine traditional meal in the best riverside restaurant in Paris,* **Le Voltaire** *(27 quai Voltaire, 7th; tel: 01 42 61 17 49; moderate); the latter also runs a café next door, serving light meals and drinks.*

Musée de la Magie

Now you see it, now you don't...

Map reference: page 41, H4
11 rue St-Paul, 4th
Tel: 01 42 72 13 26. www.museedelamagie.com
Metro: St Paul. Bus: 69, 76
Open: Wed, Sat, Sun 2–7pm; closed July and Aug. Shop. Admission charge.

A steep staircase directly off the street leads down into a 16th-century cellar with vaulted ceilings, crammed with 3,000 objects and documents tracing 200 years of the history of magic and illustrating the conjurer's art. The unusual collection of objects was assembled by renowned magician Georges Proust (a descendant of Marcel) and is playfully presented across a series of themed rooms. Secret boxes, handcuffs, magic wands and other tricks of the trade are displayed in glass cases; an impressive collection of 19th-century mechanical figures takes up a section of its own. One room is devoted to optical illusions, another to Grandes Illusions – the age-old classics of death- and gravity-defying tricks, the most universal of which must be the sawing in half of the magician's assistant.

Visitors are given a talk on the history of magic (in French), and a fairly basic magic show is staged. If your French is up to it, you can even join the Ecole de Magie, where classes for beginners and the more advanced are held every Saturday. The museum shop sells books and tricks for budding magicians.

FOOD AND DRINK: There is no end to the number of restaurants in the area, but two that are located a few feet away from the museum are good options. **Le Rouge-Gorge** *(8 rue St-Paul, 4th; tel: 01 48 04 75 89; inexpensive), a rustic bistro, has food from Southern France and good Corsican wines.* **Thanksgiving** *(20 rue St-Paul, 4th; tel: 01 42 77 68 28; moderate) serves home cooking Louisiana-style.*

The First Distribution of Crosses of the Legion of Honour, 14th July 1804, by Jean-Baptiste Debret (1812).

Musée de la Marine

The history of France as a seafaring nation

Map reference: page 42, C3
Palais de Chaillot, place du Trocadéro, 16th
Tel: 01 53 65 69 69. www.musee-marine.fr
Metro: Trocadéro. Bus: 22, 30, 63
Open: Mon, Wed–Sun 10am–6pm; closed Tues.
Shop. Admission charge.

Model of the ship *Louis XV*, burned by the English at the Battle of La Hogue (1692).

Battleships, cannon barrels and carved figure-heads of forbidding mythological women are a useful reminder to Parisian landlubbers of France's long maritime tradition. While naval warfare, Texel, Trafalgar et al loom large, the museum also treats navigation and seafaring in general.

The distance from the sea and constricted space mean that the focus of this rather strait-laced museum is inevitably, on models and paintings: therefore, the ornate *Canot de l'Empereur* (Imperial barge) is a particular treat. The dazzling white and gold vessel was built in a record 21 days in 1810 for Napoleon, who used it only once to visit the docks at Antwerp. Rowed by 28 oarsmen, the trident-bearing Neptune and sea monsters surge at the prow, while the cabin is surmounted by a crown borne by four cherubs. Its last voyage was in 1922 and it has been docked at the museum since 1945.

The marine paintings spread around the museum include battle scenes by Vignon, Isabey, Rossel, Crépin and Gudin, views of ports and portraits of admirals and explorers. The most outstanding works in the museum's art collection are undoubtedly Joseph Vernet's 13 large panoramic canvases of the principal ports of France. Commissioned in 1750 by the Marquis de Marigny, Director of the Buildings of France under Louis XV, they combine Vernet's almost documentary interest in topography as he faithfully recorded the urban landscape, with magnificent, luminous skies. The series includes *Antibes, Marseille, Toulon, Bayonne* and *Bordeaux*, although Vernet abandoned the project before completion.

Hundreds of ship models, often of superb craftsmanship, cover everything from historic battleships and three-masted schooners to langoustine fishing boats and primitive canoes. Among the particularly fine

models dating from the 17th and 18th century, are the intricately rigged *Louis le Grand* and the *Royal* – 1:12 scale models built for teaching purposes at the naval school at Rochefort. The display continues into the merchant navy with steamships and cargo vessels, followed by models and vintage posters of the luxury passenger liners, the *Normandie, Atlantique* and *Titanic*.

The development of modern marine warfare is traced from the first torpedoes, invented in the 18th century, to the rapid transformation of the navy at the end of the 19th century – from sailing fleet to battleships of World War I, to nuclear submarines and France's trouble-hit new aircraft carrier, *Charles de Gaulle*. Other displays take in navigational instruments, including finely painted compasses, brass sextants and pocket sundials, sections about ship-building and rope-making, whale teeth engraved by prisoners and giant lighthouse lenses.

A large window looks onto the restoration workshop, where you can watch models being made and repaired.

*FOOD AND DRINK: **Le Totem Restaurant** at Musée de l'Homme, see page 193.*

Tilting compass, 18th century.

Musée de la Monnaie de Paris

French coinage through the ages, traced in the city's former mint

Map reference: page 40, E4
11 quai de Conti, 6th
Tel: 01 40 46 55 35. www.finances.gouv.fr
Metro: Odéon. Bus: 70, 24 or 27
Open: Tues–Fri 11am–5.30pm, Sat–Sun noon–5.30pm; closed Mon. Visits to the workshop by appointment Wed and Fri at 2.15pm. Shop. Admission charge.

With the arrival of the euro, French coinage turned a decisive page in its history, which began in around 300 BC and is traced with admirable clarity in this ancient mint. The building commissioned by Louis XV and completed in 1777 is a remarkable Neo-classical mansion on the banks of the Seine, with sober austere lines by the architect Jacques-Denis Antoine. The minting of French currency has long since moved out of the capital, but official weights and measures are still made in the workshops, which can be visited by prior arrangement. The most interesting of the collections on display are the medals of Pierre-Jean David d'Angers. Excellent audio-visual aids and exemplary presentation make this a compelling visit.

*FOOD AND DRINK: Timeless wine bar **Taverne Henri IV** (13 place Pont Neuf, 1st; tel: 01 43 54 27 90; inexpensive) serves a selection of open sandwiches and carefully chosen wines. For a more international feel, try the converted nightclub **Alcazar** (62 rue Mazarine, 6th; tel: 01 53 10 19 99; moderate), Sir Terence Conran's contribution to Parisian gastronomy.*

Musée Jean Moulin

Jean Moulin (1899–1943), a national hero remembered in street and school names throughout France.

Documents and footage of the liberation of France by French forces and the Resistance

Map reference: page 42, D5
23 allée de la 2e DB, 15th, Montparnasse station
Tel: 01 40 64 39 44
Metro: Montparnasse-Bienvenue. Bus: 91, 92, 95, 96, 28, 58
Open: Tue–Sun 10am–5.40pm; closed Mon. Shop. Research facilities/library. Admission free.

This is not the easiest of museums to find, as its location in the Jardin Atlantique, above Montparnasse mainline station, is quite unexpected (you walk through the station to reach the stairs that lead up to it). It is shared by two national heroes – as revealed by its rather wordy full title: *Mémorial du Maréchal Leclerc de Hauteclocque et de la Libération de Paris & Musée Jean Moulin*. General Leclerc was the aristocrat from northern France who liberated Paris and it was Jean Moulin, a southern republican, who spearheaded resistance to the German occupation.

The memorial museum was opened in 1994 to mark the 50th anniversary of the Liberation of Paris. French texts and documents (most of them with English translation) chart the wartime course of Leclerc's victories and Moulin's underground movement. On the first floor, the liberation of Paris is replayed every 15 minutes as a montage of archival footage flashes across a panorama of 14 screens. The insurrection launched by Colonel Rol-Tanguy, commander of the FFI and resistance forces in Paris, cuts to the liberation of the city by Leclerc and the Americans and celebrations interrupted by German snipers.

Jean Moulin has come to embody the ideals of the French republic. The exhibits explore his different facets as a man, artist, prefect, resistance

leader and martyr. But there is no attempt to probe one of the great mysteries of Resistance historiography: who betrayed him to the Gestapo?

More documents and displays on the French Resistance and World War II can be seen the Army Museum *(see page 167)* and the Musée de la Resistance in Champigny *(see page 203)*.

FOOD AND DRINK: See Musée Bourdelle, page 153, and Musée de la Poste, page 180.

Musée de Notre-Dame de Paris

History of a Gothic masterpiece

Map reference: page 41, F4
10 rue du Cloître Notre-Dame, 4th
Tel: 01 43 25 42 92
Metro: Cité or St-Michel-Notre-Dame. Bus: 24, 38, 47, 96
Open: Wed, Sat–Sun 2.30–6pm and public hols. Admission charge.

T he modest exhibits on display offer a fragmented look at the history of France's most famous cathedral. It was here on the Ile de la Cité that Paris began. The island on the Seine was first settled by a Celtic tribe, the Parisii. Centuries later, the Romans realised the advantage of the position and developed the settlement for themselves. The oldest displays are of Gallo-Roman relics dug up in the cathedral square, in the form of pottery, coins and jewellery. Those who want to delve deeper into the city's early history should visit the Musée Carnavalet *(see page 47)* and the Musée des Antiquités Nationales *(see page 198)*.

A Dutch painting from the mid-17th century provides the earliest impression of the cathedral interior, which then looked like a gloomy art gallery with pictures hanging from every column. A series of etchings portray it in a different light, as a vast, splendid theatre for public prayer and processions.

Although the Revolution stripped Notre-Dame of its artistic treasure (and briefly rededicated it as a "temple of reason"), it soon resumed its role as the parish church of France. An engraving depicts the coronation of Napoleon on 2 December 1804.

The occupational hazards of being an archbishop in revolutionary Paris are well documented. In 1848, the peacemaking Monseigneur Affrée

climbed the barricades in Faubourg St-Antoine and was mortally wounded. Monseigneur Sibour was stabbed at St-Etienne-du-Mont during the Ste-Geneviève procession. Lastly, Monseigneur Darboy was taken hostage, incarcerated and executed during the Communard uprising in 1871.

Old lithographs reveal Notre-Dame as being at the centre of a densely populated medieval quarter dotted with small churches (St-Barthélémy, St-Denis-de-la-Chartre, St-Germain-le-Vieux, St-Landry, etc.). Apart from the cathedral, virtually all of it was razed during Haussmann's modernisation of the city in the 19th century. A letter signed by Victor Hugo (who had recently published *The Hunchback of Notre-Dame*) and Ingres, among others, recalls the campaign which resulted in the restoration of the cathedral from 1854 to 1864. An interesting watercolour dated 1839 shows a view of the southern façade before Gothic revivalist, Eugène Viollet-le-Duc, began restoration work. Viollet not only restored the cathedral, he also devoted himself to the repair of its furniture and religious objects.

FOOD AND DRINK: Les Bouchons de François Clerc (12 rue de l'Hôtel-Colbert, 4th; tel: 01 43 54 15 34; moderate) serves classic French food on the Left Bank with a list of 75 wines and champagnes. See also Musée Adam Mickiewcz, page 158.

GOTHIC SPLENDOUR

Paris has two of the finest Gothic churches in the Western world, both on the Ile de la Cité. The construction of **Notre-Dame Cathedral** *(open daily 8am–6.45pm; admission free)* began in 1163 on the site of a Romanesque church that had been built on the foundations of a Carolingian basilica, which in turn had been built on the site of a Roman temple. It took 200 years and several generations of architects and craftsmen to finish. Its twin towers and spire soar to the heavens with dramatic grace, and the magnificent rose windows, portals and flying buttresses are the hallmarks of its elegant beauty. Like all medieval churches, Notre-Dame was painted on the inside as a means for a largely illiterate population to learn the Bible stories. The use of colour was meant to glorify God and breathe life into the sculptures.

Across from Notre-Dame is the Palais de Justice, behind whose imposing walls lies the **Sainte-Chapelle** *(open daily 9.30am–6pm in summer, 10am–5pm in winter; admission free)*. This fragile-looking chapel in High Gothic style was built to shelter the Crown of Thorns, bought from the Emperor of Constantinople by Louis IX. The interior is bathed in coloured light shed by 15 magnificent stained-glass windows, depicting over 1,000 scenes from the Bible.

Musée de la Poste

Transportation of the written word through the ages and a survey of French philately

Map reference: page 40, A6
34 bd de Vaugirard, 15th
Tel: 01 42 79 23 45. www.laposte.fr/musee
Metro: Pasteur, Montparnasse. Bus: 28, 48, 89,
91, 92, 94, 96
Open: Mon–Sat 10am–6pm; closed Sun and
public hols. Shop. Wheelchair access. Research
facilities/library. Admission charge.

Occupying several floors of a forbidding building near the Maine-Montparnasse complex, the Postal Museum presents a surprisingly dynamic collection of postal paraphernalia. Run by the state postal service, it explores the different and often ingenious methods used for the delivery of written communications through the centuries. Take the lift to the fifth floor and work your way through 4,000 years of postal delivery from foot messengers and horses, stagecoaches and sailboats, to steamships, trains and planes. Dogcarts, stilts and pneumatic tubes were among the more unorthodox methods used. During the siege of Paris in the Franco-Prussian war (1870–71), mail was secreted out of the besieged city in bottles floated down the Seine, by loyal carrier pigeons, and in hot-air balloons.

A fine collection of French and foreign stamps invites perusal, alongside other exhibits such as post-boxes and uniforms.

*Food and Drink: **Ty Breiz** (52 bd de Vaugirard, 15th; tel: 01 43 20 83 72; inexpensive). Sweet and savoury crêpes washed down with a bowl of cider.*

Above: Elaborately engraved model of a postal wagon (1844).

Right: *The Semaphore of Love*, coloured engraving (late 18th–early 19th century).

France's answer to Jack the Ripper – serial killer Henri Landru pictured here in 1921 just before his execution for the murder of ten women.

trials of the century for the murder of a *demimondaine*, her maid and 11-year old daughter.

Moving into the 20th century, exhibits show the development of investigative policing, with early photos of crime scenes, mug shots and case notes of convicted murderers next to their murder weapons. The display of anti-Nazi propaganda posters next to orders for the detainment of Parisian Jews speaks volumes about Paris' role in World War II.

FOOD AND DRINK: For fresh fish and vast seafood platters try **Le Bar à Huîtres** *(33 rue St-Jacques, 5th; tel: 01 44 07 27 37; moderate). See also Musée du Moyen Age, page 81.*

Musée de la Préfecture de Police

Parisian crime and punishment

Map reference: page 42, F4
Hôtel de Police, 1 bis, rue des Carmes, 5th
Tel: 01 44 41 52 50
Metro: Maubert Mutualité. Bus: 24, 47, 63, 86, 87.
Open: Mon–Fri, 9am–5pm and Sat 10am–5pm.
Admission free.

Make your way past the officers on duty to the second floor of this 5th *arrondissement* police station. The no-frills display of documents, engravings, posters, photos, uniforms, murder weapons and other crime- and punishment-related objects is presented in chronological order to illustrate key events in the history of the Paris police from the 17th century to the present day.

Among the documents and decrees from the revolutionary period you can find Louis XVI's court summons and a prison register with Danton's name alongside arrest warrants and execution certificates, a guillotine blade, ration cards, and engravings of fires, massacres and barricades in the city streets. In spite of the dryness of the display, this section gives you a real sense of the violence, chaos and fear that reigned in revolutionary Paris.

Highlights of the 19th-century section include a reproduction of Giuseppe Fieschi's *Machine Infernal* – a line of gun barrels used in the Corsican revolutionary's assassination attempt against King Louis-Philippe in 1835. Leering from a glass case is the gruesome wax model of the head of Italian aristocrat Pranzini, a notorious swindler, seductor and murderer who was condemned to death in 1888 in one of the great show

Musée du Service de Santé des Armées

Moving testament of medical history as seen through the eyes of the army

Map reference: page 42, E5
Place Alphonse-Laveran, 5th
Tel: 01 40 51 40 00
Metro: Gobelins. RER: Port-Royal. Bus: 83, 91, 38.
Open: Tues–Wed noon–5pm, Sat 1–5pm, Sun 1.30–5pm; closed Mon, Thur and Fri.
Admission charge.

Behind the magnificent Val de Grâce church is an ancient Benedictine convent, which Anne of Austria used as a second royal residence. It was here that she vowed to build a magnificent church if God blessed her with a son. In 1638, after 21 years of marriage, she gave birth to the future Louis XIV. True to her word, seven years later, the future king, accompanied by his mother, laid the first stone of the church, which was designed by Mansart and later finished by Lemercier. It was not until the Revolution that the convent was taken over and used as a military hospital; it is this medical history that is celebrated in the museum.

A potentially maudlin subject is rendered fascinating by the recently restored collection. The need for field treatment and the sheer number of casualties in World War I forced the pace of medical progress, though re-creations of early trench hospitals and emergency rooms show the shocking conditions under which the army medical corps wor' These exhibits are supported by some goo' screen computer displays (in French) antique medical instruments and a f pharmacy jars are beautifully pres moving sketches of war. If you can form a group and reserve in advance, it is possible to extend your tour to the rooms of the ancient convent.

FOOD AND DRINK: Sample an aperitif in the atmospheric Closerie des Lilas (171 bd du Montparnasse, 6th; tel: 01 40 51 34 50; expensive), one of Ernest Hemingway's favourite spots. Nearby is one of the best wine bars-cum-restaurants on the Left bank, Le Mauzac (7 rue de l'Abbé de l'Epée, 5th; tel: 01 46 53 75 22; inexpensive), with a delightful terrace on a quiet, tree-lined street.

Musée du Vieux Montmartre

Memories of Bohemian Montmartre

Map reference: page 42, E1
12 rue Cortot, 18th
Tel: 01 46 06 61 11
Metro: Lamarck-Caulaincourt. Bus: 64, 80.
Open: Tues–Sun 11am–6pm; closed Mon.
Shop. Tour groups in English (advance reservations only). Admission charge.

If there is anything left of the "old Montmartre", of impoverished artists and writers, cabarets and brothels, it is this 17th-century manor, the oldest house on Butte Montmartre, an area once characterised by cottages and gardens. Set in a tranquil garden with a vineyard next door (the only one in Paris), it feels surprisingly out of the way, as most of Montmartre was in the days of Toulouse-Lautrec.

The main house was the home of Roze de Rosimond, an actor in Molière's theatre company. Like his master, Rosimond died during a performance of *Le Malade Imaginaire* (The Hypochondriac). It is now a museum devoted to the old artists' community and its former inhabitants. Many artists had studios here, including Renoir, Dufy, Suzanne Valadon and her son Maurice Utrillo.

Although the museum contains no major works of art, it has several floors of minor paintings, documents and photographs that recall what life on the historic hilltop was like. Of course, most visitors are curious about Bohemian Montmartre, and its story can be pieced together from the memorabilia of artists who lived and worked on the *butte* (hill). The museum's pride and joy is Toulouse-Lautrec's famous poster *Le Moulin Rouge*, in which Louise

Detail from the lively *Parce Domine* fresco painted for Le Chat Noir, the famous Black Cat cabaret, by Adolphe Willette.

FAR LEFT: *Le Divan Japonais,* Toulouse-Lautrec, 1893.

LEFT: painted sign for Le Lapin Agile, a popular Montmartre haunt for struggling artists and writers.

Musée du Vin

Wine museum in the vaulted cellars of a former monastery

Map reference: page 42, C4
Rue des Eaux – 5 square Dickens, 16th
Tel: 01 45 25 63 26. www.museeduvinparis.com
Metro: Passy. RER: Tour Eiffel-Champ de Mars
Bus: 72
Open: Tues–Sun 10am–6pm; closed Mon.
Guided tours in English on reservation.
Admission fee includes a glass of wine.

Weber (known as La Goulue, or the Glutton) dances the can-can. You can no longer order an absinthe in the reconstructed interior of Utrillo's favorite café – l'Abreuvoir – but you can rub its rare 19th-century zinc countertop (almost all of the originals were seized by Germans during the Occupation for use in armaments) and eye an assortment of empty absinthe bottles. [For those curious about the history of this banned substance, there is an Absinthe Museum *(44 rue Callé, open: June–Sept Wed–Sun, Oct–May Sat–Sun 11am–6pm; tel: 01 30 36 83 26)* in Auvers-sur-Oise, a village 35 km (22 miles) north of Paris which attracted many artists, including Van Gogh.]

The other main focus of the museum is on the long, often brutal history of Montmartre. It is said that the Romans beheaded St Denis, the patron saint of France here. Legend has it that he got up and walked away carrying his own head. During the Middle Ages, the *butte* was occupied by a Benedictine abbey, which was destroyed during the Revolution. The last abbess, Marie-Louise de Montmorency-Laval, was sent to the guillotine despite being 71, deaf and blind. The land was then quarried for gypsum (plaster of Paris), which became the *butte's* major industry before tourism.

A couple of display cases are devoted to the Commune, the working-class uprising that began in Montmartre and ended with 20,000 summary executions in 1871, and to the construction of Sacré Coeur in the years that followed. Before leaving be sure to stop and take in the splendid views of Paris.

FOOD AND DRINK: Aux Négotiants (27 rue Lambert, 18th; inexpensive). Serves simple plats du jour, generally meat-based. See also Espace Salvador Dali, page 154.

Set in a quiet corner of the 16th *arrondisse-ment,* this little museum celebrates the age-old crafts and traditions of wine-making and is worth a detour for anyone with a passing interest in wine and the history of viticulture.

The collection of traditional tools used in all the wine-making processes – from planting and harvesting to coopering and bottling – and other wine-related objects are displayed in the limestone cellars of the former Passy monastery. This was built at the close of the 15th century by the Minim Friars, a mendicant order who cultivated vines on the Chaillot hillside. They produced a light red wine that Louis XIII apparently liked to drink on his way back from hunting in the Bois de Boulogne. Wine-making ceased here when the monastery was closed down during the Revolution,

The museum is owned and run by the Conseil des Echansons, an association that promotes France's wine producers. At the end of the tour, you are invited to enjoy a glass of wine and, if you have lunch here, entrance to the museum is free.

FOOD AND DRINK: The museum restaurant (reserve for lunch, tel as above; moderate) is set in the three arched rooms used by the Passy monks to store their wine. It's an à la carte menu of regional dishes. The kitchen closes for lunch at 3pm but the wine bar serves cold cuts and cheese platters with wine until closing time.

CIMETIÈRE DE MONTMARTRE

The Montmartre cemetery, just west of rue Lepic, reflects the artistic and theatrical past of the area. The tombs are elegantly sculpted and those buried beneath are appropriately famous. Here lie Stendhal (Henri Beyle), Alexandre Dumas, Degas, Nijinsky, Berlioz and Offenbach, the diva Dalida and director François Truffaut. Toulouse-Lautrec's can-can model, Louise Weber, is also buried here.

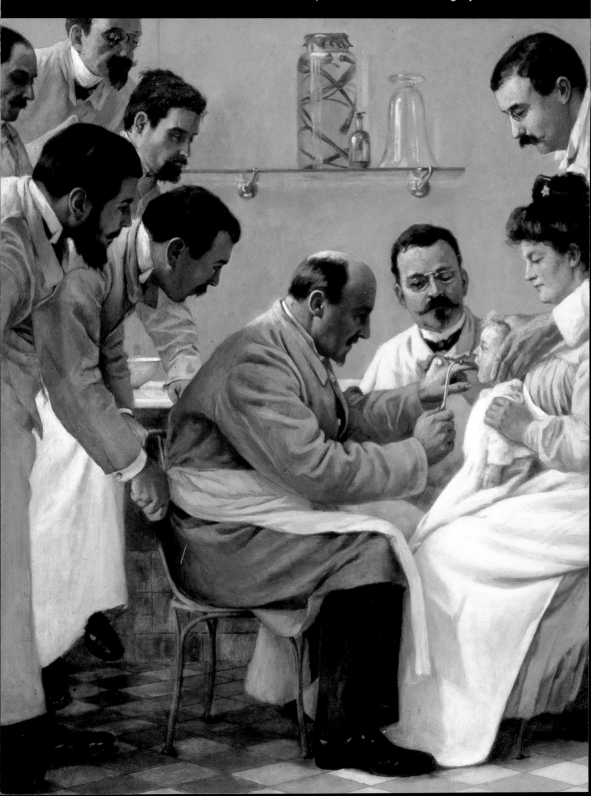

Science and Nature

Assorted museums of science, medecine, technology, natural history and anthropology, showcasing France's great achievements in scientific invention and discovery from Foucault's pendulum to the Mirage jet

Musée des Arts et Métiers

The oldest museum of science and technical innovation in Europe

Map reference: page 41, G2
60 rue Réaumur, 3rd
Tel: 01 53 01 82 00
www.cnam.fr
Metro: Arts et Métiers, Réaumur-Sébastopol
Bus: 27, 47
Open: Tues–Sun 10am–6pm, Thurs until
9.30pm. Wheelchair access. Research
facilities/library. Tour groups in English
(advance reservations). Admission charge.

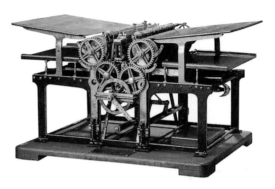

Edison's tin-sheet phonograph (1878).

This showcase of technical art and innovation is one of the most original museums in Paris, especially since its complete renovation in 2000. It belongs to the Conservatoire National des Arts et Métiers, a prestigious technical college founded by Abbot Henri Grégoire in 1794, during the height of the Terror which followed the Revolution. Grégoire was a man ahead of his time (and church), who agitated for the rights of French Jews and the abolition of slavery and signed the Declaration of the Rights of Man.

The museum is housed in the medieval Priory of St-Martin-des-Champs on the Right Bank, just north of the Marais. The tour through the history of scientific endeavour begins in a narrow attic on the second floor and ends in the airy chapel. On the way, you pass over 3,000 items from its collection of 80,000 objects and 15,000 drawings, classified and exhibited in seven "domains": scientific instruments, materials, construction, communication, energy, mechanics and transport. Each of these sections is arranged in chronological order.

The section devoted to scientific instruments covers the breadth of technical innovation from 7th-century astrolabes to the Cray super-computer. The world's first calculating machine is a star attraction: mathematician and philosopher, Blaise Pascal, perfected it in 1642 to help his father in his occupation of tax collecting. Its eight tiny wheels add and subtract while carrying over automatically. Antoine Lavoisier, the father of modern chemistry, happened to be a tax collector as well and was beheaded for that reason during the French Revolution. He used his considerable wealth to build the first laboratory – a network of glass vials connected by copper conduits, and enormous copper scales are displayed here.

The porous relationship between science and art is one of the revelations of the museum. Many of the early machine tools in the mechanics section, for example, were created by master watchmakers. Louis XVI loved to make things on a lathe – an unusual passion for an absolute monarch – and had his craftsmen build one fit for a king. The royal lathe displayed here is not only a fine precision tool but a work of art in polished steel. The same section includes one of Europe's largest collection of automatons, humanoids, mechanical musical instruments and toys.

In the communication section, the history of printing quickly moves from Gutenberg to the golden age of the press, with 18th-century sideshows like Chappe's optical telegraph. Then photography takes the stage, a technology as revolutionary to its day as the microchip is to ours. There is a wide assortment of the earliest cameras, many by Daguerre, and an 1839 daguerreotype. The Lumière Brothers' first cinematograph – a nondescript square black box with a big lens – takes pride of place. The section ends with the Apple Computer.

Perhaps the most extraordinary sight in the entire museum is *Eole*, Clement Ader's 1897 steam-powered, bat-winged flying machine hanging above the main staircase (in the transport section). Built between 1894 and 1897, out of wood, silk, and a few odd pieces of brass and aluminium, Ader's "bat" flew 300 metres (984 ft) on a foggy day in 1897, before it crashed back down to earth. Unfortunately, Ader could not raise the money for further trials.

At the bottom of the staircase stands the world's first true automobile, the Fardier de Cugnot, a massive, steam-powered tricycle designed and built by the French military engineer in 1769. Intended as an artillery carriage, the vehicle successfully carried four passengers for 20 minutes at the blazing speed of 3.6 km (2¼ miles) per hour.

The crowning glory of the museum is the 11th-century chapel (indeed, one could argue for a visit beginning here). On entering, you pass Leon Foucault's 1855 steel, brass and lead pendulum (immortalised in Umberto Eco's novel *Foucault's Pendulum*), suspended from the vault, its plane of swing rotating in relation to the earth's surface. By hanging his pendulum from the top of the Panthéon's dome in 1851, Foucault publicly proved that the world was round and rotated.

The chapel has been restored to its polychrome Gothic glow and equipped with a metal and glass walkway that transports you right up into the nave of the church. On the way, you can examine vintage cars and aeroplanes from above and below, including *Blériot XI*, the featherweight wood and canvas plane that made the first flight over the English channel in 1909. It forms an odd contrast to the ungainly *L'Obéissante* on the chapel floor – the world's first bus, which was powered by steam in 1873 and reached a top speed of 30 kmph (19 mph). A 1:16 scale model of the Statue of Liberty, itself a radical innovation in metallurgy, holds court over this unique spectacle of human invention.

FOOD AND DRINK: Chez Omar (47 rue de Bretagne, 3rd; tel: 01 42 72 36 26; inexpensive): couscous served in an old brasserie setting, popular with artists and the chattering classes. Au Bascou (38 rue Réaumur, 3rd; tel: 01 42 72 69 25; moderate): a varied menu of generous dishes from the Basque country, such as squid, roast lamb, sweet stuffed peppers, pipérade and smoked tuna.

RIGHT: *La Pascaline*, the adding machine invented by Blaise Pascal for his father, a tax collector.

FAR RIGHT: *The Insertion of a Tube*, Georges Chicotot (1889–1907).

Musée de l'Assistance Publique-Hôpitaux de Paris

One thousand years of Parisian hospital history

Map reference: page 41, F5
Hôtel de Miramion, 47 quai de la Tournelle, 5th
Tel: 01 40 27 50 05
Metro: Maubert-Mutualité. Bus: 24, 47, 63, 86, 87
Open: Tues–Sun 10am–6pm.
Admission charge.

This 17th-century mansion served as the city's Central Hospital Pharmacy until 1974. It now makes an evocative place to study hospital history. Five thousand items – paintings, engravings, sculpture, pharmaceutical objects, medical instruments, and uniforms – document the lives of patients, care-givers and doctors from the Middle Ages to the end of the 19th century. Its greatest treasure is the *Book of Working Life*, by Jean Henry (1482), one of several illuminated manuscripts that are kept in cloth-covered display cases.

The abandonment of newborn babies was a depressing fact of life in Paris for many centuries. Witness the baby deposit box *(tour d'abandon)*. Installed in the wall of the Hôpital des Enfants Trouvés, it worked like a revolving door. Parents used it to drop off babies without being seen (although, hoping that they would reclaim their child one day, the parents often swaddled their baby with an identifying object).

France's first baby formula bottles are kept in a case labelled *le biberon meutrier* (the killer bottle), because they were difficult to sterilise and resulted in the deaths of thousands of children. A more successful innovation was the "milk bar", depicted in three large canvases, which distributed milk to working-class mothers.

FOOD AND DRINK: Le Reminet (3 rue des Grands-Degrés, 5th; tel: 01 44 07 04 24; moderate): a snug setting for very good, updated bistro cooking.

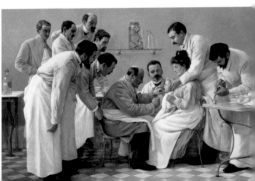

Cité des Sciences et de l'Industrie

A vast state-of-the-art science museum with hands-on exhibits for children

Map reference: page 43, H1
Parc de la Villette, 30 av Corentin, 19th
Tel: 01 40 05 80 00. www.cite-sciences.fr
Metro: Porte de la Villette. Bus: 75, 139, 150,
152, 250A, PC
Open: Tues–Sat 10am–6pm, Sun until 7pm;
closed Mon and public hols.
Restaurant/café. Shop. Wheelchair access.
Research facilities/library. Audio-guide in
English. Admission charge; supplement payable
for planetarium visits and films in La Géode
(for reservations tel: 08 92 68 45 40).

Stargazing
in the
Planetarium.

The district of La Villette in northeastern Paris was originally a "city of blood, meat and its trade", a vast abattoir supplying households and restaurants with beef. Its transformation into a giant cultural complex was one of the most inspired of Mitterrand's *grands projets (see page 31)*. The Parc de la Villette is now one of the liveliest and most popular family attractions in Paris, attracting more than 5 million visitors a year.

The park

The sprawling park is criss-crossed with waterways, some of them dug by Napoleon, and futuristic red follies – small pavilions housing mini-exhibits, snack bars and children's attractions – dot its green spaces.

To the south of the park, the cavernous 19th-century iron and glass Grande Hall, formerly the cattle market, provides an airy space for trade fairs, exhibitions and concerts. Le Zénith, also south of the canal, is a huge venue used for pop concerts. In the corner beyond sits the elegant, white Cité de la Musique, Paris's museum and national conservatory of music – one of the city's most daring structures *(see page 163)*.

La Cité des Sciences et de l'Industrie occupies the northern end of the park. The complex was originally built to be an ultra-modern slaughterhouse but was never finished. Instead, it was transformed by architect Adrien Fainsilber into one of the world's leading science museums. The vast, blue-girdered steel and glass structure is a remarkable sight. Plant life grows in its large bioclimatic greenhouses, and light streams through two enormous domes in the roof. A deep moat surrounds the main building and the shiny, perfect sphere in front of it, known as La Géode, houses a gigantic wraparound cinema.

Explora

The Cité's permanent exhibition, Explora, is arranged on two immense floors with mezzanines. The southern gallery (level 1) offers an ambitious tour of modern industrial society and its use and abuse of the natural world. There are six areas: Automobiles, Aviation, Space, Oceans, Environment and Energy, as well as a Garden of the Future where fruit and vegetables, some of them cloned, are flourishing in rock wool, peat and bark.

The role of French science and industry is represented by a nuclear Mirage IV jet, an Ariane 5 rocket and a talking Renault (explaining, in French, how its parts are recycled); but the emphasis is on the universality of the scientific revolution and the questions – practical and theoretical – that it poses for the future. You can launch a rocket using water and compressed air as propellants, step into the changing room of an orbital station, and discover why wheat in outerspace grows in all directions; the laws of aerodynamics are demonstrated to anyone who grabs the joystick of one of the flight simulators. However, you will also have to ponder, in the Environment section, the impact of man's 9 billion tonnes of rubbish a day (50 percent more than a decade ago) and the issues of global climate change, acid rain and deforestation.

TOP: Hands-on activities in the Cité des Enfants.

ABOVE: A Mirage IV jet.

In Expression and Behaviour, an odorama demonstrates that smells are stronger if we simultaneously watch a film with associated images. Choose Your Identity takes place in a "changing room", where you try out a vast wardrobe without taking your clothes off. And a double mirror reveals the "true" self – the one that everyone else sees (because there is no inversion of left and right). The Images section takes you from Renaissance pinhole-enhanced optics to contemporary pixellisation (producing video and TV images with red, green and blue phosphor dots), fast and slow motion perspective and special effects.

The northern gallery and mezzanines on level 2 take a stab at the themes of Life and Health, Medicine, Biology, Light Games, Rocks and Volcanoes, and Stars and Galaxies. It also has a Planetarium that illuminates a dome with 10,000 stars (every hour from 11am–5pm, shows last about 30 minutes; the audio-guide includes a translation. The Theatre of Birth (*Théâtre de la Naissance*) begins with an encounter between a sperm cell and ovum and ends with the birth of a child. Diet and Health (*Alimentation et Santé*) asks why people eat what they eat: crickets and caterpillars in Africa, Guinea pigs in the Andes, lizards in India, and frogs in France. Light Games offers futile grasps at The Untouchable Spring (*le ressort intouchable*) and the chance to mix the colours in Bubble Soap Paintings (*le tableau de savon*).

Stars and Galaxies has a most unusual set of scales that measures your weight on the moon, Mars and Jupiter. The Muon Show (*le théâtre des muons*) introduces quirky things – invisible particles produced by colliding cosmic dust and air molecules – that go bump in the atmosphere. Thanks to a machine called a cosmophone, we can see and hear them as they bombard us at the speed of light.

The northern gallery on level 1 is divided into five areas: Mathematics, Sounds, Expression and Behaviour, Computer Science, Images. The overarching themes are of sense perception and communication. This is a hands-on place where visitors participate in mind-bending DIY experiments involving light, sound and perception.

The physics of sound are a revelation: parabolic screens transmit a conversation between two people standing 17 metres (56 ft) apart; long tubes test the velocity of sound; the wave of a wrist makes music in the Percussion Booth (*percussions virtuelles*); and the *spatialisateur* packs the entire spectrum of sounds perceptible to the human ear into one 10-minute concert. The Inertial Merry-Go-Round (*Manège Inertiel*) demonstrates something we earthlings don't normally notice – the power of the Coriolis force created by the earth's rotation. This force is one of the things that causes winds and currents.

Aquarium and *Argonaute*

The aquarium has 200 species of fish, crustaceans and molluscs from Mediterranean coastal waters representing flora and fauna found at a depth of up to 50 metres (164 ft). A decommissioned "hunter-killer" submarine has been towed from the sea and up the Seine to a mooring next to the Géode. The 1957 diesel-electric *Argonaute* displays the ins and outs of underwater navigation. A 40-man crew led a claustrophobic existence inside its 50-metre (164-ft) hull, toiling in temperatures as high as 50°C (122°F) with no water for showers. The advent of nuclear submarines made the vessel obsolete.

From 3-D to Omnimax

Hi-tech film is one of the highlights at La Cité. The Louis-Lumière cinema (on the ground floor) shows 20-minute movies in 3-D every half hour. The Cinaxe – a simulator outfitted with the same equipment used to train airplane pilots and train engineers – moves the spectactors in sync with the film they are watching.

The Cité's ultimate film experience is inside the giant silvery sphere known as La Géode. It is one of the world's largest geodesic domes, and France's first omnimax movie theatre. Images on its 1,000-sq metre (10,765-sq ft) screen are ten times larger than in a normal film and the digital sound comes at you from all directions. Most 3D films shown are either science or nature and wildlife documentaries (one projection per hour).

Cité des Enfants

The Cité des Enfants is a completely separate place for children. Pre-schoolers (ages 3–6) can put on tot-sized hard hats and construct or tear down a building on a miniature building site equipped with cranes and pulleys. Older children (5–12) talk to robots and play at being TV anchorpersons in their own television studio.

FOOD AND DRINK: The Cité has two cafés with a limited menu and a restaurant. In fine weather, the Parc de la Villette is ideal for a picnic. Across the street from the Cité de la Musique conservatory, **Au Bœuf Couronné** *(188 av Jean Jaurès, 19th; tel: 01 42 39 44 44; expensive) is a throwback to the days when the neighbourhood was carnivore heaven. Beef tartare,* bourguignon, pot au feu *and* entrecôtes *are house specialities.*

Display dedicated to volcanoes, showing how they are formed and why they erupt.

An impressive, if gruesome, array of surgical instruments through the ages.

Musée d'Histoire de la Médecine

Surgical instruments and medical tools

Map reference: page 41, E5
12 rue de l'Ecole de Médécine, 6th
Tel: 01 40 46 16 93
www.univ-paris5.fr/SMUSHMED.HTM
Metro: Odéon. Bus: 21, 27, 38, 63, 87
Open: Mon–Wed, Fri–Sat 2–5.30 pm; closed
Thurs, Sun and public hols.
Admission charge.

Surgeons, medical students and lovers of old-fashioned museums will feel at home here. Those who feel faint at the sight or thought of blood will not. The walls of this musty museum are lined with dozens of display cases full of surgical and medical instruments, including rare items from ancient Egypt and medieval Europe. Many of them were crudely adapted for their purpose and deployed before the advent of anaesthetic or sterilisation. Medicine has come a long way since the practice of trepanning – drilling holes in people's heads to let the demons out. The toolkits for the bleeding of patients are another reminder of how dangerous it was to receive medical treatment.

Doctors did, on occasion, heal people. Witness the serpentine instrument of the type used to operate on Louis XIV's anal fistula. It brought great renown to an otherwise incompetent surgeon who had already killed several of his children with repeated bleedings and overdoses of emetics and purgatives (all standard practices of the time). The most grisly object is a table created for Napoleon III, which shows that Belle Epoque tastes could be just as bloodthirsty as the Middle Ages. It is crafted out of symmetrically sliced organs, dried blood, tanned ears and a calcified foot.

FOOD AND DRINK: See Musée du Moyen Age, page 81.

Musée National d'Histoire Naturelle

A complex of natural history museums, a zoo and a maze set in the grounds of the Jardin des Plantes

Map reference: page 41, G6
Jardin des Plantes, 57 rue Cuvier, 5th
Tel: 01 40 79 30 00. www.mnhn.fr
Metro: Monge, Gare d'Austerlitz, Jussieu
Bus: 24, 57, 61, 63, 65, 67, 89
Opening times: see individual museums.
Restaurant/coffee shop. Shop. Wheelchair
access. Research facilities/library. Tour groups
in English (advance reservations only).
Admission charge.

The Jardin des Plantes (the botanical gardens) was established in 1636 by King Louis XIII as a source of medicinal herbs to keep the king and his family healthy. The oldest tree in Paris, a false acacia planted in 1635, is here. The garden expanded during the 1700s, with the addition of a maze, amphitheatre and exhibition galleries. Then French revolutionaries added a small zoo and renamed it the Musée National d'Histoire Naturelle.

In 1889, the Galerie de Zoologie was opened in the grounds of the botanical garden. Its object was to display, conserve and study the millions of specimens brought back by European naturalists and explorers travelling the world. Armed with Linnaeus' "kingdom, genus, species" system, they attempted to identify and classify all living things and study their transformation through time. Lamarck, Cuvier and Darwin drew on their work to develop the theory of evolution.

After World War II, the zoological gallery fell into disrepair and in 1965 it was declared a public hazard and promptly closed. Twenty years later the majority of the museum's 7 million skeletons, insects, stuffed birds and mammals was transferred to a vast underground research centre called the Zoothèque, and work began on renovating the building and transforming it into an exhibition space. The Grande Galerie de l'Evolution was finally opened in 1994.

The herd of African animals takes centre stage in the Grande Galerie de l'Evolution.

Grande Galerie de l'Evolution

The objective of the Grande Galerie *(open: Mon, Wed–Sun 10am–6pm, Thur until 10pm, closed Tues and public hols)* is to illustrate principles of evolution and dramatise the impact of human behaviour on the environment. The Hall has retained elements of a 19th-century museum – parquet floors, iron columns, display cases – but the interior space has been completely modernised and equipped with interactive displays (mostly in French) examining everything from micro-organisms to the global ecosystem.

The visit begins with an exploration of the marine environment, where life began. First to greet you in this sombre space are the skeletons of two whales hunted in the 19th century. The rest of this level is subdivided into the diverse marine environments: the open water environment, coastal environment, coral reefs, hydrothermal springs and the ocean floor. One of the planet's strangest creatures is preserved here. The cœlacanth is the oldest known vertebrate and a deep-sea resident when the brontosaurus roamed the earth 370 million years ago. It swims like a quadruped and eats only twice a year. Believed extinct, this fish was found in 1938 in a fishing net off the coast of South Africa. There have been several other sightings since.

The next level explores the diversity of land environments, from the African savannah and Sahara to the tropical rainforests of the Americas and the ice fields of the Arctic and Antarctic regions. The museum's *pièce de résistance* is the

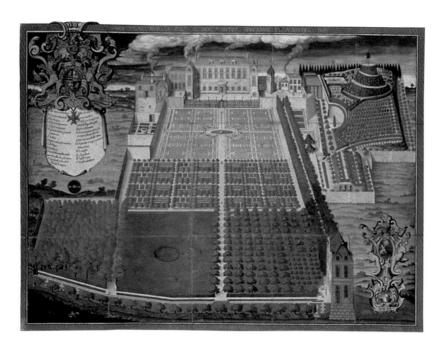

great herd of stuffed African animals that sweeps through the atrium. Armadillos, warthogs, miniature deer, ocelots, tapir, wild pigs, zebras, giraffe and elephants appear to be marching in unison through the African veldt. Lights rise and fall in 30-minute cycles to simulate day and night on the savannah. A soundtrack joins in with bird cries and animal noises. Video tapes around the display explain the behaviour of animals in their natural habitats.

The upper-level galleries explore everything from DNA to the impact of human activity on biodiversity. There is also a hall of discovery for young people (exhibits in French only) and an illuminated counter that gives the population of the world and flashes its alarming rate of increase. Man as a "factor in evolution" is studied as a hunter, domesticator of plants and animals, and polluter. One of the most striking exhibits is a plastic cube containing a week's worth of garbage from a "typical" Parisian family.

Paris, the "city of light", is revealed to be a city of trapped heat as well, and remarkably poor in flora and fauna – only two species of tree, both imported, dominate the boulevards.

Off the second floor is a gallery of extinct and endangered species. Out of the crypt-like darkness emerge stuffed creatures such as the blue hippopotamus, Chinese and Sumatran tigers, and the mountain gorilla. A wondrous clock chimes out the hours, originally designed to keep time for Marie Antoinette while she amused herself in the Petit Trianon.

Galerie de Paléontologie

The palaeontological museum *(open: Mon, Wed–Sun 10am–5pm; Sat–Sun until 6pm from Apr to Oct)* is something of a relic itself. The décor of the iron and glass 19th-century building is full of magnificent details that anticipated the Art Nouveau style. The poet Paul Claudel called it "the most beautiful museum in the world" when 10,000 visitors rushed past the doors on its inauguration in 1898. Today, it is neglected. Most of the visitors are French schoolchildren, and their minders' pleas of *"touchez pas"* ("don't touch") reverberate constantly.

The display may be old-fashioned, but the collection itself is impressive. In the ground-floor gallery, devoted to comparative anatomy, the order begins with man and works its way back through evolution to the fish. On the way, there are a thousand mounted skeletons and a mind-boggling array of exhibits behind glass, including jars of pickled primates' organs and foetuses of Siamese twins.

The first floor is even more impressive. Again, there are several thousand specimens, but this time representing a period of 600 million years. They are displayed in the order in which they disap-

ABOVE LEFT: The Jardin Royal, laid out in 1636 by the order of Louis XIV, for the cultivation of medicinal plants.

ABOVE: *The blue-faced parrot* (c. 1801–5).

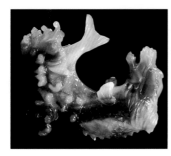

peared from earth. So the looming skeleton of the woolly mammoth, unearthed in Siberia, is near the entrance. Look out for the Mosasaure de Maastricht. Discovered in 1770, this skull (though mostly what you see is jaw) became an object of fascination throughout Europe. It was this item that put Cuvier, the father of modern palaeontology, on the path towards his theory of the extinction of species.

Galerie de Minéralogie, Géologie et Paléobotanique

The mineral gallery *(open: Mon, Wed–Sun 10am–5pm; Sat–Sun until 6pm from Apr to Oct)* contains 600,000 mineral samples displayed in an elegant, Neo-classical building built between 1830 and 1837. The Salle des Cristaux Géants (the Giant Crystal Room) lives up to its name with its collection of 80 rarer than rare giant crystals, one of which took 22 years to extract from the earth. The *Grands prismes accolés de quartz* are a pair of Brazilian crystals weighing approximately 700 kg, (1540 lb) while the *Groupe de quartz en cristaux parallèles*, also from Brazil, weighs in at 380 kg (840 lb). The largest crystal of all weighs 3 tonnes.

The Salle du Trésor (Hall of Treasure) contains a vast collection of precious and semi-precious stones, many of which came from French royal collections. There are also specimens of gold from California, pyrargyrite, a silver mineral from Peru, and an intense blue fluorite discovered in 1975 in central France.

The gallery of palaeobotany, in the same building, retraces the history of the vegetable world since its beginnings on earth. The exhibit actually begins in front of the building, where the stump of a tree – a relative of the California Redwood, which grew near the Musée d'Orsay 35 million years ago – is on view.

La Galerie d'Entomologie

The entomology gallery *(open: Mon–Fri 1–5pm)* is home to the preserved remains of 2,000 of the world's most interesting insects, grouped around five biogeographic regions. From the Région Holarctique, which includes North America and the temperate areas of China and Japan, comes the strange, metallic blue scarab beetle *(Hoplia cœrulea)*. Look out for the Criquet de Madagascar *(Phymateus saxosus)*, in the Région Afrotropicale, surely the world's most bizarre cricket. The Papilio antimachus is the largest African butterfly and Thysania aggripina, from Brazil, is the world's largest lepidoptera (moth).

Ménagerie

This, the world's first zoo *(open: daily 9am–6pm, until 6.30pm in summer)*, along with Schoenbrunn in Austria, was created in 1794 by the French revolutionary government and actually built under Napoleon. Ever since, it has served the twin purposes of amusement and science, and many rare species have found Paris a good place for the mating game. In terms of numbers, the zoo's population never recovered after 1870–71, when many of the animals were slaughtered and eaten during the siege of Paris. The more unusual Microzoo is devoted to microscopic organisms, which visitors can examine through microscopes accompanied by recorded commentary (in French). Many of these micro-organisms live in our homes and in our own bodies.

Food and Drink: Café de la Mosquée (39 rue Geoffroy-St-Hillaire, 5th; inexpensive), in the neighbouring Paris mosque, is perfect for a mint tea and baklava break. The mosaic courtyard is shaded by fig trees and cooled by a fountain. There is also a restaurant that serves couscous and tagines. L'Écureuil (3 rue Linné, 5th; moderate): A wine bar/restaurant with regional cooking from southwestern France and a selection of wines well suited to plats du jour like cassoulet, stuffed cabbage and salade landaise. La Petite Légume (36 rue Boulangers, 5th; inexpensive) is a vegetarian hole in the wall that serves "best of the earth" meals at two tables or wrapped up to take away.

Musée de l'Homme

Museum of Mankind

Map reference: page 42, C3
Palais de Chaillot, 17 place du Trocadéro
(entrance in the west wing), 16th
Tel: 01 44 05 72 72. www.mnhn.fr/mnhn/bmh
Metro: Trocadéro. Bus: 22, 30, 32, 63, 72, 82.
Open: Mon, Wed–Sun 9.45am–5.45pm; closed Tues and public hols.
Restaurant/coffee shop/bar. Bookshop. Research facilities/library. Wheelchair access.
Admission charge.

France's most important museum for anthropology, ethnology and prehistory possesses 735,000 objects from all over the world. It is an important scientific institution that has done much to advance the world's knowledge of human culture (the research library contains 180,000 volumes). But some of the exhibits seem rather jumbled and you might find yourself disorientated by closing time (the guardians simply ring the burglar alarm). The Surrealists loved this place and so do most kids. Fortunately, the museum has won a recent fight for survival, but will lose its ethnology collections in 2004 to the new Musée des Arts Premiers on quai Branly (near the Eiffel Tower), promoted by President Chirac *(see page 32)*.

An interactive exhibit connected to United Nations databases, *Six milliards d'hommes* (6 billion human

beings) allows you to enter your age into a computer and find out what the world's population was when you were born, and see how many people that were born the same year as you are still alive. It also poses alarming questions about a future world of 12 billion people. *Tous parents, Tous différents* (All related and all different) uses the results of modern genetics to explain why human bodies look so different even though humans are genetically alike.

The first-floor *Nuit de Temps* (Night of time) traces human evolution from primates to the discovery of writing. The rest of the exhibits are arranged according to geographical region. In the Galerie d'Africa Noire, a mask from Gabon, the *Masque Blanc Fang*, is one of the African artefacts credited for the aesthetic revelations that led to Picasso's *Les Demoiselles d'Avignon* and the birth of Cubism.

A la Rencontre des Amériques (Discovering the Americas) is perhaps the most interesting section of all. It was renovated for the 500th anniversary of the European discovery of the New World, which it covers from Alaska to Tierra del Fuego. Most impressive is the pre-Columbian art. The reconstruction of a Mayan temple and the suspended Incan bridge are less so. An Incan mummy (in foetal position) is said to have inspired Edvard Munch's painting, *The Scream*. The masks, totems, and wooden shamans from British Columbia represent one of the most important collections of its kind in Europe.

Ceremonial mask from the Ivory Coast (late 19th century).

"Duho" ceremonial seat, Taino, Haiti (15th century).

Palais de la Découverte

Another voyage of scientific discovery

Map reference: page 40, A2
Av Franklin-D-Roosevelt, 8th
Tel: 01 56 43 20 21. www.palais-decouverte.fr
Metro: Champs-Elysées-Clemenceau. Bus: 28, 42, 49, 52, 63, 72, 73, 80, 83
Open: Tues–Sat 9.30am–6pm, Sun until 7pm; closed Mon and public hols.
Book and giftshop. Wheelchair access. Research facilities/library. Admission charge.

The Salon de la Musique features 500 instruments from five continents. The collection highlights the importance of music to virtually all cultures, past and present, as well as the phenomenal variety of materials used for music-making (take a look at the massive crystals of the Vietnamese lithophone). World music concerts are sometimes held in the salon and, with a bit of a luck, you might see the 16-piece gamelan orchestra from Java (an ensemble of bamboo xylophones, gongs and wooden and metal chimes) in action. Three programmes can be heard on headphones in a pair of cabins.

The Salle des Arts et Techniques displays a collection of tools from all over the world sorted, unusually, by purpose rather than by geography or culture.

*Food and Drink: The food in the museum's trendy **Totem** restaurant (tel: 01 47 27 28 29) is unremarkable, but the view of the Eiffel Tower is superb.*

The Palais de la Découverte was the world's first interactive museum. It was inaugurated during the 1937 Universal Exhibition as a showcase for the adventure and spectacle of science. It remains eternally popular with Parisian kids, despite the pull of the newer Cité des Sciences *(see page 187)*. Spectators, young and old, are invited to participate in "experiments" in astronomy, biology, chemistry, mathematics and physics, which take place at regular intervals (held in French but often self-explanatory). The single most popular demonstration is the unmissable Électrostatique, in which volunteers are attached, two at a time, to a 300,000-volt generator that makes their hair stand completely on end before "grilling" them in the Cage de Faraday.

In another hall, an electric eel generates enough energy to illuminate a light bulb. At *L'Ecole des Rats* (The School for Rats) next door, you can watch the long-tailed rodents running a labyrinth, pushing pedals, opening doors and swinging on gym bars. The 3-D *Voyage dans la Cellule* (Journey through a Cell) gives you an idea of what your 10 billion cells are up to and how they replicate and divide (in French again but with superb graphics). The planetarium offers a lot of time travel within its 15-metre (49-ft) circumference – back to the past and the Paris night sky as it looked 14,000 years ago, and ahead to future solar and lunar eclipses. It also adjusts its perspective to visualise the solar system as it looks from another planet.

The Palais de la Découverte hosts some of the best temporary exhibitions in Paris on subjects as diverse as the Big Bang and the Lost World of Pompeii.

*Food and Drink: **Spoon** (14 rue du Marignan, 8th; tel: 01 40 76 34 44; expensive): France meets the Pacific Rim in a mix-and-match menu from superchef Alain Ducasse. The wine list is packed with New World vintages.*

This prehistoric rock painting, one of many found in the Tassili N'Ajjer plateau in Algeria, depicts tribesmen coming to the aid of an injured fellow warrior.

The interior offers a near perfect look, from bathroom to salon, at bourgeois life in Paris at the end of the 19th century. Pasteur's *objets d'art* (many of them lavish gifts from foreign royalty) decorate the home, as well as personal odds and ends such as his wife's unfinished knitting and the cocked hat and sword that he wore to the French Academy. Many of the sketches and portraits are by Pasteur, who was an artist as a young man.

The tour ends in Pasteur's crypt. His wife preferred to keep him in the institute rather than transfer his remains to the Panthéon. The neo-byzantine decoration – marble columns, polychrome mosaics of vines, mulberry branches and hops – was inspired by the churches of Ravenna, but also reflects the emerging Art Nouveau style of its time.

Pasteur in his Laboratory by Albert Edelfelt, 1855.

FOOD AND DRINK: *see Musée de la Poste, page 180.*

Musée Pasteur

The last residence of brilliant chemist and bacteriologist Louis Pasteur

Map reference: page 42, D5
Institut Pasteur, 25 rue du Docteur Roux, 15th
Tel: 01 45 68 82 83
www.pasteur.fr/pasteur/activites/histoire.html
Metro: Pasteur. Bus: 39, 48, 70, 89
Open: daily 2–5.30pm; closed Aug and public hols. Research facilities/library. Tour in English (no reservations necessary). Admission charge.

The vast apartment where Louis Pasteur lived for the last seven years of his life (1888–95) has been left virtually unchanged. It was built for him as part of the Institut Pasteur, the world-famous scientific institution which now occupies two buildings.

A guided tour (English or French) begins in a gallery full of Pasteur's scientific instruments and specimens. A recording sums up, in a few words, his revolutionary achievements: proving that micro-organisms cause fermentation and disease; saving the French silk industry from a moth disease; pasteurising beer and wine; and, most spectacularly, creating a life-saving vaccine against the rabies virus, long before anyone knew what a virus was.

The display cases contain more than 1,000 objects: there are the crystals demonstrating molecular asymmetry (Pasteur was a trained geologist), and test tubes of beef gelatin and rabbit marrow that he used to develop vaccines.

Musée de Radio France

The golden age of broadcasting

Map reference: page 42, B4
116 av du Président Kennedy, 16th
Tel: 01 42 30 33 83.
www.radio-france.fr/chaines/radio-france/musee
Metro: Passy. RER: Kennedy-Radio France
Bus: 22, 52, 70, 72
Open: Mon–Sat, tours at 10.30, 11.30, 2.30, 3.30, 4.30; closed Sun and public hols. Wheelchair access. Tours in English (advance reservations, tel: 01 42 30 15 16). Admission charge.

The monumental white building on the Seine (designed by Henri Bernard in 1963), which houses the headquarters of the state-run radio, also has a museum of radio and TV. Although relatively unknown, it is the finest collection of its kind in Europe, with 500 exhibits which range from the optical Chappe telegraph (1793) to on-line radio. The star attractions include the transmitter used by Eugéne Ducretet in 1898 to establish a radio connection between the Eiffel Tower and the Panthéon; and France's first TV studio. The guided tour includes a look at a recording studio. You can also attend a free concert in the largest studio on some evenings.

FOOD AND DRINK: *Bar Antoine (17 rue La Fontaine, 16th; moderate). Tiny Art Nouveau bar/bistro.*

Further Afield

A selection of museums, galleries and gardens worth visiting in the suburbs and satellite towns of Paris, with a special section on the imposing châteaux that make perfect day-trip destinations

Musée de l'Air et de l'Espace

Magnificent men and their flying machines

Aéroport de Paris-Le Bourget, 93352 Le Bourget
Tel: 01 49 92 71 99. www.mae.org
RER: Line B5 from Chatelet or Gare du Nord,
(avoid the non-stop trains that go straight to
Charles de Gaulle airport), then bus 152, or a
20-minute walk
Open: Tues–Sun 10am–5pm (until 6pm
May–Oct); closed Mon.
Book and giftshop. Wheelchair access.
Planetarium. Admission charge.

The museum at Le Bourget, in the outlying northeastern Paris district of Saint-Denis, traces the history of aviation and space exploration from the earliest flights in balloons to the latest in rockets. It would be hard to imagine a more fitting place than Le Bourget to celebrate the achievements of pioneering pilots and astronauts. In 1915, the town became the principal airfield for French World War I pilots. The first postal service planes flew from here in 1918 and, a year later, commercial service took off. Charles Lindbergh landed at Le Bourget on 21 May 1927, after a solo, transatlantic flight of 33 hours, 30 minutes.

Le Bourget's former 1937 airport now houses 180-plus planes ranging from the primitive 19th-century Otto Lilienthal hang-glider to a prototype Concorde and an Ariane rocket from the European space programme. Biplanes, fighter planes, passenger planes and stunt planes, jets and rockets are parked on the ground (including on the runway outside) or suspended from the ceiling. Almost all of them are original, and there are elevated catwalks so you can look at them from above or below.

The Grande Galerie has two rooms devoted to the hot-air balloon, which was invented in 1783 by the Montgolfier brothers and soon adopted by the military for reconnaissance. A vast assortment of the first flying machines chronicles the era of wooden biplanes and seat-of-the-pants flying. The main protaganists of World War I dogfights are represented, including the German Foker and the Spad VIII, with which French ace Guynemer shot down 17 enemy planes. The "Deperdussin" monocoque was the first plane to fly 200 km (124 miles) an hour (in 1913). A catwalk passes through the engine cabin of a Zeppelin airship that once bombed Britain.

A showcase for French aviation.

Le Hall de L'Espace, newly equipped with video and interactive displays, documents the conquest of space from the first Sputnik to France's Ariane rocket (models I and V are out on the runway). Le Hall de l'Entre Deux Guerres et l'Aviation Légère (interwar years and light aviation) explores the golden age when airplanes first crossed oceans, circled the globe and opened unexplored territory. The bus-like Farman F60 Goliath, vintage 1919, was used for the first regular passenger flights between Paris and London. There are also early helicopters.

Le Hall des Prototypes et de l'Armée de l'Air (prototypes and the air force) is a convincing display of French aerospace prowess since World War II and includes the Mirage, Leduc, Trident and Griffon.

Le Hall Concorde occupies an old hangar. You can walk through a Concorde prototype, which is surprisingly narrow, and peruse the most famous fighter planes of World War II (the Spitfire, Mustang, etc.). Also on display is the first jet plane built at the end of the war by the ingenious Heinkel (partly out of wood because they had no more steel).

*FOOD AND DRINK: There is nothing to eat on the vast museum premises (just a couple of vending machines), but there are several restaurants across the street and two reliable and reasonably priced brasseries near the station: **L'Aviatic** and **Les Sports**, on avenue de la Division-Leclerc (corner of Jean-Jaurés).*

The Montgolfier brothers launch their first hot-air balloon in front of a royal audience and 13,000 spectators (1783).

La Dame de Brassempouy. This prehistoric sculpture carved from a mammoth tusk is the world's oldest human face.

Musée des Années 30

Art, furniture and architecture of the 1930s

28 av André Morizet, 92100 Boulogne-Billancourt
Tel: 01 55 18 46 41
Metro: Boulogne-Jean Jaurès. Bus: 52
Open: Tues–Sun 11am–6pm; closed Mon and public hols
Book and giftshop. Wheelchair access. Guided tours in English (by reservation, tel: 01 55 18 46 64). Research library. Admission charge.

This is a homage to the creative interwar years, a time when the towns of Boulogne and Billancourt were the source of innovations in art, architecture and industry. Between them, they were home to a vast Renault factory *(there's a small* **Renault Museum** *at 27 rue des Abondances; tel: 01 46 05 21 58; metro: Pt de St-Cloud; open: Tues, Thurs 2–6pm; free)* and to the most important French film studios. This stretch of the Seine was also a cross-current of avant-garde architecture.

The museum focuses on the artists, architects and designers who lived in the area *(see also Musée Jardin Paul-Landowski, page 202)*. The collection covers currents in Modernism, including monumental sculptures by the Martel brothers, still lifes by Juan Gris, fashion plates and works by numerous minor figurative painters. But the museum's strength lies in its holding of furniture prototypes and architectural drawings and models, notably those relating to the town's avant-garde villas built by Perret, Le Corbusier, Lurçat and Fischer.

FOOD AND DRINK: The cinema complex next to the museum has a small café. For a serious appetite, go to the friendly **Café Pancrace** *(38 rue d'Aguesseau; inexpensive).*

Musée des Antiquités Nationales

France's most notable archaeology museum

Place du Château, 78103 St-Germain-en-Laye
Tel: 01 34 51 53 65
RER: line A (a 25-minute journey from metro station Charles de Gaulle-Etoile)
Open: Mon, Wed–Sun 9am–5.15pm; closed Tues.
Book and giftshop. Wheelchair access. Guided tours (by reservation, tel: 01 34 51 65 36). Research library. Admission charge.

Bronze Age cup, bracelet, ring and hairsprings finely crafted from gold.

The Musée des Antiquités Nationales occupies the gloomy, heavily restored Château of St-Germain-en-Laye in a chic Paris suburb. Human history begins as a labyrinth of display cases full of ancient earthenware vessels, broken blades, shield bosses and arrowheads eaten away by rust. The individual pieces may be uninspiring, but the collection in its entirety is awesome – and it only gets better as you progress through the millennia. Ancient French history is spread across eight *domaines* (sections).

In the world of early hunters and gatherers, fire, hunting, death, war, love and religion all appear in their art. There is a prehistoric stag and a curvaceous 22,000-year-old *Venus*. The ivory *Dame de Brassempouy* is the world's oldest human face (22,000 BC), while the *Bison de la Grotte de la Madeleine* (13,000 BC) seems strikingly modern.

The Bronze Age and Iron Age collections give way to the long history of Celtic and Roman Gaul and the Early Middle Ages. The tomb of a Celtic prince is a prelude to the model of the siege of Alésia, the battle in which the Romans, led by Julius Caesar, annihilated the Gauls and their leader Vercingétorix (taken to Rome afterwards in chains). The 3rd-century Mosaïque de St-Romain-en-Gal, which depicts the season's labours, is a star attraction.

La Salle d'Archéologie Comparée, in the former ballroom of François I, displays a collection of 6,000 objects from five continents.

FOOD AND DRINK: **Le Chais du Roy** *(3 rue de la Surintendance, across from the château; moderate): solid bistro provisioned by the local market and the owners' own vineyards.*

The museum also has a section dedicated to poet Paul Eluard, one of the founders of the Surrealist movement, who was born in St-Denis.

The Battle of Bourget, V.A. Poirson (1887).

FOOD AND DRINK: Le Melody, just down the street (no. 15), is the chicest choice. The less expensive Le Boeuf (no. 20), despite the name, has a lot of duck on the menu.

Musée de la Céramique

Greek terracotta, Dutch delftware, Italian faience, Islamic ceramics and, of course, porcelain made in Sèvres

Place de la Manufacture, 92310 Sèvres
Tel: 01 41 14 04 20
Metro: Pont de Sèvres, then bus 169, 171 or 179.
Open: Mon, Wed–Sun 10am–5.15pm; closed Tues. Book and porcelain shop. Wheelchair access. Admission charge.

Musée d'Art et d'Histoire de la ville de St-Denis

Poets, revolutionaries and Carmelite nuns

22bis rue Gabriel-Péri, 8th
Tel: 01 42 43 05 10. www.ville-saint-denis.fr
Metro: St-Denis Porte de Paris
Open: Mon, Wed–Fri 10am–5.30pm, Sat–Sun 2–6.30pm; closed Tues and public hols.
Book and giftshop. Admission charge.

The Carmelite convent (founded in 1625) that houses this museum narrowly escaped destruction in 1972 before being turned into a museum of local history. The original architecture was kept intact and the life of the convent's former occupants is one of the museum's most interesting aspects. Nuns' tombstones surround the cloister, and the maxims that are still painted on the walls reveal how rigidly abstemious their lives must have been ("the pleasure of dying without pain is well worth the pain of living without pleasure").

Their austere cells on the first floor are filled with religious art pertaining to the Carmelite order and objects that they used in daily life, such as a spinning wheel. The paintings by Guillot depict the nuns' caring for the sick (and, disconcertingly, bleeding them). Look out for the cell occupied in the 18th century by Louise de France, the daughter of Louis X. The former refectory is dedicated to medieval archaeology and also features a well-preserved apothecary.

The second floor offers something completely different. The displays here chronicle the 1871 uprising of the Paris Commune through paintings, engravings, posters and satirical drawings (this period was France's golden age of political caricature). The Communards' 72 days of ruling Paris ended with their defeat and a bloodbath of 30,000 summary executions.

Founded in 1824, the museum in Sèvres has amassed one of the world's most complete collections (100,000 objects) of the ceramic arts. At the entrance, the visitor is greeted by a statue of the great French ceramicist Bernard Palissy (c. 1510–89; see pages 73–74). The ground floor covers Chinese, Byzantine and Cypriot pottery, and has a rich collection of Islamic ceramics. The museum also has a notable Italian Renaissance collection. Among its most precious pieces is an extremely rare dish (1525) from Faenza in northern Italy (hence the term, faience), which depicts the Biblical tale of Joseph finding the bowl hidden in Benjamin's bag. Although faience is thought to have originated in Spain, it was in Italy that it flourished.

Faience plate of Moorish design, 15th-century.

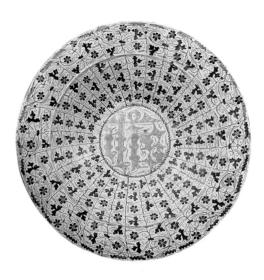

Pride of place goes to Sèvres porcelain on the first floor. Stop to admire the pair of grand Etruscan-style vases – one depicts Napoleon arriving at the Napoleon Museum (later the Louvre) with wagonloads of art from defeated Italy *(see pages 18–22)*, the other portrays the education of the Ancient Greeks. The rest of the floor represents other French and European ceramics from the 17th–18th century. The third floor is used for temporary exhibitions.

Musée Maurice Denis

Fine works by a mystical artist and his Nabis associates

2bis rue Maurice Denis,
78100 St-Germain-en-Laye
Tel: 01 39 73 77 87
RER: line A (25 minutes from metro station Charles de Gaulle-Etoile), then bus A, or a 15-minute walk
Open: Wed–Fri 10am–5.30pm, Sat–Sun 10am–6.30pm; closed Mon–Tues.
Book and giftshop. Admission charge.

It would be hard to exaggerate the charm of this stately building buffered by woods and gardens in the smart suburb of St-Germain-en-Laye. It was built in the 17th century for Madame Montespan, the mistress and secret wife of Louis XIV, to provide shelter for the poor and orphans of the town. Painter Maurice Denis (1870–1943) pur-

A Lady having Tea, Maurice Denis (1893).

chased Le Prieuré (The Priory), as he renamed it, in 1915, and lived and worked on the estate for the rest of his life. Denis was a follower of Gauguin and the main theorist of the Nabis movement that Gauguin's use of vivid colour and patterning had inspired. He was a deeply religious man and dedicated much of his time to restoring the chapel, which he had re-sanctified, painting frescoes and designing stained-glasses windows.

Alongside the work of Maurice Denis (paintings, graphic art, stained glass, furniture and mosaics), many other artists are represented, most of whom were associated with the Nabis group: Gauguin, Sérusier, Vallotton, Bonnard, Vuillard, Ranson, Redon and Mucha. It was the ambition of the Nabis to break down the artificial boundaries between craftsmanship and so-called fine art and to integrate art into daily life. As well as paintings and sculptures you can admire the furniture, fans, glassware, tapestries and graphic art that they produced.

FOOD AND DRINK: see Musée des Antiquités Nationales, page 198.

Giverny – Fondation Claude Monet

Claude Monet's house and gardens

Rue Claude Monet, 27620 Giverny
Tel: 02 32 51 28 21. www.fondation-monet.com
Train: Trains for Vernon depart from Paris St-Lazare mainline station: a 45-minute journey followed by a short bus- or taxi-ride from Vernon station to Giverny. You can rent bicycles at the station in summer.
Open: Tues–Sun 10am–6pm Apr–Oct (last ticket sold at 5.30pm); closed Mon and Nov–Mar. Café. Book and gift store. Seed and flower shop. Wheelchair access. Admission charge.

The undisputed master of Impressionism, Claude Monet spent 43 years of his life in Giverny, from 1883 until his death in 1926. Strange as it may seem, none of his original paintings are on display here – (most of Monet's work is divided between the Musée d'Orsay *(see page 86)*, the Musée de l'Orangerie *(see page 106)*, and the Musée Marmottan *(see page 105)*. Nevertheless, half a million people flock here each year to see the gardens that he created and immortalised in his art.

FAR LEFT: Monet's garden at Giverny.

LEFT: Poster advertising the Sunday Bal des Canotiers (Boaters' Ball) in Bougival.

The premises are entered through the light-drenched atelier (now a gift shop) in the back, where Monet painted his vast canvases of water lilies. The interior of the house is full of Japanese furniture, prints and ceramic vases, and his precious collection of Japanese engravings covers the walls of several rooms. Along with his gardens, the prints were a major source of inspiration. Most of the original furniture has disappeared and the blue and yellow dining room is a reconstruction. The most appealing room is the kitchen, with its row of copper pots and yellow crockery that Monet designed himself. By all accounts the artist was also a great cook.

The two gardens, Le Clos Normand and Le Jardin d'Eau, are linked by a subterranean passage. The former is more traditional and rectangular, inspired by formal 18th-century designs, with archways of climbing plants and rows of bluebells, pink peonies, roses, nasturtiums, poppies and hibiscus.

The Water Garden, formed by a tributary of the Epte, lies further away, shaded by weeping willows. Here is the celebrated Japanese Bridge and the lily pond. "It took time for me to understand the lilies", wrote Monet. "I had planted them for pleasure; I cultivated them without a thought to painting them. . . then, suddenly, I experienced the revelation that there were magic worlds in my pond. I grabbed my palette and since then it is the only thing that I paint."

FOOD AND DRINK: *Les Nymphéas* (*99 rue Claude Monet; tel: 02 32 51 39 31; moderate), a restaurant and tearoom, is opposite the museum. There is a country-style restaurant up the road in the* Hotel Musardière (*123 rue Claude Monet; tel: 02 32 21 03 18; moderate*).

Musée de l'Ile de France

Uncovering the city's suburbs and satellite towns

Château de Sceaux, 92330 Sceaux
Tel: 01 41 13 70 41
RER: B2 to Sceaux, then bus 192 or 197 (or a 15-minute walk)
Open: Mon, Wed–Sun 10am–5pm Oct–Mar; 10am–6pm Apr–Sept; closed Tues and public hols. Book and giftshop. Admission charge.

This museum is an introduction to the rural and royal past of l'Île de France. Essentially Paris and its suburbs and satellite towns, the Île de France extends about 80 km (50 miles) to the east, west and south of Paris and about 48 km (30 miles) to the north. Today, the area contains the greatest concentration of wealth and economic power of any region in the European Union.

The museum explores four themes: the estate of Sceaux itself – once a rival to Versailles; the royal châteaux, such as St-Cloud, and the original château

The Portière of the Famous from the Gobelin tapestry factory (18th century).

of Sceaux, which have disappeared; the countryside from the 17th to the 20th centuries; and the French ceramic industry. Portraits in the Grand Salon present the estate's most famous owners – Louis XIV's finance minister, Colbert, and the dukes of Maine and Penthièvre – while paintings in the Petit Salon, such as *La Leçon d'Astronomie de la Duchesse du Maine*, offer a few suggestive details about their lives. Ceramics are a highlight with objects from Creil, Choisy, Montereau and Gien.

*FOOD AND DRINK: The chateau park has a kiosk that serves crêpes; the cheap and cheerful **Auberge du Parc** (6 av du Président-Franklin-Roosevelt) caters to the Lycée across the street.*

Musée Jardin Paul-Landowski

Tribute to a monument builder

14 rue Max-Blondat, Boulogne-Billancourt
Tel: 01 55 18 46 41
Metro: Boulogne-Jean Jaurès
Open: Wed, Sat–Sun 10am–noon and 2–5pm;
closed Mon–Tues, Thur–Fri.
Bookshop. Admission charge.

Sculptor Paul Landowski (1875–1961) worked in this garden atelier from 1906 until his death in 1961. He received many important commissions for public monuments. His most famous work is *Le Christ* (1931), the statue on top of Corcovado mountain in Rio de Janeiro – 33 metres (108 ft) high and weighing 1,000 tonnes (1,100 tons).

Two studio rooms and the garden are filled with statues, statuettes, sketches and models for his monuments. Among them are the extraordinary fragments of the *Temple of Man*, designed to depict the history of humanity but which was never completed, and a model of the monument that he made to commemorate those who died in Algeria, but which was destroyed after the Algerian War of Independence. He was also responsible for the mausoleum of Sun Yat Sen in Nanking, the *Wall of the Reformation* in Geneva, as well as many familiar sights in Paris, such as the *Monument to the Glory of French Armies* on Place Trocadéro and the tomb of Maréchal Foch (1937) at Les Invalides.

(Combined tickets for this museum and the Musée des Années 30, see page 198, are available.)

FOOD AND DRINK: see Musée des Années 30, page 198.

One of the Renaissance Museum's prize exhibits is the so-called Charles V Ship, a mechanical clock that chimes the hour with drums and cannon (late 16th century).

Musée de la Renaissance

Decorative and fine art of the Renaissance

Château d'Écouen, 95440 Écouen
Tel: 01 34 38 38 50
Train: from Gare du Nord to Écouen, then bus 269 (or a 20-minute walk through the forest)
Open: Mon, Wed–Sun 9.45am–12.30pm 2–5.15pm; closed Tues and some public hols.
Book and giftshop. Admission charge.

The Château d'Écouen is a masterpiece of Renaissance architecture that ranks alongside Chambord and Blois. It was built from 1538–55 for the Duc de Montmorency, the Royal Constable and favourite of François I. The building underwent several reincarnations over the centuries; it has been a prison, a hospital and a school. Today, the château houses the French Renaissance collection – 8,000 items from the 16th century – moved here in 1977 from the Cluny museum in Paris (now dedicated solely to the Middle Ages, *see page 78*).

The period interiors, jewellery, stained glass, porcelain, armour, sculpture and art are of an extraordinary quality and diversity. The collection is full of unusual surprises, too, such as the Turkish ceramics and the mechanical golden ship that can ring out the hours with drums and cannon. The star attraction is the *David and Bethsheba* series, the most beautiful Renaissance tapestries preserved in France.

Food and Drink: The château has a small café/restaurant with a terrace. Nearby Montmorency has La Paimpolaise (30 rue Gallieni; tel: 01 34 28 12 05; inexpensive) for Breton crêpes and seafood.

Musée de la Résistance

The story of the French Resistance told through documents, photos and art works

Parc Vercors, 88 av Marx Dormoy, Champigny-Sur-Marne
Tel: 01 48 81 00 80. www.musee-resistance.com
RER: Line A2 to Champigny-St-Maur, then taxi or bus 208 (2 km/1 mile)
Open: Tues–Fri 9am–12.30pm and 2–5.30pm, Sat–Sun 2–6pm; closed Mon, public hols and on weekends in summer.
Bookshop. Admission charge.

This 19th-century house overlooking the Marne river contains one of the largest collections of Resistance documents in France. Five rooms of audio-visual exhibits offer a comprehensive presentation of the events leading up to World War II and the occupation of France from 1942 to 1944. Documents, photos and newspapers bear witness to the number and variety of people from all walks of life who risked deportation and death to liberate France. More than a few of them were talented artists, as demonstrated in a gallery of their art work. If you have no knowledge of French, however, you're at a disadvantage. Apart from a wall of guns and one or two pieces of sabotage equipment, the majority of the collection is made up of documents for which there are no English explanations.

The museum's small park is named after the French hero, Vercors, who founded Editions de Minuit, France's underground press under German occupation.

Food and Drink: La Guinguette L'Île Martin-Pêcheur (41 quai Victor-Hugo; tel: 01 49 83 03 02; moderate). Experience a typical guinguette – here, the tradition of the riverside ball lives on in this dance hall-cum-café. Each year on 14 July, a "Miss Guinguette" competition is held here by the Association Culture Guinguette.

Musée Mémorial Ivan Tourgueniev

Turgenev's luxurious Paris *dacha*

Les Frênes, 16 rue Ivan-Tourgueniev, Bougival
Tel: 01 45 77 87 12
Metro: La Défense, then bus 258
Open: Sun from Easter to Christmas 10am–6pm (or by appointment, Apr–Sept).
Book and giftshop. Research library. Concerts. Admission charge.

This peaceful retreat on the banks of the Seine was the scene of a celebrated salon frequented by the luminaries of the day, among them the composers Saint-Saens and Fauré, opera diva Pauline Viardot and writers Henry James, Flaubert, Zola and Daudet. They were all friends of the Russian novelist, Ivan Turgenev, who lived here for several years before his death in 1883.

The library and study have been faithfully recreated in accordance with Turgenev's descriptions, right down to the samovar. There are family portraits of his close friends, the Viardots, and a selection of original letters and first editions of his books in Russian and French. The bedroom, done out in Turgenev's favourite shade of green, is where he died in 1883.

Solomon meeting the Queen of Sheba, detail of the magnificent painted fireplace at the Château d'Ecouen (16th century).

C H A T E A U X

Equestrian Museum and royal stables

The Equestrian Museum *(Musée Vivant du Cheval, tel: 03 44 57 13 13, www.musee-vivant-du-cheval.fr; admission charge)* is housed in the former royal stables (Grandes Ecuries), within 10 minutes' walk of the château; spectacular dressage displays take place in the stables' central rotunda three times daily *(at 11.30am, 3.30pm and 5.15pm)*. The stables themselves are impressive – according to popular belief their instigator, Louis-Henri, Duke of Bourbon (1692–1740), was convinced that he would be reincarnated as a horse and so undertook to build a future home fit for an equestrian king.

Chantilly's Grand and Petit Châteaux.

Chantilly – Musée Condé

A moated château and its prize collection of artworks plus a grand equestrian museum in the horse-racing capital of France

Chantilly (40 km/25 miles northeast of Paris)
Tel: 03 44 62 62 62
Getting there: By road – from Paris, either take the N16 or the A1 autoroute to the exit at Survilliers-St-Witz. By train – Gare du Nord to Chantilly-Gouvieux (approximately 30 minutes), plus a 30-minute walk or short taxi ride (Taxis Chantilly, tel: 03 44 57 10 03) to the château.
Open: Mon, Wed–Sun Mar–Oct 10am–6pm, Nov–Feb 10.30am–12.45pm and 2–5pm; closed Tues. Grounds open daily.
Shop. Guided tours available by request. Booking obligatory for groups (tel: 03 44 62 62 60). Discovery tours and workshops arranged for children. Wheelchair access to the gardens only. Admission charge.

Although the name Chantilly is synonymous with the unusual quartet of whipped cream, lace-making, porcelain and horse-racing, the biggest crowd-puller here (on non-race days, at least) is the town's magnificent château. Chantilly is a great place to take children – the interior of the palace is aimed at adults, but boat trips and balloon rides are both on offer in the château's extensive grounds. For those in search of a little horse play, there's also an Equestrian Museum in the town.

Equestrian statue at the Musée Vivant du Cheval.

Art and architecture

The château, which is divided into two main parts – the Petit and Grand Châteaux – was built between the 16th and 19th centuries for a succession of powerful French dynasties: the Orgemont, Montmorency, Bourbon-Condé and Orléans families. Most of what is standing today dates from the 19th century, since the 14th-century foundations of the Grand Château were razed to the ground during the Revolution.

Between 1875 and 1885 new buildings were erected by Honoré Daumet to house the art collections of Henri d'Orléans, Duke of Aumale (1822–97) and his son Louis-Philippe. The latter donated Chantilly to the Institut de France in 1886, stipulating that the original hang of the artworks be maintained; the collection is hence arranged according to each painting's dimensions, regardless of school or period, and the effect is neat but eccentric.

There are two main galleries in the museum: the Deer Gallery, a former banqueting room now hung with tapestry hunting scenes, and the Picture Gallery, which features works by Poussin, Watteau, Nattier, Delacroix and Corot. At one end of the Picture Gallery is a rotunda housing two gems: *The Loreto Madonna*, attributed in 1979 to Raphael, and Piero di Cosimo's *Simonetta Vespucci*. Also notable is the circular Tribune, the walls of which are covered with masterpieces by Poussin, Van Dyck, Watteau, Delacroix and Ingres, and the Sanctuary, home to Raphael's tiny but exquisite *Three Graces*.

Included in the price of your entrance ticket is a guided tour *(except Sun afternoons and public holidays in summer)* around the Great Apartments of the Prince de Condé on the first floor of the Petit Château. There are nine rooms, of which the most interesting is the Large Monkey Room, whimsically decorated with chinoiserie panels. A separate guided tour of the private apartments of the Duke and Duchess of Aumale, in the Petit Château, is also offered.

The palace grounds

If you've had your fill of art, make for the grounds: a formal French garden designed by André Le Nôtre; a Romantic rambling English garden (1817) by Victor Dubois; and an Anglo-Chinese garden set around the Hameau (hamlet), a rustic-style group of cottages erected in 1774, which served as a model for Marie Antoinette's dairy at Versailles.

The Hameau is about 20 minutes on foot from the main château and can be reached by motorised boat, which costs extra but enables you to tour the château's moat and Grand Canal, also laid out by Le Nôtre. Another fun attraction is Chantilly's huge helium balloon, the largest of its type in the world. For a small fee, and weather-permitting, the 10-minute balloon ride offers splendid bird's-eye views of the château, its gardens, the former royal stables and the surrounding countryside.

FOOD AND DRINK: A range of meals and snacks are available at La Capitainerie (tel: 03 44 57 15 89; moderate), in the basement of the château. Outdoor dining and afternoon teas, including some mouth-watering patisserie and ice creams, are on offer by the Hameau (moderate).

Fontainebleau

The seat of sovereigns from Louis IX to Napoleon III and a glittering example of French Mannerism

Fontainebleau (60 km/37 miles southeast of Paris)
Tel: 01 60 71 50 70. www.rmn.fr
Getting there: By road – take the Fontainebleau exit on the A6 autoroute, and the château is 16 km/10 miles away, on the edge of the town of Fontainebleau. Parking is available in town. By train – Gare de Lyon to Fontainebleau-Avon (approx. 50 minutes). From the station, take the "Château" bus or make the 30-minute walk through the town. Trains out of Paris are infrequent (roughly one every hour), so check before travelling (tel: 08 36 35 35 35; www.sncf.com). Open: Mon, Wed–Sun 9.30am–5pm; closed Tues and 12.30–2pm Nov–Apr.
Shop. Audio-guides in English. Guided tours. Wheelchair access. Admission charge.

The crowning glory of the town of Fontainebleau is the former royal residence on the fringes of the town centre. Louis IX called Fontainebleau "his wilderness", François I likened trips here to "coming home", and, from his exile in St Helena, Napoleon I called this palace "the true home of kings". It was here that the Revocation of the Edict of Nantes was signed by Louis XIV in 1685, and that Napoleon I signed his first act of

Rosso's painting at Fontainebleau. The elephant sports a fleur-de-lys and salamander (François I's emblem) on its crown and is said to represent the king.

abdication in 1814, before taking his leave for Elba from Fontainebleau's double horseshoe staircase – the front area of the château is hence now called the Farewell Courtyard. More recently (1945–65), Fontainebleau made its mark as the headquarters of the military branch of NATO.

An evolving estate

It is known that a fortified castle stood on the site of the present château as early as the 12th century, the remains of which are now integrated into the Oval Courtyard's square-shaped keep. From 1528, François I (1494–1547), an ardent huntsman keen to make the most of the 100 sq km/40 sq miles of dense forest in the Fontainebleau area, enlisted the services of the artists Francesco Primaticcio and Sebastiano Serlio to transform the existing buildings into a grand Mannerist palace (he had been impressed by this style of architecture during his conquests in Italy). The style, typified by the use of motifs in direct opposition to their accepted meaning or context, is now inextricably linked with this palace, so much so that it is often referred to as the First Fontainebleau School. François, a patron of the arts, made his new château a centre of artistic excellence and brought paintings by da Vinci (the *Mona Lisa*, now in the Louvre) and Raphael and priceless sculpture, tapestries and furnishings here.

The next monarch to make a grand impression on Fontainebleau was Henri IV (1553–1610). During his reign, the wing housing the Deer Gallery, Diana Gallery (built for Henri's wife, Marie de Médicis), the Dauphin's entrance and the buildings around the Kitchen (or Henri IV) Courtyard was added.

Renovation work and additions were carried out under monarchs from Louis XIV (1638–1715) to Louis XVI (1754–93), but with the latter came the French Revolution, and Fontainebleau was no longer the home of kings. While the Revolutionary years were bleak for Fontainebleau, since the palace was stripped of its contents and left to ruin, Napoleon's reign proved more favourable. By 1803, the French conquerer had founded a military school here and in 1804 he began a full refurbishment of the palace, mostly in the then-fashionable Empire Style, characterised by winged lions, palmettes and Egyptian-style sphinx motifs. Napoleon also converted the Small Apartments for his personal use.

After the Restoration, Louis Philippe (1773–1850) continued to renovate the château, refurbishing much of the interior. Napoleon III (1808–73) carried on Louis Philippe's work, and the Empress Eugénie (1826–1920) had new salons installed and opened a Chinese Museum in the Great Pavilion. Note that access to some areas (Small Apartments, Napoleon Museum and Chinese Museum) is limited; call ahead on 01 60 71 50 70 to check times.

If you're visiting Vaux-le-Vicomte *(see page 208)*, you could combine this with a trip to Fontainebleau, since the two châteaux are within 16 km/10 miles of each other and on the same train line.

FOOD AND DRINK: There are no eating facilities at the château itself. However, it's only a 5-minute walk into town, where there are numerous cafés, brasseries and restaurants.

Malmaison

The favourite home of Josephine Bonaparte

Av du Château de Malmaison, Rueil-Malmaison (15 km/9 miles southwest of Paris)
Tel: 01 41 29 05 55
www.mairie-rueilmalmaison.fr
Getting there: By metro – RER A to La Défense, then bus 258, or RER to Rueil plus a 20-minute walk through the town. By road – from Paris, head for Porte Maillot towards La Défense; go through the tunnel at La Défense in the direction of the N13 Rueil/St-Germain; continue to place de la Boule, take the A13 (av du M. Joffre) and carry straight on until the A13 becomes av Napoléon Bonaparte; av du Château is on your left.
Open: Wed–Mon 10am–noon, 1.30–5pm (summer) and 9.30am–noon, 1.30–4.30pm (winter), closed Tues.
Shop. Guided tours. Audio-guides in English. Wheelchair access to ground floor and gardens. Admission charge (combined with Bois-Préau).

Fontainebleau, seen from the Farewell Courtyard.

In the quiet suburb of Rueil-Malmaison is one of the most delightful châteaux within easy access of the French capital: Malmaison, the former home of Josephine Bonaparte, first wife of Napoleon I.

The estate passed through various hands until 1799, when it caught the eye of Madame Bonaparte. She reputedly had to borrow money for the down-payment from the previous owner's steward – a sum that Napoleon repaid on his return from conquering Egypt. Josephine engaged the services of the up-and-coming architectural duo of Percier and Fontaine to renovate the existing building in the then-fashionable Neo-classical style, characterised by simple, geometric forms and minimal extraneous decoration, and in 1805 she employed garden landscaper, L.M. Berthault, to work on the grounds.

While Malmaison was initially used by the consular couple purely as a country retreat, by 1800 Napoleon was spending an increasing amount of time here, even holding official meetings on the estate. In 1809, since Josephine could not give her husband his much-needed heir (despite having two children by her first marriage to Viscount Alexandre de Beauharnais), Napoleon nullified the marriage. He gave his former wife the Malmaison estate and it was here that she spent most of her time until her death in 1814.

Touring the château

Highlights on the ground floor include a monumental billiard table by Mathurin-Louis Cosson, two ethereal paintings by Gérard and Girodet on the subject of Ossian in the lavish Gilded Drawing Room, and a magnificent harp topped by an Imperial eagle by Cousineau in the Music Room. Also of note are the Pompeiian-style dancers that are delicately painted on stucco on the walls of the dining-room, Napoleon's quirky, tent-style Council Room and his Library, the ceiling of which is dotted with Neo-classical busts of authors from Ovid to Voltaire.

The first floor shows the Imperial couple's private apartments, although little of what is now on display is original: much of the furniture, mostly in the Empire style favoured by Napoleon, has been sourced from the Tuileries and other former royal residences. Most striking on this floor are paintings including Gérard's portrait of Napoleon in his coronation robes (c. 1805–10), Henri-François Riesener's *Empress Josephine* (1806), Louis-Albert-Ghislain d'Albe's *General Bonaparte*

(1796–7) and Jacques-Louis David's famous *First Consul Crossing the Alps* (1801). Most of the second floor is dedicated to displaying the contents of the former Empress's wardrobe, for which she was especially renowned.

Before you leave, take time to explore the gardens, which are landscaped in the rustic style typical of English country gardens. Look out for the massive cedar tree on your right as you stand with your back to the house – it was planted in 1800 to celebrate Napoleon's victory at Marengo.

Other attractions in the château include the Osiris Pavilion, which is named after the current owner and is home to a decorative arts collection, and the Carriage Pavilion, built in 1830; the coaches in the latter include Napoleon's field landau used in his Russian campaign and the hearse used in St Helena for Napoleon's funeral.

Tickets to Malmaison cover entry to Bois-Préau *(Musée du Château de Bois Préau, 1 av de l'Impératrice, 92500 Rueil-Malmaison; tel: 01 47 49 20 07)*, although, at the time of writing, this château, now a Napoleonic museum, was closed for renovation.

FOOD AND DRINK: Although there is no restaurant at the château itself, the grounds are lovely, so you could come prepared with a picnic if the weather's fine. Otherwise, there are numerous eating places in nearby Rueil.

David's magnificent *First Consul Crossing the Alps at the Grand-St-Bernard Pass*, on show at Malmaison.

The rear façade of Vaux-le-Vicomte, complemented by Le Nôtre's elegant French-style gardens.

Vaux-le-Vicomte

The former home of Louis XIV's one-time Finance Minister, Nicolas Fouquet, and considered to be the forerunner to Versailles

Maincy (60 km/37 miles from Paris)
Tel: 01 64 14 41 90. www.vaux-le-vicomte.com
Getting there: By road – from Paris, take the A6 to the Fontainebleau exit; follow signs to Melun, then take the N36 and D215. By train – Gare de Lyon to Melun (40 minutes), then by taxi (approx. 15 euros each way) 7 km/4 miles to the château; there is a taxi rank by the station car park – if there are no taxis waiting, there is a placard showing numbers to call to order one.
Open: daily end Mar–mid-Nov 10am–1pm and 2–6pm, and mid-Nov–end Mar to groups only and by prior arrangement.
Shop. Audio-guides in English. Guided group tours by reservation only (tel: 01 64 14 41 90 or visit www.vaux-le-vicomte.com). Wheelchair access to the gardens. Admission charge.

Visitors in search of Classical French architecture, impressive formal gardens and a good dose of intrigue should be satisfied by a trip to Vaux-le-Vicomte. The château, in the heart of the Seine-et-Marne countryside, was built as the home for Louis XIV's Superintendent of Finances, Nicolas Fouquet, protégé of Cardinal Mazarin and one of the most promising young politicians of his day. Fouquet was a man of exquisite taste and a keeper of impeccable company, with the fabler La Fontaine, the dramatist Molière and the writers Madame de Scudéry and the Marquise de Sévigné among his close friends.

The château

In 1656, Fouquet engaged Louis Le Vau (architect), Charles Lebrun (painter) and André Le Nôtre (garden designer) to construct a cutting-edge home on land bought in 1641 with inheritance money. On 17 August 1661, Fouquet hosted a grand house-warming party, with an impressive programme of events including a first performance of Molière's *Les Fâcheux*, music by Lully, a firework display and A-list invitee, Louis XIV, as guest of honour.

Fouquet, however, had not reckoned on kingly jealousy, nor the double-dealing (if you believe the Vaux spin) of Colbert, another of Louis's chief ministers and Fouquet's arch rival. Guilty or not, in September 1661, the master of Vaux was arrested by the Muskateer d'Artagnan and thrown into jail on charges of embezzling state funds; he died in prison 19 years later.

Meanwhile, Louis XIV engaged the services of Fouquet's design trio to transform the hunting-lodge at Versailles *(see page 209)* into a palace fit for a king. Vaux was stripped of its furnishings and returned to Fouquet's wife only in 1673. In 1705 it passed into the hands of the Maréchal de Villars, and in 1764 was sold to the Duc de Choiseul-Praslin, Louis XV's naval minister. In 1875, although the château was in a state of disrepair, it was bought by the French industrialist Alfred Sommier, who set about restoring it to its former glory; the château opened to the public in 1968. The current owner, Count Patric de Vogüé, is Sommier's great-grandson.

Vaux is more than just a good yarn, however. The rural location of the château, although inconvenient for car-less visitors, makes a trip here a welcome antidote to the bustle of Paris. The building itself, set on a stone terrace surrounded by an artificial water-filled moat, is a fine example of the harmonious traditional French style, and the lavish interior decoration – a riot of gilding, elaborately decorated wainscoting, glittering crystal and exquisite paintwork by Lebrun – is impressive.

The gardens

The crowning glory of Vaux, however, is Le Nôtre's handiwork – the first garden to be laid out in what is now known as the French style. This is characterised by geometric lines, intricate parterres, the use of optical illusions, which make elements in the garden seem closer than they actually are, and clever water management. If you don't have the energy to hike to the end of the gardens and back, you could hire one of the pint-sized golf buggies (deposit by credit card and driving licence required) that can be driven around much of the grounds and even through Le Nôtre's 1,000-m/328-ft long Grand Canal. Novelty boats *(Nautils)* can be hired on the canal.

Fountain displays are staged every second and last Saturday of the month from April to October (3–6pm), and candlelit evenings are held from 8pm until midnight on Saturdays from mid-May to mid-October plus some bank holidays. Entry tickets cover admission to outbuildings in the château grounds where Vaux's carriage collection is on display.

FOOD AND DRINK: Great-value meals, including Provençal salads and hot main courses, plus soft and alcoholic drinks, are available at the château's L'Ecureuil restaurant (tel: 01 64 14 41 90; inexpensive). A shaded terrace and indoor seating make this an ideal eating place, whatever the weather.

Versailles

France's premier former royal residence

Versailles (21 km/13 miles southwest of Paris) Tel: 01 30 83 78 00. www.chateauversailles.fr/en Getting there: By RER – C5 to Versailles-Rive Gauche. By train – Paris Montparnasse to Versailles-Chantiers or Paris St-Lazare to Versailles-Rive Droite. By bus – 171 from Pont de Sèvres to Versailles-Place d'Armes. By road – take the A13 towards Rouen and exit at Versailles-Château; park in the place d'Armes. Palace: open daily except Mon; May–Sept 9am–6.30pm, Oct–Apr 9am–5.30pm.

This costume for Louis XIV's *Grand Carrousel* musical extravaganza is attributed to Gissey, chief designer of the court costumes and decorations of Versailles.

Grand and Petit Trianon: open daily except some public holidays Nov–Mar noon–5.30pm, Apr–Oct noon–6.30pm. Coach Museum: Mar–Nov, Sat and Sun 2–5pm only. Gardens: open daily except in very poor weather, Apr–Oct open 7am, Nov–Mar open 8am, closed 5.30–9.30pm depending on season. Shop. Prior booking (recommended to avoid queuing) possible via website. Audio-guides and tours in English (tel: 01 30 83 77 88 for group bookings; individuals should reserve in person at entrance D; average tour: 1 hr 30 minutes). Wheelchair access (entrance H). Admission charge (reduced after 3.30pm) except on first Sun of each month, Oct–Mar.

The Hall of Mirrors is adorned by Lebrun's masterly ceiling, which depicts the achievements of Louis XIV's 72-year reign.

Versailles, symbol of pre-Revolutionary royal decadence and the site of such historic events as the signing of the Treaty of Versailles, marking the end of World War I, is now France's third most-visited monument. Although most of the château can be covered in a day, to assimilate fully the wealth of historical, political and architectural information connected with this incredible place (and, on a purely practical level, to co-ordinate guided visits to the various areas of the château), you might need to devote two days to the task. (If you spend one day at Versailles, you should be able to see the château's main sections plus the gardens.)

Louis XIII and Louis XIV

Despite its current palatial scale, the estate had humble beginnings. In 1623, Louis XIII, a passionate huntsman, chose to build a lodge near the town of

Versailles to the west of Paris, in order to take advantage of the thick forest in the vicinity. In 1631, he commissioned his head architect, Philibert Le Roy, to upgrade the lodge; Le Roy's buildings flank what is now known as the Marble Courtyard, a marble-paved recess at the end of the Royal Courtyard (the space dominated by an equestrian statue of Louis XIV in front of the palace). Further changes were made to the old palace from 1661–68 under Louis XIV; the new young king charged his architect Louis Le Vau (supposedly head-hunted, along with the painter Charles Lebrun and the landscape gardener André Le Nôtre, after Louis saw their work at Vaux-le-Vicomte, *see page 208*) to embellish the existing buildings.

Versailles was still too small to cope with the King and his entourage, however, and, with the aim of creating a monument to commemorate his realm and a building fit to house King, Court and Parliament, in 1668 Louis commissioned Le Vau to extend the palace further. These changes were controversial – Le Vau enveloped the existing palace in a new building (the current white-stone block that backs onto the gardens and houses the State Apartments), inciting criticism from various quarters – the memorialist, the Duc de Saint-Simon, wrote, "the beautiful and the ugly, the vast and the restricted, were stitched together". Other additions at this time include the blue-and-white porcelain Grand Trianon.

From 1678, Jules Hardouin-Mansart, who had risen to fame as designer of the Invalides church in central Paris, took over as principal architect. This was a period of prolific building at Versailles, since in 1682 the château became the official Court residence and the seat of the French government – an arrangement that enabled Louis, a firm believer in his position as absolute monarch (*"L'Etat c'est moi"* – I am the state), to maintain strict control over both the affairs of state and the behaviour of his courtiers. Under Mansart's artistic eye the Hall

of Mirrors (Galerie des Glaces), North and South wings, stables, Grand Lodgings (staff accommodation) and Orangery were constructed. In 1687, Mansart redesigned the Grand Trianon, and from 1699 to 1710 his Royal Chapel was erected.

Louis XV to the Revolution

Although the Court returned to central Paris during the Regency of 1715–22, upon his proper accession to the throne Louis XV moved his court back to Versailles. He commissioned the architect Ange-Jacques Gabriel to refurbish the private apartments of the king and royal family and, from 1762–64, to build the Petit Trianon, to the northwest of the estate. Between 1768 and 1770 Gabriel built the imposing Royal Opera, which was inaugurated on 16 May 1770 to mark the marriage of the Dauphin (Louis XV's grandson and the future Louis XVI) and Marie Antoinette. In 1771, Gabriel redesigned Mansart's crumbling North Wing in the classical French style, fronted by a colonnaded pavilion.

The main architectural addition to the château under Louis XVI, who moved to Versailles with the aim of putting a healthy distance between himself and the increasingly discontented Parisian mob, was the Hameau (hamlet), built for Marie Antoinette between 1783 and 1787. Louis's faith in the impenetrability of Versailles proved futile, however, and on 6 October 1789 he was taken from the château with the rest of the royal family and forced to return

The Seine (1687), by Etienne Le Hongre, and the rear of the palace.

to the Tuileries Palace in Paris. Louis, the last king in the Bourbon line, was guillotined on 21 January 1793, in the present-day place de la Concorde.

From Napoleon to World War II

After the Revolution, the palace was looted and the estate fell into disrepair. Following Napoleon's marriage to his second wife, Archduchess Marie-Louise in 1810, he considered moving here, but his plans never came to fruition. The couple did, however, enjoy retreats in the Grand Trianon, and the Emperor gave the Petit Trianon to his sister Pauline.

Future occupants of the château did little to benefit it. Louis-Philippe of Orléans, France's king from 1830 to 1848, carried out renovation work, notably on the colonnaded pavilion of the South Wing, but his transformation of parts of the château into a museum "To all the Glories of France" took its toll on the buildings. During the late 19th and the 20th century Versailles's main function was as the site of military headquarters: the Germans made it their headquarters in the Franco-Prussian War, the Allied War Council sat here during World War I, and in World War II, from 1944 to 1945, the Allies had their headcamp here.

The main palace

For visiting purposes, the château is divided into several areas. The main part, which may be accessed without a guide, includes the lavish State Apartments of the King and Queen (Grands Appartements), notably the King's State Bedroom in which the monarch's every move was scrutinised by a league of courtiers. Also in this section is the Queen's bedchamber, which looks as impressive as it must have done when Marie Antoinette was forced to leave the palace in 1789, and the vast Hall of Mirrors. This, the ultimate glass corridor, described by the Marquise de Sévigné as a "sort of royal beauty unique in this world", features 17 arched windows opposite 17 corresponding mirrored arcades; the decorative vaulted ceiling is embellished by captions by the playwright Jean Racine and 30 paintings by Lebrun, which are framed by stucco work. All manner of artistic devices, from *trompe l'oeil* to allegory and fake perspective are exploited to depict notable civil and military events from the first 17 years of Louis XIV's mammoth 72-year reign. It was in this room that the Treaty of Versailles was signed to signify the end of World War I. Tour guides advise that the best time to visit this west-facing gallery is the afternoon, when the sun streams in.

Other highlights of this main tour include, in the Hercules Room, the ceiling painting *The Apotheosis of Hercules* (1733–6), by François Lemoyne, and, in the Battle Gallery towards the end of the tour, a copy of the imposing behemoth *The Crowning of the Empress Josephine at Notre-Dame* (1804) by Jacques-Louis David. The work shows Napoleon crowning his wife, having reputedly only moments before snatched the crown from Pope Pius VII, who had been invited to perform the official act.

For a supplement – beware, these are charged for most "extras" at Versailles, making visits pricey – access is granted to Louis XIV's private bedroom and the apartments of the Dauphin and Dauphine. If you plan to visit this part of the château and the main section described above, note that the two parts are accessed via different doors (Entrance A for the main section, C for the King's chamber, while groups enter at Entrance B); it's worth checking which queue is shorter and visiting that part of the house first, since you should only have to queue once. To avoid queuing altogether, book for tickets for the château in advance of your visit via the château's website *(see page 209)*. Guided tours on offer include: the private apartments of Louis XV, Louis XVI and the Opera; the Opera and Royal Chapel; the apartments of Madame de Pompadour and Madame du Barry; and Marie Antoinette's suite (tel: 01 30 83 77 88 for times).

The Olympian Gods and Goddesses, all with Features of Members of the Royal Family (1670) by Jean Nocret, Versailles.

The Trianons and Hameau

The two other main buildings on the estate are the Grand and Petit Trianon, both located to the northwest of the estate, at one end of the strip of water that runs perpendicular to the main body of the Grand Canal, around 30 minutes on foot from the main château. If you don't fancy the walk, you could take the miniature train that runs regularly from the château, along the Grand Canal and across to the two Trianons and back. Bicycles and horse-drawn carriages may also be hired in the grounds.

The single-storey, Italianate Grand Trianon was erected by Louis XIV as a miniature palace in which he would be able to find respite from the pomp and circumstance of life in the main château. Le Vau's original design of 1670, decorated in blue-and-white delftware porcelain, was replaced in 1687 by the marble architecture of Hardouin-Mansart that still stands today. The Grand Trianon was looted during the Revolution and later redecorated in the existing Empire style for Napoleon I and his second wife Marie-Louise. Since Charles de Gaulle stayed here during his presidency, one wing of the Grand Trianon is reserved for the French Head of State.

The Petit Trianon was built for Louis XV in the Greek style by Gabriel from 1762 to 1768, as a retreat for the king and his mistresses Madame de Pompadour, then Madame du Barry. The gardens were designed by the scientist and botanist Bernard de Jussieu and later re-landscaped in the rambling English style for Marie Antoinette, who was given the Petit Trianon upon her accession to the throne. Also linked with Marie Antoinette is the Hameau, a cluster of thatched cottages designed by architect Richard Mique and built just northeast (10 minutes' walk) of the Petit Trianon. The official Versailles guidebooks stress that these rustic-style buildings were not erected, as popularly believed, so that the Queen could play at being a shepherdess, but as a dairy where food for the royal estate was produced.

The gardens and park

If you've had your fill of architecture and interior decoration, it may be time to visit the château's gardens and park. These are the work of André Le Nôtre, who grappled with narrow hillocks and marshland to create the ultimate formal-style French playground for Louis XIV.

A principal feature in the park is the Grand Canal, an artificial ornamental stretch of water that covers an area of 44 hectares (105 acres) and which can be explored by boat. Around the canal, a network of pathways, fountain basins, hidden groves studded with statuary based on classical and mythological figures, and painstakingly sculpted trees and bushes, radiates out symmetrically and on several levels. Note that there is an extra charge to enter the gardens on Sundays, when the fountains come to life and 17th-century music blasts over the parterres. (While it's fabulous to see Louis's gardens in watery splendour, Sunday is the worst day on which to visit the château's interior, as it can become almost unbearably overcrowded.)

Other sites to visit at Versailles include the Jeu de Paume indoor real tennis courts, situated just outside the Versailles estate, on the rue du Jeu de Paume, and Hardouin-Mansart's Great and Small Stables, located below the Parade Ground, between St-Cloud, Paris and Sceaux avenues. The stables are now home to Versailles' Carriage Museum.

FOOD AND DRINK: There are several cafés and restaurants within the château grounds, including a cafeteria (moderate) by the Chapel Royal courtyard, some pleasant eating areas in the gardens, notably La Flottille (tel: 01 39 51 41 58; moderate) on the terrace next to the canal, and open-air eating areas (inexpensive) serving snacks in the groves on either side of the Latona Garden and Royal Avenue. In summer, kiosks are dotted around the estate, and there are stalls selling cans and snacks at the château entrance.

FAR LEFT: *Apollo's Chariot*, Versailles, by Jean-Baptiste Tuby.

LEFT: Marie Antoinette's chocolate-box Hameau.

"I have just been to Versailles, where everything is grand and everything is magnificent."
– Madame de Sévigné.

Essential information

Visiting the Museums

The Paris Museums Pass

Although municipal museums are free, the national museums and the majority of privately run museums charge an entrance fee *(see box on page 215)*. If your plan is to visit as many museums as you can during your stay, it's worth investing in a **Carte Musées Monuments**. This pass allows free entry into more than 70 museums in and around Paris, though it doesn't cover special exhibitions. A list of participating museums and monuments comes with the pass. At time of press prices were: €13 for a one-day pass, €26 for a 3-day pass and €39 for a 5-day pass. Passes are on sale at main Metro and RER stations, museums, branches of FNAC, tourist offices and from the Eurostar ticket desks.

When to Visit

Most museums close either on Monday or Tuesday, and some also close on public holidays (especially on 1 May). Major museums stay open all day, but smaller ones often shut for a long lunch from noon or 12.30pm until about 2.30pm, or in some cases open only in the afternoon. As a rule, ticket offices close at least half an hour before the museum does.

The major museums draw big crowds on weekends, especially on Sunday when there are reduced rates. If you can, try to visit them on weekdays. The "big three" all have late-night openings: the Louvre is open until 9.45pm on Monday and Wednesday; the Musée d'Orsay is open until 9.45pm on Thursday; and the Centre Pompidou stays open until 9pm every day except Tuesday.

You can prebook the Louvre if you want to avoid queues, and high-profile temporary exhibitions – particularly at the Pompidou and the Grand Palais – are best prebooked. (Telephone numbers and opening times are given at the beginning of each museum review.)

State and municipal museums

The Réunion des Musées Nationaux (RMN) runs 33 national museums. These are free for under-18s and the unemployed and offer reduced rates for 18–25 year olds. They are free for all on the first Sunday of the month (Versailles from Nov–Mar).

RMN museums in Paris are: Musée du Louvre, Musée de l'Orangerie, Musée Picasso, Musée du Moyen Age, Musée Delacroix, Musée Hébert, Musée d'Orsay, Musée Rodin, Musée Gustave Moreau, Musée des Arts d'Afrique et d'Océanie, Musée des Arts Asiatiques – Guimet, Musée d'Ennery, Musée des Arts et Traditions Populaires, Musée Henner. RMN museums in the Paris environs include: Musée du Château de Fontainebleau, Musée de Versailles et de Trianon, Musée des Antiquités Nationales, Musée des Châteaux de Malmaison et Bois-Préau, Musée de la Céramique, Musée de la Renaissance.

All municipal museums and galleries run by the Mairie de la Ville de Paris (MVP) are free. These are: Musée d'Art Moderne de la Ville de Paris, Maison de Balzac, Musée Bourdelle, Musée Carnavalet, Musée Cernuschi (closed until 2004), Musée Cognacq-Jay, Mémorial de la Libération de France et Musée Jean Moulin, Petit Palais – Musée des Beaux-arts de la Ville de Paris (closed until 2003), Musée de la Vie Romantique, Maison de Victor Hugo and Musée Zadkine.

Children's Museums

After Disneyland, the Parc de la Villette is the capital's most popular attraction for children. It contains the Cité des Sciences et de l'Industrie *(see page 187)* and the Cité de la Musique *(see page 163)*, as well as the giant wraparound Géode cinema that shows 3-D IMAX films, and Cinaxe, a flight simulator.

Other good museums for entertaining and educating the kids include: the Grande Galerie de l'Evolution, the revamped natural history museum crawling with stuffed animals *(see page 190)*; the Musée des Arts d'Afrique et d'Océanie, which has live crocs in the basement *(see page 121)*; the Musée Grevin, populated with villains and heroes in wax *(see page 174)*; the Musée de la Poupée, a small doll museum with a shop and hospital *(see page 116)*; and the Musée de la Magie, where magicians perform tricks *(see page 175)*. Anyone excited by boats and planes should visit the Musée de la Marine *(see page 177)* or the Musée de l'Air et de l'Espace *(page 197)*. The Catacombs *(see page 171)* are often enjoyed by older kids with a taste for the macabre.

A visit to one of the châteaux featured at the end of the book is a great day out for all the family.

Public Holidays

1 January, *Jour de l'An* (New Year's Day); *Lundi de Pâques* (Easter Monday); 1 May, *Fête du Travail* (May Day); 8 May, *Victoire 1945* (VE Day); *L'Ascension* (Ascension Day); *Lundi de Pentecôte* (Whit Monday); 14 July, *Fête Nationale* (Bastille Day); 15 August, *l'Assomption* (Feast of the Assumption); 1 Nov, *Toussaint* (All Saints' Day); 11 November, *Armistice 1918* (Remembrance Day); 25 December, *Noël* (Christmas Day).

Banks and post offices close on these dates and so do many museums *(see individual entries)*. In August many small shops and restaurants close as Parisians leave the city in droves for their annual holiday. This is a great time to visit Paris and its museums as it is much quieter.

Tourist Offices

Office de Tourisme et des Congrès de Paris (Paris Convention and Visitors' Bureau)

127 av des Champs-Elysées, 8th Paris; tel: 08 36 68 31 12. www.paris-touristoffice.com; Metro and RER A: Charles-de-Gaulle-Etoile, George-V; open daily 9am–8pm; closed 1 May.

Information desk with booklets and leaflets on Paris and its attractions; reservation desk for hotels; ticket bookings for shows and exhibitions; sightseeing desk for coach tours, river cruises, travel passes and museum passes. It also has a bureau de change and telephones. Other branches can be found at the Gare de Lyon *(Mon–Sat 8am–8pm)* and by the Eiffel Tower *(daily May–Sept 11am–6.40pm).*

Syndicat d'Initiative de Montmartre

21 place du Tertre, 18th; tel: 01 42 62 21 21; Metro: Anvers, Abbesses; open daily 10am–7pm. This tourist office is dedicated to the promotion of Montmartre.

Getting Around

The Paris Metro and RER

Run by the Régie Autonome des Transports Parisiens (RATP), the Paris Metro is one of the world's oldest subway systems, and some of its stations are almost historic monuments. It is used by approximately 9 million people every day. Despite that, it is quick and efficient. The Metro operates from 5.30am, with the last train leaving end stations at 12.30am. Its comprehensive map (reproduced at the back of this guide) and signposting make it virtually impossible to get lost. The lines are identified by numbers, colours and the names of their terminals, so Line 4 running north is shown as Porte de Clignancourt, while going south it is Porte d'Orléans. Follow the orange correspondance signs to change Metro lines.

The Metro runs in conjunction with the RER (suburban regional express trains), which operates five main lines, identified as A, B, C, D and E. RER trains run daily every 12 minutes from 5.30am to midnight.

Tickets and passes

The Metro and the bus system use the same tickets. A book or *carnet* of 10 tickets, which is available from bus or Metro stations and some *tabacs* (tobacconists), offers a considerable saving. Another option is the Paris Visite card, valid for one, two, three or five consecutive days on the Metro, bus and railway in the Paris/Ile de France region. The card also entitles you to a discount at several tourist sites and can be bought from main Metro, RER and SNCF stations.

For shorter stays, you can buy the **Mobilis card**, which allows an unlimited number of trips for a day on the Metro, bus, suburban SNCF, RER and the night buses, extending as far as Disneyland Paris. It can be bought in all Metro stations.

A **Carte Orange** allows unlimited travel on the number of zones of your choice on any public transport system for a month. A **Carte Jaune** gives you unlimited travel from Monday to Monday. To buy either of these you need to take along a passport photograph to any Metro or SNCF station. Sign your card and copy its number onto your ticket – you will be fined by ticket inspectors if you fail to do this.

For further information on the Paris Metro and RER network, and their current tariffs, contact RATP (tel: 08 36 68 41 14 for 24-hour information in English, or visit: *www.ratp.fr).*

Buses

Taking the bus is a pleasant way to see the city but can be much slower than the Metro because of traffic. Tickets can be bought from the driver or from Metro stations, as buses accept the same tickets as the Metro. Remember to punch your ticket, and not your travel card, in the *compositeur.*

Buses don't automatically stop, so when you want to get off push one of the request buttons and the *arrêt demandé* ("bus stopping") sign will light up. Each bus has a map of its route posted at the front and back and at every bus stop. Most buses run from 6.30am to 8.30pm, although some routes continue until 12.30am.

A night service, the **Noctambus**, leaves Place de Châtelet (av Victoria or rue St-Martin) at 1.30, 2.30, 3.30, 4.30 and 5.30am on 10 routes. Travel passes are valid on the bus and stops are marked by a black-and-yellow owl logo. Look out for the **Balabus** service at certain stops. It visits the main tourist sites every Sunday and on public holidays (11 April– 26 September 12.30–8pm). The tour lasts about 50 minutes.

Taxis

Paris has almost 500 taxi ranks, but be careful to hail only a genuine taxi – one with a light on the roof – as other operators may charge exorbitant fares. The white light will be on if a cab is free, while a glowing orange light means that the taxi is occupied.

Maps

A recommended supplement to the maps in this book is the laminated *Insight Fleximap to Paris*. Frequent visitors to Paris should consider investing in a copy of *Paris par Arrondissement* – the Paris equivalent to the London A-Z available from bookshops *(librairies).*

Telecommunications

Telephones

Most public phone boxes in Paris are card-operated. **Phone-cards**, or *télécartes*, can be bought from kiosks, tobacconist's and post offices. You can also make calls from post offices, which have both coin- and card-operated phones. To call long-distance, ask at one of the counters and you will be assigned a booth – you pay when your call is over. Cafés and *tabacs* often also have public phones, which usually take either coins or, in the case of the more old-fashioned models, *jetons* – coin-like discs bought at the bar.

All telephone numbers in France have 10 digits. Paris and Ile de France numbers begin with 01; freephone numbers begin 08 00; premium rate numbers begin 08 36 and mobile phone numbers begin 06. For French directory enquiries and the operator, ring 12; international directory enquiries is 3212.

To call other countries from France, first dial the international access code (00), then the country code: Australia 61, UK 44, US and Canada 1. It's worth remembering that you get 50 percent more call-time for your money if you ring between 10.30pm and 8am on weekdays, and from 2pm at weekends.

Post Office

The French post office is run by the PTT *(Poste et Télécommunications)*. The main branches are open 8am–7pm on weekdays and 8am–noon on Saturday. Stamps *(timbres)* are available at most tobacconists and other shops selling postcards or greetings cards.

Emergency and Medical Services

Ambulance (SAMU): 15
Fire department (Sapeurs Pompiers): 18
Police: 17
Emergencies from a mobile: 112
Emergency doctors (SOS Médecins): 01 47 07 77 77
Emergency dentists (SOS Dentaire): 01 43 37 51 00
24-hour pharmacy: Dhéry, 84, av des Champs-Elysées; tel: 01 45 62 02 41.
In all emergencies **SOS Help** operates an English helpline from 3–11pm daily: 01 47 23 80 80

Newspaper and Magazine Listings

To find out what is going on in the capital, try *L'Officiel des Spectacles* or *Pariscope* (which has a section in English). Both magazines come out on a Wednesday and give cultural listings for the week, with full details on museums, galleries, exhibitions, theatres, concerts, cinemas, nightlife, etc.

Both *Le Monde* and *Le Figaro*, the two main national broadsheets, produce a weekly Paris listings supplement, also published on a Wednesday.

Useful Websites

www.paris-touristoffice.com Official site of the Frence tourist office, with information on hotels, sites, events, exhibitions, etc.
www.rmn.fr The national museums' site
www.paris-france.org and *www.mairie-paris.fr* Sites run by the Mairie de la Ville de Paris (the city council) giving general information on Paris.
www.musexpo.com Guide to museums and exhibitions
www.magicparis.com Information on travel, shops, hotels, etc.
www.pariscope.fr The weekly listings magazine online
www.ratp.fr The official Paris transport system site
www.pagesjaunes.com The French Yellow Pages
www.meteo.fr The weather
www.france.com General information on France

There are numerous internet cafés around the city centre. The **Virgin Megastore** on the Champs-Elysées has its own cyber café and opens until midnight. The Champs-Elysées branch (No. 66) of **easyEverything** (one of four) is open 24-hours a day. **Café Orbital** *(13 rue de Médicis, 6th)* is open 10am–10pm every day except Sunday when it opens in the afternoon until 8pm.

For up-to-date information on Paris museums and news on current exhibitions look at the Insight website **www.insightguides.com**.

Tours

Coach tours of the city are run by **Cityrama** *(tel: 10 44 55 61 00; www.cityrama.com)* and **Paris Vision** *(tel: 01 42 60 30 25)*. They cover the main sights with a commentary but do not stop along the way. **Parisbus** runs double-decker buses that stop at Trocadéro, the Eiffel Tower, the Louvre, Notre Dame, the Musée d'Orsay, the Opéra, the Arc de Triomphe and the Grand Palais. You can hop off, sightsee, then catch a later bus. A commentary runs in English and French *(tel: 01 43 65 55 55)*. **Paris L'Open Tour** runs a similar service *(tel: 01 43 46 52 06)*.

Banks and Money

Most banks are open all day from 9am–5pm Monday to Friday, though some close for lunch between 12.30 and 2.30pm. All banks are closed on public holidays, often from noon the day before. ATM machines outside banks and post offices will allow you to withdraw euros using your own debit or credit card (remember your pin number). The accepted cards are marked on the machines.

Shopping

Traditionally in France, most shops close for lunch at around noon and open again at 2.30pm, but in Paris, many shops remain open all day and do not close until 7pm. Food shops, especially bakers, tend to open early. Most boutiques and department stores open about 9am, although some do not open until 10am. Few shops open on Sunday, except for in the Marais district in the 4th *arrondissement* where most of the boutiques are open for business.

Further Reading

Art and Architecture

Art in Focus: Paris Linda Bolton (Bulfinch Press; Studio Editions, 1995). A tour of Paris museums, paintings, applied arts, and architecture.

A Propos de Paris, by Henri Cartier-Bresson (Thames & Hudson, 1998). More than 130 stunning black-and-white photographs of the French capital, taken by Cartier-Bresson over a period of more than 50 years.

Brassai: The Eye of Paris, by Richard Howard (Abrams, 1999). Part-biography, part-catalogue of a photography exhibition of Brassai's pictures organised by Houston Fine Arts Museum.

Dictionary of Art and Artists, by Peter and Linda Murray (Penguin, 1997). A concise but comprehensive reference book with good potted artists' biographies

The Oxford Dictionary of Art, edited by Ian Chilvers and Harold Osborne (Oxford University Press, 2001). Another solid reference companion.

French Art: The Ancien Régime 1620–1775, by André Chastel (Flammarion, 1995). Sweeping history of French painting, sculpture and architecture during the reigns of Louis XIII, XIV, and XV.

Guide to Impressionist Paris: Nine Walking Tours to the Impressionist Painting Sites in Paris, by Patty Lurie and Darryl Evans (Bulfinch, 1997). The locations that inspired painters such as Monet, Pissaro, and Renoir.

A Life of Picasso Vols I, II and III, by John Richardson (Jonathan Cape, 1996).

Monet's Garden, by Vivian Russel (Frances Lincoln; Stewart Tabori & Chang, 1991). A full account of the creation and evolution of Monet's garden.

Paintings in the Louvre, by Lawrence Gowing (Stewart, Tabori & Chang, 1989). Illustrations and commentary covering more than 800 European paintings.

Paintings in the Musée d'Orsay, by Robert Rosenblum (Stewart, Tabori & Chang, 1989). The French Impressionists, the academics against whom they rebelled, and the Post-Impressionist era.

Paris: Capital of the Arts 1900–1968, by Sarah Wilson (Thames & Hudson, 2002). Fascinating look at Paris as a hotbed of creativity.

Symbolist Art, by Edward Lucie-Smith (Thames & Hudson, 1981). A good introduction to Puvis de Chavannes, Moreau, Redon et al in relation to their international equivalents.

History and Society

France 1845–1945, by Theodore Zeldin (Oxford University Press, 1980). Five-volume magnum opus by the social historian.

The French, by Theodore Zeldin (Harvill Press, 1997). A one-volume guide to the hearts and minds of the French with pointers on "how to laugh at their jokes" and "how to love them."

Transforming Paris: The Life and Labors of Baron Haussmann, by David P. Jordan (Simon & Schuster, 1994). Illustrated account of the controversial urban planner who swept away much of *vieux* Paris to create the capital of the Belle Epoque.

The Age of Illusion: Art and Politics in France, 1918–1940, by Douglas and Madeleine Johnson (Rizzoli, 1987). Between-the-wars Paris when it was the world capital of the avant garde.

Paris: A Century of Change 1878–1978 by Norma Evensen (Yale University Press, 1979). An illustrated architectural history of a century in the life of Paris.

The Rape of Europa: The Fate of Europe's Treasures in the Third Reich and the Second World War by Lynn H. Nicholas (Knopf; Papermac 1995). Account of the systematic looting of Europe's art treasures by the Nazis and the restitution efforts of curators, in Paris and elsewhere, following the war.

Madame de Pompadour (Harper and Row, 1958) and *The Sun King* (Penguin, 1995), by Nancy Mitford. The daily life of the king, the court and the government in the 17th century.

A Woman's Life in the Court of the Sun King, the letters of Duchesse d'Orléans. Introduction and translation by Elborg Forster (Johns Hopkins University Press, 1984). Insights into 17th-century court life.

Literature

The Oxford Companion to French Literature, by Sir Paul Harvey and J.E. Heseltine. (Oxford University Press, 1959).

The Hunchback of Nôtre-Dame (1831); *Les Misérables* (1862), by Victor Hugo (most have been translated in the Penguin Classics series)

Eugénie Grandet (1833); *Old Goriot* (1834), by Honoré de Balzac. Just two selected titles from Balzac's monumental *Comédie Humaine* (many have been translated in the Penguin Classics series).

Remembrance of Things Past (1913–32) by Marcel Proust. The great French novel written in bed. The classic Scott Moncrieff translation is published by Penguin.

Time Out Book of Paris Short Stories, ed. Nicholas Royle (Penguin, 1999).

Foucault's Pendulum, by Umberto Eco (Picador, 1988). Mystery-thriller that begins under the ever-swinging pendulum in the Musée des Arts et Métiers.

Other Insight Guides

Insight Guide France is the major book in the French series covering the whole country, with features on food and drink, culture and the arts. Other Insight Guide titles include *Brittany, Normandy, The French Riviera* and *Provence & the Côte d'Azur*.

There are also numerous French titles in the smaller *Pocket Guide* and *Compact Guide* series, including *Paris*. The foldable *Insight Fleximap to Paris* is a useful, easy-to-use companion to this guide.

Other cities in the *Museums and Galleries* series include New York, Florence and London.

Art & Photo Credits

Permissions

Every effort has been made to trace the copyright holders, and we apologise in advance for any unintentional omissions.

Works of art have been reproduced with the permission of the following copyright holders:

The Spirit of our Time, (detail), 1909 by Raoul Hausmann ©ADAGP, Paris and DACS, London 2002, cover

Young Women of Provence at the Well by Paul Signac ©ADAGP, Paris and DACS, London 2002, 2

The Terrace in the Country, 1908 by Georges Braque ©ADAGP, Paris and DACS, London 2002, p28t

To My Wife, 1933–44 by Marc Chagall ©ADAGP, Paris and DACS, London 2002, p28b

Kiki de Montparnasse in a Red Jumper and a Blue Scarf by Moise Kisling ©ADAGP, Paris and DACS, London 2002, p29

The Turkish Bath by Martial Raysse ©ADAGP, Paris and DACS, London 2002, p33

Seven Virtues & Seven Vices, 1983 by Bruce Nauman ©ARS, NY and DACS, London 2002, p34

La Fée Electricité (detail), 1937 by Raoul Dufy ©ADAGP, Paris and DACS, London 2002, p36

La Grande Anthropométrie Bleue, 1960 by Yves Klein ©ADAGP, Paris and DACS, London 2002, p56

Palombe (detail), 1994 by Frank Stella ©ARS, NY and DACS, London 2002, p57

Composition with Two Parrots, 1935–39 by Fernand Leger ©ADAGP, Paris and DACS, London 2002, p58

The Spirit of our Time, 1909 by Raoul Hausmann ©ADAGP, Paris and DACS, London 2002, p59

Nu de Dos à la Toilette, 1934 by Pierre Bonnard ©ADAGP, Paris and DACS, London 2002, p60

Odalisque in Red Culottes by Henri Matisse ©Succession H Matisse/DACS 2002, p62

Self Portrait, 1901 by Pablo Picasso ©Succession Picasso/DACS 2002, p90

The Bathers, 1918 by Pablo Picasso ©Succession Picasso/DACS 2002, p91

Portrait of Dora Maar, 1937 by Pablo Picasso ©Succession Picasso/DACS 2002, p92t

La Femme à la Poussette by Pablo Picasso ©Succession Picasso/DACS 2002, p92b

Jeunes Filles à la Mouette, 1917 by Pierre Bonnard ©ADAGP, Paris and DACS, London 2002, p96

Three Figures Sitting on the Grass, 1906 by André Derain ©ADAGP, Paris and DACS, London 2002, p97

Nu Dans le Bain, 1937 by Pierre Bonnard

©ADAGP, Paris and DACS, London 2002, p98

La Mariée Devissée, 1921 by Jean Crotti ©ADAGP, Paris and DACS, London 2002, p99bl

Bronze Spider by Louise Bourgeois ©Louise Bourgeois/VAGA, New York/DACS, London 2002, p99r

La Nuit, 1902 by Aristide Maillol ©ADAGP, Paris and DACS, London 2002, p103

Deux Jeunes Filles by Aristide Maillol ©ADAGP, Paris and DACS, London 2002, p104

Hommage au Douanier Rousseau, 1996 by Robert Combas ©ADAGP, Paris and DACS, London 2002, p135

Reclining Figure 1951 Permission Henry Moore Foundation: p136

Bicycle Wheel, 1963 by Marcel Duchamp ©Succession Marcel Duchamp/ADAGP, Paris and DACS, London 2002, p138

The Triumpher, 1973 by Jean Dubuffet ©ADAGP, Paris and DACS, London 2002, p155

The House of Victor Hugo by André Dignimont ©ADAGP, Paris and DACS, London 2002, p157

Credits

Arcaid/Richard Bryant: 32t, 32b
Arcaid/John Edward Linden: 133
Arcaid/Richard Einzig:146
Arcaid/Paul Raffery: 148r
Arcaid/Ben Johnson: 149
AKG London/Robert O'Dea, 3

AKG/Erich Lessing: 17, 30t, 67t, 105l, 159, 186l, 195, 200
AKG London: 24t, 26, 28 94, 96, 99l, 105r, 148l, 153t, 157l, 158, 159l, 168, 172, 181, 194b
AKG Berlin/Elie Bernager: 173m, 173b
The Art Archive/Musée de L'Armée Paris/Dagli Orti: 19
The Art Archive/Carnavalet, Paris/Dagli Orti: 50
The Art Archive/Musée Guimet, Paris/Dagli Orti: 118, 123, 124, 125l
The Art Archive/Musée du Louvre, Paris/Dagli Orti: 66, 68, 71, 75
The Art Archive/Musée d'Orsay, Paris/Dagli Orti: 83
The Art Archive/Victor Hugo's House, Paris/Dagli Orti: 157t
Jerry Dennis/Apa: 30b, 57, 79, 82t, 93, 136, 135b, 162, 164l, 164r, 167t, 173t, 174b, 175
Annabel Elston /Apa: 45, 171
Bibliothèque Centrale M.N.H.N: 191t, 191b, 192tr
Bridgeman Art Library: 10 & 11, 13, 15t, 16, 22, 24b, 28, 29, 31, 33, 34, 38 & 39, 55, 62t, 62b, 63, 76t, 80tr, 80bl, 80br, 82b, 89, 90, 95, 108, 115t, 133, 177t, 193, 194t, 199b, 209b
Bridgeman Art Library/ Flammarion: 12
Bridgeman Art Library/Giraudon: 18, 21, 25, 36, 51t, 51b, 69, 70, 73r, 78, 87r, 87l, 88, 91, 92t, 107b, 121r, 122, 151, 170b, 196, 201tr, 210 & 211
Bridgeman Art Library/ Giraudon/Lauros: 14, 23, 20, 36 & 37, 53, 54b, 72, 73l, 74b, 80tl, 85b, 97, 100, 101b, 106, 107t, 114, 157r, 170t, 176, 177b, 199t, 201b
Bridgeman/J.P Zenobel: 68r
Bridgeman Art Library/Peter Willi: inside cover, 6 & 7, 8 & 9, 20, 27b, 58, 59, 67b, 71, 74t, 76b, 77, 81t, 81b, 86, 89, 98, 155b, 180t, 180b
Bridgeman/Roger-Viollet, Paris: 15
Bridgeman/Visual Art Library, London: 85t

G.Berizzi/RMN: 119
Cité des Sciences et de L'Industrie/Pascal Prieur: 187
Cité des Sciences et de L'Industrie/Arnaud Legrain: 189b
Cité des Enfants and Techno Cité: B. Baudin 188t, Michel Lamoureux 188b
CNAC/MNAM. Dis. RMN Marc Domage: 132, 137
Marc Dubrocca: 160t
EDF Espace Electra: 134
L'Institut du Monde Arabe: 131
L'Institut du Monde Arabe/ P Maillard 130t, 130b
Foundation Dina Vierny/Musée Maillol: 103, 104
Fondation Coffim: 132, 135
Ministère de la Culture-France: 142, 145t, 145b
M.N.H.N.: Erik Gonthier 192tl
Musée de l'Air et de l'Espace: 197t, 197b
Musée de l'Armée: 166
Musée de l'Armée/ Straessle: 167b

Musée d'Art et d'Histoire du Judaisme/Nicolas Feuillie: 120
Musée d'Art et d'Histoire du Judaisme/Mario Goldman: 121l
Musée des Arts et Métiers: L Bessol: 185
Musée des ATP: RMN, 109
Musée de l'Assistance Publique-Hopitaux de Paris: 184 (detail), 186br
Musée Association Les Amis d'Edith Piaf: 165
Musée Henri Bouchard: 152
Musée du Cristal Baccarat: 111t, 111b
Musée du Parfum Fragonard: 115b
Musée Jacquemart- André: 101t, 102
Musée Cernuschi: 126, 127b
Musée de la Chasse et de la Nature: 110
Musée Dapper/Hughes Dubois: 127t, 128b
Musée des Art Forains: 169
Musée Grevin: 174t
Musée d'Histoire de la Medecine: 189t

Musée de la Mode et du Costume: 113
Musée de Montmartre: 182t, 182b, 183
Musée Jean Moulin: 179
Musée National d'Art Moderne, Pompidou Centre: 56, 60
Musée d'Histoire Naturelle/ L. Bessol: 190
Musée de la Poupée: 116 & 117
Topham Picturepoint: 23t, 27t, 129, 147, 201tl, 204t, 206
Topham Picturepoint/ John Hodder: 213
Lisa Lou (Courtesy of the Fondation Cartier): 35
Clare Peel/Apa: 163, 204b, 207, 208, 210, 212bl, 212br
P.M.V.P (Photothèque des Musées de la Ville de Paris): 47, 49l, 49r
P.M.V.P Legraces/PH Joffre: 52
P.M.V.P/P H Ladet and R Briant: 54t
P.M.V.P: P H Joffre: 99r
P.M.V.P: P H Ladet: 160, 161
RMN: 128t, 209t

RMN/Beatrice Hatala: 92b
RMN/J. L'hoir: 125r
RMN/Bulloz: 154
RMN/J.G. Berizzi: 155, 198t
RMN/Gerard Blot: 202
RMN/Lagiewski: 205
RMN/Popovitch: 150, 156t
RMN/Franck Raux: 156b
RMN/R G Ojeda: 198b, 203
Roland Gegryck: 112

Map/floorplan production
Stephen Ramsay

© 2002 Apa Publications GmbH & Co. Verlag KG (Singapore branch)

Cover illustration created from works of art inside this book. Cover concept and design: Klaus Geisler

INSIGHT GUIDE MUSEUMS AND GALLERIES OF
PaRIS

Art Director and Designer
Klaus Geisler
Production **Sylvia George**
Cartographic Editor **Zoë Goodwin**

Index

● **Museums and galleries reviewed are shown in bold**